Re-thinking the Day of YHWH
and Restoration of Fortunes
in the Prophet Zephaniah

DAS ALTE TESTAMENT IM DIALOG

an outline of an old testament dialogue

Band /Vol. 2

Herausgegeben von / edited by
Michael Fieger & Sigrid Hodel-Hoenes

PETER LANG
Bern · Berlin · Bruxelles · Frankfurt am Main · New York · Oxford · Wien

Michael Ufok Udoekpo

Re-thinking the Day of YHWH and Restoration of Fortunes in the Prophet Zephaniah

An Exegetical and Theological Study of 1:14-18; 3:14-20

PETER LANG

Bern · Berlin · Bruxelles · Frankfurt am Main · New York · Oxford · Wien

Bibliographic information published by Die Deutsche Bibliothek
Die Deutsche Bibliothek lists this publication in the Deutsche Nationalbiblio-
grafie; detailed bibliographic data is available on the Internet at ‹http://dnb.ddb.de›.

British Library Cataloguing-in-Publication Data: A catalogue record for this book is
available from *The British Library*, Great Britain

Library of Congress Cataloging-in-Publication Data

Udoekpo, Michael Ufok.
Re-thinking the day of YHWH and restoration of fortunes in the prophet
Zephaniah : an exegetical and theological study of 1:14-18; 3:14-20 / Michael Ufok
Udoekpo.
p. cm. – (Das Alte Testament im dialog = An outline of an Old Testament dialogue ;
v. 2)
Includes bibliographical references and index.
ISBN 978-3-0343-0510-5
1. Bible. O.T. Zephaniah–Criticism, interpretation, etc. I. Title.
BS1645.52.U36 2010
224'.9606–dc22

2010040781

Die Herausgeber bitten die Leserinnen und Leser um Verständnis für die knappe
deutschsprachige Bibliographie. In Anbetracht der Herkunft des Autor sind die
Herausgeber bereit, die Bibliographie in der Form zu publizieren.

Cover design: Thomas Jaberg, Peter Lang AG

ISSN 1662-1689
ISBN 978-3-0343-0510-5

© Peter Lang AG, International Academic Publishers, Bern 2010
Hochfeldstrasse 32, CH-3012 Bern, Switzerland
info@peterlang.com, www.peterlang.com, www.peterlang.net

Printed in Switzerland

Table of Contents

Acknowledgements

The present work is a thoroughly revised and updated version of my doctoral dissertation accepted in the Faculty of Theology at the Pontifical University of St. Thomas, Aquinas (Angelicum), Rome. As I reached the final stage of preparation of this unique theological-exegetical manuscript for publication I recount with deep gratitude the memory of God's blessings upon me during my long, difficult and lonely years of academic journeys in the area of biblical studies (Scriptures) in the United States, Middle East (Egypt, Israel and Jordan) and in Rome. I owe far more than I can say, to my former Bishop, Most Rev. Dr. Camillus A. Etokudoh, my Bishop-elect, mentor and friend, Rt. Rev. Msgr. Camillus R. Umoh, Msgr. S. U. Etok, the Vicar General and the Diocesan Administrator, priests, religious and lay faithful of Ikot Ekpene Diocese, my family, friends, colleagues, sponsors, teachers and professors who over these years have supported me morally, materially and personally.

My thesis moderator in Rome, Prof. Joseph Agius, O. P., deserves my gratitude. He was very helpful. He originally encouraged me to improve on the language of the dissertation and offered many valuable suggestions. I am also thankful to my censor, Prof. Theodore Mascarenhas, SFX for his friendly, critical and constructive examination of this work. Both of these scholars were inspiring to me. Professors Phan Tan Thanh, the Dean and Rev. P. Glenn Morris O. P., the Secretary General of Angelicum and his assistance, Rev. Sr. Collete Keane, O. P., Luke Buckles, O. P., the Rector of the Convitto and Paul Murray, O. P., were also very encouraging to me.

In the United States I am indebted to Dr. Jean-Pierre Ruiz of St. John's University, New York, my professor, teacher and mentor of long standing who has always been present whenever I needed his advice both on academic and other life issues. This book, I should say, is a tribute to him and my other professors both in the Biblical Studies and Semitic Departments at the Catholic University of America, Washington DC who impacted and shaped my theological and exegetical skills in the sacred science. I would like to particularly mention with gratitude, Prof. Dr. Michael Weigl of the Institute für Alttestamentliche Bibelwissenschaft, Vienne who while at Washington DC led a group of us on an impressive study trips and excavation to Egypt and Jordan. He taught and introduced me to the Prophet Zephaniah, during an exegetical doctoral seminar in the Fall of 2006 on „the Late-Pre-exilic Prophets (Nahum, Habakkuk and Zephaniah)." I am profoundly grateful to all my professors.

The support and hospitality offered me by Revs. Nicholas Figliola, Don Baier, Terry Staple, Charles Ehrhart, Deacons Monte, Sonny and families, the staff and the parishioners of St. Frances Cabrini Church of the Diocese of Rockville Centre, New York and of St. Louis Parish, Arlington Diocese, Virginia and by the Josephites' Community, Washington D.C., during these long years of studies and research are appreciated.

Again, to Archbishop Carlo M. Vigano, Msgr. Fortunatus Nwachukwu I am grateful for their moral support. I would also love to thank my friends at the Pontifical Biblical Institutes and Angelicum, Rome (Frs. Joseph Nalpathilchira and John B. Perianayagam), Prof. Fredrick Bliss and Sister Columba Cleary, O.P. with her community members who re-read and edited this work earlier. I am grateful to Rev. Dr. Pius Akpan Benson for his warm friendship and encouraging conversation. Pius also from the Deutschland generously revised my German citations. Sources of strength and support also came from friends / families like Drs. Anselm Etokakpan, Donatus Udoetteh, Felix Akpabio, Frs. John Bakeni, Francis Adedigba, Francis Chiawa, Vincent Awongo, Matthew Udoh, John Idio, Mr/Mrs Werner Doris Debis, Mr/Mrs Bill and Mary-Ann Bowden, Mr/Mrs Wally-Judith Sweeney, Ms Genevieve Hogan, Mr/Mrs Joseph Alice Fazio, the family of Nnaettok, Alva Hinton and family, Mr/Mrs Barth Ebong, Mr/Mrs Sylvester-Ekatteh Umoh, Teresa Jumbo, Joseph/Josephine Sciberras, Jenet/Joyce Lang, Dr. Emmanuel Akpan and Greg Tarquinio.

My greatest debt of thanks also goes to the family of Evelyn Nabbah and the Berrie Foundation who sponsored me in Rome for the academic years of 2008/2009 and 2009/2010, respectively. I remain grateful to Angelica Berrie, Prof. Rabbi Jack Bemporad, the Berrie Fellows (Cohort II) and to all who have contributed to my success, including those not mentioned here. I am thankful to Sara Negro, and the editorial staff of Peter Lang in Switzerland for their offer of April 23, 2010 and for selecting and recommending this work to the editors of *Das Alte Testament im Dialog* (DATID). I owe a special debt of appreciation to them for accepting and raising this work for publication in Vol. 2 of this professionally and internationally-oriented series. The valuable suggestions of Dr. Michael Fierger also improved the quality of this work.

My sincere appreciation also extends to Bishop William Murphy and Msgr. Bob Brennan, Msgr. Brian Mcnamara, Msgr. Thomas L. Spadaro and the entire faith community of the Church of the Good Shepherd of the Diocese of Rockville Centre, New York, my last home before the publication of this work. Finally, my deepest and tearful thanks to my parents, who sowed in me the faith, but now gone with the hope of salvation. To my brothers, sisters, nieces, nephews and all my relations, thank you for your love, support and prayers.

Holbrook, New York
July, 2010   Michael Ufok Udoekpo

Foreword

For several decades now many scholars have published works on specific themes as they relate to theological thoughts and oracular sayings of both the Major and Minor Prophets of Israel. As scholarly interest in the prophets continue to increase by the day, these publications also continue to multiply, even as the Old Testament prophets seem to be determined and ever ready to unfold in their prophetic pronouncements deeply significant meanings that were never thought of before. Thus even though several scholars from different perspectives and contexts have made significant contributions to the understanding of the prophets, such understanding has never been final, definitive or exhaustive.

What we have said above applies with equal force to the prophetic oracles of Zephaniah. Although many scholars have studied and written on this less-read minor prophet of Israel, his three-chapter work has continued to unfold new levels of meanings over the years. The oracles of Zephaniah belong to a dark period in the history of Judah because about one hundred years before Zephaniah's time the Northern Kingdom of Israel had been invaded and carried into exile by foreign powers on account of infidelity and idolatry. Under the leadership of two successive evil kings, Manasseh and Amon, the people of Judah also fell into worship of false gods.

The prophecy of Zephaniah highlights the nature of the relationship that exists between YHWH and his people. It was meant to warn the people, especially the tribe of Judah of God's approaching wrath and judgment. And as Zephaniah predicted, God punished His people and the surrounding pagan nations through a superior foreign power. Not even a brief religious renewal under the good king Josiah was enough to turn the tide of paganism and false worship that carried Judah toward certain destruction. And so it was that judgment came to Judah in about 586 B.C.E., when the Babylonian warlord, Nebuchadnezzar, invaded the area, destroyed the city of Jerusalem and carried its leading citizens into captivity in Babylon.

The most significant theological contribution of Zephaniah is to be found in his message of judgment encapsulated in the concept of the "Day of YHWH" or "Day of the Lord" which he adapted from earlier Old Testament biblical traditions and contextualized it in a way that suited his theological purposes. Zephaniah portrays this great day as a time of trouble and distress, darkness, trumpet and alarm (1:14–15). The "Day of YHWH" is directly linked to the nature of God who is Holy. Because God is Holy, He demands holiness and righteousness in His people, and will judge those who continue to sin and rebel (1:17). But the Lord also is merciful and faithful to His promise. To the committed remnant He offers encouragement and protection from the approaching dark day (2:1–3). And to the righteous He promises the final realization of the covenant which He sealed with Abraham hundreds of years earlier. People of all nations will gather to worship the Lord (2:11; 3:9). His own people will be renewed in righteousness (3:11–13). And the King of Kings Himself will rule in their midst (3:15).

In his book, *Re-thinking the Day of YHWH and Restoration of Fortunes in the Prophet Zephaniah,* Michael Ufok Udoekpo has made an invaluable contribution to the understanding of the theology of Zephaniah, especially his concept of the Day of YHWH, by undertaking an exegetical and theological study of Zeph 1:14–18 and 3:14–20. In order to establish his originality and the purpose of his work the author has undertaken an exhaustive examination of the opinions presented by other scholars on Zephaniah's concept of the Day of YHWH. In doing this he discovered that many scholars who have written on the Day of YHWH in Zephaniah did not address some critical, textual, literary and theological issues that make Zeph 1:14–18 and 3:14–20 a theological continuum. Aside from this it is also to be noted that prior to Michael's work there was never any systematic exegetical and theological study of the Day of YHWH and the restoration of fortunes in the prophet Zephaniah. This work therefore has overcome the limitations and shortcomings of earlier scholars by offering a more comprehensive exegetical and theological study of Zephaniah, his concept of the Day of YHWH and the restoration of fortunes.

Michael Ufok Udoekpo is to be highly commended for making available to the reading public this special contribution to the understanding of prophet Zephaniah. In a simple and easy-to-read style, the author is able to carry along both biblical scholars and ordinary readers breathtakingly till the end. His work will continue to remain monumental among many other works published on the prophets, particularly Zephaniah. With great joy I congratulate Michael Ufok Udoekpo and recommend his great work to all and sundry, especially those who are interested in gaining more insights into the message of Zephaniah.

Donatus Udoette
Department of Religious and Cultural Studies
University of Uyo – Nigeria

Abbreviations

General Abbreviations

AB	Anchor Bible
ABD	Anchor Bible Dictionary (D. N. Freedman et al. eds.)
ATh NT	Abhandlungen zur Theologie des Alten und Neuen Testamentss
AJT	American Journal of Theology
ATR	African Traditional Religion
ATSAT	Arbeiten zu Text und Sprache im Alten Testament
BAG(D)	W. Bauer, W. F. Arndt, and F. W. Gingrick (3rd ed.: and F. W. Danker), Greek-English Lexicon of the NT and Other Early Christian Literature
BASOR	Bulletin of the American Schools of Oriental Research
BCE	Before Common Era
BDB	F. Brown, S. R. Driver, and C. A. Briggs, Hebrew and English Lexicon of the Old Testament
BDF	F. Blass, A Debrunner, and R. W. Funk, A Greek Grammar of the NT
BEI	Biblia Hebraica Interlinieare
Bib	Biblica
BiKi	Bibbel und Kirke
BN	Biblische Notizen
BSac	Bibliotheca Sacra
BZAW	Beihefte zur ZAW
BZNW	Beihefte zur ZNW
CAT	Commentaire de l'Ancien Testament
CBQ	The Catholic Biblical Quarterly
CR	Currents in Research
DH	Deuteronomistic History
EDNT	Exegetical Dictionary of the New Testament
EM	Encyclopedia Migraith =Encyclopedia Biblica (Heb)
ExpTim	Expository Times
ETL	Ephemerides Theologicae Lovanienses

EvTh	Evangelische Theologie
GS	Gaudium et Spes
HCOT	Historical Commentary on the Old Testament
HUCA	Hebrew Union College Annual
HThKAT	Herders theologischer Kommentar zum Alten Testament
ICC	International Critical Commentary
IDB	G. A. Buttrick (ed.), Interpreter's Dictionary of the Bible
ILB.PT	I Libri Biblici. Primo Testamento
ISBE	G. W. Bromiley (ed.), International Standard Bible
ITC	International Theological Commentary
JBR	Journal of Biblical Journal
JRT	Journal of Religious Thought
JSJ	Journal for the Study of Judaism in the Persian, Hellenistic, and Roman Periods
JSOT	Journal for the Study of the Old Testament
JSOTSup	Journal for the Study of the Old Testament Supplement
JSS	Journal of Semetic Studies
JTSA	Journal of Theology for Southern Africa
KAT	Kommentar zum A. T. E. Sellin (ed),
LXX	Septuagint
MT	Masoretic Text
NJBC	New Jerome Biblical Commentary
NA	Nostra Aetate
NSBT	New Studies in Biblical Theology
NT	New Testament
OBO	Orbis biblicus et Orientalis
ÖBS	Österreichische biblische Studien
OCB	The Oxford Companion of the Bible (eds. Metzger & Coogan)
OTG	Old Testament Guides
OTL	Old Testament Library
OT	Old Testament
PBC	Pontifical Biblical Commission
ResQ	Restoration Quarterly
RSR	Recherches de science religieuse
SBL	Society of Biblical Literature
SBLSP	SBL Seminar Papers
SBLSymS	SBL Symposium Series

20

SBT	Studies in Biblical Theology
SDB	Stuttgarter Bibelstudien
TDNT	Theological Dictionary of the New Testament
ThD	Theology Digest
TLOT	Theological Lexicon of the Old Testament
UR	Unitatis Redintegratio
VT	Vetus Testamentum
VTSup	VT, Supplements
WMANT	Wissenschaftliche Monographien zum Alten und Neun Testament Welt des Orients
WUNT	Wissenschaftliche Untersuchungen zum Neuen Testament
ZSTh	Zeitschrift für systematische Theologie

Abbreviations of the Books of the Bible

Gen	Genesis		1 Macc	1 Maccabees
Exod	Exodus		2 Macc	2 Maccabees
Lev	Leviticus		Job	Job
Num	Numbers		Ps(s)	Psalms
Deut	Deuteronomy		Prov	Proverbs
Josh	Joshua		Eccl	Ecclesiastes
Judg	Judges		Song	Song of Songs
Ruth	Ruth		Wis	Wisdom
1 Sam	I Samuel		Sir	Sirach
2 Sam	2 Samuel		Isa	Isaiah
1Kgs	1 Kings		Jer	Jeremiah
2Kgs	2 Kings		Lam	Lamentations
1 Chr	1 Chronicles		Bar	Baruch
2 Chr	2 Chronicles		Ezek	Ezekiel
Ezra	Ezra		Dan	Daniel
Neh	Nehemiah		Hos	Hosea
Tob	Tobit		Joel	Joel
Jdt	Judith		Amos	Amos
Esth	Esther		Obad	Obadiah

Jonah	Jonah	Eph	Ephesians
Mic	Micah	Phil	Philippians
Nah	Nahum	Col	Colossians
Hab	Habakkuk	1 Thess	1 Thessalonians
Zeph	Zephaniah	2 Thess	2 Thessalonians
Hag	Haggai	1 Tim	1 Timothy
Zech	Zechariah	2 Tim	2 Timothy
Mal	Malachi	Titus	Titus
Matt	Matthew	Phil	Philemon
Mk	Mark	Heb	Hebrews
Lk	Luke	Jas	James
Jn	John	1 Pet	1 Peter
Acts	Acts of the Apostles	2 Pet	2 Peter
Rom	Romans	1, 2, 3 Jn	1, 2, 3, John
1 Cor	I Corinthian	Jude	Jude
2 Cor	2 Corinthian	Rev	Revelation
Gal	Galatians		

General Introduction

A. Preamble

The prophecy of Zephaniah is a compendium of prophetic thoughts on the nature of YHWH's relationship with His people.[1] This theological message is communicated in the concept of the Day of YHWH (יום יהוה) by Zephaniah.[2] It is a prominent concept in the OT studies. Zephaniah adapted this concept from earlier traditions and uses this expression more than any other OT Prophet. He uses it mostly when he wants to emphasize the notion of a God who loves, who judges, and punishes (Zeph 1:14–18) and rewards (Zeph 3:14–20).

With this notion Zephaniah reminds us that YHWH not only judges on His Day but he also shows mercy and inspires hope. He restores fortunes (שׁוב שׁבות) and saves His repentant people (3:14–20). He reminds us that human history though mingled with hope and expectation, is guided by ultimate judgment, revelation and intervention of YHWH, the Sovereign of creation. It is an affirmation that YHWH is always in the midst of His People (Zeph 3:15c; 17e), whom they are called to constantly seek. It is a dialectical experience of judgment (1:14–18) and restoration (3:14–20), which has its basis in human repentance and God's love and mercy. It stands inseparable from the problem of biblical or prophetic eschatology, since the prophets enabled

---

1   Brevard S. Childs, *Introduction to the Old Testament as Scripture* (Philadelphia: Fortress Press, 1979), 462.

2   יום יהוה/ἡ ἡμέρα τοῦ κυρίου/Day of YHWH or Yahweh/ Der Tag YHWHs and the Day of the Lord will be used interchangeably in this study. Of course YHWH is a common symbolic name for the God of Israel. It represents God's dynamic, active intervention and presence among the people of Israel (Exod 3:14). This is translated in the LXX as κύριος (Lord).

Israel to look back creatively at its past, judge the present and anticipate the future.[3]

B. Status *Quaestionis* and Motivations

The search for the meaning, origin and significance of this dialectical
experience, encapsulated in יום יהוה (the Day of YHWH) is a path
many biblical exegetes, theologians and historians of religions have
walked, significantly in the scholarly past, without a consensus. It remains highly debatable among various methodological approaches or
schools of thoughts. This obvious skepticism and lack of theological
monophony on the root meaning of יום יהוה (the Day of YHWH), is
clearly reflected in the available wide spectrum of scholarly opinions
today.[4]

For instance, in his 1899 lectures on "Hebrew, Jewish and Christian
Eschatology from Pre-prophetic Times till the Close of the New Testament Canon," which later appeared in *A Critical History of the Doctrine
of a Future Life in Israel, in Judaism and in Christianity*, R.H. Charles
pointed out that there existed prior to Amos a popular belief or expectation of the Day of YHWH, in the Israelite community.[5] This con-
scious perception was based on the covenant tradition, which had guar-
anteed Israel, "the Day," when YHWH will conquer His enemies in
battle on their behalf.

Charles' thought influenced John M.P. Smith, who also believed on
the existence of a poplular notion of the concept of the Day of the
Lord among the Israelite community before the preaching of the prophet

---

3   David P. Reid, *What Are They Saying About the Prophet?* (New York: Paulist
     Press, 1980), 11.
4   Details of some of these views will be the subject of Chapter One.
5   R.H. Charles, *A Critical History of the Doctrine of Future Life and Israel, in
     Judaism and in Christianity* (London: University Press, 1913), 85–86.

Amos.[6] Hugo Gressmann linked the Day of YHWH to the "popular eschatological belief" among the Israelites.[7] Sigmund Mowinckel on the other hand thought the motif was primarily to be understood within the context of Israel's cultic life of the New Year's Festival, borrowed from the Canaanites and Babylonian religions.[8]

In the 1940s Ladislav Černy and his school rejected Mowinckel's theory and argued that the meaning of the concept should be traced to the day of divine decree.[9]

Gerhard von Rad, and his school, in the 1950s, emphasized the Holy War *(Der heilige Krieg)* motif.[10] This was followed by the theophanic description of Meir Weiss, and the mediating role emphasized by Frank M. Cross in the 1960s.[11]

Most of these studies were not only addressed to the problem of prophetic eschatology or reduced to methodological debates, but were done exclusively of the overall *Dodekapropheton* (the Twelve Prophets).[12]

---

6   John M. P. Smith, "The Day of Yahweh," *AJT* 4. vol. 5 (1901): 505–533.

7   Hugo Gressmann, *Der Ursprung der israelitisch-jüdischen Eschatologie* (Göttingen: University Press, 1905) cited in K. J. Cathcart, "Day of the Lord," in *Anchor Bible Dictionary*, vol. 2 (ed. David N. Freedman et al., New York: Doubleday, 1992), 82–85.

8   See Sigmund Mowinckel, *Psalmenstudien II: Das Thronbesteigungsfest Jahwes und der Eschatologie* (Kristiana: Dybwad 1922) cited in Ladislav Černy, *Day of Yahweh and Some Relevant problems* (Praze: Nakladem Filosoficke Fakulty University Karlovy, 1948), 33–41.

9   Černy, *Day of Yahweh,* 73–77.

10 Gerhard von Rad, "The Origin of the Concept of the Day of Yahweh," *JSS* 4 (1959):102–103; Idem, *The Message of the Prophets* (New York: Harper, San Francisco, 1965), 95–99.

11 Meir Weiss, "The Origin of the 'Day of the Lord' – Reconsidered," *HUCA* 37 (1966): 29–62; Frank Moore Cross, "The Divine Warrior in Israel's Early Cult," in *Biblical Motifs: Origins and Transformation* (ed., Alexander Altman. Cambridge: Harvard University Press, 1966), 11–30.

12 There are several titles for the Book of the Twelve (the Twelve) Minor Prophets, *(Prophetae Minores = Latin)*, Dodekapropheton (German), οι δωδεκα προφηται or τον δωδεκαπροφητον *(ton dōdekaprophēton* = Greek). In this work these titles shall be used interchangeably to refer to the Twelve prophets in the MT order (Hosea, Joel , Amos, Obadiah, Jonah, Micah, Nahum, Habakkuk, Zephaniah, Haggai, Zechariah and Malachi) and *LXX* arrangement (Hosea, Amos, Micah

Even those scholars who later took on studies in Zephaniah and the Day of YHWH left out many of the critical, textual, literary and theological issues that bind together Zephaniah 1:14–18 and 3:14–20. The theology and salvific significance of the Day of YHWH, especially as uniquely expressed in Zephaniah 1:14–18 and 3:14–20 were minimally treated, if not completely neglected.

In other words, prior to this study, there has not been any systematic and coherent exegetical-theological study of the Day of YHWH (יום יהוה) and the restoration of fortunes (שוב שבות) in the prophet Zephaniah, a much lesser known or lesser read prophet.[13] Its rich theological, ecumenical and pastoral relevance to the study of the NT and the pluri-religious communities today, especially for the church in Africa (living side-by-side with ATR and Islam) is yet to be critically explored in the OT research. This constitutes part of my motivation for this work.

Joel, Obadiah, Jonah, Nahum, Habakkuk, Zephaniah, Haggai, Zechariah and Malachi). Scholars have also agreed that it is called "Minor Prophets," not because the content or theological message is less relevant or not important, but because of the relative length of the material content compared to larger books like Isaiah, Jeremiah, Ezekiel, and Daniel.

13 A few years ago I walked into one of the branches of the Bank of America in the United States with a copy of the Commentary on Zephaniah by Adele Berlin. I was comfortably seated by one of the bank officials who also happened to be a pastor of one of the Christian churches. When I responded to his inquiry with regard to the text in my hand, he surprisingly went into the inner chamber of the bank to confirm with his church member (bank staff) that there was a prophet by name, "Zephaniah, "in the Bible. I had similar experience in Israel, on February 2010 with a Jewish friend who confessed his lesser familiarity with the text of the prophet, and promised to go back and read it up.

C. Purpose of this Study

This study therefore, aims at overcoming the limitations and inadequacies of these past studies. It aims at filling-in these neglected gaps. This work aims at a more coherent and comprehensive exegetical and theological reassessment of the concept of the Day of the Lord in the prophetic traditions, particularly in the prophet Zephaniah. While reassessing this concept in selected passages of the prophetic tradtions, their relationship to Zephaniah and to the rest of the Twelve Minor Prophets, to the Deuteronomistic History, and to other Old Testament passages, particularly Psalm 126 shall be examined. The study will highlight areas of Zephaniah's creative adaptation, modification and contextualization, *vis-à-vis* his *Sitz-im-Leben*. This thesis argues that the judgment, threats, punishment and justice heard in Zephaniah 1:14–18, is not the end, but rather, an anticipation of the joy, salvation, hope and restoration or reversal of fortunes (שבות/*šᵉbût* שוב/*šûb*) evident in Zephaniah 3:14–20.

Moreover, the study aims at stressing the relevance and the theological values of the enduring message of repentance, humble trust and hope against hope, which Zephaniah offers people who yearn for peace irrespective of their cultural background and nationality. For Zephaniah, YHWH's day has no boundary. It is universal and unlimited to all cultures. It is an invitation to repentance and a reassurance of God's love and promises, which Jesus makes the foundation of his own life and teaching (Matt 11:29; Luke 6:20).[14] This work, as will be demonstrated in the chapters that follow, challenges us to be the "Zephaniahs" of today, and bearers of the message of hope, peace, justice and perseverance in seeking the Lord. This has meaning since the suffering and wrath heard in Zephaniah 1:14–18 is a foreshadowing of the hope, joy, and restoration of fortunes in Zephaniah 3:14–20. It means that the

---

14   D.J. Moeller, "Zephaniah, Book Of," in *The New Catholic Encyclopedia*, vol. 4 (ed. Berard L. Martherter et al., New York: Thompson & Gale, 2003), 918–919.

present, even if it is arduous, can be lived and accepted, if it leads toward a goal,[15] the restoration of fortunes by YHWH.

D. Key Working Definitions and Limitations of this Study

Terms and phrases like the "Day of YHWH," the "restoration of fortunes," and "eschatology," run through this thesis. Although they will be discussed fully in the progress of this work, their broad definition here serves to limit the perspective and fine-tune the scope of the present work. The prophets before Zephaniah, particularly Amos, changed the popular and positive notion of the Day of YHWH from that of the day in which God will fight a battle to defeat the enemies of Israel, bring them blessings and prosperity, to a negative notion of the Day of Judgment and accountability (Amos 5:18–20). On this Day, YHWH demonstrates his sovereignty and control over all creation and nations. This uniquely Israelite concept of God who involves himself in human history is well recalled, summarized and intensified in the three chapters of the Book of the prophet Zephaniah.

For Zephaniah the "Day of the Lord," is a day of YHWH's intervention in human history. It is a day of judgment, covenant renewal, a call for repentance and reassurances of God's love. This judgment is particular (Zeph 1: 4–10) and universal (Zeph 1:2–3, 18; 3:18–20). The immorality, idolatry, arrogance and pride of Judah and other nations would make this day one of wrath, distress, tribulations and utter destruction (1:14–18). But in spite of these misfortunes, Zephaniah reassures his audience of hope, salvation and restoration of fortunes. Members of this audience included, the non-arrogant, the remnant, the righteous, the humble poor, the non self-sufficient-rulers and the

---

15   Benedict XVI, Encyclical Letter, *Spe Salvi* (Vatican City, Libreria Editrice Vaticana, 2007), 3. See also Thomas Aquinas, *Summa Theologica* Ia IIae, q. 40, a.1, where this perseverance of holding on to the "goal" is interpreted as the Christian hope.

contrite of heart (Zeph 3:14–20). In other words, for Zephaniah, the Day of the Lord is both a day of judgment and a day of the restoration of fortunes of His people.

The restoration of fortunes (שבות/$š^e b\hat{u}t$ שוב/$š\hat{u}b$), in this thesis is not restricted to a political implication of the "return from captivity or exile." It embraces the social, moral, economic and religious reversal of fortunes. It has to do with the entire well-being of Israel, and human persons of all times and cultures.[16] This study understands that mercy would be the final work of God, who inspires hope. To a remnant of Israel composed of the "poor and a humble people of the land," (3:12ff), the proclamation would resound "Shout for joy O daughter of Zion, the Lord has annulled your judgment. YHWH, the warrior and savior is in your midst. He will rejoice over you with happy songs and renew you by his love, make you famous among nations, when he will restore the fortunes of Israel (3:14–20).[17] This window of hope is more intensified in the theology of Zephaniah, than in earlier prophetic traditions.[18] It has an inclusive implication of the entire history of redemption and fits into the broad OT and prophetic understanding of eschatology. This key concept as used in this study deserves an explanation here.

1. Defining the OT and Prophetic Eschatology

The term, "eschatology" comes from the Greek word "ἔχατον" meaning "furthest," "last," or "final."[19] In contemporary biblical exegesis, eschatology refers generally to God's future intervention to end the present course of events. This definition is subject to interpretation depending

16   This will be discussed in detail in Chapter Three.
17   See D. J. Moeller, "Zephaniah, Book of," 918–919.
18   See Carroll Stuhlmueller, *Amos, Hosea, Micah, Nahum, Zephaniah, Habakkuk* (OT 15; Collegeville Bible Commentary. Collegeville, MN: The Liturgical Press, 1986), 97. Here Stuhlmueller stresses that "Zephaniah's way of handling offenses enabled prophecy to take its first steps toward the apocalyptic style, more evident in such writings as Ezekiel 38–39 and fully developed in Daniel 7–12."
19   Richard N. Soulen, R. Kendall Soulen, *Handbook of Biblical Criticism* (3rd revised and expanded edition; Lousville/London: Westminster Jon Knox, 2001), 55.

on the aspect of biblical literature under investigation and the interpretative position that is adapted.[20]

In the OT understanding eschatology is not restricted to the narrow understanding of the term as the study of the doctrine of the last things, such as death, judgment, heaven, hell, and the nature of the resurrection of Jesus.[21] It is a change of course in human history through divine intervention, within God's plan of salvation. It is the realization of God's plan of salvation. Perhaps, the more reason why Johannes Lindblom, in 1962, critically observed that if eschatology is a doctrine of the end of the world and the history of mankind, there is no eschatology at all in the Old Testament prophets.[22] This study focuses on prophetic eschatology.

Early Israel had no doctrine of the end of the world, the last judgment, and the resurrection to eternal life beyond the grave as such. In other words, eschatology in this context must be seen in a sense adapted to the general character of the prophetic message by utilizing the idea of the two ages ("this age" and the "age to come"), rather than that of the end of all things.[23] Lindblom stresses that passages which describe the new age may be said to express a *positive eschatology*, while those which speak of the end, express what he calls a *negative eschatology*. Here the predictions refer to Israel as having a *national eschatology*. If the eschatology is widened to include the world and all mankind, we may appropriately speak of a *universal eschatology*. And when the age to

---

20   See Soulen, *Biblical Criticism*, 55–56; David L. Petersen, "Eschatology (OT)," 575, where he suggests that the following three things should be kept in mind while discussing OT eschatology: (1) the term is used with widely different meaning; (2) the term as applied to OT literature dates back to only the nineteenth century; (3) the term though sounds new, is reminiscent of a systematic treatment of Israelites thoughts and traditions. More so, eschatology, senso *stricto* (an apocalyptic, cataclysmic and new age of conflict followed by utopic bliss and individual fate, after life), is different from the eschatology which is most often innately communal and cosmic in reference.

21   Soulen, *Biblical Criticism*, 55.

22   Johannes Lindblom, *Prophecy in Ancient Israel* (Philadelphia: Fortress Press, 1962), 360.

23   Lindblom, *Prophecy*, 360.

come is thought of as an age of happiness and bliss, we have *eschatology of salvation (Heilseschatologie)* in contrast to eschatology of misfortune *(Unheilseschatologie)*.[24]

Similarly, John Bright confirms that if we define eschatology *senso stricto*, much as it would be understood in dogmatic theology, it is probably improper to speak of eschatology in connection with the pre-exilic prophets, including Zephaniah.[25] In fact in biblical scholarship John J. Collins suggests that eschatology, broadly speaking, "refers to the expectation of any decisive change in the course of history through the intervention of God."[26] Whether this change is national or cosmic cannot be strictly isolated since the plan of salvation envisaged various eschatological stages.

Hans Schwarz, in his recent studies on OT and NT eschatology rightly singles out three main relevant points with regard to OT eschatology in particular.[27] They include the human destiny, the last judgment, and the promise of hope for a Messiah. The last point emerged fairly late, while the first one (human destiny) is the earliest.[28] Schwarz observes that Israel was sandwiched between the Mesopotamian and Egyptian eschatological cultures. But the OT writings do not demonstrate these issues of death and life as found in these other cultures.[29]

---

24   Lindblom, *Prophecy*, 362.

25   John Bright, *Covenant and Promise: The Prophetic Understanding of the Future in the Pre-Exilic Israel* (Philadelphia: The Westminster Press, 1976), 18.

26   John J. Collins, "Old Testament Apocalypticism and Eschatology," in *NJBC* (eds., Raymond E. Brown, Joseph Fitzmyer and Roland E. Murphy; New Jersey: Prentice Hall, 1990), 298.

27   For an interesting exposition of Christian Eschatology, see Hans Schwarz, *Eschatology* (Grand Rapids, MI: Eerdmans, 2000), 107–172.

28   Schwarz, *Eschatology*, 31.

29   See Schwarz, *Eschatology*, 32–33. Here a detailed analysis of "death and the hereafter" consciousness in Egypt and Mesopotamia is presented. In Egypt there are the Pyramid Texts from the third millennium, the Coffin Texts (2000 B.C.E.) and the Book of the Dead (1500 B.C.E). These are all literature that deal with the journey of the dead into the afterlife, and a guide to the living, that they would know what to expect once they died. In Mesopotamia, particularly Assyria and Babylonia, the texts concerning the hereafter are parts of the twelfth table of the Gilgamesh Epic and Ishtar's journey into the netherworld.

For Israel the emphasis on this life was based on her understanding of God, who not only had a plan to save Israel, but had acted and shown His mighty power in liberating them from Egypt with a promise of blessings and prosperity in the future, sealed with the covenant with Abraham (Gen 12:1–9; 15:1–21; 17:1–27), Moses (Exod 19–24) and David (2 Sam 7:1–17) and with Jesus in the NT (Matt 1:1–17; Luke 1:55–73).

It was based on the Patriarchal, Davidic and Sinaitic traditions.[30] God was a God of life, blessing and prosperity. The end usually desired by the Israelites was death in old age with their sons and children around them (Gen 49:33), provided they fear the Lord (Prov 10:27).[31]

Just as emphasis was on this worldly aspect of life, early death was understood as punishment for godlessness (1 Sam 2:32). However there were a few occasions where some were taken up to God in heaven (Enoch, Gen 5:24; Elijah, 2 Kgs 2:11). This demonstrated a special blessing given to those who lived an outstanding life before God while here on earth. It is in the later part of the OT, in the second Temple and in the NT times that resurrection is mentioned "Of those who are sleeping in the land of dust, many will awaken, some to everlasting life, some to shame and everlasting disgrace. Those who are wise will shine

---

30   David L. Petersen, "Eschatology (OT)," *ABD* 2: 575–79. See also Soulen, *Biblical Criticism*, 55. Here Soulen strongly affirms that eschatology is fed by numerous strands of bliblical tradition, including, God's promises to the ancestors (Gen 49:8–12; Deut 33:13–17; cf Num 23:21). Also see details of some of these events of salvation history *(Heilsgeschichte)* in Thomas P. McCreesh, "Salvation History," in *The New Dictionary of Theology* (eds. Joseph A. Komonchak, Mary Collins and Dermot A. Lane; Bangalore: Theological Publications, Gill and Macmillan, 1996), 929–931. Here God's deeds for the salvation of the world are narrated (Exod 14–15:21; Deut 5:15; 6:20–23; Josh 24:6–7; Isa 51:10): the divine purpose (Exod 19:1–6), Israel became God's people (Deut 4:1; Josh 1:2–6), recognizing creation (Gen 12–50), sin and punishment (Gen 1–11), God's covenant (2 Sam 7), exile (1 Sam 12:13–15), prophetic justice (Amos 6; Hos 10; Isa 5), the call to trust in God (Isa 7:4–17) and a transformed vision of the future (Zeph 3:14–20; Jer 31:31–34) and the apocalyptic and NT visions of the fulfillment of the prophecies (Matt 13; Lk 4).
31   Schwarz, *Eschatology*, 36–37.

as brightly as the expanse of the heavens, and those who have instructed many in uprightness, as bright as stars for all eternity" (Dan 12:1–3).[32]

In fact, for Israel, God's judgment was first conceived as judgment here on earth and during our lifetime (Deut 32:35). One was expected to fear and trust in God, who is holy and gracious. God judges anyone who ignores his precepts and laws, including Israel. God is not just a God of promise and threat. He brings his promises and threats to reality. It was a judgment within the frame of history that was constantly modified by the prophets.[33]

In other words, this was a familiar concept that was already rooted positively in the ancient culture of Israel.[34] They believed the anticipation of a definitive divine intervention through which God would first bring judgment on his people and then, in the farther future, would deliver, restore, and thus bring them to his triumphing purpose. Zephaniah expanded on the past prophetic traditions, especially of Amos 5:18–20, a pattern of communicating this expectation. Prophets among other things attacked the religious, social, and moral abuses of which the nation was guilty.

---

32 Schwarz, *Eschatology*, 38.

33 See Jürgen Moltmann, *Theology of Hope: On the Ground and the Implications of a Christian Eschatology* (trans. J. W. Leitch; New York: Haper & Row, 1967), 104–105 cited in Schwarz, *Eschatology*, 43. Here Moltmann demonstrates with great passion his conviction that God's promises in the life of Israel was constantly modified and expanded.

34 See Th. C. Vriezen, "Prophecy and Eschatological," in VTSup, vol 1, *Congress Volume: Copenhagen 1953* (Leiden: Brill, 1953), 199–229 cited in Schwarz, *Eschatology*, 43. What is interesting here is Vriezen's contribution to the understanding of Israel's notion of eschatology. Although he was aware of the risk of this division that may overlap, he categorized the development of this understanding as follows: (1) pre-eschatological period/pre-classical prophetic period, when Israel's hope is only political and purely nationalistic (2) proto-eschatological period (Isaiah and his contemporizes), when the vision of a new people and a new universal kingdom begins to emerge (3) actual eschatological period (Deutero-Isaiah and his contemporaries), when the kingdom of God is not only seen as coming in visions, but as changing the world and (4) transcendental-eschatological period of apocalyptic expectation: salvation is expected not to come in this world, but either spiritually in heaven or after a cosmic catastrophe in a new world.

They also criticized in the strongest terms the policies of state which its leaders follow. They were not only the conscience of their people, but were also social critics of their society. The prophets would declare that the nation was under judgment, facing imminent danger on the Day of YHWH.[35]

Usually their message was not just this declaration of judgment, but also hope and salvation. For example in Isaiah, the hope for a new future, with a universal scope of salvation, which would come to influence Zephaniah, is intensified and expanded. Some have suggested that Isaiah be called, "the first preacher of the eschatological expectation." Isaiah expected a complete destruction to be followed by a universal salvation. This salvation was no longer confined to Israel, but opened to the world.[36]

Indeed, the prophets usually looked beyond the judgment they were announcing and anticipating that God will come again in mercy and love to restore his glory and their fortunes, establishing his rule over them, in righteousness and peace.

Zephaniah built on these traditions followed by Deutero-Isaiah who introduced the suffering servant of YHWH (Is 42:1–4; 49:1–6; 50:4–11; 52:13–53:12) as a fulfillment of that promise made to David (Isa 55:3). This promise is believed in the NT to have been fulfilled in the person of Jesus Christ, the Messiah, and the High Priest (Heb 4).[37]

---

35   Bright, *Covenant and Promise*, 15. See also Emil A. Wcela, *The Prophets: God's Spokesmen through the Years* (God's Word Today. A New Study Guide to the Bible; New York: Publo Publishing, 1980), 9–12. Here Wcela stresses that at their best, the prophets were defenders of true faith in Yahweh: they would condemn false steps Israel might be taking in working out its relationship with Yahweh, encourage a certain way of life or direction in which Israel ought to move, defend moral or social values. At times, they would condemn the king for his abuse of power.

36   Th. C. Vriezen, *An Outline of Old Testament Theology* (Newton, MA: Bradford, 1958), 360.

37   See Schwarz, *Eschatology*, 46–54 for detail study of the significance of "Messiah" and the expansion of Messianic hopes in the apocalyptic period. Also Mowinckel, in *He That Cometh*, 187–257 though from a cultic perspective has done extensive study on the significance of these texts of the Suffering Servant of YHWH (Isaiah 42–53). He observes that, "the church has from the very beginning seen in Jesus Christ the true fulfillment of these prophecies."

Similarly, Bright writes that "this promise for future salvation is one of the most distinctive features in the message of the prophets. He stresses that it is this, perhaps more than anything else, which serves to bind the OT unbreakably with the NT, in a single canon of Scripture."[38]

In other words, the promise heard in the OT is fulfilled in the NT. It is the OT that provides the historical background for the eschatological proclamation of Jesus in the NT, which is not within the scope of this work.[39] However it is worth noting that it is within this context that

---

38 Bright, *Covenant and Promise*, 15.

39 See Schwarz, *Eschatology*, 61–103. Here, Eschatology in the NT is discussed in full to include: the Jewish context, the eschatological figure of Jesus (his eschatological message of the Kingdom, his self understanding, Jesus and the question of the future), the eschatological proclamation of the evangelists, the emphasis on the present in John's gospel, the eschatological message of Paul, and the eschatological scope of the early church. Other studies on Christian eschatology by Schwarz include: Adolf von Harnack, *What is Christianity?* (trans., Th. B. Saunders. New York: Harper, 1957), 54 ("the kingdom of God for him is already present in the hearts of men"), Johannes Weiss, *Jesus' Proclamation of the Kingdom of God* (1892) (trans., with intro., Hyde Hiers and David Larrimore Holland (London: SCM, 1971), 132–33 ("for him the kingdom is totally otherworldly, and its realization is up to God alone and not reliant on human action"), Albert Schweitzer, *The Mystery of the Kingdom of God: The Secret of Jesus' Messiahship and Passion* (trans., Walter Lowrie. New York: Macmillan, 1950), 60 (he identifies with "consequent eschatology." For him, "we do not know anything about Jesus's earlier development – "at his baptism the secret of his existence was disclosed to him, that he was the one whom God had destined to be the Messiah"), Marcus J. Borg, *Jesus in Contemporary Scholarship* (Valley Forge, PA: Trinity Press International Press, 1994), 57 (for him "the kingdom of God is not a definite concept, but a symbol pointing to the kingship of God, the divine power and sovereignty, compassion and justice. Jesus invited the present hearers to 'enter' it and have their lives shaped by it"), C. H. Dodd, *The Parables of the Kingdom* (New York: Scribner, 1961), vii (This world has become the scene of divine drama. It was a "realized eschatology" because in Jesus the eternal entered decisively into history), John A. T. Robinson, *Jesus and His Coming: The Emergence of a Doctrine* (London: SCM, 1957), 136–37 (he sees no evidence of the second coming of Christ), Oscar Cullmann, *Salvation in History* (trans. S. G. Sowers et al., London: SCM, 1967), 179–80 (Jesus expected the coming of the *eschaton* in the near future, but did not occur, but the future

O. Cullmann and J. Jeremias rightly see eschatology as fulfillment and promise.[40] For them salvation is already present and guarantees the not yet of its final realization. Hence, eschatology implies a present reality and a future expectation.[41] By eschatology as in OT criticism, and in the prophetic traditions this study shall broadly and mostly be referring to Israel's orientation toward the immediate future, with a wider implication for Christian hope or final drama of salvific history fore-

---

remain unchanged. Jesus was also aware of the interim period, the time of the church. The idea of immediate coming was as a result of the tension between the salvation which has occurred in Jesus and the final salvific act yet to occur), idem *Christ and Time: The Primitive Christian Conception of Time and History* (trans. F. V. Filson; London: SCM, 1962), 84–185 (stresses present and future dimensions of eschatology).

40   See also Soulen, *Biblical Criticism*, 55–56. Here, in my own opinion, Soulen has rightly and summarily observes different ways scholars and theologians have broadly approached the subject of eschatology by simply drawing a broad distinction between prophetic eschatology and apocalyptic eschatology or apocalypticism to differentiate between (a) expectation concerning the future found in the prophetic warnings/promise in the OT and (b) expectations concerning an imminent crisis characteristic of apocalyptic literature. The later flourished in the 2nd Temple and NT (200 B.C.E.–200 C.E.); and its major examples are in Daniel 7–12 and Revelation. Though prophetic eschatology and apocalyptic eschatology are continuous in many aspects, Soulen notes, their characteristic emphases differ. The Prophets addressed issues of status, relationships, prosperity etc., within the present world, where God was at work guiding things toward fulfillment or consummation; while the apocalypticists warned of God's intervention from the beyond, in radical disjunction with history, to destroy and re-create the world. Prophetic eschatology announces God's activity within the arena of the present world; apocalyptic eschatology announces God's plans to interrupt and end history because it is heading in a direction contrary to God's will. For him "J. Jeremiah developed perhaps the most adequate view of NT's presentation of eschatology. This is the position that in Jesus we have "inaugurating eschatology." See also; George W. E. Nickelsburg, "Eschatology (Early Jewish)," *ABD* 2: 579–594; D. E. Aune, "Eschatology (Early Christian)," *ABD* 2: 594–609.

41   Soulen, *Biblical Criticism*, 56.

36

shadowed by Zephaniah 3:14–18.[42] It is a change of course in human history through the divine intervention, within God's plan of salvation, which is present with the implication of a future expectation or the final drama of salvation history. The prophets enabled Israel to look back creatively on its past, judge the present and anticipate the future. The Day of YHWH envisioned by Zephaniah is an eschatological day of judgment with a future day of renewal and restoration of the fortunes of the remnant who repent, and in which a new work of YHWH brings about salvation to Israel to an extent hitherto unknown.

2. The Limitations of this Study

Following our definition of prophetic eschatology, with its present and future implications, the question of discerning whether the Day of the Lord in Zephaniah was a historical or an eschatological event is often very difficult to decide.[43] It poses a limitation to this study.

In other word, the distinction or the demarcation between the historical and the eschatological in the prophet Zephaniah, as in all other prophets is difficult to make.[44] This study sees the Day of the Lord as both historical and eschatological in Zephaniah. It is both a present and a future reality. The day will occur in history as well as in the final drama of history, the realization of God's plan of salvation.[45]

---

42 See Reid, *What Are They Saying About the Prophet?*, 48–59. Here the OT and prophetic understanding of the future, time, promise and fulfillment are fully discussed. He defines Israel's future as the organic outreach of the religious decisiveness with which the Israelites choose to own their turf in the present.

43 See Willem Vanggermeren, *Interpreting the Prophetic Word* (Grand Rapids, Zondervan, 1990), 174–175 where it is rightly stated that "though the Lord's act of judgment takes place throughout the history of redemption, each act foreshadows the final judgment."

44 Eugene H. Merrill, *Kingdom of Priests: A History of Old Testament Israel* (Grand Rapids; MI: Baker, 1987), 457.

45 See Greg King, "The Day of the Lord in Zephaniah," *Bibliotheca Sacra* 152 (January–March 1995): 31–32.

It is also worth noting from the beginning that particular attention and detailed exegesis in this work shall concentrate on the two *pericopae* of Zephaniah 1:14–18 and 3: 14–20. While we study these texts in great details, references will need to be made to the texts that precede and follow them (Zeph1–3).[46] Even though the Day of the Lord (יום יהוה) is an attractive theological and eschatological concept in the circle of Israel's prophets of diverse historical times and settings, the scope of this work does not permit detailed analysis of all the prophets. Effort shall rather be concentrated on emphasizing how Zephaniah adapted, modified and contextualized this concept from past traditions to suit his own *Sitz-im-Leben*. This is done by studying only selected Day of YHWH passages in the Twelve Minor Prophets as well in the Major Prophets (Isaiah, Jeremiah, and Ezekiel) and Psalm 126 which shares similar theological themes, poetic and literary features with Zephaniah. In comparing Zephaniah with the prophetic literature, Amos 5:18–20 shall always be used as a case study since it is almost unanimously agreed among scholars that the Day of YHWH was first heard in Amos, the first of the classical prophets.

Similarly, while comparing Zephaniah with the DH (Deut–2 Kings) this study will not engage in detailed analysis of each of the books of the DH. Rather, with examples from selected passages of the DH we shall sketch in broad outlines or stress those common theological themes that run through Zephaniah, the remaining Minor Prophets and the DH. The similarity of language and literary features, and shared socio-historical contexts among these texts shall be demonstrated by this study. The relevance of these contacts and sharings shall also be stressed.

In sum, this work limits its focus mainly to the theology of Zephaniah and its values for today, especially as conveyed by the concepts of the Day of YHWH and restoration of fortunes. It basically argues that although there might be tribulations and judgment, restoration will be the final work of God to a remnant of Israel and to the nations who trust and seek refuge in YHWH alone.

---

46 See my proposed working-structure of the Book of Zephaniah in Chapter Two of this study.

E. Contributions and Originality

Given the narrow and exclusive approaches of past scholars to the study of the Day of YHWH, and a lack of a coherent, systematic and exegetical-theological study of Zephaniah 1:14–18 and 3:14–20 in the history of OT research, this study is an original attempt to fill that void. It intends to open the door, at least to a highlighting of those aspects of Zephaniah's theology which are often neglected or omitted in OT studies. It will also permit scholars, exegetes and theologians of different fields of specialization, especially of diverse Christian cultural backgrounds, to break out from those narrow boundaries to which the Day of YHWH investigation has often been confined.

Besides this renewed investigation this work attempts a creative and original insight into the salvific, forward-looking implication and universal relevance of Zephaniah's texts to the NT and to the the contemporary world of multi-religious communities, in a particular way to the Church in Africa. Elements of interreligious and cultural dialogue are identified. This is also unprecedented in the history of the study of the Day of YHWH in Prophet Zephaniah. This thesis serves to highlight the fact that YHWH's primary goal in judgment, punishment and justice (Zeph 1:14–18) is to renew the fellowship of his people of all cultures with Himself. With it, we are reminded that our future depends on how we respond ethically to the demands of the present. It also serves as a reassurance of YHWH's promises and love, the renewal and restoration of the fortunes (שבות/šᵉbût שוב/šûb) of his remnant people (Zeph 3:14–20).

F. Method and Methodology

Since the Day of YHWH is a concept that developed and passed through a historical tradition, this study will use the tools of various historical-critical methods of exegesis, supplemented by literary criticism. With the historical-critical method, this study will examine the meaning and significance of this concept within the historical context or the *Sitz-im-Leben* of the prophets, especially Amos. This is aimed at demonstrating how and why Zephaniah adapted, modified, contextualized or reinterpreted this theme to suit his own life situation. Literary criticism will help to deal with the question of authenticity, structure, final form, genre, poetic and other linguistic features that characterize Zephaniah 1:14–18 and 3:14–20. Hopefully this will lead us to a clearer understanding of the theological meaning and pastoral significance of the texts under investigation.

This dissertation contains six concise Chapters with a summary result and a general concluding portion. Additional information in these Chapters is assigned to the footnotes. Chapter one surveys the history of research, and various methodological approaches employed by various scholars from the 1940s towards the general meaning or interpretation of the Day of YHWH. The historical background of Zephaniah: person, text and content, date, authorship of the book and his socio-historical context are considered in this Chapter. This will help to highlight the theological message of the prophet. Recent studies on Zephaniah as a whole and on his concept of the Day of YHWH in particular, shall be studied.

Chapter Two focuses on Prophet Zephaniah. It dwells on his overwhelming theme and on the theology of the "Day of YHWH," adapted from past prophetic traditions.[47] The structure of Zephaniah will be examined so as to determine the textual limit and literary integrity of Zephaniah 1:14–18. The unit of Zephaniah 1:14–18 will be given a fresh translation, using tools of textual criticism to determine Zephaniah's prophetic woes and oracles. This is followed by a detailed exegesis of Zephaniah 1:14–18. The message of the Day of Judgment that fills Zephaniah 1:14–18 is a foreshadowing of the theology of divine promises, hope and restoration of fortunes (Zeph 3:14–20), discussed in the following Chapter.

---

47 Gaetano Savoca, *Abdia-Naum, Abcuc-Sofonia: nuova version, introduction e commento* (ILB.PT 18; Milano: Paoline Editoriale Libri, 2006), 145.

Chapter Three discusses in detail the theology of the restoration of fortunes in the Prophet Zephaniah (3:14–20). It focuses on the usages of (שבות/šᵉbût שוב/šûb) (restore fortunes), translates, delimits and exegetes the passage (Zeph 3:14–20) within the overall book of Prophet Zephaniah. The poetic and literary features, as well as the theological-eschatological themes and elements of this prophetic text are discussed. This study suggests that the joyful cheers (רני) of the people in 3:14–20, reverse the bitter cry of the warrior (מר צרח שם גבור), the wrath (עברה), distress and tribulation (צרה ומצוקה), ruin and desolation (שאה ומשואה), darkness and gloom (חשך ואפלה), the terrible clouds (ענן וערפל), the cry of war with trumpet blast (שופר ותרועה) and the hostility (צרר) of Zephaniah 1:14–18.

Zephaniah not only adapted past traditions, but also actualized them in his life situation. Chapter Four will re-examine the "Day of YHWH" in the past prophetic traditions especially in Amos 5:18–20. This will serve to create the setting for the comparative study of this concept in Zephaniah and in other prophets. It will also serve to shed more light on the concept of the Day of YHWH in Zephaniah and stress Zephaniah's creative adaptation, modification and contextualization of his theological message. This of course challenges us today to constantly adapt the vitality of the Word of God and to patiently seek its meaning in history and tradition through faith.

Since these texts are not isolated from the rest of the OT, especially, the Twelve Minor Prophets, attempts will be made to underline such relationship with a goal of emphasizing the specificity of Zephaniah's uniqueness in the following Chapter. Taking cognizance of this inter-relatedness of our texts with other OT passages and traditions, Chapter Five examines the place or the relationship of Zephaniah 1:14–18 and 3:14–20, with the Books of the OT, especially with the entire three chapters of the Book of Zephaniah, the *Dodekapropheton*, DH and Psalm 126. Zephaniah's creative way of adapting and contextualizing the concept of the Day of YHWH shall be foregrounded. This will help us recognize better the pastoral roles of the prophets who helped Israel put language on its experiences.[48] They helped to reinterpret Israel's

---

48   Reid, *What Are They Saying About the Prophets?*, 33–34.

reality as her creative, living, challenging and actualizing memory.[49] Zephaniah challenges each of us to live responsibly in the ambience of history, on the twilight of a new tomorrow which we hopefully choose. This choice embodies that pattern of living fully in the present, anticipating the future, enlivened and enabled by the life-giving tradtions of the past.

Chapter Six affords this study as an opportunity to step back and reflect on the theological relevance and contemporary values of Zephaniah 1:14–18 and 3:14–20 to the larger human society, the NT and religious communities, particularly the Church in Africa. Since the socio-political, religious, cultural and moral problems encountered by Zephaniah, are also confronted by the Church and the pluri-religious society of today, including the Church in Africa, the ecumenical and interreligious values of this study shall be stressed.[50]

Finally, the result of this study will be summarized in the general concluding section, underlining the enduring theological message of Zephaniah. YHWH judges and punishes the arrogant, and the idolaters. This punishment expressed in forms of wrath and utter devastation is provoked by sin and the bad choices of human beings. It is aimed at the renewal of true friendship and fellowship with the Lord. Repentance, hope, faith and humble trust in God alone are true settings for such renewal, God's blessings, divine promises, prosperity and restoration of fortunes.

---

49   See Adele Berlin, *Zephaniah: A New Translation with Introduction and Commentary* (AB 25A; New York: Doubleday, 1994), 13–16. Here she recognizes the vast intertextual relationship of Zephaniah with the entire Hebrew Bible.

50   See John Paul II, *The Church in Africa: Post-Synodal Apostolic Exhortation Ecclesia in Africa* (Nairobi, Kenya: Pauline Publicaiton, 1995), 61–62. Here the importance of inculturating the faith, the gospel and theology is emphasized, because "a faith that does not become culture is not fully accepted, not entirely thought out, not fully lived."

Chapter One

A Survey of the History of Research on the Day of YHWH and General Background of Zephaniah

1.1 Day of YHWH Studies and Multiple Schools of Thought

The search for the meaning, origin, and significance of the concept of the Day of YHWH (יום יהוה) is a path many biblical exegetes, theologians, historians of religions and historiographers have walked significantly in the scholarly-past, but without a consensus. Surprisingly, in spite of the centrality of this concept in the Old Testament and in Hebrew religion there has not been a major systematic investigation of it, particularly in the theology of Zephaniah.

Some scholars have dealt with it partially in various chapters of their books, while some merely commented on previous commentaries made on it. A handful of scholars have also made some substantial remarks on the background and historical origin of this concept, but with little insight into its contemporary theological values. Many others are not even aware that there is a prophet called Zephaniah. Although this chapter is devoted to a step-by-step survey of these past approaches, its result will help us to establish a distinguishable methodological framework which will enable us discuss relevant prophetic passages that influenced Zephaniah's theology of the Day of YHWH. It will also help us appreciate the place of this concept in the history of OT studies.

1.1.1 Studies on the Day of YHWH Prior to 1950

Prior to 1950, R.H. Charles, John Merlin Powis Smith, Hugo Gress-mann, Sigmund Mowinckel, Ladislav Černy and H. Wheeler Robinson are among those scholars whose opinions on the study of the Day of YHWH would come to influence generations of exegetes, historians and theologians. In his 1899 Lectures on "Hebrew, Jewish and Christian eschatology from pre-prophetic times till the Close of the New Testament Canon," which later appeared in, *A Critical History of the Doctrine of a Future Life in Israel, in Judaism, and in Christianity*, R.H. Charles observed that there existed before Amos a popular belief and expectation of the Day of YHWH. This was a day when YHWH will conquer His enemies in battle. It was a day when YHWH would challenge and judge Israel's adversaries.[1] Charles' contribution would be perceived in subsequent exegesis, although he has also been strongly criticized by modern scholars. K.J. Cathcart, for example, critically observed that given the title of Charles' lectures, he may have misunderstood eschatological hopes to be part and parcel of the Day of YHWH. Cathcart believes that since "eschatology proper," arose in the exile, an eschatological aspect of the Day of YHWH belongs to the late prophecy.[2]

In 1901, John M.P. Smith wrote a lengthy article "The Day of YHWH," in his effort to trace the origin of יום יהוה in the Hebrew Bible. Like Charles, Smith agrees on the popular notion of the Day of YHWH. For him, "the origin of the idea of the Day of YHWH must be sought in the pre-prophetic stage of Israel's history."[3]

Smith traces the initial appearance of the Day of YHWH idea in the Hebrew Bible, to the prophecy of Amos, in the prosperous times of Jeroboam II (788–747 B.C.E.). He argues that, prior to Amos's prophecy, this idea pre-existed in the thought and consciousness of the people. For these people, the Day of YHWH (יום יהוה) simply meant the time

---

1 Charles, *A Critical History of the Doctrine of Future Life in Israel*, 85–86.
2 K.J. Cathcart, "Day of Yahweh," in *ABD* 2: 84.
3 John M.P. Smith, "The Day of Yahweh," *AJT* 4, Vol 5 (1901): 505–533.

or desired period when an era of great glory and prosperity would be inaugurated for Israel, as a special nation with a divine mission.[4]

This hope for a great and immediate future for this unique nation through the help of YHWH was fostered by tradition and by an outgrowth of the general Semitic conception of a God-ordained commission. This mission presupposed extension of the sphere of the divine authority and sovereignty. It also presupposed a source of inspiration and courage in the great work of the conquest of Canaan. The hope for the Day of YHWH, according to Smith, was developed and strengthened by the realization of the progress witnessed in the nation's history, impressed upon the consciousness of the citizens by the prophets.[5]

Indeed, besides the implication of a God-given commission, there was the conception of YHWH as a Living and True God who prevails over other gods, since ancient Israel was certainly a polytheistic and monolatrous[6] culture, YHWH living side by side with other Canaanites neighbors.[7] Smith identifies the political relation of early Israel with

4   Smith, "Day of Yahweh," 505. Here, Smith makes reference to Yahwistic and Elohistic passages of a pre-prophetic thought of God's promises to a special and unique nation (cf. Gen 12 :1–10; 18:18ff.; 27: 28–29; Exod 19: 4–5; 34:10–11; Num 23:9–10; 24:17).

5   Smith, "Day of Yahweh," 508–509.

6   See Robert Karl Gnuse, *No Other Gods: Emergent Monotheism in Israel* (JSOT 241; England: Sheffield Academic Press, 1997), 315 and Nili Fox, "Concept of God in Israel and the Question of Monotheism," in *Text, Artifact, and Image: Revealing Ancient Israelite Religion* (ed. Gary Beckman and Theodore J. Lewis; Rhode Island: Brown Judaic Studies, 2006), 326–345 where scholars are almost of a consensus that, Monolatry is basically the oneness of the godhead only in reference to worship as there is an ontological plurality of knowledge of gods. It is a synonym for "henotheism," "the exclusive worship of a tribal-national deity which did not deny the reality of patron deities of other people." Cf John Bright, *A History of Israel* (4th ed. Louisville/London: Westminster John Knox Press, 2000), 145. In ancient Israel for example, Baal, El, Asharah, etc, existed side by side with worship of YHWH. Polytheism is the recognition and worship of many or a plurality of gods.

7   See Gnuse, *No Other Gods*, 62–128 and Mark. S. Smith, *The Early History of God: Yahweh and the Other Deities in Ancient Israel* (2nd ed.; Grand Rapids, MI: Eerdmans, 2002), xii–xxxxvi for a detailed and impressive research, history and debate, stressing the gradual, evolutionary and revolutionary process of the

outside nations as another element that emboldened the early notion of יום יהוה (the Day of YHWH). Given the fierce battles and conflicts associated with the process of settlement in Canaan during the period of the Judges and early kings, Smith believes that Israel had adopted a policy of conciliation toward the Canaanite's neighbors and "strangers."[8]

In the light of the above argument Smith concludes that "the popular conception of the Day of Yahweh was that of a great day of battle on which Yahweh placed himself at the head of the armies of Israel and led them through an overwhelming victory over all their enemies."[9]

Smith insists that it was in the hands of Amos that the concept of the Day of YHWH underwent a transformation to be later followed, adapted, and modified and contexualized by subsequent prophets like Isaiah, Joel, Jeremiah and Zephaniah.[10]

However, Smith sums up his work, which some scholars thought was too general, by outlining the common elements that characterize the Day of YHWH in the prophetic literature.[11] They include the contextualization of the concept by each prophet, as their consciousness of the divine increased. There was also the recognition of the fact that the present age was only temporary and that it must give way to a better and glorious one, on the coming Day of YHWH. Connected to this Day of YHWH was the picture of great catastrophic dramas in the natural world. The Day was also thought to be serving punitive purposes. The time of the coming of the Day was indefinite, though for the most part it was conceived of as being near at hand.[12]

---

movement of monolatrous early Israel culture, by convergence, assimilation and differentiation in the pre-exilic era to a radical monotheistic culture during the exile (586–538 B.C.E.), with its climax in the time of Second Isaiah.

8   Smith, "Day of Yahweh," 510.

9   Smith, "Day of Yahweh," 512.

10   Detail traditions of the concept of יום יהוה (the Day of YHWH) in the prophetic literature will be treated in Chapter Two of this work.

11   Černy, in *The Day of Yahweh*, 32 (whose work will be discussed later), thought that Smith's "connection between the idea of the Day of Yahweh and the general Semitic ideological background was rather too general and external."

12   Smith, "Day of Yahweh," 530–531.

Finally, the Day of YHWH was represented as introducing a new political state, since the prophets were patriots, loyal to Israel and Judah as well as to YHWH. The concept of the Day of YHWH reflected from generation to generation the political and social *Sitz-im-Leben* of the nation.[13]

After Charles and Smith came Hugo Gressmann, who in 1905, with the influence of Herman Gunkel,[14] observed that there existed in Israel an ancient prophetic popular eschatology. This popular expectation was a living element in the people's faith.[15] Using the Day of YHWH in Amos 5:18–20 as his starting point, Gressmann believes in the mythological origin of eschatology, which he divided into "*'Unheils-echatologie'* and *'Heilseschatologie'*."[16] Just as Palestinian eschatological ideas originated from ancient Oriental myths, the Hebrew eschatology

---

13   Smith, "Day of Yahweh," 533.

14   See detailed ideas of Gunkel, as cited by Černy in *Day of Yahweh*, 33–41. Gunkel belongs to "Die Religionsgeschichtliche Schule" ("History of Religions School"). Having studied Genesis 1 and Revelation 22, he asserts in his work, *Schöpfung und Chaos in Urzeit und Endzeit* (Göttingen: University Press, 1895), that "we too have turned for the solution of many problems set by eschatology, as well as for the understanding of a number of difficult terms, constantly recurring in all periods of its development, to the oldest stock of Semitic mythology, that came from Babylonia, the source of Hebrew Eschatology." See also Richard N. Soulen and R. Kendall Soulen, *Handbook of Biblical Criticism* (3rd edition, expanded and revised; Louisville: Westminster John Knox Press, 2001), 161 for detailed explanation of *"Religionsgeschichtliche Schule."* It is explained as "the name given to a group of Protestant scholars in Germany, who, at the turn of the 20th cent., sought to understand the history and literature of ancient Israel, Judaism, and early Christianity by situating them within the history of Ancient Near Eastern Religions generally."

15   Details of Gressmann's views can also be found in Johannes Lindblom, *Prophecy in Ancient Israel* (Philadephia: Fortress Press, 1962), 316–317.

16   Hugo Gressmann, *Der Ursprung*, 157–246. See also Lindblom, *Prophecy*, 316–317. Here the following criticism leveled against Gressmann gives us a deeper insight into Gressmann's notion of eschatology, that "what German scholars call eschatology is not eschatology at all. A theophany has itself nothing to do with eschatology. The oracular style, frequently used by the prophets, gives their untterances an irrational character, in some measure reminiscent of eschatological sayings. Purely historical events are often clothed in the mythological garb."

he said is of foreign geographic and ethnic origin that came to influence the prophetic books.[17]

Gressmann, in my own opinion, may also share in the criticism levelled against Charles, that it is doubtful if one can talk of eschatology in a proper sense, especially in Babylonian and Egyptian cultures before the Exile. Gressmann, with the influence of his master Gunkel, spent much time on the speculative mythological origin of the Day of YHWH. He did not dedicate much time to the theological relevance of this prophetic concept.

Gressmann was followed by Sigmund Mowinckel and his school, whose cultic theory of the identification of the Day of YHWH with YHWH's enthronement, not only challenged his predecessors, but would also come to influence generations of scholars after him. Joseph Agius considers Mowinckel's theory a major one, but feels that it was based on the latter's importation of Babylonian religion upon Hebrew religion.[18] Mowinckel believed that the Old Testament does not speak of a world-catastrophe. For him, there is no authentication of the existence of such a theory in the ancient Oriental world.

However, he believes that "Yahweh of the Old Testament was a God of the same type as Marduk, Tammuz, or the like; and the religious texts of Israel were to be interpreted in accordance with their supposed Babylonian patterns."[19] He interpreted the Hebrew religion and liturgical Psalms in the light of the Babylonian New Year Festival.[20] In his studies of these Psalms, he identified the features of the ancient Israelite New Year Festival, in which one of the central ideas was the enthronement of YHWH as king of the world, the symbolic representation of His victory over His enemies, both the forces of chaos and the historical enemies of Israel.[21] The theory offers no explanation of the

---

17   See the rest of the summary of Gressmann's theory in Černy, *Day of Yahweh*, 32–41.

18   Joseph Agius, "Amos, Pecoraio di Tekoa," (Lectures, Pontificia Università San Tommaso D'Aquino, Rome, March 27, 2009).

19   Sigmund Mowinckel, *He That Cometh* (Trans. G. W. Anderson; New York: Abingdon Press, 1954), 25.

20   For example, Psalms include Pss 24, 47:8; 93:1; 96:8; 97:1.

21   Mowinckel, *He That Cometh,* 25–26.

authentication of the uniqueness of Israel's eschatology. Mowinckel basically argues that the Israelite New Year Festival was the enthronement festival of YHWH, and rejects the existence of a popular eschatological belief before the Prophet Amos. He sees the Day of YHWH originally as a day of YHWH's manifestation or epiphany in the cult of the New Year Festival. It was the day of His festival, when YHWH as a king came and wrought salvation and victory for His people.[22]

The result of this victory was the renewal of creation, election, and the covenant, and these ideas and rites were from the old fertility festivals which lay behind the historical festival.[23] During this New Year Festival there was, as in other near Eastern patterns, (e.g. the celebration of the enthronement of Marduk), a symbolic repetition of the accession to the throne or a procession, in which Yahweh, represented by the Ark, went up to his palace in the temple.[24] In other words, Mowinckel had the pattern of *akîtu* festival before him and this influenced his understanding and explanation of the Hebrew Psalms, and the attempt to reconstruct the *cultus* underlying them.[25]

Mowinckel's theory has been widely criticized by scholars, including Robinson, Černy, von Rad and Roland de Vaux. According to Roland de Vaux, the formula YHWH *Malek* (YHWH is king) found in the Psalms is not a formula of enthronement as Mowinckel suggested. It is impossible, if not unthinkable, to see who, according to Israel's religious concepts, could have enthroned Yahweh, since He himself posseses all power. Moreover, in the Babylonian texts, and in those Egyptian texts which can be compared with them, the words, 'Marduk is king'

22 Mowinckel, *He That Cometh*, 145.
23 Mowinckel, *He That Cometh*, 26.
24 Mowinckel, *He That Cometh*, 26.
25 For detailed appraisal of Mowinckel's theory see, Sigmund Mowinckel, *Psalmestudien, II.* as cited and extensively discussed by Černy, *Day of Yahweh*, 41–49; Mowinckel, *He that Cometh,* 52–59; and the literature cited by Roland de Vaux, *Ancient Israel: Its Life and Institutions* (Grand Rapids, MI: Eerdmans, 1997), 526–529; Frank Moore Cross, *Canaanite Myth and Hebrew Epic: Essays in the History of the Religion of Israel* (Cambridge: Harvard University Press, 1997), 79–80.

are not a formula of enthronement either. Rather they are an acclamation, a recognition of Marduk's power as acting as a king.[26]

Stressing recently the views of Roland de Vaux, that the Pslams suggested by Mowinckel were not "Enthronement Psalms,' but psalms about the kingship of Yahweh, Agius refreshingly points out that Mowinckel's theory was insufficiently based on ancient methodological studies of *Enuma Elish* and the application of the result of this study on Hebrew religion. For Mowinckel to arrive at his conclusion by a tendentious comparison of Marduk's enthronement festival in ancient Babylon with the portion of the Psalms that has "God's reign," is not sufficient to define or trace the origin of the Day of YHWH, to the passages of the Psalms (47:8; 93:1; 97:1), as the Day of enthronement of YHWH *(Der Tag Jahwäs ist der Thronbesteigungstag)*.[27]

Attention is drawn to the argument of Roland de Vaux that there is no evidence in the Bible that Israel celebrated a New Year festival. Among the Jews, the New Year feast, the *Rosh ha-Shanah*, is one of the feasts of the years which came up only in later Judaism. There is no mention of it in the liturgical text, or in the pre-exilic historical texts.[28] That Marduk reigns over creation during spring and loses control over creation or nature when the leaves, trees and creation wither in winter cannot be applicable to YHWH, since YHWH is always in charge of His creation.[29]

Prior to Roland de Vaux, other scholars, especially H. Wheeler Robinson, cleverly suggested that Mowinckel's own theory of the Day of YHWH might be described as the reverse of Gressmann's.[30] Whereas Gressmann derived the day from the eschatology, Mowinckel derives the eschatology from the day.[31]

Going by the analysis of Robinson, the enthronement was the nucleus of an elaborate mythology going back to creation and symboli-

---

26 de Vaux, *Ancient Israel*, 505.

27 Agius, "Amos, Pecoraio di Tekoa," (Lectures, Pontificia Università San Tommaso D'Aquino, Italy; Rome, March 27, 2009). See also de Vaux, *Ancient Israel*, 505.

28 See de Vaux, *Ancient Israel*, 502–504 for details of these celebrations.

29 de Vaux, *Ancient Israel*, 504–505.

30 H. Wheeler Robinson, *Inspiration and Revelation in the Old Testament* (Oxford: Oxford University Press, 1946), 140.

31 Robinson, *Inspiration and Revelation*, 140–141.

cally initiating the New Year. The blessings which are sought are declared to be already given and there is a cultic cry namely, 'YHWH has become King.' The implication of this is that the earthly king is the representative of the heavenly King.[32] He is a principal conduit and source of divine grace.

Robinson had also observed that although many scholars acknowledged the existence of a New Year's Festival in Israel with the enthronement of YHWH as King, the festival is nowhere named amongst the three primary Hebrew festivals.[33] Robinson was referring to the following feasts in Exodus 23:14–17:

> Three times a year you will hold a festival in my honor. You will observe the feast of unleavened bread. For seven days you will eat unleavened bread, as I have commanded you, at the appointed time in the month of Abib, for in that month you came out of Egypt. No one will appear before me empty handed. You will also observe the feast of the grain of harvest, of the first fruit of your labors in sowing the fields, and the feast of ingathering, at the end of the years, once you have brought the fruits of your labors in from the fields. Three times a year all your men folk will appear before the Lord, Yahweh.[34]

Robinson moved from noticing the absence of a Mowinckel's New Year Festival in Exodus 23:14–17, to detailed arguments against the identification of the festival with the Day of YHWH. Mowinckel bases his argument by emphasizing the reference to the kingship of YHWH in the Enthronement Psalms and also in eschatological passages like Micah 4:6–14, Zechariah 14:8–10, Isaiah 33 and Deutero-Isaiah. Robinson believes that the passage in which Mowinckel appeals for proof of identity are not those in which the 'Day of YHWH' occurs.[35] Equally un-

---

32   Robinson, *Inspiration and Revelation*, 140–141.
33   Robinson, *Inspiration and Revelation*, 141–143.
34   Other similar quotations, will be taken from *The New Jerusalem Bible* except indicated otherwise.
35   See detailed treatment of these Psalms of enthronement and its criticism in Hans-Joachim Kraus, *Psalms: A Continental Commentary* (2 vols.; trans. Hilton C. Oswald; MN: Fortress, 1993); Claus Westermann, *Praise and Lament in the Psalms* (trans., Keith R. Crim and Richard N. Soulen; Alanta: John Knox Press, 1981), esp., 145–151 on "songs of enthronement of Yahweh" (Isa 52, Pss 47, 93, 96, 97, 98, 99).

convincing is Mowinckel's claims that the New Year Festival was the source of eschatology.[36]

Robinson's significant contribution includes the fact that we may instructively compare the relation of eschatology to the Enthronement Festival, with that between prophecy by word and the symbolic acts of the prophets. These acts did not generate prophecy, but implied it. They gave concrete reality to the prophetic word and were felt to be YHWH's own initiation of His activity through the prophets. Therefore, Mowinckel's cult-drama theory was an expression of faith in YHWH's kingship.

Robinson subscribes to the older view concerning the Day of YHWH as that of a battle, in which YHWH manifests Himself in an extraordinary way on behalf of his people. It was Amos, he reiterates, who reversed this popular notion, emphasizing final judgment on Israel and the world.[37] As the title of his work, *Inspiration and Revelation in the Old Testament* suggests, this position gives a revelatory value to the meaning of the Day of YHWH. The Day of YHWH brings to focus the manifestation of YHWH's purpose in history.

In other words, the character of the Day illumines the nature of revelation. YHWH is shown to be victorious within the present world-order, and on the stage of human history. Finally, the Day of YHWH ushers in a new era of faith, peace, justice and prosperity on earth.[38]

In 1948, Ladislav Černy in his work, *The Day of Yahweh and Some Relevant Problems*, challenged Mowinckel's notion of the origin of the Day of YHWH as dependent on the kingship of YHWH, and on the yearly enthronement of the king during the New Year Cultic-Dramatic festivals. In my own opinion, Černy made a remarkable contribution and insight to the study of יום יהוה (the Day of YHWH), that deserves a brief summary here.

In fact, Černy believes that the study of יום יהוה (the Day of YHWH), is not only the most interesting, but also the most important of all the teachings of the Hebrew prophets. This concept touches on the intel-

36   Robinson, *Inspiration and Revelation*, 143.
37   Robinson, *Inspiration and Revelation*, 143.
38   Robinson, *Inspiration and Revelation*, 145.

lectual, emotional, mythological, theological, spiritual, ritual, ideological and social dimensions of the Hebrew religion. It is the basic notion of Hebrew eschatology, which he defines as "a doctrine concerning the conditions and means of the survival of the community and of the individual.[39]

Černy went on to examine and trace the sources of this concept to the Hebrew conception of time. He analysed the different meanings of the word יום (day) with some foreign parallels with statistics of the phrase, יום יהוה (the Day of YHWH). Černy also noted other peculiar phrases, composed with the word יום (day).[40] He asserts that there existed in Babylonia and Assyria, an accurate sense of observation of time. In Babylonia and Assyria it partly depended on cult and mythology; but in the Hebrew, this was not the case.

In Hebrew, words such as, יום (day) or שנה (year) sometimes convey different meanings. Černy gives an example with the phrase "these three times" (זה שלש רגלים), found in Balaam's story in the Book of Numbers 22:28, 32 and 33. The root of the word רגלים (feet), is the substantive segholate רגל meaning "the foot." Literally this could be taken to mean "three feet," highlighting the Hebrew association of time with space."[41]

---

39 Černy, *Day of Yahweh*, vii–viii.

40 See Černy, *Day of Yahweh*, 1–26 for the details of this interesting source – critical analysis.

41 See also F. Brown, S. Driver and C. Briggs, *The Brown-Driver-Briggs Hebrew and English Lexicons: With an appendix containing the Biblical Aramaic* (Peabody, MA: Hendrickson Publishers, 2005) for an elaborate listing of the usages of רגל to include: a human foot, feet of animals, of tables. Černy, in his *Day of Yahweh*, 2–5 has also discussed other Hebrew words with different or spatial meanings which is beyond the scope of this work such as; פעם- "a beat," "foot," "step," "anvil", in Isaiah 41:7; קדם "front", in Isaiah 9:11 "east", in Proverbs 7:12," and "former time", in Isaiah 23:7, and the word דור in Isaiah 38:12, means habitation/dwelling, if its root is the verb דור, "to heap up," "to pile." But originally it meant "to go about," "to move in a circle." But in Isaiah 13:20 and Jeremiah 50:39, עד־דור ודור mean "from age to age," "from generation to generation", or "through all the ages." *BDB* also lists it as "heap up, pile," "dwell,", "period, generation" of men living in a particular time, duration, age, present, past and future, generations characterized by quality or condition.

Černy discusses the different meaning of the Hebrew word יום with some parallels in foreign expressions. He draws attention to the fact that in the Old Testament יום (day) occurs about 2285 times with different meanings, connotations and usages. This includes for instance, the measuring of some quantity (Gen 8:22, Isa 33:26) and valuation of quality ("on the day of the battle" 1 Sam 13:22). It is to the latter group, according to analytical Černy, that יום יהוה (the Day of YHWH) belongs, as one indefinite day in the future, without anything being determined either as to its duration or as to its particular connection with the definite number of days in the year.[42]

42   Since Černy, in his *Day of Yahweh*, 5–7, has given a detailed and very extensive lexical analysis and classification of יום in the Hebrew Bible, it will be fruitless to repeat them here, except to draw our attention to an updated analysis of יום, by E. Jenni in *TLOT* 2: 526–39. Jenni observes that the substantive "day" is common in other Semitic languages. In the OT *yôm* (day) occurs (sg.1, 452×), (dual, 5×), (pl., 842×) and total (2,304×). The adverb, *"yôm mâm"* (by day, during the day 55×). He classifies the basic meaning of *"yôm"* to include (a) day, from sunrise to sundown, (b)"day of 24 hours," (c) vague word for "time, moment," (d) day as point in time, (e) adverbial expression form with *"yôm"* such as *"hayyôm hazzeh"* (this day = today). Other adverbial usages are: (1) *kol-hayyôm* = the whole day or always, ever, as in Gen 6:5; Exod 10:13, (2) ביום אחד = in one day, in the same day, simultaneously as in Gen 27:45; Lev 22:28; 1 Sam 2:34; (3) ביבם אחר = some other time as in 2Sam 18:20, (4) יום, יום = daily, day by day as in Gen 39:10; Exod 16:5; Isa 58:2, (5) *layyôm* = daily, per day (Exod 29:36, 38; Num 7:11, (6) *wayᵉhî hayyôm*= once upon a time, or it happened that or there was (1 Sam 14:1; 2 Kgs 4:8, 11, 18; (7) k (ᶜh) *yayyôm* = now (1 Sam 9:13, 27; Isa 58:4, (8) *hayyôm* = on this day (1 Kgs 13:11; "by day" (Hos 4:5). Other basic meanings are: the pl. *yômîm* which indicates a particular number of (calendar) days (Gen 1:14; Job 3:6, days of the year); "days" modified by a subsequent generation of person which refer, in most cases to the "days of one's life, or to one's family lifetime; indeterminate point in time, as well as idiomatic usage of yāmim to mean "year." Jenni adds that *yôm/yâmîm* not only indicates an actual unit of time, but develops further into the most important temporal usage in the OT, for expressing moments and time e.g, עולם/עת. Also יום יהוה (the Day of YHWH) is used theologically which occurs in this form in Isa 13:6, 9; Eze 13:5; Joel1:15; 2:1, 11; 3:4; 4:14; Amos 5:18 (twice), 20; Obad 15; Zeph 1:7, 14 (twice) and in Mal 3:23 making it a total of 16 times. Jenni also observes that the Qumran literature uses יום, (day) without any significant change from the OT. In the *LXX*, ἡμέρα is used to mean "time."

He went on to discuss how the word יום (day), or its equivalents are used in some Semitic inscriptions like, the Moabite stones and the Aramaic papyri from Elephantine.[43] The goal of this lengthy analysis is to challenge and reject Mowinckel's views of linking the Day of YHWH to the annual celebration of the enthronement of the ancient king. Černy argues that in Babylonia or Assyria, there existed many feasts, some of which were even celebrated more than once a year. For Černy, the real יום יהוה (Day of YHWH) was different from that discussed by his predecessors, particularly Mowinckel.[44]

Furthermore, he made a statistical study of the occurrences of יום יהוה (the Day of YHWH), particularly in the prophetic literature, as well as other similar phrases, composed with the word יום (day), which quite often are connected with hopes, promises, expectations, as well as fortunes.[45] Borrowing from the prophetic passages, Černy defines the Day of YHWH, as the day of divine decree (Isa 10:22–23; 28:21; Ezek 39:8; Zeph 2:2; Mal 3:19, 21). It is a day of darkness (Amos 5:18, 20; Joel 2:2, 3:4, 15), a dreadful day (Joel 2:11; 3:4; Mal 4:5), a destructive day (Ezek 7:25), and a dangerous day.[46]

Although Černy's contribution has been quite significant, his definition of eschatology and the Day of YHWH is not quite satisfactory.

---

43   See, Černy, *Day of Yahweh*, 8–17, for detailed discussion of this, as well its parallels in the cuneiform inscriptions of the Sumerians and the Babylonians.

44   Černy, *Day of Yahweh*, 17. However, we have already discussed the theories of his predecessors, including Mowinckel, whose influence; he observes in pp. 49–52, affected the Myth-and-Ritual" School. That is, those English Scholars who generated volumes of research work on Egyptian, Babylonian, Canaanite and Hebrew religions based their positions on the principle that " the early inhabitants of the Ancient Near East, like other people were not occupied with general questions concerning the world but with certain and similar practical and pressing problems of daily life." The implication of this, which Černy continues to reject, for example is that, the central feature of the Egyptian and Babylonian ritual systems being the fact that the king is for the well-being of the community, and hence is regarded as divine. He represents in the great seasonal rituals as the annual New Year Festival.

45   Černy, *Day of Yahweh*, 17–26.

46   Černy, *Day of Yahweh*, 26.

The latter is too vague, while the former sounded pessimistic. He spent much time like his predecessors arguing about the origin and the sources of the Day of YHWH, neglecting the theological significance of this important concept for the Christian and religious communities. He laid too much emphasis on the disastrous outlook of the Day of YHWH, as against his few words of hope and restoration, which he passively mentioned in the last paragraph of his work.[47] The fact of the centrality of the theme of the Day of YHWH in the Twelve Minor Prophets was not mentioned at all.

1.1.2 Studies on the Day of YHWH in the 1950s and 1960s

Besides Černy's monograph on the *Day of Yahweh*, studies on this important biblical concept continued to characterize OT research, in the 1950s and 1960s. But these studies appeared mostly in the form of articles and in chapters of books.[48] Uppermost in my mind is H. H. Rowley, who in 1956 devoted the seventh section of his work, *The Faith of Israel: Aspects of Old Testament Thought*, to the discussion of יום יהוה (the Day of YHWH). Rowley recognizes that throughout the OT, there is a look to the future. He stresses that "Israel believed that

---

47 His quotation of Jan Amos Komenský, in *Day of Yahweh*, 106, contextualizing the Day of YHWH within the historical *Sitz-im-Leben* of the Czech nation after the battle of the White Mountain at Prague in 1621, though very impressive, was too little. He wrote: "I trust God that after the passing of the storm of wrath which our sins brought down upon our heads, the rule of thine affairs shall again be restored to thee, O Czech people!" This sense of restoration, which I think the Day of YHWH anticipates is also well highlighted in his quotation of Micah 4:3ff "And he shall judge among many people, and rebuke strong nations afar off; and they shall beat their swords into ploughshares, and their spears into pruning hooks; nation shall not lift up a sword against nation, neither shall they learn war anymore," (see also, Isa 2:2–4).

48 Detailed critical studies on the Day of YHWH are not common and hence, K. J. Cathcart in *ABD* 2: 84, also affirmed that "although the concept of the Day of Yahweh has often been investigated, surprisingly there has not been any major study of it in recent times."

while there was a brief period of innocence and bliss at the opening of history, the real climax and crown of history lay in the future."[49]

Israel had firm assurances that 'the best is yet to be,' though that assurance was rooted in God, and not in the mere expression of human optimism. These elements of hope and optimism were found in her thought from the beginning.[50] Rowley traces the root of the Day of YHWH in the prophetic literature, back to the Book of Amos (5:18ff). It was from here that subsequent prophets, including Joel (2:2), and Zephaniah (1:14ff) adapted the message of the Day of the Lord.

Similar expressions, Rowley observes, are also found in passages in the Prophet Isaiah (24:20; 25:9), described as the "golden age." While in some passages the Day of the YHWH was conceived of as night at hand (Isa 13:6; Ezek 30:3; Obad 15), but all conceived it as a time of the divine breaking-in into history in a spectacular fashion. While God was believed to be always active on the plane of history, using nature and men to fulfill his ends, the Day of YHWH was thought of as a day of his more direct and clearer manifest action.[51]

Rowley maintains that although most of the predictions of the prophets, concerned issues of their own times and contexts, these passages were of the future, pointing to the time when God's wrath will consume all that is evil, and usher in the age of bliss. Rowley is convinced of the sovereignty of YHWH. He believes that lines should not be drawn too sharply between prophecy and apocalypticism.[52]

Moreover, the "golden age," Rowley thinks, is not only universal, but it has a fundamentally religious basis, such that, there shall not only be a unity of rule, but all shall reflect his will. It is not just a political and economic reality, but mostly moral and spiritual, and it dreams of enduring peace (Mic 4:3–4; Isa 2:4). Rowley recognizes obedience, divine promises, universalism in the Day of YHWH, expressed

---

49 H.H. Rowley, *The Faith of Israel: Aspects of Old Testament Thought* (London: SCM Press, 1956), 177. I will like to draw attention here that this work was originally "The James Sprunt Lectures" delivered at Union Theological Seminary, Richmond, Virginia, in 1955.

50 Rowley, *Faith of Israel*, 177.

51 Rowley, *Faith of Israel*, 179.

52 Rowley, *Faith of Israel*, 180.

in Deutero-Isaiah and in post-exilic Judaism.[53] He discusses this day as Messianic, a day when prophecies would be fulfilled. The early Church, he stresses, indicated the importance of this messianism by attributing the word, "Christ" to Jesus.[54]

Rowley went ahead to opine that Isaiah 61:2, which Jesus read in the synagogue (Luke 4:16ff) of Nazareth, defines the acceptable year of YHWH. This, according to him, underlines not only the Day of YHWH, but the day of vengeance and judgment of God.[55] But just as in Amos, this is not the end, for the prophet is sent to comfort the mourners, the afflicted and the oppressed.

Rowley further went on to observe that the phrase "Son of Man," which is found in several OT and NT passages, in Psalm 8, Daniel 7, 1 Enoch, and particularly on the lips of Jesus in the Gospels (Matt 24:17–28; Mk 13:14–26 and Luke 17:22–37), represents a different line of approach to the conception of the Day of YHWH, whose fusion with the Davidic leader should not be pushed back earlier than the time of Christ. For him, the fact that both the Davidic Messiah and the Son of Man[56] were found side by side in the circles of those interested in apocalyptic phenomenon is not to be denied.[57] Also the figure of the Suffering Servant of Deutero-Isaiah, whose mission was to do justice and judgment as well as bring law and order to everyone (Isa 42:1–4; 49:1–6; 50:4–11; 52:13–53:12), is one of the various approaches to the thought of the Day of YHWH, and all remain related together, since they are all associated with the same theme of the coming of the Kingdom.

Rowley concludes that the OT concept of the Day of YHWH and the establishment of God's sovereignty is not only fulfilled in the NT, the Church, but is also based on the unwavering faith of Israel, that humans were created in the image of God.[58] Although Rowley's ap-

---

53   Rowley, *Faith of Israel*, 181–82.
54   Rowley, *Faith of Israel*, 187.
55   Rowley, *Faith of Israel*, 193.
56   For the use of "Son of Man" in the Gospels see Joseph Ratzinger/Pope Benedict XVI, *Jesus of Nazareth* (trans., Adrien J. Walker; New York: Doubleday, 2007), 321–355.
57   Rowley, *Faith of Israel*, 196–97.
58   Rowley, *Faith of Israel*, 201.

proach to the Day of YHWH, from multiple perspectives, makes his studies very complicated, his emphasis on judgment, future joy and faith in the sovereignty of YHWH is very insightful.

In contrast to Rowley's approach and those of his predecessors, in 1958 Gerhard von Rad, published an important little work, *Der Heilige Krieg im Alten Israel.*[59] This work challenges Mowinckel and generates sustainable debate on the theme of the Day of YHWH. In it, von Rad describes Israel's sacral warfare as an institution of the era of the Judges, limited to the defensive wars of Israel. Gerhard von Rad warns against rushing for an admission of evidence, for the study of the concept of the Day of YHWH.[60] He argues that we should not look for the meaning, origin and significance of the Day of YHWH, merely from within the cultic context, as suggested by Mowinckel.

Gerhard von Rad basically argues that "the Day of Yahweh encompasses pure events of war, the rise of Yahweh against his enemies, his battles and his victory."[61] He argues that, of the several texts (Isa 2:12;

59   See Gerhard von Rad, *Der Heilige Krieg im Alten* Israel (AThNT 20; Zurich: 1951), cited in Cross, *Canaanite Myth*, 88. But see details of the 1958 translation of the original small eighty-four page work in von Rad, *Holy War in Ancient Israel* (trans., and ed., Marva J. Dawn; Grand Rapids, MI: William B. Eerdmans Publishing Company, 1991). There it is rightly observed by Ben C. Ollenburg that, the term "holy war" is directly rooted in the OT, although it does speak of the "wars of Yahweh," (1 Sam 18:17; 25:28; Num 21:14). Hence, "these wars are Yahweh's wars (מלחמות יהוה). The enemies are Yahweh's enemies (איבי יהוה; Judg 5:31; 1 Sam 30:26), and the one who acts is YHWH. For further details see von Rad, *Holy War,* 44–51.

60   Cross, *Canaanite Myth,* 88. In Islam this defensive warfare is referred to as, *jihād* = war in a limited sense or "spiritual warfare." For details see, Peter C. Craigie, *The Problem of War in the Old Testament* (Grand Rapids, MI: William B. Eerdmans Publishing Company, 1978), 22–26.

61   Gerhard von Rad. "The Origin of the Concept of the Day of Yahweh," *JSS* 4 (1959): 97–108. For von Rad, the prophets took the notion of the "Day of YHWH," from the old Holy War theory or tradition, but broadened it to embrace the universal as well as the cosmic sphere. The summary position of Von Rad's teaching or theory on the Day of YHWH are also found in von Rad, *Old Testament Theology,* vol 2 (trans. D.M.G. Stalker; New York: Haper San Francisco, 1965), 119–125; Idem, *The Message of the Prophets* (New York: Harper San Francisco, 1965), 95–99.

13:6, 9; 22:5; 34:8; Jer 46:10; Ezek 7:10; 13:5; 30:3; Joel 1:15; 2:1, 11; 3:4; Obad 15; Zeph 1:7, 8, 14–18; Zech 14:1), Amos 5:18–20, which is usually considered the earliest key passage and departing point for the study of Day of YHWH, offers an insufficient definition and study of the concept and its tradition.

He believes that Amos 5:18–20 is not unequivocal in its mention of the Day of YHWH. Also, the long poem in Isaiah 2:9–22, with its repeated refrain, deals much more with the general results and effects which the coming of YHWH is to have, than with the thing itself and its concrete accompaniments.

In these passages, we hear of people fleeing and throwing away their idols in the process.[62] Without question, it was the intention of the narrator to attribute the cause of victory to Yahweh alone. In other words, von Rad appeals for a contextual study of the texts in the following words:

> Let us, however, suppose that the correct procedure in the elucidation of an exegetical problem such as this is that we should not confine ourselves to the examination of the occurrences and their meaning in their own immediate context. Form criticism and the investigations of the history of tradition have taught us that terms as important as these seldom appear alone, but are as a rule associated with a whole complex of ideas which have definite recurring themes of whose presence careful account must be taken….we must adopt a broader exegetical basis than can be provided by an examination of the term itself, and must include the whole of the textual unit in which the term appears along with its constitutive concepts.[63]

62   von Rad, *Message of the Prophets*, 95. See also *Holy War*, 49 where it is clear that in no way did the act of the war exlude belligerent activity on the part of Israel.

63   von Rad, *Old Testament Theology*, vol 2, 120. In other words, Holy War in Ancient Israel, from the point of view of von Rad is dependent on form criticism. Holy War for him, is determined not just by tradition but, by institution. This is rooted back to form criticism pioneered by Hermann Gunkel and the studies of Albrecht Alt. von Rad's thought is reflected in his earlier work on the "Form-critical Problem of the Hexateuch." Here he argues that the account of the Conquest in Joshua fits together with the Pentatuech to form Hexateuch. See Ben C. Ollenburger's comment on "form criticism" in the introductory section of *Holy War*, 13–16.

Truly, von Rad, in this passage, recommends the study of "self con-tained units" when searching for the meaning of Day of YHWH in a biblical text. Some of these texts include Isaiah 13 (Poem on Babylon), 34 (Oracle against Edom), Ezekiel 7 (Oracle against Egypt), and Joel 2 (Locust in Judah). For him, these are the most suitable and unequivo-cal take-off points for the study of יום יהוה (the Day of YHWH).[64] Gerhard von Rad notices that Isaiah 13 begins with a call to war, and encourages warriors to get ready for the battle. The Oracle against Edom in Isaiah 34 is constructed in like manner.[65] Moreover, Ezekiel 30 is also an elaborate poem and a single unit.[66] It is a proclamation of the Day of the Lord against Egypt. Verse 1–9 is worth quoting here:

> The word of Yahweh was addressed to me as follows, 'Son of man, prophesy and say, "the Lord Yahweh says this: Howl: Disaster day! For the day is near, the Day of Yahweh is near, it will be a day of dark with cloud, a time of doom for the nations...That day, I shall send messengers to terrify the carefree Cushites, and anguish will overtake them on the day of Egypt. It is coming soon.[67]

These passages are not only self-contained units, but their context de-picts the war-like and disastrous nature of the Day of the Lord. Simi-larly, in Joel 2:1–11, von Rad thinks, the prophet is definitely equating the imagery of the locusts with the armies of the Day of YHWH, march-ing into battle, and is thus able to draw on the whole range of war concepts connected with the Day of YHWH.[68]

With regard to the text of Zephaniah (1:7–18), which will be taken up later in the appropriate section, von Rad acknowledges it as the most important source for a detailed discussion of the Day of YHWH. He calls it a single unit, which discusses the Day of YHWH, beginning

64   von Rad, *Old Testament Theology*, 120.
65   von Rad, *Old Testament Theology*, 120.
66   von Rad, *Old Testament Theology*, 121.
67   von Rad, *Old Testmaent Theology*, 121, Here von Rad believes very strongly that these texts as well as those of Ezekiel 7 make plain that the prophecy deals with the Day of YHWH.
68   von Rad, *Holy War*, 121. Here the concept of the Holy War is not only discussed in Joel, but the Holy War origin of the concept is confirmed.

with the "cry that the day of Yahweh is near."[69] He singles out verse 7, especially the phrase, "Yahweh has prepared a sacrifice (זבח)," where "sacrifice (זבח), as a metaphor, runs through other passages and texts that deal with the Day of YHWH (Isa 36:6; Jer 46:10; Ezek 34:17).[70] Moreover, like the "sacrifice (זבח), in Zephaniah, von Rad stresses that the use of "blood" (דמם) in Jeremiah 46:10 also indicates the context of war.[71]

In other words, von Rad sees similarities in these texts in their portrayal of sacral war, painted by images of the call to warriors and military personnel to gather for the battle of YHWH,[72] sanctification of the army,[73] panic among the enemy forces, sacrifices, streaming of blood, distress, wailing and changes in the natural order and the resultant total annihilation. The widespread employment of these concepts in the prophets suggests that we are dealing with a well-established component part of eschatological tradition. It is, for him, the stereotyped cry by which men were summoned for military services in earlier times, or a cry which men once went out into battle with YHWH as their "Commander-in-Chief."[74] The high point of this Holy War, von Rad stresses, was formed by the *hērem* (חרם), the consecration of the booty to Yahweh. As was the case for the entire Holy War, this too was a cultic phenomenon since human beings and animals were slaughtered, gold

---

69 von Rad, *Old Testament Theology*, vol. 2, 122.

70 von Rad, *Old Testament Theology*, 122.

71 von Rad, *Old Testament Theology*, 123.

72 See also von Rad, *Holy War*, 41–42 for the description of this theory. Here it is noted that, "once the army had gathered in the camp, it was called "the people of Yahweh" (עם יהרה or עם אלהים cf. Judg 5:11, 13; 20:2)."

73 See von Rad, *Holy War*, 42. Here it is further noted that "the army stood under severe sacral regulations. The men were *"consecrated"* [קדש; Jos 3:5]. They submitted to sexual renunciation (1 Sam 21:5; 2 Sam 11:11–12)."

74 von Rad, *Message of the Prophets*, 98–99. Idem, *Holy War*, 52–74; 95–115. Also see, Roland De Vaux, *Ancient Israel; Its Life and Institutions* (trans. John McHugh; Grand Rapids, MI: Eerdmans, 1961), 214–67; Craigie, *The Problem of War in the Old Testament*, 21–54 for a detailed theological study of military institutions, wars and Holy War in ancient Israel's tradition, particularly how the old tradtion of the Holy War once again found its speakers in the prophet.

and silver and the like went as קֹדֶשׁ into YHWH's treasury (Josh 6:18–19 cf 1 Sam 15).[75]

This study agrees with von Rad's suggestion that the origin of the Day of YHWH is to be found in the Holy War traditions. These wars occur in the biblical tradition where YHWH fought by Himself. They are also those wars which people fought on behalf of YHWH. However, the theological point here is the fact that YHWH was the architect of every victory and success. But like any proposal, von Rad's "Holy War" motif has over the years, generated heated scholarly debates and criticisms.

Uppermost in my mind is Meir Weiss, who in 1966 published an elaborate article, "The Origin of the "Day of the Lord"-Reconsidered." This well written work is a reaction to, or is based on the influence of K.-D. Schunk, "Strukturlinien in der Entwicklung der Vorstellung vom 'Tag Y's'."[76] In it, Weiss revisited this debate from Jerusalem in a forceful manner.[77] He thinks that von Rad's "Holy War" theory is vulnerable to criticisms. Granting, von Rad's conclusion that יוֹם יהוה (the Day of YHWH) encompasses a pure event of war, this war-element, Meir Weiss stresses, is still far from being constitutive in the prophecies on the Day of YHWH, considering the prominent place which the concept of the Lord as a "man of war" occupies in biblical faith.[78]

Weiss points to those prophecies that threaten warlike attacks executed by the Lord without alluding to the Day of the Lord. He questions the difference between the Day of the Lord and the days in which

---

75   See von Rad, *Holy War*, 49–50.

76   K.-D. Schunk, "Strukturlinien in der Entwicklung der Vorstellung Vom 'Tag Y's," *VT* 14 (1964): 320ff, cited in Meir Weiss, "Origin of the Day of the Lord," 29, argues critically among other things, that "Es besteht nicht der geringste Anlass, die durch von Rad entwickelte Herleitung des Vorstellungskreises vom 'Tag Y's' aus den Traditionselementen des Heiligen Krieges in Frage zu stellen," (= there is no slightest cause to question von Rad's derivation of the concept of the Day of YHWH from the traditional circle of the Holy War – [my translation]), as against the widely disputed cultic interpretation of Mowinckel.

77   Meir Weiss, "The Origin of the "Day of the Lord – Reconsidered," *HUCA* 37 (1966): 29–62.

78   Weiss, "Origin of the "Day of the Lord," 30.

the Lord will fight his enemies. In other words, he argues that if von Rad considers the announcement of the prophets regarding the Day of YHWH as a bold actualization of the old tradition of the Holy War (cf. 1 Sam 15), he is still far from defining the constitutive elements of the prophecies about the Day of the Lord. According to him, von Rad has not characterized adequately the essential aspects of the concept.[79]

Weiss argues that among the Day of the Lord texts, according to von Rad's theory, that contain Holy War elements,[80] a majority is to be found in Isaiah 13 and Joel 2. For him, these are the two prophecies which betray a certain affinity to each other and which do not belong to the earliest prophecy about the Day of the Lord.[81] Weiss draws an example from the texts of Isaiah 13:3, Zephaniah 1:7 and Joel 4:9. In Isaiah 13:3, the Lord designates his special or purified guest to carry out the Holy War on the Day of the Lord (אני צריתי למקדשי), while in Zephaniah 1:7d it is stated that, "he has consecrated his guest," (הקדיש קריו). In Joel 4:9 we read, "Proclaim this among the nation, prepare for battle," (קראו זאת בגוים קדשו מלחמה).

This phrase, הִקְדִישׁ קְרֻאָיו (Zeph 7:1d) is paratactically related to כִּי־הֵכִין יְהוָה זֶבַח ("For the Lord has prepared a sacrifice", v 7c).[82] It is the image of the "sacrifice" that leads to the "consecrated guest." Weiss argues that one cannot find in the expression הקדיש קראיו ("he has

79   Weiss, "Origin of the "Day of the Lord," 31.

80   These elements (which we have already alluded to) as contained in Table A of Weiss's "Origin of the "Day of the Lord," include: "call to battle," "consecration to war," fright, discouragement, panic," "ban," and "changes in the natural spheres (in the sky, darkening of the celestial bodies, darkness, clouds, thunder and quaking).

81   Weiss, "Origin of the "Day of the Lord," 31.

82   See the explanation of "Parataxis," in Soulen, *Biblical Criticism*, 134–135. There it is observed that it is derived from Greek meaning "to place beside." In grammar generally parataxis refers to the coordination of clauses without indicating their syntactic relation. See also the explanation of this paratactic style in David E. Aune, *The Westminster Dictionary of New Testament & Early Christian Literature & Rhetoric* (Louiseville: Westminster John Knox Press, 2003), 236. For Aune, it "is a stylistic structure in which clauses and sentences are strung together (like in the case of Zeph 1:7c and d) without conjunctions or combined with coordinate conjunctions."

consecrated his guest") an allusion to the sacral conduct of war.[83] But it seems Weiss fails to see the metaphorical use of these terms.

With regard to קדשו מלחמה (preparing for battle in Joel 4:9), he invokes the argument of J. A. Soggin that one has first of all to take into consideration that various prophecies use the root קדש in connection with wars obviously not related to the Day of the Lord. This verbal phrasing does, therefore, not necessarily reveal anything about the origin of the Day of the Lord, but rather the prophecy as such "moves in that atmosphere of the Holy War tradition."[84] The participants in the war of the Day of the Lord are alluded to as "my sanctified guests," only because in that war, God manifested himself. As in Joel 4:9 and Zephaniah 1:7, the preparation for war is commanded in the language of sanctity on account of God's presence there, just as it is in the cases of theophany in general.[85]

Moreover, Weiss argues that as to the fourteen "self-contained" texts themselves, it should be noted that five of them (Isa 34; Joel 1, 3; Obad 15; Zeph 1:7, 14), which constitute more than a third of the total, have not been found to contain any allusion whatever to an event of war.[86]

Gerhard von Rad, in his quest for the origin of the concept of the Day of the Lord found his way into the Holy War tradition, not to the origin of the concept of יום יהוה (the Day of YHWH). Gerhard von Rad while embracing the methodological principle of *Formgeschichte*

---

83   See Weiss, Origin of the "Day of the Lord," 32 for a detailed debate over these passages, once used by von Rad himself to refute Mowinckel's theory of the cultic origin of the Day of the Lord, since הקיש can also be used metaphorically.

84   J. A Soggin, "Der prophetische Gedanke über den heiligen Krieg, als Gericht gegen Israel," *VT* 10 (1960): 81ff cited in Weiss, Origin of the "Day of the Lord," 32. Moreover, this קדש מלחמה is absent in the book of Deuteronomy which von Rad regards as an outstanding expression of the Holy War idea. In Joshua 3:5; 1 Sam 16:5 and in Exodus 19:10ff, people were invited to sanctify themselves not for Holy War.

85   Weiss, "Origin of the "Day of the Lord," 34.

86   See Weiss, "Origin of the "Day of the Lord," 37–38, for an extensive and detailed debate on this.

(form history)[87] and *Überlieferungsgeschichte* (history of transmission)[88] neglected the methodological principle that details of historical things must not be deduced from that which is not possible, but from general opinions with particular reference to individual circumstances.[89]

However, Weiss on a positive note says that von Rad is right in claiming that Amos 5:18 is not sufficient to be unequivocally used as the only suitable starting point, for an examination of the Day of the Lord. But his conclusion based on "self-contained" prophecies in the light of Amos and Isaiah 2 is methodologically mistaken.[90] Weiss also has a problem with those who adopt the view of pre-prophetic origin (the popular notion) of the Day of YHWH. How is it that the Day does not appear in the extra-prophetic literature? No satisfactory answer has been provided.

From here, Weiss went on to argue and demonstrate how the Day of the Lord, which appears in different and divergent forms in biblical books, poses a perplexing problem for those who follow the pre-prophetic origin theory.[91] Weiss thinks that on close examination, the Day of YHWH was neither a firm formula nor a *terminus technicus*. For him, there is no strong evidence that the audience was familiar with this usage. Weiss therefore, believes that the best conclusion to Amos 5:18 is that the phrase יום יהוה (Day of YHWH) was understood by

---

87   See the analysis of "Formgeschichte," in Soulen, *Biblical Criticism,* 61–64. It may be "loosely defined as the analysis of the typical forms by which human existence is expressed linguistically; traditionally this referred particularly to their oral, preliterary state, such as legends, hymns, curses, laments etc."

88   See Soulen, *Biblical Criticism,* 198–199, for a detailed analysis of the meaning of "history of transmissiion" or "tradition history."

89   See Weiss, "Origin of the Day of the Lord," 39, where he interestingly cites Aug. Boeckh's *Encyklopedie und Methodologie der philologischen Wissenschaften* (Leipzig: 1877), 56 which originally states that, "Die Einzelheiten sollen nicht… deducirt werden, was bei historischen Dingen nicht möglich ist, aber sie sollen hervorgehen aus seiner allgemeinen Anschauung, und diese muss sich wieder in jedem einzelnen Theile bewähren" (= "the details should not be deduced, which are not possible with regards to historical things, rather they should result from their general view and these must prove its worth in every individual part").

90   Weiss, "Origin of the "Day of the Lord," 40.

91   Weiss, "Origin of the "Day of the Lord," 45.

his audience, who heard it for the first time from this prophecy.[92] In other words, this expression in Amos was adapted and modified by later prophets including Isaiah, Joel, Jeremiah and Zephaniah.[93]

He concludes that the motif-complex and phraseology of the Day of the Lord did not originate in the popular belief tradition of Israel but was actually originated in a phrase coined by Amos in the course of his polemic with his contemporaries about the manifestation of the Lord. This motif-complex of יום יהוה (Day of YHWH) for Amos was not traceable to von Rad's Holy War tradition, but has its roots in the motif-complex of the theophany-descriptions, where Amos had stumbled over the concept that would influence subsequent prophets as well as later eschatological versions.[94]

Not many would agree with Weiss in his detailed criticism of von Rad, nor does he have the final say on the development of the concept of the Day of YHWH. It is more popular among scholars today including the present author that Amos did not originate the phrase but its written form was first found in the prophetic literature of the Prophet Amos. Also Weiss may have overlooked the fact that when von Rad speaks of the link between the Day of the Lord and the Holy War, he is simply referring to the origin of the concept. It was later that the notion of the Day was applied to any saving experience.

Frank Moore Cross and his student Patrick Miller, though mildly critical of von Rad, see in von Rad the logic of rooting the Day of YHWH to the events of the Holy War. Cross critically observes that von Rad holds onto his theory because he agrees with the School of Alt that only individual tribes entered the land, or infiltrated it, and that the traditions of the conquest are a secondary complex composed of unitary traditions of individual tribes.[95]

---

92   Weiss, "Origin of the "Day of the Lord, "45–46.
93   Weiss, "Origin of the "Day of the Lord,"48–57.
94   Weiss, "Origin of the "Day of the Lord," 60.
95   Cross, *Canaanite Myth*, 88. Also in his approach to the the history of Israel as a whole, von Rad was heavily indebted to his own teacher, Albreach Alt. Alt's most important studies are compiled in *Essays on Old Testament History and Religion* (Oxford: Basil Blackwell, 1966).

Cross believes that Mowinckel's and von Rad's opinions on the origin of the Day of YHWH can be reconciled. The Day of YHWH is both the day of YHWH's victory in battle and the day of YHWH's royal festival. The cult of Israel is nothing but an amalgamation of imagery from the Holy War tradition with that of creation-kingship motifs. It is a dramatic reenactment of the Exodus and the conquest. The primary reason for this is that YHWH the heavenly warrior, masterminded actions in both of these events. The conquest so understood, according to Cross, is not a historical event, but a construct of the *Heilsgeschichte* School. Hence, he thinks, von Rad fails to deal with the origin of the Holy War in Israel, and in turn with the mythological elements in the Holy War, as practised by earliest Israel, and indeed as practised by pre-Yahwistic and non-Israelite peoples.[96] This led him to conclude that the theories of Mowinckel and von Rad are reconcilable and complementary. It is for him the wedding of the "Myth and Ritual School," with the "History of Redemption School."[97]

He took on the study of Psalm 24, in order to substantiate his position. According to Cross, Psalm 24 is a celebration of the kingship of YHWH, and his role as creator. It is a hymn chanted in procession that commemorates YHWH's military victory for early Israelite communi-

---

96 See Cross, *Canaanite Myth*, 89 for further treatment of the Holy War in Israel as well as a detailed study of the cosmic and methodological elements in sacral warfare.

97 See Cross, *Canaanite Myth*, 82–85 for details, where Cross critically reviews the strengths and weaknesses of the *"Heilsgeschichtliche Schule"* and the "Myth and Ritual" approaches to the early cult and came to a conclusion that, the development of Israel's cultic themes and institutions is far more complex than envisaged by either of these schools. It involves the amalgamation of the mythological and historical memory materials even in the earliest corpus of ancient poetry, law, and epic traditions. In the *Heilsgeschichtliche* School, obviously the concentration has been on the cult of the tribal league; while in the Myth and Ritual School, the focus has been on the cult in the time of the monarchy largely through the influence of the ideology of the Holy War. This influence results in or leads finally to the ideology of the apocalyptic. Therefore, the Day of YHWH is the day of victory in holy warfare. It is also the Day of YHWH's festival when the ritual conquest was enacted in the procession of the Ark, the procession of the King of Glory (מלך כבוד).

ties. This combination of themes is highlighted in Isaiah 51:9–11, with eschatological implications in general, and the Day of YHWH in particular.[98] The Day of YHWH as a pure event of war, when YHWH arose and defeated His enemies in battle, is not far removed from the Day of YHWH's manifestation, the day of festival, and the day of YHWH's enthronement when the Lord would come to provide salvation and prosperity for His people.[99]

Patrick D. Miller, Cross's student who was also influenced by von Rad's ideas and arguments on the Holy War, commends Frank M. Cross, Jr., for pointing out that the conflict between the views of von Rad and the older view of Sigmund Mowinckel is not as real as it may seem. For him, in fact the Day of YHWH imagery comes out of the tribal league Holy War traditions as they were carried through the royal *cultus* in the association of ritual conquest with the enthronement.[100] Miller invokes the 1962 argument of R. Bach to support the position of von Rad.[101] Miller further suggested that the warlike language in prophetic literature connotes more than theophany, or metaphorical calamity. They represent the participation of the divine council as a cosmic or heavenly army in the eschatological wars of YHWH, whose military activities were associated with the Day of YHWH, and which involved a joint participation of human and earthly forces or divine and heavenly armies.[102]

In other words, it generally signals the participation of the whole cosmos in the wars of YHWH. When YHWH calls His council, His

---

98 Frank Moore Cross, "The Divine Warrior in Israel's Early Cult," *Biblical Motifs: Origins and Transformation* (ed. Alexander Altmann; Cambridge: Harvard University Press, 1966), 11–30. See also *Canaanite Myth*, 79–90.

99 Cross, *Canaanite Myth*, 91–111.

100 Patrick M. Miller, "The Divine Council and the Prophetic Call to War," *VT* 18 (1968): 100.

101 See also Miller, "Divine Council," 100, where he aptly cited R. Bach, *Die Aufforderungen zur Flucht und zum Kampf in altestamentlichen Prophetenspruch* (WMANT IX; Neurkirchen Kreis Moers, 1962) in which Bach demonstrated the *Sitz-im -Leben* of the Gattungen of prophetic oracles which involve a summons to battle and those involving a summons to flight is the Holy War of early Israel. He insists that a number of these oracles of course have to do with the Day of YHWH.

102 Miller, "Divine Council," 101.

heavenly army to fight, all creation participates in it, just as it did in His wars for Israel in early times (Deut 33:2–5; 26–29; Jos 5; 10:12–13; Judg 5:20; Ps 68:8–30).[103] It is evident that despite the criticism on von Rad, this study lines up with Cross and Miller and those scholars we have discussed, all of whom think that von Rad has a point to make.

Cross and Miller rightly, believe that the two theories are reconcilable. They take the position that the origin of the Day of YHWH is not completely divorced from the Holy War *(Der Heilige Krieg)* tradition of Israel, as these traditions were carried through the royal cult. But Cross and Miller's Schools themselves have not yet produced a systematic study of the texts of the Day of YHWH.[104]

The investigation of the origin and meaning of the Day of YHWH did not end with Mowinckel, von Rad, Cross or Patrick Miller. Ralph W. Klein, in his 1968 work, "The Day of the Lord," questioned "what does it mean for Yahweh to have a Day?"[105]

In his search for an answer to this question, he reviewed earlier studies highlighting the significance of YHWH's participation on His Day.[106] He also stressed the impact and effect of this day.[107] Klein discusses

---

103 Miller, "Divine Council,"100–107. Miller makes an effort to cite some of those passages filled with the imagery that is reminiscent of YHWH's battle as a Divine Warrior against cosmic or divine enemies as well as Israel's historical enemies. He also discusses in some great detail, Isaiah 13:1ff; Joel 4:9ff; Jeremiah 51:27–28; Isaiah 40:26 and 45:12; 2 Kings 6: 15–19 and 2 Kings 7:6 where imagery of YHWH as a Divine Warrior is found.

104 K. J. Cathcart, "Day of Yahweh," in *ABD* 2: 85.

105 Ralph W. Klein, "The Day of the Lord," *Concordia Theological Monthly*, 39 (1968): 517.

106 Klein, "Day of the Lord," 517–20. Here he observes that, one of the fullest descriptions of the Day of YHWH is in Zephaniah 1: 15–16, as compared with Joel 2:2, and a number of these terms of description imply theophany, which is central to its interpretation as Holy War or cultic festival.

107 Klein, "Day of the Lord," 521–22. According to him, these effects include, the way in which the enemy is completely mesmerized (Isa 13:7ff; Jer 47:4; Ezek 7:14, 17, 27); Panic (Isa 22:5); agony (Isa 13:8; Ezek 30:16, Joel 2:6); imminence in character (Zeph 1:7, 14); few survivors will be recorded (Amos 5:19) and no hiding place for YHWH's enemies (Isa 2:10).

objects of YHWH's wrath.[108] He also discusses the Day of YHWH and eschatology.[109] His discussion on Joel and the notion of the Day of YHWH,[110] as well as the significance of this Day of YHWH for today, is impressive. Although, Klein's studies lack detailed analysis of specific biblical texts, his application and call for contextualization of the Day of YHWH to our contemporary life situation, is highly commendable.[111]

108 Klein, "Day of the Lord," 522–523. Here he stresses on the false optimism of Israel and Judah as special people, who by engaging in injustice and abuse of cultic rites become objects of YHWH's wrath (Amos 5:21–24); the proud and lofty (Isa 2); evil, arrogant and ruthless people (Isa 13); faithless people (Isa 22); people who engage in violent, and abominable ways (Ezek 7); those who gloat and rejoice over Judah's fall (Obad) and against all evil doers (Mal 4). However, repentance, trembling and fear of YHWH can usher in God's mercy.

109 See Klein, "Day of the Lord," 523–24. Here he attempts to observe whether the Day of YHWH is in itself an eschatological concept, especially in pre-exilic texts. How is eschatology to be defined? Narrowly, it could be defined as the doctrine of the things which concern the end of the world and the new hope that lies on the other side of history; or it means the catastrophic ending of the physical order and the beginning of a new spiritual order. On a number of occasions the day of YHWH is clearly understood as a past event (Lam 1:12; 2:1, 21–22; Ezek 13:5 and 34:12). But if eschatology, Klein continues to argue, is broadly seen as the study of ideas and beliefs concerning the end of the present world order, and the creation of a new order, thus emphasizing the intra-historical character of many of the happenings, then we can conveniently say that the pre-exilic prophets did have an eschatology of doom; hence, they looked forward to a new day when YHWH would intervene to reactivate His election and covenant.

110 Klein, "Day of the Lord," 524–25. Here, invoking the studies of Hans Walter Wolff, "Dodekapropheton, Joel" in *Biblischer Kommentar*, 14, 5 (Neukirchen Vluyn: Neukirchen Verlag, 1963), Klein recognizes the extensive treatment of the Day of YHWH in Joel. Chapter One is devoted to lament, emphasizing the seriousness of the current locust plague and drought, which symbolize the imminent fulfillment of the day of the Lord. Chapter Two escalates the distress from the contemporary locust plague to the final, eschatological turmoil. The tone of the book undergoes a dramatic transition (2:18) for the remainder of the text is devoted to a reassuring of a New Jerusalem, including a complete and final victory over all the nations.

111 See Klein, "Day of the Lord," 525, where he boldly suggests that, "when justice in the community is not a goal of the people of God, when war, poverty, prejudice, and other sins are accepted as inevitable, when security is predicated on an

1.1.3 Studies on the Day of YHWH in the 1970s and 1980s

While in search for the meaning and significance of this concept, A. Joseph Everson, recognized יום יהוה (Day of YHWH), as a central theme in prophetic thought about the future. He reviewed past scholarly opinion, including those of Mowinckel, von Rad, Charles, Fensham and Meir Weiss on the Day of YHWH, in his effort to contribute to the debate on the best way to comprehend or define the character and nature of יום יהוה (Day of YHWH).[112] This, according to Everson, can be accomplished by sticking to the reading and studying those texts which form the basic field of evidence for the study of the tradition.[113] Everson dwells on five texts which not only interpret past his-

---

ethnic or ecclesiastical heritage that endeavors to lock the saving God in a box, then the confrontation with the living God is as horrible to contemplate as the marital pictures of the prophetic day of Yahweh."

112 A. Joseph Everson, "The Day of Yahweh," *JBL* 93 (1974): 329. He points out that F. Charles Fensham in his "Possible Origin of the Concept of the Day of the Lord," *Biblical Essays* (Bepeck, South Africa: Potchefstroom Herald, 1966), 90–97 suggested another perspective of this study. Fensham, he said "maintains that the Day of YHWH should most properly be viewed against the background of covenant traditions as the event of the execution of treaty curses."

113 Everson, "Days of Yahweh," 330. Here, he interestingly reiterated the 16 occurrences of יום יהוה in prophetic literatures in seven prophetic Books (Isa 13:6, 9; Ezek 13:5; Joel 1:15; 2:1, 11; 3:4; 4:14; Amos 5:18[2×], 20; Obad 15; Zeph 1:7, 14[2×]; and Mal 3:23). The phrase is also found in three additional texts, but with minor variations יום ליהוה = day of the Lord, day belonging to the Lord [translations are mine] (Isa 2:12; Ezek 30:3; Zech 14:1). Other related phrases are: ביום עברת יהוה = in/on the day of the Lord's wrath (Ezek 7:19; Zeph 1:18); [ב]יום אף יהוה =[in/on] the day of the Lord's anger (Zeph 2:2, 3, Lam 2:22); ביום חרון אפו = on the day of His burning anger (Lam 1:12; ביום אפו = on his day of anger (Lam 2:1). Additional variations include: ביום זבח יהוה = on the day of the sacrifice of the Lord (Zeph 1:8); יום נקמה = the day of vengeance (Jer 46:10); יום נקם ליהוה = the day of vengeance of the Lord (Isa 34:8); ויום נקם לאלהינו = and a day of vindication/vengeance by our God (Isa 61:2); כי יום נקם בלבי = for the day of vengeance (was/had been) in my heart (Isa 63:4); יום מהומה ומבוסה ומבוכה = a day of tumult, subjugation and confusion (Isa 22:5). Other references to specific "days" in the prophetic literature include: the day of whirlwind (Amos 1:4); the evil day

torical events, but in which he believes specific references to the tradition are present.[114]

Based on these texts, he came out with three conclusions. First, these texts are interpretations of past events. Second, these texts provide a basic perspective for understanding all the Day of YHWH texts. Finally, the Day of YHWH concept is used in the prophetic literature in connection with the realities of war, the memories of war or the anticipation of new occasions of war.[115] Everson's study, in my own judgment, like previous studies, still lacks an in-depth analysis of specific texts of the Day of YHWH tradition and their relevance today. He did not give adequate attention to its role in the rest of the Twelve Minor Prophets. It is mostly a commentary on past studies. He began by recognizing the centrality of the Day of YHWH in the thoughts of the prophets about the future, but later seems to highlight more of those texts which, according to him, deal with past historical events. Everson also went on to discuss the connection of the Day of YHWH traditions with wars, without qualification, sending mixed signals as to his definite position and ending on a very unsatisfactory note. A detailed and close reading of the Twelve shows that the theme not only runs through the Twelve Minor Prophets, but that the word "day" could be used in several senses within the historical context of a particular prophet, and it still refers to the phrase, in question, יום יהוה (the Day of YHWH). This will be extensively substantiated in subsequent chapters.

(Amos 6:3); the day of trouble (Isa 37:3; Jer 51:2; Ezek 7:7; Nah 1:7); the day of visitation (Isa 10:3); the day of Median (Isa 9:3); the day of Jezreel (Hos 1:11); and the day of Egypt (Ezek 30:9). There are also numerous expressions such as "in the latter days," "behold the days are coming," and the declaration, "in that day," which alone occurs almost 200 times in the prophetic literature.

114 In "Days of Yahweh," 331, Everson lists these texts to include: Lamentations 1; 2; Ezekiel 13:1–9 , which looks back on the destruction of Judah and the fall of Jerusalem in 588-86 BCE; Jeremiah 46:1–12 , which describes the destruction of an Egyptian army at the battle of Carchemish in 605, and Isaiah 22:1–14, which looks back on the destruction in Judah and Jerusalem's escape during the campaign of Sennacherib in 701,

115 Everson, "Days of Yahweh," 335–37.

Another scholar, Yair Hoffmann also dwelt on this concept. He believes very strongly that the "Day of the Lord" is inseparable from the overall problem of biblical eschatology, and to some extent, it is a reflection of the different approaches to that subject.[116] He lined himself up with earlier scholars in determining the limit or the extent of the study or usage of the phrase, יום יהוה (Day of YHWH).[117]

He concludes his studies with the following recommendations: First, יום יהוה (the Day of YHWH) should be appreciated as a phrase which developed and passed through a long traditional process of growth. When evaluating its significance, the *Sitz-im-Leben* of the earlier prophets should be taken into consideration.

Second, it is important to realize that Amos did not use it as a definite or technical term, but it gained such a character during the time of Zephaniah, 150 years after Amos. Third, Amos used it in the context of theophany, regarding certain events connected with the appearance of God.[118] He suggests, contrary to Everson that יום יהוה (the Day of YHWH) was never used to describe days or events in the past but future events. It was never a non eschatological term, and once it had crystallized as a term, it had an eschatological significance. Similar phrases, unlike the position of Everson, were generally intended to be variations on the eschatological term, and such variations could be used, according to Hoffmann, both in eschatological and non-eschatological scriptures.[119]

Michael S. Moore wrote six years after Yair Hoffmann. He historically studied in great detail the theology of the Prophet Zephaniah. He acknowledged the centrality of the prophecy of Zephaniah in the exposition of the prophetic announcement of יום יהוה (the Day of

---

116 Yair Hoffmann, "The Day of the Lord as a Concept and a Term in the Prophetic Literature," *ZAW* 93 (1981): 37.

117 Unlike earlier scholars, Hoffmann in his "Day of the Lord," 39 highlights that with regard to whether the יום יהוה was a definite concept or not, traditional Jewish exegetes thought it was not a definite term. For example in the Targum, T. Jonathan never translated the phrase יום יהוה, because he did not expect it to be a definite term. Rashi, Ibn Ezra and Maimonides also thought it was not a definite term.

118 Hoffmann, "Days of the Lord," 50.

119 Hoffmann, "Days of the Lord," 50.

YHWH).[120] Moore commendably devoted the rest of his article to categorizing earlier studies into the tradition-critical approaches (von Rad and his school, Fensham); myth-and-ritual approaches (Mowinckel and his school); history of religion approaches (Jean-Georges Heintz),[121] theophanic approaches (Černy, Meir Weiss, J. Jeremias),[122] and the mediating hypotheses of Frank Moore Cross, already discussed.[123]

120 He actually invoked Arvid S. Kapelrud, *The Message of the Prophet Zephaniah* (Oslo: Universitetsforlaget, 1975), 80; von Rad, "Origin of the Concept of the Day of Yahweh," 102, and many others to drive home his point. See also See Michael S. Moore, "Yahweh's Day," *ResQ* 29 (1987): 193–208, for a detailed impressive renaissance of this study.

121 Actually here, Jean-Georges Heintz in his "Oracles prophetiques et 'guerre sainte' selon les achieves royales de Mari et l'Ancient Testament," (*VTSup* 17; Leiden: Brill, 1969), 112– 138, probably drawing from earlier studies of Černy, *Day of Yahweh*, 10–17 , built a case against the "Holy War" theory of von Rad. Heintz disagrees with von Rad's stand that the study of the origins of יום יהוה concept be limited to those OT texts which explicitly mention the Day of YHWH. Heintz in his studies attempts to highlight and link von Rad's *Der Heilige Krieg* theory in connection with the Akkadian phrase *ūmūšū qerbū* = "his days are near", and to link it to the biblical phrase כי קרוב יום יהוה = "for the Day of YHWH is near," as representative of a stereotyped battle cry in the ancient Near East. See also, Heintz, "Aux origins d'une expression biblique: ūmūšū qerbū, in A. R. M., X/6, 8?" *VT* 21(1971): 528–540.

122 See J. Jeremias, *Theophanie* (Neurkirchen: Neukirchiener Berlag, 1965), 97– 100 for details of his views.

123 See Moore, "Yahweh's Days," 204, where he qualifies Cross's interpretation of the Day of YHWH motif as attractive. He rightly observes that Cross anchors his study in his other thesis joining together the Canaanite myth and Hebrew Epic. For Cross, Moore reiterates, the motif of YHWH as "divine warrior," finds traditional meaning both in exodus conquest traditions of YHWH Sabaoth's march toward Jerusalem from Sinai (Judg 5:4–5; Deut 33:2–3; Exod 15) and in those texts from the Jerusalem cult tradition describing YHWH as the Warrior who conquers the primordial elements of Chaos in Canaanite/mythological terms (Pss 24:7–10; 132). He suggests that the conquest/divine warrior traditions were somehow preserved in the so-called "Gilgal cultus," (basing the reconstruction of the "liturgy" of such cultus on tradtion-critical hypotheses which seek to explain the events of Joshua 3– 5 and the ancient characteristics of the poetical form and content of Exod 15) before their latter reworking by the Deuteronomistic historians. These traditions were later transformed and mythologized during the monarchical era, in a process which served ultimately to

Moore finally calls for a dynamic and pluralistic approach towards the interpretation of the Day of YHWH, since by the time of Zephaniah his contemporaries would have understood the significance of his prophetic message, within their own historical context.[124]

Although Moore's article is basically a renewed reflection on past studies and a categorization of those opinions into different schools of thought, his recommendation of flexibility and adaptation of several procedural steps, in the face of pluralism of methods of biblical exegesis, especially with regard to passages and concepts common to both Testaments, is in my own judgment, highly commendable.[125]

---

give the "Divine Warrior," motif 'depth," such that it was later picked up in the apocalyptic prophecies. Examples of this intertwine of two complex traditions of cosmic warfare with the theme of conquest is evident in biblical texts (Isa 40:3–6; 35; 51:9–11; 62:24–28; Hos 2:16–17).

124 See Moore, "Days of Yahweh," 208, where he passionately, invokes upon his suggestions, the assertion made by Franz D. Hubman, in his *Untersuchung zu den Koffessionen: Jer 11:18–12:6 und Jer 15:10–21* (Stuttgart: Echter Verlag, 1978), 309 that "Definitive judgments on weighty problems are more often resolved by a combination of arguments from several procedural steps."

125 See the following studies where there has been a profound and general recent acknowledgement of the turmoil and shifts of exegetical methodologies and mutual dialogue between diachronic and synchronic method: Robert Morgan with John Barton, *Biblical Interpretation* (Oxford: Oxford University Press, 1988); Raymond E. Brown and S.M. Schneiders, "Hermeneutics," in *NJBC* (ed., R.E. Brown, J.E. Fitzmyer and R.E. Murphy; Englewood Cliffs: Prentice-Hall, 1990), 1144–65; Joseph A. Fitzmyer, *The Biblical Commission's Document "The Interpretation of the Bible in the Church," Text and Commentary* (Subsidia Biblica 18, Rome: Biblical Institute Press, 1995); Sandra M. Schneiders, *The Revelatory Text: Interpreting the New Testament as Sacred Scripture* (Collegeville, Minnesota: Liturgical Press, 1999); S.L. McKenzie, and S.R. Haynes, eds., *To Each Its Own Meaning: An Introduction to Biblical Criticisms and their Application* (rev. ed.; Louisville, London: Westminster John Knox Press, 1999); Odil Hannes Steck, *Old Testament Exegesis: A Guide to the Methodology* (trans. James D. Nogalski; 2nd ed.; Resources for Biblical Study 39; Atlanta: Scholars Press, 1998); Michael Weigl, "Current Research on the Book of Nahum: Exegetical Methodologies in Turmoil?" *CR* 9 (2001): 81–130; William L. Countryman, *Interpreting the Truth: Changing the Paradigm of Biblical Studies* (New York: Trinity Press International, 2003); D.A. Knight, Foreword, *Methods of Biblical Interpretation; Excerpted from the Dictionary of Biblical Interpretation* (Nashville: Abingdon Press, 2004).

1.1.4 Studies on the Day of YHWH in the 1990s to Date

Richard H. Hiers, in 1992 reaffirmed that the "'the Day of the Lord" is a central feature of the prophets' message to their contemporaries. It is dominant in Isaiah, Joel and Zephaniah." What is interesting in his studies unlike those studies before him is that Hiers throws more light on the similarity in meaning that occurs when the following expressions are used: "that day," "the day of," and "the day when."

For him, they are often used interchangeably with the fuller expressions or in context. He cited Isaiah 2:12–22, Jeremiah 46:10 and Ezekiel 7:5–27, as clear examples, of these interchangeable usages.[126] In most cases, Heirs affirms the same meaning is suggested.[127] In his brief article, Hiers touches on quite a number of יום יהוה (the Day of YHWH) issues in a refreshing manner, including YHWH's judgment against nations,[128] against Israel, Judah or Jewish people,[129] future deliverance or blessing for Israel, Judah, nations and creations.[130] He also observes that similar terms occur in the NT contexts with reference to the future appearance or return of Jesus as their Κυρίος, since the Jews and early Christians read the OT יום יהוה (the Day of YHWH), as η ημέρα τοῦ κυρίου in their LXX.[131]

126 Richard H. Hiers, "Day of the Lord," *ABD* 2: 82.
127 Hiers, "Day of the Lord," 82.
128 For Heirs, a few scattered passages seem to refer to Yahweh's previous acts of judgment against foreign nations, like "the day of Median" (Isa 9:4), referring to the Midianites earlier defeat. But most others refer to YHWH's future punishment of various nations. Most of the prophetic books contain oracles against foreign nations.
129 See Hiers, "Day of Yahweh," 82 where he gives detailed texts demonstrating that the classical prophets warned their contemporaries in Israel and Judah that the "Day of Yahweh" would come upon them in the form of cosmic or meteorological catastrophes or of powerful enemy armies which will bring YHWH's judgment against them for violating the covenant requirements of the law.
130 See also Hiers, "Day of Yahweh," 83, where he implicitly challenges or contradicts some past scholars who restricted the significance of the Day of YHWH to past events. Some 60 occurrences of the "Day of YHWH" and similar expressions refer to the future time when YHWH would reestablish the fortunes of Israel, Judah or the Jewish people and other nations.
131 Hiers, "Day of the Lord," 83.

K. J. Cathcart's article which we have already alluded to, also force-fully takes stock of past approaches to יום יהוה/ἡ ἡμέρα τοῦ κυρίου (the Day of the Lord). He calls for a distinction between a primary day of YHWH's intervention with limited effect and a secondary day with a universal cosmic judgment, suggesting that there is an organic conti-nuity between prophetic preaching and apocalyptic eschatology.[132]

Recently, in 1997 Rolff Rendtorff cautioned against limiting the concept and the implication of the Day of YHWH, to those texts which specifically use the construct chain, יום יהוה (the Day of the Lord). Rendtorff argues that the concept of the Day of YHWH has shown not only its dominant presence in the passages of the Book of the Twelve, but has also demonstrated a significant promise of a unifying theme.[133]

Rendtorff was followed by James D. Nogalski who in his 1999 work, "The Day(s) of YHWH in the Book of the Twelve," searched relent-lessly for an appropriate identification and usage of the Day of YHWH in the Book of the Twelve. He concluded that based on thematic and verbal links, the concept of the day of divine intervention provides a literary cohesion to the writing of Hosea through Obadiah, suggesting the involvement of the rest of the Twelve. He believes these links in-clude more than just the phrase יום יהוה (the Day of the Lord).[134]

From the verbal and thematic arguments of Nogalski, and others, we come to the linguistic and philological investigation of Ishai-Rosenboim Daniella. Writing from Israel, Daniella disagrees with Yair Hoffmann and those scholars who restrict the study of the Day of YHWH to those passages that the construct form, יום יהוה (the Day of YHWH) occurs. Daniella calls this construct form a "collocation," or *nomen regens* and *nomen rectum*, and the later qualifies the former."[135]

132 K. J. Cathcart, "Day of Yahweh," 84–85.
133 Rolff Rendtorff, "How to Read the Book of the Twelve as a Theological Unity," *SBLSP* (1997): 420–432. See also James D. Nogalski and Marvin A. Sweeney, *Read-ing and Hearing the Book of the Twelve* (SBLSymS 15; Atlanta: SBL, 2000), 75–87.
134 James D. Nogalski, "The Day (s) of YHWH in the Book of the Twelve," *SBLSP 1999; One Hundred and Thirty-Fifth Annual Meeting: November 20–23, 1999* (SBLSymS 38; Atlanta: SBL, 1999), 617–42.
135 For details, see Daniella Ishai-Rosenboim, "Is יום חי (the Day of the Lord) a Term in Biblical Language?" *Biblica* 87 (2006): 395.

Daniella linguistically and philologically identifies these collocations in the Hebrew Bible as well as in other sources. Daniella concludes that the collocation יום הי in the Bible is not a term, nor a key to the study of the Day of YHWH. Rather, this collocation may be replaced by others such as; the day of anger, the day of the anger of the Lord, that day.[136] The absence of this collocation does not eliminate or disqualify a prophecy from the list of prophecies dealing with the concept of the Day of YHWH.[137]

Although Daniella's linguistic and philological approach appears complicated and devoid of theological substance, the point is well driven home that in discussing the Day of the Lord, scholars should not limit their discussion to prophecies in which we find the specific collocation, יום הי, since the criteria for defining a prophecy as one of the Day of the Lord are definite motives, characteristic of that time in which God will appear.[138]

Also recently in 2007, Balakrishnan Sobhidanandan in his Doctoral Dissertation, accepted in the Faculty of Theology at The Pontifical University of St. Thomas Aquinas, theologically approached the concept of the Day of YHWH in the Prophet Joel.[139] This work was less focused on the linguistic, literary and textual analysis of the book of Joel, within the context of the Twelve Minor Prophets. But the traditional "Cultic" and "Holy War" approaches to this concept was well discussed. In Joel, the Day of YHWH is not only a day of judgment symbolised in the swarm of locusts (Joel 1:15; 2), but a day of hope, YHWH's intervention in history, a glorious future and salvation for the repentants in the valley of Jehoshaphat, made possible by the merciful acts of YHWH.[140]

---

136 The Tetragrammaton יח םוי is the author's way of rendering the "Day of the Lord" or "The Day of Y.'"

137 Ishai-Rosenboim, "Is יה םוי (the Day of the Lord) a Term," 397–401.

138 Ishai-Rosenboim, "Is יה םוי (the Day of the Lord) a Term," 401.

139 Balakrishnan Sobhidanandan, "The Day of the Lord in the Book of Joel: A Day of Judgment" (PhD diss., Rome: Pontificia Studiorum Universitas A. S. Thoma Aquino. 2007).

140 See, Sobhidanandan, "The Day of the Lord" 61–69.

These surveys of past studies testify to the non-fundamental agreement among scholars as to the best approach to defining the origin, meaning and nature or significance of the Day of YHWH. It is clear that members of these various schools of thought paid more attention to the historico-religious, cultic, mythical and theophanic origin of the concept, with little attention to textual and theological implications and thematic unity of the concept of the Day of YHWH that runs like a thread throughout the entire Book of the Twelve, which this study intends to demonstrate. In the past studies not much of the theological, social, and cultural relevance of the Day of the Lord has been discussed. Its ecumenical and interreligious values were also not noticed. In fact, Zephaniah, the focus of this present work, was relegated to the background, and if discussed, it was done in passing. It was not done in a satisfactory manner. This brings us to the general background of Zephaniah and to the study of the Day of YHWH.

1.2 Background of Zephaniah and Studies on his Day of YHWH

Before turning our attention to the survey of specific studies on the Prophet Zephaniah, particularly on the Day of YHWH, a general survey of the background of Zephaniah is necessary. This includes a brief review of his person, date and the socio-historical context of his message. This will help foster a better appreciation of his overall theology in subsequent chapters.

The Book of Zephaniah is the ninth of the Twelve Minor Prophets in both MT and LXX ordering.[141] It consists of three chapters, fifty-three verses, with a central theological theme of יהוה יום (the Day of

141 In the MT the Twelve Minor Prophets are arranged as follows: Hosea, Joel, Amos, Obadiah, Jonah, Micah, Nahum, Habakkuk, Zephaniah, Haggai, Zechariah, and Malachi; while in the LXX we have, Hosea, Amos, Micah, Joel, Obadiah, Jonah, Nahum, Habakkuk, Zephaniah, Haggai, Zechariah and Malachi.

YHWH). Chapter One, after the superscription (1:1) opens with the announcement of doom on creation, humans and animals (1:2–3), then the focus of the judgments move to Judah and the idolaters and sinners there (vv 4–6). They must prepare for the Day of YHWH (vv 7–18).

Chapter Two predicts judgment and misfortunes on several nations, after a window of hope and exhortation to repentance and change of heart (vv 1–15). Chapter Three discusses judgment and misfortunes on Jerusalem. This came as a result of recklessness, abuses of power and offices by her priests, judges and rulers (vv 1–8). This is followed by a promise of hope, and a note of joy. The sovereign and victorious YHWH will calm Israel's fear and gather the dispersed ones. He will make them popular and restore the fortunes of their remnants (vv 9–20). In other words, the judgment and threats heard in the first two chapters, anticipate the hope, joy and salvific message of the latter part of chapter three (vv 14–20). What about the person of the prophet?

1.2.1 The Person, Style and Historical Origin of Zephaniah

The search for the personality of Zephaniah and his historical origin has always left scholars with different answers.[142] The name צפניה (Zephaniah) means, "the Lord hides," "he whom the Lord hides," or "the Lord has cause to be hidden,"[143] and *JHWH protegge, nasconde,*[144]

---

142 H. Ferguson, "The Historical Testimony of the Prophet Zephaniah," *JBL* (1883): 42–59; Kapelrud, *The Message of Prophet Zephania,* 41–42; Gene Rice, "The African Roots of the Prophet Zephaniah," *JRT* 36 (1979): 21–31; Carroll Stuhlmueller, *Amos, Hosea, Micah, Nahum, Zephaniah, Habakkuk* (Collegeville Bible Commentary, Old Testament 15; Collegeville, MN: The Liturgical Press, 1986), 99; Maria Eszenyei Széles, *Wrath and Mercy: A Commentary on the Books of Habakkuk and Zephaniah* (trans. George A. F. Knight. ITC; Grand Rapids; MI: Eerdmans, 1987), 61–64; Feinberg, *Minor Prophets,* 221; John M. Berridge, "Zephaniah (Person)," *ABD* 6:1075; Adele Berlin, *Zephaniah: A New Commentary with Introduction and Commentary* (AB 25A; New York: Doubleday, 1994), 31; J. Vlaardingerbroek, *Zephaniah,* (HCOT; leuven: Peters, 1999), 11–13 and Savoca, *Abdia-Naum, Abacuc-Sofonia,* 145–46.

143 Feinberg, *Minor Prophets,* 221; Széles, *Wrath and Mercy,* 62.

144 See Savoca, *Abdia-Naum, Abacuc-Sofonia,* 145.

It is a derivation of the Hebrew root צפן, "to conceal, hide, treasure," which is frequently employed with reference to YHWH's treasured ones "צפוניך" (Ps 83:4), the concealment of YHWH's servants from evil (Pss 27:5; 31:21), or even as a designation for YHWH's "treasured" or "cherished" city of Jerusalem (Ezek 7:22).[145]

This name occurs in 1 Chronicles 6:21 (son of Tahath); Jeremiah 21:1; 29:25, 29; 52:24 (the priest Zephaniah, son of Maaseiah); Zechariah 6:10, 14 (father of Josiah, and unknown relation to King Josiah). This suggests "Zephaniah," was a common name in Israel. The form צפניהו is also found in Jeremiah 37:3.[146]

In other words, in the OT this name is attributed to four persons: the priest, Zephaniah, son of Maaseiah, the father of Josiah, the son of Tahath and the prophet during the reign of Josiah (640–609 B.C.E.).[147] It is the latter, found in the superscription (Zeph 1:1), that scholars widely believe best expresses the question of the historical origin of Zephaniah.[148]

---

145 Sweeney, *Zephaniah*, 47. See also N. Arbuckle, "Zephaniah," in *A New Catholic Commentary on Holy Scripture* (eds., Reginald C. Fuller, Leonard Jonson and Conleth Kearns; New Jersey: Nelson, 1969), 718 and Savoca, Abdia-Naum, Abacuc-Sofonia, 145.

146 Sweeney, *Zephaniah*, 47.

147 Berridge, "Zephaniah (Person)," *ABD* 6:1075.

148 Nothing seems to be known about this prophet outside of this superscription with its present significance "the Lord protects." But some scholars had thought or translated it as a noun confessing "Zaphon is YHWH." Zaphon was an important Canaanite god who gave his name to 'Zaphon,' the mythical mountain home of gods. This proposal Sweeney, *Zephaniah*, 47 recognizes is "based on a reading of the root צפן in relation to the noun צפון "north," and the appearance of the omicron in the LXX's rendition of the name as Σοφονιας. However, the usage of "Zaphon," with the implication of the northern mythological home of the Canaanites gods in Ugaritic literature, is no longer popular. This study settles with the obvious one, "YHWH protects." See further details of the explanation of these usages in A. Peter, *Die Bücher Zefanja, Nahum und Habakuk* (Düsseldorf: Patmos-Verlag, 1972), 29–31; P. R. Ackroyed, et al. eds., *The Books of Joel, Obadiah, Jonah, Nahum, Habakkuk and Zephaniah* (London: Cambridge University Press, 1975), 153–154; Berlin, *Zephaniah*, 31; Vlaardingerbroek, *Zephaniah*, 30–31.

Savoca affirms this when he writes that "Della personalità di Sofonia non abbiamo altre informazioni fuori da quelle che possiamo dedurre dal libretto a lui attribuito."[149]

In the superscription we read, "The word of the Lord which was addressed to Zephaniah, son of Cushi, son of Gadaliah, son of Amariah, son of Hezekiah; in the days of Josiah son of Ammon, King of Judah." This superscription which contains Zephaniah's genealogy is unique and unusual.[150] It is a mystery.[151] It is different from the heading of other prophetic books. For instance, in Isaiah, Jeremiah, Joel and Jonah, reference to the name of the father is not a genealogy, but has similar import as our contemporary last names.[152]

These diversities or the uniqueness of Zephaniah's superscription leave scholars guessing as to the root origin of Zephaniah.[153] Széles thinks that probably the author of Zephaniah 1:1 wants to establish the fact that Zephaniah came from a royal background, well vested in Judean culture. He is witnessing to the fact that King Hezekiah was his great-grand-father.[154]

149 Savoca, *Abdia-Naum, Abacuc-Sofonia*, 145. That is to say "we do not have much information about the personality of Zephaniah outside what is attributed to him in the Book."

150 See Rice, "African Roots," 21, where it is even suggested that, Zephaniah came from Africa; Vlaardingerbroek, *Zephaniah*, 11.

151 Széles, *Wrath and Mercy*, 62.

152 Vlaardingerbroek, *Zephaniah*, 11 went on to rightly observe that in Amos 1:1; Mic 1:1; Nahum 1:1 there is a different description. In Zech 1:1, the indication of a father and grandfather is not a genealogy, but somehow expanded last name. In the case of Obadiah, Habakkuk and Haggai, there is no further designation of any kind.

153 See Stuhlmueller, *Amos, Hosea, Micah, Nahum, Zephaniah, Habakkuk*, 99. Here it is observed that, "Zephaniah's father is called Cushi, which is an Ethiopian name. Zephaniah refers to Ethiopia negatively in 2:12, but more positively in 3:10. While his father mixed African blood into Zephaniah's Israelite origins, his other ancestors reach back four generations to Hezekiah, very likely the King of Jerusalem."

154 Széles, *Wrath and Mercy*, 62. See Sweeney, *Zephaniah*, 48 where it is highlighted that it was Abraham Ibn Ezra, the twelfth century, Spanish-Jewish commentator, who made such identification. Ibn Ezra argued that, Amariah ben Hezekiah must have been the brother of the Judean King Manasseh ben Hezekiah and who demonstrated that the chronology of four generations is appropriate for a prophet who spoke during Josiah's reign.

Széles's thoughts reecho Rice, who observed earlier that the most plausible inference from the exceptional character of Zephaniah's genealogy is that the last name member, Hezekiah, was a person of unusual significance, who reigned around 727/715–698/687 B.C.E.[155] It is also argued that some passages of Zephaniah, for example, Zephaniah 1:8–9, betray a certain familiarity with the court and the customs prevailing there.[156]

Some objections have been raised against the identification of King Hezekiah here. It is argued that the text of Zephaniah 1:1 does not explicitly call the Hezekiah of Zephaniah's ancestry King. Some scholars contend that the identification is impossible on chronological grounds. They argue that whereas there are four generations from Zephaniah's ancestor, Hezekiah, there are only three from King Hezekiah through his successors on the throne, namely; Manasseh (698/687–642 B.C.E.), Amon (641–640 B.C.E.), and Josiah (640–609 B.C.E.).

It is also difficult to identify Amariah as the older brother of Manasseh. No son of Hezekiah named Amariah is known, although Amariah is listed in 2 Chronicles 31:15 as one of the Levites appointed by Hezekiah to distribute freewill offerings in the cities of the priests.[157] Manasseh was only twelve years old when he succeeded his father as king in Jerusalem (2 Kgs 21:1), which indicates that Hezekiah fathered him at the age of forty-two, following his revolt against Sennacherib (2 Kgs 18:1–2) of Assyria. Here it is stated that Hezekiah was twenty-five years old when he became king and ruled for twenty-nine years. This makes it unlikely that Hezekiah had other sons prior to Manasseh.[158]

The time between King Hezekiah (715–687 B.C.E.) and Zephaniah, who is generally regarded as being active around 630 B.C.E, is

155 Rice, "African Roots," 21. See also W. F. Bright, "The Chronology of the Divided Monarch of Israel," *BASOR* 100 (1945): 16–22; Michael D. Coogan, *The Old Testmaent: A Historical and Literary Introduction to the Hebrew Scriptures* (New York: Oxford University Press, 2006), 526–533, where he has rightly observed that the chronological data for the dates of the reigns of Ahaz, Hezekiah and Manasseh are inconsistent.
156 Vlaardingerbroek, *Zephaniah*, 12.
157 Sweeney, *Zephaniah*, 48.
158 Sweeney, *Zephaniah*, 48.

extremely short for four generations.[159] Also, the expression "king of Judah" does not occur in apposition to the name of Hezekiah. In the Peshitta, Hilkiah instead of Hezekiah is attested. Vlaardingerbroek believes there are no compelling arguments for or against the position that the identity of King Hezekiah is meant here in the text of Zephaniah 1:1. But lack of clear evidence or concrete information requires that the debate be left open.[160]

There has also been a lively discussion of Zephaniah's father Cushi.[161] According to Vlaardingebroek, there are some scholars, particularly J. Heller, who thinks that the later editor redacted Zephaniah 1:1, which originally referred to "Zephaniah son of Cushi," to position Hezekiah who was a well known king in its place. Cushi then was taken as a proper name, but not a gentilic one. Zephaniah, the spiritual father of Josiah's reformation, now becomes a descendant of the earlier king and reformer, Hezekiah.[162]

On the other hand, Sweeney observes that although Cushi is presented here as a proper name, it appears in the common gentilic form that refer to Ethopians, Nubians, or people from the land of Cushi (Num 12:1; 2 Sam 18:21, 22, 23, 31, 32; Jer 13:23; 38:7, 10, 12; 39:16).[163] This has generated tremendous debate among scholars with regard to the African ancestry or root of Zephaniah.[164]

According to J. Daniel Hays, part of the reason why such a debate is lively is because Cushites ruled Egypt from 715 BCE until 663 BCE, during which time the relationship between Cushite-ruled Egypt and Judah were cordial, both in terms of commerce, political affairs and for

159 Rice, "African Roots," 21–22.
160 Vlaardingerbroek, *Zephaniah,* 13.
161 Rice, "African Roots," 21–31; Vlaardingerbroek, *Zephaniah*, 12; Széles, *Wrath and Mercy*, 62; Sweeney, *Zephaniah*, 48.
162 Vlaardingerbroek, *Zephaniah*, 12.
163 Sweeney, *Zephaniah*, 48–49. However, Ethiopia is identified with Cushi. It is here used in its biblical sense of that portion of the Nile valley south of Syene, modern Aswan (Ezek 29:10), corresponding roughly to the modern state of Sudan.
164 See Rice, "African Root," 21–31.

military purposes.[165] In other words the Cushites had an impressive presence in Palestine throughout the seventh century during which Zephaniah preached, although Cushite presence in Egypt ended in 663 BCE when the Assyrians destroyed the Thebes, few years before the actual ministry of Zephaniah.[166]

Although Vlaardingerbroek dismisses that neither Zephaniah 1:1 nor 2:12 offer any support for this, it was certainly possible for Judeans or Israelites to have African ancestry. In the light of this, Rice argues that the study of the roots of the prophet Zephaniah is not the only biblical subject that does not permit the satisfaction of a definitive answer. Moreover, there is nothing that prevents us, according to Rice, from the identification of the Hezekiah recorded in the book of the prophet Zephaniah, or of Zephaniah's ancestry with King Hezekiah, nor with the identification of Cushi with one of Ethopian descendants. However, Zephaniah's significance depends not on his roots but on his message. He was God's instrument for every people and nation and race (Zeph 3:10).[167]

Besides being of a Judean or African origin, Széles suggests that Zephaniah seems to have had the opportunity to interact with members of the ruling circle in Judah. This is evident in Zephaniah's apparent familiarity with his environment and cultural repertoire. Zephaniah, she stresses, knew not only his city but also his geography, his political and religious leaders. For example, Zephaniah in his preaching gives precise topographical descriptions of Jerusalem.

He preached about the royal palaces (1:8–9), the temple and its neighbors (1:10–11), the merchants (1:11). He preached about the

---

165 J. Daniel Hays, *From Every People and Nation: A Biblical Theology of Race* (NSBT 18; Downers Grove; IL: Inter Varsity Press, 2003), 121.

166 Hays, *From Every People and Nation*, 122.

167 See Vlaardingerbroek, *Zephaniah*, 12; Sweeney, *Zephaniah*, 49. See also Hays, *From Every People and Nation*, esp. 105–139. Here, opinions of scholars on the possible origin of Zephaniah are extensively discussed. Racial issues in the prophetic literaure *vis-à-vis* the relationship of Zephaniah with Cushi are discussed, as well as the possibility of a Judean having an African ancestry. Most important for this study is Hay's emphasis on the universality of salvation exemplified in Zephaniah's genealogy.

old city (1:12–13) and the new city (1:10–11). He demonstrated his knowledge of territories outside Jerusalem and Judah as well. These include, the seacoast dominated by the Philistines (2:4–5), Nineveh in the north (2:14), Ammon and Moab in the east (2:8–10) and Egypt to the south (2:12).[168]

Besides, he was a social critic of his time. He was also well acquainted with the preaching of earlier and contemporary prophets that will be discussed in Chapter Four. He shares the vocabulary and linguistic tools with other writings like the Wisdom Literature and the Psalms. He uses words like מוסר "correction" (3:2,7); דל "humble, lowly," עני "poor, submissive" (3:12); בקש/דרשה "seek" (1:6; 2:3); משפט "judgment" (3:5); רני/בת־ציון "rejoice/shout for joy/daughter of Zion" (3:14) and שבות/שוב "restore/fortunes" (3:20).[169]

In terms of style, Zephaniah appears in a steady line of continuity with the prophecy of the south. With Amos and Isaiah, he centers upon the remnant, the Day of YHWH, sin and chastisement. Other similarities in prophetic style include a phrase like, "seek the Lord" which links Zephaniah with Amos (Amos 5:4–7, 14–15; Zeph 2:3). Others are the customary forms of curses (Amos 5:11; Zeph 1:13), which have already been mentioned. Zephaniah's language is unique, clear, correct and sincere.[170]

In my judgment, Zephaniah's existence is authentic, although no one has complete and concrete information about his origin. This lack of complete information about his person and origin should not distract us from recognizing the place of the sovereignty of YHWH, who elects Zephaniah as God's instrument, irrespective of nationality or race. Besides, being God's instrument and messenger his message is relevant to people of all times and cultures, since God cannot be tied to any ethnic community. He preached in the time of King Josiah (640– 609 B.C.E.), which is highly significant for this study as well.

---

168 Széles, *Wrath and Mercy*, 63.
169 See also, Széles, *Wrath and Mercy*, 64.
170 See Stuhlmueller, *Amos, Hosea, Micah, Nahum, Zephaniah, Habakkuk*, 97– 98.

1.2.2 The Timing and the Socio-Historical Setting

A discussion on the timing, dating or the socio-historical setting of the prophecy of Zephaniah has always formed a significant part towards a clearer understanding of the theology of this prophet. The debate in my own judgment concentrates mostly on the late pre-exilic and early exilic period. There is hardly any commentator on Zephaniah who has not attempted a discussion on this highly sensitive issue.[171]

Nogalski presents three good summary positions with regard to the dating of Zephaniah. Some date Zephaniah prior to the Josianic reforms begun in 622 B.C.E., while some see Zephaniah's work as part of those reform processes after 622 B.C.E. There are also those in the third group who argue for the period of Jehoiakim/Eliakim (608–598 B.C.E.).[172]

Those in the first school of thought argue that the cultic or spiritual abuses mentioned in Zephaniah, fit in with practices prevalent during and immediately after the reign of Manasseh (698/687–642 B.C.E.), Josiah's grandfather. They argue that Zephaniah was instrumental in initiating the reforms of Josiah. Roberts for instance belongs to this catergory. He argues that there are no good reasons to doubt the historical information of superscription (1:1). Robert stresses that Zephaniah's portrayal of the rampant idolatry, syncretism and corrupt behavior among the royal and religious officers in Jerusalem (1:4–6, 8–9; 3:3–4) testifies that Zephaniah preached in the early days of Josiah

---

171 Some of them uppermost in my mind are; Ferguson, "The Historical Testimony of the Prophet," *JBL* 3 (1883): 42–59; Donald L. Williams, "The Date of Zephaniah," *JBL* 82 (1963): 77–88; Kapelrud, *Message of Prophet Zephaniah*, 41–44; Langohr, G., "Le Livre de Sophonie et la critique de l'authenticité," *ETL* 52 (1976):1–27; Stuhlmueller, *Amos, Hosea, Micah, Nahum, Zephaniah, Habakkuk*, 96–97; J.J.M. Roberts, *Nahum, Habakkuk, and Zephaniah* (OTL; Philadelphia: Westminster, 1991), 163–164; Ehud Ben Zvi, *A Historical-Critical Study of the Book of Zephaniah* (BZAW 198; Berlin: Walter de Gruyter, 1991), 325–357; Patterson, *Nahum, Habakkuk, Zephaniah*, 275–278; Nogalski, *Literary Precursors*, 173–215; Berlin, *Zephaniah*, 33–42; Vlaardingebroek, *Zephaniah*, 13–17; Savoca, *Abdia-Naum, Abacuc-Sofonia*, 148–50.

172 Nogalski, *Literary Precursors*, 178.

prior to the reforms of 622 B.C.E. (2Kgs 22:3–23:25). It is also argued that Zephaniah, while preaching, did not mention the name of the King in person, but rather, בני־המלך (sons of the King). Perhaps, Josiah was too young by then to be burdened with the responsibility of condemnation for idolatry and syncretism.[173]

The Second group of scholars argues that Zephaniah preached during the reform of Josiah, although the reform did not actually begin in full swing until the discovery of the "Law Book."[174] The third group advocates for the time of Jehoiakim. Members of this group include eminent scholars like Donald Williams and J. Philip Hayatt.[175] They argue against the first two groups by highlighting the overwhelming evidence of the book of Zephaniah which, they presumed, might be the possible basis for the position taken by the first two groups.

William, in particular, thinks this evidence is nothing else but the imminent destruction of Jerusalem (Zeph 1:4, 10–11; 3:1–4). He observes that those who argue for the dating of Zephaniah as testified in the superscription believe that Zephaniah preached during the reign of Josiah.[176]

However, the post-Josianic school, to which Williams and others belong, place the preaching of Zephaniah in the time of Jehoiakim, Jehoiachin/Jeconiah (597 B.C.E.) and Zedekiah/Mattaniah (597–586 B.C.E.). Post-Josianic arguments, though less attractive, may be summarized under the following four points.

First, the expression in the prophet Zephaniah 1:4, (the remnant of Baal) "את־שאר־הבעל" not only refers to those who survived Josiah's reforms, but fits, as well, in the time of Jehoiakim. Second, the abuses

---

173 Robert, *Nahum, Habakkuk and Zephaniah*, 163. See also, Berlin, *Zephaniah*, 34; Nogalski, *Literary Precursors,* 179; and Vlaardingerbroek, *Zephaniah*, 13–14 for details of this position.

174 Nogalski, *Literary Precursors*, 179.

175 J. Philip Hayatt, "The Date and Background of Zephaniah," *JNES* 9 (1950): 27. He argues that "if there was a Scythian threat to Judah in the period shortly before 621 (and that is very doubtful!), it certainly was not great enough to call forth Zephaniah's vivid description of the great Day of Yahweh which he pictures as bringing cosmic catastrophe, not simply the devastation of Judah."

176 Williams, "Date of Zephaniah," 79.

described in Zephaniah 1:13, 17; 2:2, 7 and 3:1–8 re-echo deuteronomic language, that existed in the time of Josiah and after him. Third, the cynicism of Zephaniah 1:12 "הקפאים על־שמריהם" (those who stagnate over the remains of their wine/lee), indicates some kind of disappointment in the reforms after the death of Josiah. Fourth, the references to Moab and Ammon in Zephaniah 2:8ff, become understandable in the reign of Jehoiakim, based on his actions described in 2 Kings 24:2.[177]

It is also argued that in the case of the dating of the time of Josiah, the genuineness of the prophecies against foreign nations (2:4–15) cannot be maintained. Nineveh did not fall until 612 B.C.E. In fact, the oracle against Nineveh appears to be a *vaticinium ex eventu* (a prophecy from an outcome), and a prophecy against the Philistines (2:4–7) may refer to the chastisement by the Babylonians after an uprising in alliance with Judah.[178]

Nevertheless, Williams concludes his post-reformational argument by maintaining that there is no good reason to deny the date of Zephaniah's work in the period following Josiah's death (609 B.C.E.) and the death of the prophet himself, in 587 B.C.E. He argues that the name Zephaniah in 2 Kings, Jeremiah, and Zechariah refers to the same man, whose preaching is preserved in one of the books of the Minor Prophets. He believes that Zephaniah stands alongside Jeremiah as a witness to the momentous events which reshaped the political life of the Fertile Crescent in the late seventh and early sixth centuries, and formed a prelude to the fall of Jerusalem and exile.[179]

---

177 Nogalski, *Literary Precursors*, 179; Vlaardingerbroek, *Zephaniah*, 14.

178 Vlaardingerbroek, *Zephaniah*, 14.

179 Williams, "Date of Zephaniah," 88. Also see Vlaardingerbroek, *Zephaniah*, 15–16 for some of the counter arguments against the position of Williams as well as other specifications with regard to the dating of the prophecy of Zephaniah. See also Berlin, *Zephaniah*, 34–42 for list of different scholars with different positions, including E. Achtemeier who dates most of chapter 3 to 612–609, (end of Josiah's reign); J. P. Hyatt and D. Williams (reign of Jehoiakim, 608–598 B.C.E.); B. Peckham (590 B.C.E., for the first edition) and L. Smith and E. R. Lacheman (200 B.C.E.).

Finally, Berlin presents a good summary of Ehud Ben Zvi's post-monarchic dating of Zephaniah.[180] Drawing evidences from the thematic and linguistic similarities of Zephaniah's language of prophecy with the exilic and post-exilic Psalms and with the genealogies in Ezra and Nehemiah, Ben Zvi advances his arguments.[181] For Ben Zvi, the author of the book of Zephaniah was a sophisticated writer who was addressing a sophisticated audience. He was influenced by other prophetic traditions, wisdom literature, the *anawim* Psalms, the *malak* Psalms, and congregational Psalms.[182] For example, the image of the ideal community in the book of Zephaniah is one of a poor humble people without a king or royal elite, oppressed by wealthy, proud and impious enemies. The community awaits salvation from YHWH alone, since no king or national leader is expected to arise.[183]

According to Ben Zvi, this community "understands itself as a post-monarchic group whose horizon and focus is not that of creating (or recreating) a political center of power, a new and just bureaucracy, and the like. Instead, this group centers on a set of community-accepted religious attitudes, such as total reliance on YHWH."[184]

Additionally, Berlin observes that the point to be taken into consideration in this sort of argument is that the time of Josiah is not necessarily the time that the book was written, but it is the time in which the book is set.[185] In fact, the theory of late dating of Zephaniah is exciting, just like recent appreciation of the Deuteronomistic History (Deut–2 Kings) as late text,[186] though not without problems. The single most

---

180 Ben Zvi's position is well outlined in his concluding pages of his work, *A Historical-Critical Study of the Book of Zephaniah* (BZAW 198; Berlin: Walter de Gruyter, 1991), 347–358.

181 Berlin, *Zephaniah*, 36.

182 Berlin, *Zephaniah*, 36.

183 Berlin, *Zephaniah*, 36.

184 Ben Zvi, *Book of Zephaniah*, 356.

185 Berlin, *Zephaniah*, 38.

186 See Jean-Louis Ska, *Introduction to Reading the Pentateuch* (Winona Lake, Indiana: Eisenbrauns, 2006), 217–234. See also Vlaardingerbroek, *Zephaniah*,15–16 where the argument against late texts includes the fact that since King Josiah was not held accountable, does not mean that he was still a boy or a minor during the reforms. Josiah may have been spared the embarrassment and criti-

important problem that the late dating of Zephaniah must overcome is the superscription (Zeph 1:1), which clearly claims that Zephaniah preached "in the days of Josiah, son of Ammon," and not in the days of Jehoiakim.[187]

This problem has remained a historical-critical crux for scholars. Some have refused to accept the information in the superscription (Zeph 1:1) that Zephaniah preached during the time of Josiah. The moral and idolatrous situations mentioned in Zephaniah have been interpreted as a sign of persistence in the negative direction, even after the discovery of the Law Book (2 Kgs 22:8). Others think Zephaniah's preaching took place when Josiah was just a little boy. While for some as discussed, Zephaniah's preaching took place after the monarchic period and ended with Zedekiah in 586 B.C.E.

Nevertheless, this study lines up with those who believe that the preaching of Zephaniah is located within the broader socio-historical setting of the events of the seventh century B.C.E. Judah, at the end of the Assyrian domination, when the religious reforms of Josiah took place. It is true that at the beginning of the seventh century B.C.E. the Assyrian empire was approaching the threshold of its collapse, leaving several states to fight for power and space with Judah in their midst.

Prior to this, Assyria was the dominant force in the Near East under the leadership of Kings Sannacherib (705–681 B.C.E.), Esar-haddon (681–669 B.C.E.) and Ashurbanipal (669–627 B.C.E.) who conquered Egypt as well. Egypt freed itself from Assyria by 655 B.C.E. led by Psammetichus I (664–610 B.C.E.), but still nurtured their relative friendship. What led to the internal struggle that eventually weakened Assyria was the death of Ashurbanipal in 627 B.C.E. Babylon took advantage of this, led by General Nabopolosser (625–605 B.C.E.).

With the help of the Medes, Nineveh, the capital of Assyria was attacked in 612 B.C.E., and by 608 B.C.E Assyria was out of the circle of a dominating power, leaving Egypt and Babylon to fight for dominance. During this time Nabopolossar and Nebuchadrezzar II or

---

cism because he was a pious king. And the divine role of YHWH should not be ruled out.

187 Nogalski, *Literary Precursors*, 180.

Nebuchadnezzer (605–562 B.C.E.) of Babylon dominated Near East, including Egypt, in a successive fashion.[188]

The implication of these powers fighting and wounding one another is that Judah had the liberty to be on its own. Judah by this time produced important kings, Manasseh, Hezekiah's son and successor, a loyal Assyrian vassal, and Josiah, Manasseh's grandson. Following the example of his great-grandfather, Hezekiah, Josiah, Amon's son, declared independence and embarked on a very popular religious reform that Jeremiah, Zephaniah and Nahum, the prophets of this time, would come to support.[189]

Berlin is right to observe that information about Josiah in the Bible stands to be interpreted or reconstructed by historians. It is also true that while Josiah's religious and spiritual reformation is narrated in 2 Kings 22–23 and 2 Chronicles 43–45, his overall policies in relation to internal and foreign powers, except Josiah's death at the hands of Neco II of Egypt (610–595 B.C.E.), have not been stressed enough in the texts. And because the books of Kings and Chronicles had different agendas, they put the emphasis on different aspects of Josiah's reign. In the Book of Kings, Josiah is a great religious reformer, while in the Book of Chronicles he is a priest-king, with the emphasis on re-building the temple and re-establishing the Passover ritual.[190]

In my own view, since this debate as to the precise date for Zephaniah is unending, I prefer to work with the assumption that Josiah's religious reforms were part of a larger program of national reformation, transformation and purification, aimed at the reunification of all Israel under the Davidic rule and covenant traditions. Zephaniah's prophecy would have been preached to support the call for faith and hope in God and

---

188 See Coogan, *Old Testmaent,* 349–377 for a detailed and well written history of this period.

189 See Berlin, *Zephaniah*, 46 and Coogan, *Old Testament,* 349–377 where relevant texts like: 2 Kings 21–23; 2 Chronicles 33–35, Zephaniah, Nahum, the prayer of Manasseh, Habakkuk, Jeremiah and the Letter of Jeremiah, are highlighted.

190 See Berlin, *Zephaniah,* 44–47 for an extensive discussion of their portrayal of Josiah. See also Paul H. Wright, *Greatness, Grace and Glory: Carta's Atlas of Biblical Biography* (Jerusalem; Israel: Carta, 2008), 97–106.

obedience to YHWH, who continues to act in human affairs as the Sovereign of all creation. In sum, the setting is that of the reforms of Josiah, the king who acted decisively and rightly on behalf of his people.

1.2.3 Josiah's Reforms in Retrospect

In 2 Kings 22–23 and 2 Chronicles 34–36, we read that in the eighteenth year of King Josiah's reign (640/639–609), a period of turmoil in the Near East, but of economic and political and religious advantage to Judah, repairs and renovations were conducted in the Temple (2 Kgs 22:3). Josiah sent the secretary, Shaphan, on an official trip to Hilkiah, the high priest, with vital financial instructions concerning the ongoing repairs (2 Chr 34:11ff). Hilkiah gave Shaphan a "book of the Law" which he found in the temple. Having read it, Shaphan brought it to the young King Josiah (2 Kgs 22:8).[191] On hearing its contents, this young King was greatly alarmed, and asked the prophetess Huldah to consult the oracle of YHWH concerning the threat which the content of the book reflected (2 Kgs 22:11ff; 2 Chr 34: 22ff).

Huldah responded with pronouncements of doom upon the people and the land due to their apostasy, idolatry and syncretism (2 Kgs 22:15–17; 2 Chr 34:24–26). She promised Josiah safety from the forth-coming disaster, since his heart had been touched by the content of the law book, followed by his humility and obedience to YHWH (2 Kgs 2:18–20; 2 Chr 34:27–28). This was the case since Josiah had convoked an assembly for reading of the law and renewal of the covenant promises (2 Kgs 23:1–23; 2 Chr 34:29–33). This was followed by the inauguration of the reformation and purification, to implement the demands of the law book, which was discovered. All the cult objects of Baal and Asharah, the host of heavens' worship, were banished and removed from the Temple and their priests were dismissed as well (2 Kgs 23:4–5). Cult prostitution was abolished (v 7). The Moloch cult with human sacri-

---

191 Josiah was only eight years old when he ascended the throne in 640 B.C.E., and might have depended on royal officials of corrupt integrity (2 Kgs 1–2; 2 Chr 34:1–2).

fices was also abrogated (v 10). The paraphernalia of the Assyrian Shamash cult, that is, the horses which the kings of Judah had dedicated to the sun, were also exterminated (v 11). Pagan cults and altars innovated by Ahaz and Manasseh were uprooted (v 12). In fact, the king also destroyed all the cult centers that Solomon had built for the Sidonians (Phoenicians), Ammonites, and Moabites (v 13). The reformation was even extended to the then northern kingdom (vv 15–19). This was followed by the institution of the Passover celebration (2 Kgs 23:21–23; 2 Chr 35:10–18).

Many scholars have spent time arguing that the aim of the reform was not cult centralization, but only purification of all defilement. Some also have pointed out possible contradictions between the narrative in 2 Kings and 2 Chronicles, and speculate on the intention of the deuteronomistic historians.[192] This study progresses with the assumption that in as much as Josiah's religious reforms were designed for the nation's transformation and purification, the text of Zephaniah was written to support Josiah's program and effort.[193]

Richard D. Patterson seems to summarily capture the socio-political setting of Zephaniah's prophecy well in the following words:

> Zephaniah therefore lived in a critical time of transition. Externally, the Assyrian ship of state began to show the stress of age and, creaking and groaning in all its timbers and joints, floundered in the seas of economic and political adversity. The ancient near east was in the grip of climatic change…Assyria was in its death throes. Internally, the relaxing of Assyrian pressure allowed Judah and its king the liberty to pursue the cause of righteousness without fear. It was an exciting and pivotal age in which to live. Zephaniah was to prove equal to its challenges. Indeed, he may have well been the Lord's catalyst for the great reformation that would sweep across the land.[194]

In other words, the effect of the collapse of the Assyrian empire on Judah was socially, politically, and religiously positive. The people of Judah had the freedom and liberty to select their king and to think for their

---

192 See E. W. Nicholson, *Deuteronomy and Tradition*, 5–7 and Vlaardingerbroek, *Zephaniah*, 17–22 for an extensive debate on these issues.
193 Berlin, *Zephaniah*, 47; Sweeney, *Zephaniah*, 53.
194 Patterson, *Nahum, Habakkuk, Zephaniah*, 279.

well-being. They were able to manage their finances which facilitated the renovation of the temple. Social justice and righteousness were pursued without force and intimidation by a foreign power. Josiah's religious reforms were part of this larger rebuilding of a sense of nationalism and common purpose or restoration of Davidic pride. Zephaniah preached under this setting in support of Josiah's cause. He was indeed the Lord's instrument. He broke the prophetic silence that hung over Judah since Isaiah and Micah disappeared toward the end of Hezekiah's reign (715–686 B.C.E.).[195] Events of the world of Zephaniah's "Day of YHWH," are well illustrated in the following chronological table.

Chronological Table of some of the Events of the Eighth and Seventh Centuries BCE[196]

Israel	Judah	Assyria	Egypt	Syria	Events
Jehoahaz, 815–802	Amaziah, 800–783	Adad-Nirari III, 811–784		Ben Hadad III, 806…	
Jehoash, 802–786					
Jeroboam II, 786–746 *preaching of Amos/Hosea	Uzziah(Azaria),783–742, Jotham coregent, ca. 750,	*Assyria became weak	XXIII dynasty, 759–715		
Zechariah, 746–45, Shallum 745, Menshem 745–737, Pekahiah 737–36, Pekah 736–732, Hoshea 732–24, *Fall of Samaria 722/1	Jotham, 742–735 *preaching of Isaiah Ahaz 735–715 *preaching of Micah Hezekiah 715–686	Tiglath-pileser III 745–727; Shalmaneser V 826–722 Sargon II 721–705 *(invades Israel)		Razin 740–732	
Babylon colonialism	Manasseh 686–642	Sennacherib 705–681, *invades Israel (701) Esarhaddon 680–669, Ashurbanipal 668–627	*Ashurbanipal invades Egypt and sacks the Thebes 663		

195 Stuhlmueller, *Amos, Hosea, Micah, Nahum, Zephaniah, Habakkuk*, 96.
196 For dates see John Bright, *A History of Israel* (4th ed. Louisville; Westminster John Knox, 2000).

Israel	Judah	Assyria	Egypt	Syria	Events
	Amon 642–640			Medes	
Nabopolasser 626–625 *Neo Babylonian empire	*Josiah 640–609* *Jeremiah, *Zephaniah,* *Nahum	Shin-shar-ishkun 629–612 *Fall of Nineveh 612		Cyaxeres 625–585	Battle of Megiddo and the death of Josiah 609 in the hands of Neco II of Egypt
	Jehoahaz 609				
Nebuchadnezzer 605–582	Jehoaikim 609–598 * the preaching of Habakkuk				
	Jehoiachin 598/7 *preaching of Ezekiel				
	Zedekiah 597–587				
	Fall of Jerusalem to the Babylonians 586/7 Exile				Exile to Babylon 586/7

In recent years scholars including Hubert Irsigler have also devoted their time in studying Prophet Zephaniah. Uppermost in my mind is an impressive study made by Marvin A. Sweeney.[197] It may not be necessary to recycle such an extensive work here. I will rather briefly comment on his conclusions, discuss few works he never dwelt on, and highlight briefly the history of research on Zephaniah's Day of YHWH, in particular.

197 Marvin A. Sweeney, "Zephaniah: A Paradigm for the Study of the Prophetic Books." *CR* 7 (1999): 120–145. Similar significant studies include Hubert Irsigler, *Gottesgericht und Jahwetag. Die Komposition Zef 1:1–2:3, untersucht auf der Grundlage der Literarkritik des Zefanjabuches* (ATSAT 3; St. Ottilien EOS, 1977), 71–93; Rex Mason, *Zephaniah, Habakkuk, Joel* (OTG; Sheffield: JOST press, 1994), 16–58; Michael Weigl, *Zefanja und das "Israel der Armen." Eine Untersuchung zur Theologie des Buches Zefanja* (ÖBSt 13; Klosterneuburg: Östereichisches Katholisches Bibelwerk, 1994), 230–243. Also most recently Irsigler's commentary, *Zefanja* (HThKAT; Freiburg: Herder, 2002) and Weigl's Lectures/Seminar on "TRS D: Seminar on Late-PreExilic Prophets, Nahum Habakkuk, Zephaniah," (The Catholic University of America, Washington D.C., Fall 2006) have been very insightful as well.

1.2.4 Marvin A. Sweeney's Studies on Zephaniah

Concentrating on Zephaniah's studies from the mid 1970s, Sweeney acknowledged the fundamental consensus among scholars on the existence of the methodological tension on the reading of Prophet Zephaniah, namely, should Zephaniah be read diachronically or synchronically?[198] What about the present literary structure of the text? Is there any influence or indication of a later addition, reading or interpretation? These are sample questions that have occupied minds of scholars recently.[199]

Sweeney's work, in my own opinion, symbolizes a total recognition or an awareness of these problems. He is also aware of the various attempts to apply the lessons learnt from advances in exegetical theory to the interpretation of the book.

He begins with the redaction-critical analysis of Zephaniah from the mid-1970s and beyond.[200] He turns to the various attempts to interpret Zephaniah from a more holistic perspective that emerged during the same period, including various literary, historical, and theological assessments of the book.[201] He finally examines in a nut-shell, the role of Zephaniah in the currently emerging unity-approach to the study of the *Dodekapropheton*.[202]

Sweeney, still in my own judgment, rightly concludes by observing that the current research on the Book of Zephaniah as a paradigmatic book is not a monopoly of a particular scholar, or of a single method of biblical exegesis. Like other prophetic literature, Zephaniah's interpretation is dynamic, as exegetes explore different methods in an attempt to address the problems posed by the earlier scholarly opinions.[203] This present study insists that scholars in mutually exploring these methods need to continue to be aware of the theological concerns and contextual values of Zephaniah's prophecy.

198 Childs, *Introduction to the OT*, 459–61.
199 Sweeney, "Zephaniah: A Paradigm," 119–120.
200 Sweeney, "Zephaniah: A Paradigm," 122–130.
201 Sweeney, "Zephaniah: A Paradigm," 130–138.
202 Sweeney, "Zephaniah: A Paradigm," 138–139.
203 Sweeney, "Zephaniah: A Paradigm," 140.

1.2.5 Other Specific Studies on Zephaniah's Day of YHWH

There are other studies on Zephaniah that were not discussed in detail, either in Sweeney's work or anywhere else. These include the theological and exegetical works of Charles, L. Feinberg, Roy B. Zuck, Walter C. Kaiser, Richard D. Petterson, Greg A. King, Donald E. Gowan and Johannes Vlaardingerbroek and commentary by Hubert Irsigler. I will not dwell extensively on Irsigler's commentary on *Zefanja*, since Sweeney has done justice to earlier works by irsigler, especially his 1977 disertation; *Gottesgericht* which has great influence on his views in the recent commentary. Irsigler in his 2002 commentary however, discusses the formal characteristics of Zephaniah in detail. He insists on the three steps of judgment on the Day of YHWH in the book of Zephaniah, which includes judgment against Judah and Jerusalem (Zeph 1:1–2:3), judgment against nations (Zeph 2:4–15) and judgment against Jerusalem and nations, before His salvific acts upon Jerusalem and nations (Zeph 1:1–20).[204] Let us briefly reflect on some of these other contributions not captured by Sweeney.

In his 1951 work, *Habakkuk, Zephaniah, Haggai and Malachi: The Major Messages of the Minor Prophets,* reprinted in 1990 in *The Minor Prophets,* Feinberg painstakingly and theologically delineated "Zephaniah the Day of the Lord."[205] Feinberg observes that though Zephaniah has been considered as one of the most difficult readings in the prophetic canon, his message has a definite focal point, the Day of YHWH. Zephaniah uses the expression more often than any other prophet in the Old Testament. Feinberg agrees with most scholars that in the first chapter, Zephaniah announces judgment upon Judah, followed by judgment upon several people after the call for repentance in Chapter Two. Finally, after words of judgment on Jerusalem, he promises future glory for Israel's restored remnant in Chapter Three.

---

204 Irsigler, *Zefanja*, 82–435. See also Sweeney, "Zephamiah: A Paradigm." 133–134.

205 Charles Lee Feinberg, *Habakkuk, Zephaniah, Haggai and Malachi: The Messages of the Minor Prophets* (New York: American Board of Missions of the Jews, 1951), 43–72, reprinted, in *The Minor Prophets*, Chicago, IL: Moody Press, 1990), 221–236.

Feinberg sees Zephaniah's prophecies of world judgment and final salvation for God's own people, as comprehensive.[206] Feinberg recognizes in Zephaniah his special affinities or thematic parallelism with the message of earlier prophetic traditions, like Amos, Isaiah and Jeremiah. What is particular about his studies is also his theological breakdown of Zephaniah's message into; universal judgment, visitation upon Judah, the Day of the Lord, those who seek not the Lord, the call to repentance, and judgment on Philistia, Moab, Ammon, Ethiopia and Assyria.

He also talks about the visit of the Lord, the wrath, the blessing, the millennial glory and the joy that this day will bring.[207] He goes on to stress that Thomas of Celano's (1250 A.D.) liturgical hymn, *"Dies irae, dies illa,"* ("that day is a day of wrath") was inspired by Zephaniah 1:15. But he pleads that Zephaniah's Day of the Lord, must not be viewed only in the light of chastisement, but also of blessing, promise and restoration of fortunes to the remnant nations and Israel.[208]

In 1991, Roy B. Zuck, like Feinberg, also took a theological approach. But he basically agrees with von Rad that, "Zephaniah's Day of the Lord theme draws attention to God's role as a warrior. It corresponds to the sovereign's day of conquest, a notion found in Ancient Near Eastern literature."[209] It is the central motif in Zephaniah's message. The Day is near and swift (Zeph 1:7, 14). Several nations already would be involved.

Zuck concludes that this Day of the Lord was initially realized in conjunction with the Babylonian conquest of the Near East shortly after Zephaniah's prophecy. He agrees with many scholars that this Day has a cosmic and universal dimension that transcends the time of Zephaniah.

---

206 Feinberg, *Minor Prophets*, 221–222.
207 Feinberg, *Minor Prophets*, 222–234.
208 Feinberg, *Minor Prophets*, 225–236. I think Feinberg's allusion to "King" here, at least metaphorically, goes back to the cultic/kingly motif already discussed by earlier scholars including Mowinckel.
209 Roy B. Zuck, *A Biblical Theology of the Old Testament* (Chicago, IL: Moody Press, 1991), 416.

The Day will bring cataclysmic judgment that would rival the Noahic flood in magnitude (Zeph 1:2–2:3, 18; 3:8), but God will restore His covenant to the repented or purified Zion and reassert His Mighty Rule over them.[210]

Although Zuck's view of Zephaniah's Day of the Lord may sound like a repetition of scholarly theological opinions already heard, his conclusion brings a refreshing and telescoping insight into this study. For him, Zephaniah's presentation of the Lord's Day illustrates the principle by which the prophets often merged near and far-off events, presenting one unified picture of the future in which the chronological gaps made apparent by later revelation and historical developments are not visible. One could say in the case of Zephaniah that the Babylonian conquest, which was nearly universal, given the limited geographical proportions of the prophet's *Weltanschuung* (worldview),[211] foreshadowed a greater eschatological judgment to come. Zephaniah's vision of universal restoration, Zuck suggests, will be realized after this latter phase of eschatological judgment.[212]

Walter C. Kaiser Jr.'s theological contribution, though extremely brief and repetitive in content also deserves our attention.[213] According to Kaiser Jr., although Obadiah, Joel, Amos, and Isaiah had all spoken of this Day, Zephaniah alone emphasized more strenuously the universality of its judgment while also surprisingly predicting the conversion of the nations as one of its fruits. One unique thing about Kaiser Jr's contribution is his linkage of Zephaniah's message to the Wisdom Literature.

In Zephaniah, judgment would begin with Judah (Zeph 1:4) for introducing Baalism. Judah should abandon Baal and rather "seek/consult" (דרש/בקש) YHWH. This "seeking" is an attitude of the "humble of the land" (ענוי הארץ) who turn back to worship YHWH (2:3; 3:12).

210 Zuck, *Biblical Theology*, 418.
211 See Helmut W. Ziefle, *Modern Theological German: A Reader and Dictionary* (Grand Rapids, MI: Baker, 1997), 331.
212 Zuck, *Biblical Theology*, 418.
213 Walter C. Kaiser Jr., *Toward an Old Testament Theology* (Grand Rapids, MI: Zondervan Publishing House, 1991), 223–224.

They were also known in Zephaniah 3:7 as those who "feared" (ירא)
YHWH and accepted "correction," (מוסר). For Kaiser Jr, these terms
מוסר / ירא / ענוי הארץ, link Zephaniah's message to the fear of the Lord
in Wisdom Literature.[214]

The humble of the land are those who fear YHWH and take His
counseling or correction. They are part of that remnant (שארית), who
shall "graze their flocks", on the pasture and plunder their enemies
(Zeph 2:7, 9). The remnant shall enjoy the promised blessing of
YHWH.[215]

In his 1991 *Exegetical Commentary*, Richard D. Patterson links every major section of the book of Zephaniah to his teaching on the Day
of the YHWH.[216] For him Zephaniah writes to inform his readers of
the coming Day of the Lord. He groups Zephaniah's message into two
broad aspects. First, for Zephaniah, the Day of YHWH is a day of
judgment upon all nations and peoples. Second, it is a day of purification for sin, when the redeemed of all nations shall join a re-gathered
Israel in serving God and experiencing His blessings.[217] Patterson's entire detailed exegesis in my own opinion is very impressive.

---

214 See David Winston, *The Wisdom of Solomon: A New Translation with Introduction and Commentary*. (AB 43; Garden City, NY: Doubleday, 1979), esp., 4–66; Patrick W. Skehan, and Alexander A. Di Lella, *The Wisdom of Ben Sira*. (Anchor Yale Bible 39; New Haven: Yale University Press, 1987); David Winston, "Solomon, Wisdom," *ABD* 6:120–26; Roland E. Murphy, "Wisdom in the OT," *ABD* 6: 920–31; Alexander A. Di Lella, "Wisdom of Ben-Sira," *ABD* 6: 940–45; " Fear of the Lord as Wisdom: Ben Sira 1, 11–30," in *The Book of Ben Sira in Modern Research: Proceedings of the First International Ben Sira Conference 28-31 July 1996, Soesterber, Netherlands*, ed. Pancratius C. Beentjes (BZNW 255; Berlin/New York: Walter de Gruyter, 1997), 113–133; "God and Widom in the Theology of Ben Sira: An Overview," in *Ben Sira's God : Proceedings of the International Ben Sira Conference, Durham-Ushaw College 2001*(BZNW 321; Berlin/New York: Walter de Gruyter, 2002), 3–17, where wisdom is studied in an interesting detail as the "fear of the Lord."; C. Termini, (Lectures on "Imagine e funzione della Sapienza," Rome, Pontifical University of St. Thomas Aquinas, 2008/2009).

215 Kaiser Jr., *Old Testament Theology*, 224.

216 Richard D. Patterson, *Nahum, Habakkuk, Zephaniah, The Wycliffe Exegetical Commentary* (Chicago: Moody Press, 1991), 275–388.

217 Patterson, *Nahum, Habakkuk, Zephaniah*, 281– 82.

Another scholar not given adequate attention by Sweeney was Greg King, who, like Patterson, links the specific details of every unit of Zephaniah to his message of the Day of YHWH. But Sweeney unfortunately only cited Greg King in the bibliographical section of his work.[218] In his 1995 article Greg A. King more than any other recent scholar, devoted his impressive article towards a reassessment of the Day of the Lord in "Zephaniah."[219] This reassessment, Greg King confirmed, is necessary as there had been a lack of a major systematic study of this concept in Zephaniah. Some past studies, Greg King observes, have incorrectly restricted their investigation to the precise phrase, "the Day of the Lord." But as noted already, recently there has been an increasing realization to enlarge יום יהוה (the Day of the Lord) to include the phrase: "on that day," so as to understand this concept fully and in a broader perspective of the prophetic literature, especially, the Book of the Twelve.[220]

The construct form, יום יהוה (the Day of the Lord) strictly speaking, occurs three times in Zephaniah (1:7; 2x in1:14). But a careful analysis of the context of the many other verses where the word, "day," occur leaves no doubt that they refer to the same concept. Greg King refreshingly gives an example with the phrase, "day of Yahweh's sacrifice," (1:8); "on that day" (1:9–10), and "the day of Yahweh's fury (or wrath)" as synonymous phrases for the "the Day of YHWH."[221] In fact, the word יום (day) appears in the singular about twenty times in the book of Zephaniah, and all are connected with Zephaniah's message of the Day of YHWH. Other temporal references used by Zephaniah include, "at that time," or "when that time" (1:12), to refer to the concept of the Day of YHWH. He calls this a "wholistic" approach to the book of Zephaniah.[222]

He defines the Day of YHWH in Zephaniah as a day of YHWH's intervention, a day of YHWH's universal sovereignty, a day of YHWH's

---

218 Sweeney, "Zephaniah: A Paradigm," 143.
219 Greg A. King, "The Day of the Lord in Zephaniah," *BSac* 152 (1995): 16–36.
220 King, "Day of the Lord," 16.
221 King, "Day of the Lord," 17.
222 King, "Day of the Lord," 17.

judgment as well as a day of YHWH's covenant and salvation.[223] Zephaniah expresses divine intervention with the use of terms such as הס (be silent in 1:7), פקד (to punish, visit, inspect in vv 8–9 and 12) and חפש (to search in v 12). The nature of YHWH's interventions becomes clearer in the first person declarations, such as "I will sweep off" (1:2–3), "I will stretch my hand" (1:4), "I will gather" or "take away," (3:18), "I will make an end," and I will rescue," (3:19–20). This divine involvement in human affairs, Greg King thinks, is the most salient feature of Zephaniah's proclamation of the Day of YHWH. And here the emphasis is on the proper noun, יהוה (YHWH). He is the one who intervenes in human affairs.[224] It is a day which actually "is" YHWH's, and His coming theophany is portrayed in the conceptual imagery of Warrior, Judge, and the real King of the universe."[225]

Greg King's insight not only embraces von Rad, Mowinckel and Cross's theories in a certain way, but does it with a renewed spirit. The universal sovereignty of YHWH is made clear in Zephaniah (1:2). It is also highlighted in the punishment meted out on the Philistines, Moabites, Ammonites, Cushites and Assyrians (Zeph 2). Moreover, "all the earth shall be consumed (3:8)."[226] Greg King, in a detailed fashion went on to analyze those verses which give support to the יום יהוה (the Day of YHWH), as a Day of microcosmic (1:4–13) and macrocosmic (1:2–3) dimensions of judgment and with factors responsible for such judgments.[227]

Besides being the Day of intervention and judgment, the Day of YHWH, in Zephaniah, is a Day of the implementation of the terms of the covenant between YHWH and Israel. Drawing from some covenant parallels in the book of Deuteronomy, Greg King believes that the theophanic imagery of the Day of the Lord (the rationale and description of the judgment to be meted out at that time, and the portrayal of the restoration to be granted), are all indication that the Day

223 King, "Day of the Lord," 18–30.
224 King, "Day of the Lord," 19.
225 King, "Day of the Lord," 20.
226 King, "Day of the Lord," 21.
227 King, "Day of the Lord," 22–26.

of the Lord is a day of covenant implementation.[228] He devoted the last sections of his article to stressing the historical and eschatological aspects of this day. He also used it to identify the hope and restoration elements embedded in the theology of Zephaniah, in spite of the cataclysmic, destructive and judgmental aspects implicit in the text.[229] For him it is best to read the occurrence of the Day of YHWH in Zephaniah both as historical and eschatological events.

He concludes his work on a very strong note by emphasizing the present and future goals of the Day of YHWH. The present goal was for Zephaniah to motivate his contemporaries to worship YHWH alone (1:4–6), and to seek righteousness (2:3). While his future goals consisted in pointing at the establishment of YHWH's kingdom on earth, he stressed the full vindication, redemption and glorification of the faithful (3:14–20). This will take place when YHWH is exalted King in the midst of His people, when YHWH will reign over them.[230]

This was followed by the studies of Gowan in 1998. Although his remark on Zephaniah's Day of YHWH is very scanty, he reinforced the wisdom motif earlier mentioned by Kaiser Jr. Gowan who sees the vocabularies of lowliness, humility, poverty and affliction used in Zephaniah's prophecy as a grammatical, if not a theological parallel to the Wisdom Literature. In Wisdom Literature, these terms are used as the opposite of pride, haughtiness, and scornfulness. Zephaniah has chosen these terms because the pride that leads humans to choose their own course, scorning the way of life provided by YHWH, is a major theme in Zephaniah's theology.[231]

In 1999, Johannes Vlaardingerbroek published a historical and exegetical commentary on Zephaniah. This theological commentary brought a renewed interest in the familiar tripartite division of the book. The division includes announcements of judgment against other nations; repeated announcement of judgment against Jerusalem and prom-

---

228 King, "Day of the Lord," 26–29.
229 King, "Day of the Lord," 29–31.
230 King, "Day of the Lord," 32.
231 Donald E. Gowan, *Theology of the Prophetic Books: The Death & Resurrection of Israel* (Louisville: Westminster John Knox Press, 1998), 79–84.

ise of salvation for Jerusalem and the dispersed exiles.[232] Vlaardinger-broek's study is less supportive of Paul R. House's view of Zephaniah as a mere prophetic drama, since it does not really make clear the movement from judgment to grace.[233] Before he embarks on verse by verse exegetical analysis of the three chapters of Zephaniah,[234] he discusses the provenance of Zephaniah, the man Zephaniah, time and background as well his relationship with Josiah's reforms and the Deuteronomy.[235]

In sum, Vlaardingerbroek is of the opinion that the prophecy of Zephaniah must be understood in the context of his prophetic ministry. It must be understood in the context of the import of that part of the booklet which originated with the prophet himself as well as in the context of the import of the book in its present form.[236] For example, Vlaardingerbroek believes that since Zephaniah 2:4–15 (assuming it supported the policies of King Josiah) reflects another viewpoint (Zeph 1:2–2:3; 3:1–8), then Zephaniah must have made two appearances with two imports. It is hard to tell which came first, that of total judgment (Zeph 1:2–2:3 and 3:1–8) or that of Josiah (2:4–15), since the textual sequence as usual is that of judgment against Judah, against nations, promise of salvation and restoration of fortunes. His point is that the conditions condemned in 1:2–2:3 existed before and after the reformation (3:1–8). Possibly the message of the Day of YHWH was given later when it became evident that the reformation had not really brought the dawn of a new time.[237]

He went on to say that the personal message of Zephaniah has two parts: all inclusive, eschatological judgment upon Judah and Jerusalem, with the survival of a few repentant and humble remnants for a glorious future; as well as the support for the politics of Josiah by means

232 Vlaardingerbroek, *Zephaniah*, 9.
233 Paul R. House, *Zephaniah: A Prophetic Drama* (JSOTSup 69; Sheffield: Almond Press, 1988).
234 Vlaardingerbroek, *Zephaniah*, 29–219.
235 Vlaardingerbroek, *Zephaniah*, 9–24. These last points will be discussed in detail in chapter two of this study.
236 Vlaardingerbroek, *Zephaniah*, 24.
237 Vlaardingerbroek, *Zephaniah*, 25.

of prophecies directed against neighboring nations, particularly those whose policies were against Judah. The judgment on the Day of YHWH is pictured as being near. Zephaniah's words are first of all intended for conversion of his contemporaries. But since the words of the prophets are words of God, they have been preserved to be fulfilled, even in the NT's teaching on the Day of the Lord.[238] Moreover, the restoration and salvation (Zeph 3:9–20), after judgment (Zeph 1–2), evidence the fact that, those who gave the book final redaction lived after the event of the destruction of Jerusalem in 586 B.C.E. This event is viewed as fulfillment of Zephaniah's prophecy of judgment. The Day of YHWH (יום יהוה) came upon Judah and Jerusalem, but there was still hope left.

This study agrees with Vlaardingerbroek that the terrible things said in Zephaniah 1:14ff did not close doors for hope and restoration heard in Zephaniah 3:14ff. Just as Feinberg saw Zephaniah's prophecies of judgment on the world and the final salvation for God's own people as comprehensive, Vlaardingerbroek rightly sees Zephaniah's message of all–inclusive judgment and the promise of restoration by grace, coming to a common meeting point, on the Day of the Lord.[239]

1.3 A Summary Reflection on Chapter One

This survey has shown that the concept of the Day of YHWH is not only one of the most interesting aspects of the prophetic literature in the OT research, but has attracted scholars of various generations, traditions and schools of thought. It shows that prior to 1950 and before 1980 scholars were generally engaged in defining the traditio-historical, mythical and cultic origin and significance of the Day of YHWH. Some traced it to the pre-Israelite era, some to the exodus conquest and others to the Holy War motif, while others to the combination of

---

238 Vlaardingerbroek, *Zephaniah*, 26.
239 Vlaardingerbroek, *Zephaniah*, 27.

both. Questions such as: was the concept, eschatological or non eschatological? Theophanic or non-theophanic, primary or secondary, definite or indefinite also occupied the minds of scholars, in an isolated and unsystematic manner.

Even when other newer approaches, including linguistic and philological methods, were employed, the contributions of earlier scholars like Mowinckel, von Rad, Cross and Meir were still considered relevant. The unifying theme of the Day of YHWH, which runs like a thread through the Twelve, was increasingly appreciated by scholars. The investigation of the general historical background of Zephaniah set the stage for a better appreaciation of the theology of Zephaniah, which was communicated in the motif of יום יהוה (the Day of YHWH).

Sweeney also showed an impressive general analysis and compilation of scholarly opinions on the study of Zephaniah from the mid 1970s till 1996. These opinions concentrated mostly on the question of which method should best be applied in the study of Zephaniah, diachronic or synchronic, holistic or eschatological? The theologicial, religious and ecumenical values of Zephaniah were not given a priority.

Specific studies on the Day of YHWH in Zephaniah, neglected by Sweeney, were taken up by Feinberg, Zuck, King, Gowan and Vlaardingerbroek in a more holistic and eschatological manner. Its contemporary relevance was not highlighted. But fortunately there were specific studies which made references to the "Kingly" and "Holy War" motifs suggested earlier by von Rad and others. Moreover, although Cross's mediating role was insightful; he did not present a systematic study of the texts of the Day of the Lord. And even though von Rad's theory had generated criticism and debates over the years, it remains relevant and key to our present study of the concept of the Day of the Lord in the Prophet Zephaniah.

Chapter Two

A Study of the Day of YHWH
in the Prophet Zephaniah

Up to this point, we have been dealing with the *status quaestionis* and with a general survey of the history of research on the Day of YHWH in the prophetic literature, particularly in the prophet Zephaniah. It was also vital to discuss the general historical background and setting of the prophecy of Zephaniah. In the light of this broad survey, this Chapter deals with the overwhelming theme and the exegesis of the Day of YHWH, in the Prophet Zephaniah (1:14–18), which stresses judgment and the wrath of YHWH. However, an exegesis of this unit will be preceded by an overview of Zephaniah's message followed by an examination of the text, the literary structure and the place of Zephaniah 1:14–18 and 3:14–20 in the entire book of the Prophet Zephaniah.

2.1 An Overview of Zephaniah's Message of the Day of YHWH

As the Lord's instrument, Zephaniah preached in the late pre-exilic period in order to re-conscientize his contemporaries and fellow citizens concerning the coming of יום יהוה (the Day of YHWH). This is the Day of Judgment. It is a Day of God's intervention and restoration of the fortunes of those who seek refuge in Yahweh alone. Zephaniah, God's messenger, reminded them that on this Day, there would be a judgment upon nations, Judah and Jerusalem, due to their sins of idolatry, syncretism and disobedience to YHWH.

He stressed the need for repentance which would be followed by God's promises, affirmation and assurances of God's love (3:14–17). In other words, Zephaniah emphasizes that the threats, calamities and notices of judgment (1:2–2:3), are not isolated from the messages of hope, joy and restoration of God's love and fortunes for the humble remnant (2:4–3:20).

In the prophecy of Zephaniah, YHWH is the Creator and Sovereign of the universe. He is the Chief Judge and Deliverer of His chosen people. He is also the Lord of the covenant. On that Day YHWH will appear with judgment (1:8–12) and He will make a terrible end of all the evil doers, including those who are proud (1:14–18). YHWH will pass judgment on those colonial powers, nations and those who worship false gods (2:4–15). On the other hand, a time for salvation is also on the way for the remnant and for the re-created people of the Lord. These are the humble, the lowly and those who seek refuge in the name of YHWH (3:9–20).

In other words, YHWH's ultimate goal in judgment is the purification, remaking and renewal of His people, the creation of a poor and humble people in whose midst the righteous God, the Conduit of joy and the Restorer of the fortunes of the remnant people, dwells (3:12–18).[1] Zephaniah, while condemning the particular external faults of his time for example, the worship of false gods and syncreticism (1:4–5), the adaptation of foreign customs (1:8), violence and fraud (1:11), false rituals (3:4), also recognized and condemned the interior cause of these sins, namely, pride (1:16; 2:10, 15; 3:11).

True religion, according to Zephaniah, is to seek YHWH in righteousness and humility (2:3). These are the religious qualities demanded of the remnants.[2] These messages of the Day of YHWH, as we will see in the following chapter, continue to run through the different structural units, or sections of the book of Zephaniah.

This makes sense since "the structure of the book of Zephaniah and its message," can only be fully "grasped as a dialogue between the gen-

---

1   See Kapelrud, *Message of the Prophet Zephaniah*, 61–102 for an interesting insight into the preaching of Zephaniah.

2   See Arbuckle, "Zephaniah," 718.

eral structure of the book, with the beliefs and hopes of the communities behind the text."[3] In other words, the themes of the entire book of Zephaniah, particularly our units for exegesis (1:14–18; 3:14–20), are not disconnected from its discussed historical setting nor from the literary structure of the entire book, that follows.

2.2 The Literary Structure of the Text of Zephaniah

Since more time will be spent on our specific units under study (1:14–18; 3:14–20), let me broadly remark that many commentators and exegetes agree that the book of Zephaniah, apart from the superscription (1:1), patterns itself on the familiar tri-partite eschatological prophecy of Israel's prophets. These include judgments or threats against Judah and Jerusalem (1:2–2:3), judgments and threats against nations (2:4–3:8) and divine promises to Judah/Jerusalem and to all the nations (3:9–20).[4] These tri-partite, theological structures, B. S. Childs rightly observes, could be said to have served as paradigmatic for the structure of several other prophetic writings.[5]

In fact, prior to these modern divisions, Berlin had observed the different divisions held in the Middle Ages, as well as the divisions found in the different codices. These include, *Aleppo* (seven divisions); *Leningrad* (six divisions), *Cairo* (eight divisions); *Petersburg* (nine divisions), *NRSV*

---

3   See Ben Zvi, *Book of Zephaniah,* 346. This is not to say that I agree with Ben Zvi completely, in his detailed study of the subject in pages 325–346. His logical square, mathematical analysis of the structure and message of Zephaniah is too dry with little theological flesh.

4   For this widely accepted position see Sweeney, "A Form – Critical Reassessment of the Book of Zephaniah," *CBQ* 53 (1991): 388–408; Ben Zvi, *Book of Zephaniah,* 325–346; J. S. Kselman, "Zephaniah," *ABD* 6:1078–1080; Nogalski, *Literary Precursors,* 171–215.

5   Childs, *Introduction to the Old Testament,* 458. Also see Sweeney, "Zephaniah: A Paradigm for the Study of the Prophetic Books," *CR* 7 (1999): 122–145 for detail and impressive literary-form-redactional-critical reading of Zephaniah.

(seven divisions) and the *NEB* (three divisions).[6] J. M. P. Smith breaks it into nine divisions, while J. J. M. Robert prefers four divisions (1:1; 1:2–2:3; 2:4–15 and 3:1–20).[7]

Berlin herself is very critical of Roberts's division, since Robert seems to dismiss the relevance of the literary context. Berlin prefers to work with the *Leningrad Codex* (MT text), except that she believes the superscription should be treated differently. According to Berlin, Zephaniah 1:2–9 is a vociferous announcement of doom, while verses 10–18 describe the doom in detail.[8] For her Zephaniah 2:1–4 presents the last chance for the people of Judah to repent.[9]

This is followed by Zephaniah 3:1–13, which discusses the prophet's prophecy against the overbearing Jerusalem.[10] Finally, verses 14–20, she stresses, present the future joy for Jerusalem.[11] However, Berlin, cognizant of the ongoing debate of the pre-exilic, exilic and post-exilic structures of the book, cautions that the book, as it stands should be read as a rhetorically and structurally unified work.[12]

Prior to Berlin, Richard D. Patterson also argued for the unity of Zephaniah. Patterson vehemently cautioned against denying such a unity. He divided Zephaniah into two major sections, each with five sub-units Section one is the declaration of the Day of the Lord's judgment (1:2–2:3) with sub-units of pronouncements on the earth (1:2–3), pronouncement on Judah (1:4–6), exhortation (1:7–13), information about the Day of YHWH (1:14–18) and instruction (2:1–3). Section two, presents details concerning the Day of the Lord's Judgment (2:4–3:20), with its sub-units of pronouncement on the nations (2:4–

---

6   Berlin *Zephaniah,* 17–19.
7   Robert, *Nahum, Habakkuk and Zephaniah,* 162–163 and Berlin, *Zephaniah,* 19.
8   Berlin, *Zephaniah,* 71–84.
9   Berlin, *Zephaniah,* 95–102.
10   Berlin, *Zephaniah,* 125–140.
11   Berlin, *Zephaniah,* 141–148.
12   Berlin, *Zephaniah,* 20. See also Nogalski, *Literary Precursor,* 175–176 for more detailed debate among scholars who hold that a good section of Zephaniah Chapter Three is a post exilic text.

15), on Jerusalem (3:1–7), exhortation (3:8), information (3:9–13) and instruction (3:14–20).[13]

Michael Weigl, who is viewed by some scholars as representing a renewed foray into redaction-critical work, does not shy away from this debate. Apart from minor glosses in Zephaniah 1:3c, 4b, 9a, 17c, 18b–e; 2:7ade, 9g–10c; 3:5e, 8–9, 10a, Weigl believes that the words of Zephaniah are those found in Zephaniah 1:2–3:15. Zephaniah, for him, sees YHWH's intervention in a universal perspective.[14]

Moreover, Zephaniah arranges his own oracles into three basic components (1:2–18; 3:6–15; and 3:16–20). In 1:2–18, Zephaniah takes on YHWH's settling account with Jerusalem, in the context of the universal framework. Zephaniah 2:1–3:5 discusses the judgment against nations, and associates the judgment of Jerusalem and Judah with them through the framework of this section in Zephaniah 2:1–3 and 3:1–5. Zephaniah 2:1–3 looks back to 1:2–18 and emphasizes the Day of YHWH motif; while Zephaniah 3:1–5 likens Jerusalem to the foreign nations that are also to be judged. Zephaniah 3:6–15 outlines the process by which the nations and Jerusalem will be purged to produce a new remnant constituted by the poor of the land, which represent the hope for the continuity of Israel's *Heilsgeschichte*. Zephaniah 1:1 and 3:16–20 are viewed by some scholars as a later addition.[15]

---

13 Patterson, *Nahum, Habakkuk, Zephaniah*, 281–292. See also John S. Kselman, "Zephaniah, Book of," *ABD* 6: 1077–1080, where the question of the unity of the text is further discussed. Chapters 1 and 2:12–15 are recognized by some as authentic to Zephaniah of the Josianic era with the rest of the book assigned to the exilic and post-exilic periods. But currently, most of the book is attributed to the late seventh century Zephaniah with possible expansion in the exile and post-exilic eras, e.g., 2:8–11 and 3:14–20 respectively. He broadly divided the work into oracles of disaster and judgment (1:2–3:8) and oracles of salvation (3:9–20) with eight sub-units: (1) editorial and universal judgment (1:1–6); (2) day of YHWH introduced (1:7–13); (3) apocalyptic Day of YHWH and call to seek YHWH (1:14–2:3); (4) oracles against nations (2:14–15); (5) oracles against Judah (3:1–5); (6) examples of other nations (3:6–8); (7) picture of purified nation (3:9–13), and (8) joy of the people and of YHWH himself (3:14–20).

14 Weigl, *Zefanja*, 243–244.

15 Sweeney, "Zephaniah: A Paradigm for the Study of the Prophetic Books," 128–129.

Sweeney sees the Book of Zephaniah as that which bears the central theme of the Day of YHWH. It is a prophetic exhortation (1:1–3:20), which is divided into two huge sections (1:1 and1:2–3:20), with two major sub-units. The first section is a prophetic announcement of the Day of YHWH (1:2–18). The second (2:1–3:20), according to Sweeney, is the prophetic exhortation to seek YHWH, with several sub-units, that culminate with the prophetic summons of Jerusalem and Israel to rejoice (3:14–20).[16]

Sweeney's central thesis, that follows, is recommended. He believes that although some later glosses appear in the text, the book as a whole still has a coherent structure of late pre-exilic prophecy.[17] The purpose of the book, according to him, was to preach repentance from idolatry and syncretism and to invite Israel to seek YHWH alone. The prophecy was an enormous spiritual support for King Josiah's program of national restoration, purification and reformation.[18]

In the light of the above discussion on the views on the structure of the book of Zephaniah, it is evident that the units of focus in this present study (1:14–18 and 3:14–20) fall not only into the first and the last sections of the traditional tripartite structure of threats to Judah (1:2–2:3), threats to nations (2:4–3:8), salvation and divine promises (3:9–20), but they also maintain the same positions in almost all other forms and structural proposals put forward by scholars and commentators. Therefore, this work sees the judgment and threats of the first section (1:2–2:15) converted into hope, joy, re-creation,

---

16   See the appendix of Sweeney's work, "Form-Critical Reassessment of the Book of Zephaniah," 407–408 for a summary structural diagram of the book of Zephaniah.

17   This same argument was advanced by Childs in his *Introduction to OT as Scripture*, 460 that with regards to the integrity of the oracles, there is a wider consensus among critical scholars that the present form of the book reflects genuine, late pre-exilic oracles to which has been added a layer of post-exilic material (3:9–14; 2:7, 8a, 9a, 10–11). But in spite of this, the crucial point to be made is that in the canonical process the material has been organized around a theological center. Although Childs may still be challenged with a question such as: which canon, a unity approach to the text is still recommended.

18   Sweeney, "Form Critical-Reassessment of the Book of Zephaniah," 391, 406.

salvation and restoration of fortunes in the last section (3:1–20). These structures, this dissertation argues, are all built around a common theme of יום יהוה (the Day of YHWH) and restoration of fortunes (שוב שבות).

Alternatively, the uniquely Israelite concept of God, who judges, who involves Himself in human history, and who calls people to repentance with assurances of His love, restoration and salvation, is evident in the following proposed two major structures, with five subunits each:

The Superscription (Zeph 1:1)

1. The Day of YHWH: *vis-à-vis* universal judgment on Judah and nations (1:1–2:15)
   1.1 threats of judgment upon creation and Judah (1:2–6)
   1.2 direct announcement of the Day of YHWH (1:7–13)
   1.3 description and consequences of the Day of YHWH (1:14–18)
   1.4 A call to conversion/repentance (2:1–3)
   1.5 YHWH will punish the nations (2:4–15)
2. The Day of YHWH: *vis-à-vis* Song of Joy, salvation, restoration of fortunes (3:1–20)
   2.1 YHWH will punish rulers and leaders in Judah (3:1–5)
   2.2 Like other nations, YHWH will punish the unrepentant Judah (3:6–8)
   2.3 The picture of a converted nation/humble remnant (3:9–13)
   2.4 The joy of the restored Israel and that of YHWH (3:14–18)
   2.5 YHWH restores the fortunes of his people (3:19–20)

Each of these sections within which our two units (1:14–18 and 3:14–20), are located, is not disconnected from the other and to the rest of the book of Zephaniah.

2.3 The Place of Zephaniah 1:14–18 and 3:14–20 in the Book of Zephaniah 1–3

The two units of Zephaniah 1:14–18 and 3:14–20 cannot be successfully treated without referring one to the other and to the entire 53 verses (three chapters) of the Book of Zephaniah. This has become necessary as recent scholarship on Zephaniah increasingly prefers a unity approach to the text, rather than an isolated, fragmentary approach as adopted in the past. If we may recall, the Book of Zephaniah, besides the superscription patterns itself on the familiar tri-partite eschatological, theological message of Israel's prophecy. They are generally grouped into judgments or threats against Judah and Jerusalem (1:2–2:3), judgments and threats against nations (2:4–3:8) and divine promises of restoration and salvation to Judah/Jerusalem and every nation (3:1–20), as discussed already. These tri-partite messages are all accommodated in the two major structural patterns (1:1–2:15; 3:1–20), with a circle of five sub-units each, followed by this study.

However, the sub-units of 1:14–18 and 3:14–20 are interrelated within the entire body of Zephaniah's text in many instances. Rhetorically, Zephaniah 1:7 calls for silence since the Day of YHWH is near. This Day of YHWH is seen poetically repeated in the sub-unit of verses 14–18. Thematically, Nogalski has noticed also that the motif of the Day of the Lord occurs in all sections of the entire book of Zephaniah.[19] For instance, the judgment sections exhibit judgment on Judah, as well as judgment on nations. The former is repeated in the beginning of the next section (3:1–5). In fact, it is observed that the parenetic character of Zephaniah 1:2–3:20 is reflected in Zephaniah 2:1–3, which invites the nation of Judah to seek YHWH alone.[20] Several scholars including Irsigler group this call to seek YHWH together with Zephaniah 1:2–18 on thematic reasons since both texts (Zeph 1:2–18 and 2:1–3) are

---

19   Nogalski, *Literary Precursors*, 171.
20   Hunter, *Seek the Lord*, 259–270. See also Sweeney, *Zephaniah*, 50.

116

concerned with the notion of the Day of YHWH.[21] Hence, the theme pervades the entire Book of Zephaniah.

From Nogalski's perspective, the judgment section of Zephaniah 1:2:2–2:3, in this present form, skillfully weaves together two different themes, so that it is difficult to separate them literarily from one another. These two inter-woven themes concern the judgment against Judah and Jerusalem (1:4–6; 8–13; 2:1–3) and a universal judgment against all humanity (1:2f, 14–18).[22] It is the relationship of the preceding themes with the following oracles against nations (2:4–3:8), and universal restoration (3:9–20), which Nogalski has observed that we intend to stress further.

These oracles as Nogalski has accurately observed, are a carefully constructed collection of sayings against the Philistine cities in the west of Jerusalem (2:4–7), Moab and Ammon in the Transjordan to the east (2:8–11) and the Ethiopians and Assyrians (2:12–15) in the south and north respectively. The judgment of the first section culminates in the judgment pronouncement against Jerusalem and her leaders (Zeph 3:1–8).[23] The theme of judgment in Zephaniah 1:14–18, is related with the rest of the text. It anticipates the joy and restoration of fortunes for the remnants (3:14–20).

Contextually, the phrase "the Day of YHWH" (יום יהוה), according to Greg King, the concept of the Day of YHWH appears three times in the book of Zephaniah (1:7 and two times in v. 14). But when one examines thoroughly other contexts within which the term "day" appears in Zephaniah, there is little doubt left, that they refer to the same theme of the "Day of YHWH" that runs through the three chapters. As we saw in preceding chapters, phrases like, "the day of YHWH's sacrifice," (1:18), "on that day," (1:9–10), and "the day of YHWH's fury," (1:18), are all pointing to the same central theology of Zephaniah, namely, judgment and restoration of fortunes.

Zephaniah 3:14–17, for instance functions as a prophetic response to the preceding judgments on Judah, Jerusalem and nations. In other

---

21   See Wilhelm Rudolph, *Micha-Nahum-Habakkuk-Zephanja* (KAT XIII/3; Gütersloh; Mohn, 1975), 255–256; Irsigler, *Gottesgericht*, 113–116; Roberts, *Zephaniah*, 161–163
22   Nogalski, *Literary Precursors*, 172.
23   Nogalski, *Literary Precursors*, 172.

words, the joy of the daughters of Zion in Zephaniah 3:14ff was not only long anticipated by Zephaniah 1:14–18, but it is a result of YHWH's annulment of their judgment (3:15a–d), who has invited them to overcome their fears (v 15d), since He is really in their midst (v 15c).

The YHWH who speaks in 3:18–20, is addressing the community that had once seen wrath, ruin and devastation (1:14–18). YHWH is addressing a community that had once placed their trust in military might, silver and gold. He, YHWH alone will restore their fortunes (3:14–20). Therefore, Zephaniah 1:14–18 and 3:14–20 are not only literally and syntactically related, but they are also thematically related.

The fruits of this relationship include the notions that God intervenes in human affairs in diverse manners (1:7). God rules over all creation, man, woman and animals (vv 2–3). God judges and punishes (vv 8–13). YHWH's judgment is speedy (v 14) and could be devastating (v 15). It even penetrates all kinds of fortifications and human barriers (v 16), and renders those who refuse to repent useless (v 17). This judgment, of course, is universal, regardless of tribe, tongue and language. It reaches to the ends of the earth, and affects also the rich and the poor (v 18; 2:4–15). But as far as those who trust and seek YHWH (2:1–3) are concerned, there will be hope, joy, salvation, and reversal of their misfortunes to good fortunes (Zeph 3:1–20).

However, the fact that the central theme of the Day of YHWH and the restoration of fortunes bind Zephaniah 1:14–18 and 3:14–20 together will be unfolded better, as we dwell on a thorough exegetical study of Zephaniah 1:14–18, in the next section.

2.4 An Exegetical Study of Zephaniah 1:14–18

Evidently, the text of 1:14–18 is not unconnected with the prophecy that precedes (vv 2–13), as well as with that which follows (Zeph 2–3). This is true, since the notion of the Day of YHWH, among other poetic and syntactical features, dominates the entire structure of the text, as it stands. In other words, in the book of Zephaniah, the unit of

1:14–18, is not only relevant to the other units, but it is central to the theme of the Day of YHWH (יהוה יום), which stands out in the prophecy of Zephaniah.

It is in this light, that Greg King earlier rightly argued that though the concept of the Day of YHWH appears three times in the entire book, once in Zephaniah 1:7 and twice in Zephaniah 1:14, the theme is not unconnected with several other contexts, particularly where the word "day" is used. The expressions in the texts of Zephaniah "the Day of YHWH's sacrifice," (1:7), "on that day," (1:9–10), "the Day of YHWH's wrath" (1:18), are all synonymously used with "the Day of YHWH" (יהוה יום), as found in verses 7 and 14.[24]

However, before returning to a detailed exegesis of this unit a comment on the texts and versions of the book of Zephaniah as well as a fresh translation of the unit are necessary. These ventures will enable us to discern better the prophetic message of the Day of YHWH in Zephaniah, as adopted from earlier prophetic traditions and contextualized in his own life situation.

2.4.1 Text of Zephaniah 1:14–18

Recently many scholars, including Robert, Kselman, Berlin and Sweeney have constructively engaged in a facinating reflection on different texts and versions of the book of Zephaniah, of which our literary unit (1:14:18), is a part.[25] The basic Hebrew text of the book of Zephaniah has been generally preserved in the MT of the Hebrew Bible, although there are a few obscurities (1:2, 14; 2:1–2; 3:17–19).[26] Outside the

---

24   King, "The Day of the Lord in Zephaniah," 17.
25   Robert, *Zephaniah*, 163; Kselman, "Zephaniah Book Of," *ABD* 6:1078; Berlin, *Zephaniah*, 23–31 and Sweeney, *Zephaniah*, 3–41. Several versions of Zephaniah include, the Masoretic [MT], the Septuagint [*LXX*], Scrolls from the Judean Wilderness, Targum, Peshitta, Vulgate, Old Latin texts and other textual traditions.
26   Kselman, *Zephaniah*, 1078. See also Arbuckle, "Zephaniah," 718. Here he affirms that the Hebrew Text of Zephaniah is good, except these few obscurities or alterations possibly might have been rendered by modern critical methods and by reference to the LXX.

MT, some fragments of the text of Zephaniah have survived in the Dead Sea Scrolls or Scrolls from the Judean Wilderness, in the Samaritan Pentateuch and in the scattered Talmudic quotations of biblical verses.[27]

These surviving texts, from the *Dead Sea Scrolls* include; a Hebrew fragmentary *Pesharim* (commentaries) from Qumran Cave 1, 1QpZeph (1:18–2) and Cave 4, 4QpZeph (1:12–13). Again, from the Dead Sea is the scroll of the Minor Prophets from *Muraba'at* (Mur 88), dating from about 100 C.E. This contains most of the prophecy of Zephaniah (1:1; 1:11–3:6; 3:8–20), including our specific units of 1:14–18 and 3:14–20, in a textual tradition very close to MT.[28]

There is also the basic Greek text of the book of Zephaniah, which has been studied.[29] It is true that the LXX *Vorlage* of the consonantal text of Zephaniah, while not identical to the MT, stood very close to it. This is not to say that there have not been scribal errors, omissions, glosses, different word divisions and vocalizations and a few instances of possible tendentious translations. For instance, in Zephaniah 2:11 of the MT we read the expression, כל־אלהי הארץ (all the gods of the earth). But in the LXX, it is translated πάντας τοὺς θεοὺς τῶν ἐθνῶν τῆς γῆς (all the gods of the people of the earth). Kselman thinks that this translation is due to the influence of Jewish monotheism.[30]

In addition, there is the Greek translation of the *Dōdekaprophēton*, discovered in Nahal Hever (8HevXII gr). This translation contains the

27 See a summary of this in Berlin, *Zephaniah*, 23–24. Here she warns that none of these texts (Samaritan Pentateuch, Talmudic quotations) is as complete as the MT and the textual accuracy of all of them is no more certain).

28 See Sweeney, *Zephaniah*, 3–18 for a detailed study of this MT version of Zephaniah, textual features, structure, genre, and rhetorical function, the text tradition and that of the Twelve as a whole.

29 See Sweeney, *Zephaniah*, 19–24 for a detailed study of the origins of the LXX versions, which originated from the Greek-speaking-Jewish community of Alexandria in the mid-third century B.C.E. According to the *Letter of Aristeas*, that was written to explain the origin of the LXX, the Ptolemaic Egyptian Monarch Ptolemy II Philadelphus (285–247 B.C.E) commissioned the translation of Torah into Greek in his effort to assemble all known and important books of the world in his library.

30 Kselman, "Zephaniah," 1078.

oldest known witness of the Greek text of the *Dōdekaprohēton*.[31] It contains mostly the fragment of Zephaniah 1:1–4, 13–17; 2:9–10; 3:6–7).[32] In this study, the MT text, with its apparatus and the following alternative fresh translation's arrangement[33] will be used. Occasional references shall be made to the *LXX*, the *Vulgate* and other relevant texts, where necessary.[34]

2.4.2 Translation and Textual Criticism of Zephaniah 1:14–18

The entire prophecy of Zephaniah on the nearness of the Day of YHWH's intervention, earlier heard in verse 7, is intensified in verses 14–18. The consequences and the significances of this Day of YHWH, is described in the following poetic and hymnal fashion:

קרוב יום־יהוה הגדול	14a. Near is the great day of the Lord
קרוב ומהר מאד	14b. Near with great/much speed
קול יום יהוה מר	14c. The voice of the day of the Lord is bitter
צרח שם גבור	14d. There a warrior roars
יום עברה היום ההוא	15a. A day of wrath is that day
יום צרה ומצוקה	15b. A day of distress and tribulations
יום שאה ומשואה	15c. A day of ruin and devastation
יום חשך ואפלה	15d. A day of darkness and gloom
יום ענן וערפל	15e. A day of black cloud and heavy cloud
יום שופר ותרועה	16a. A day of trumpet blast and battle cry
על הערים הבצרות	16b. Against fortified cities
ועל הפנות הגבהות	16c. And against exalted towers
והצרתי לאדם	17a. I will bring distress to the people
והלכו כעורים	17b. And they shall walk like the blinds

31 Sweeney, *Zephaniah*, 26–27.
32 Kselman, "Zephaniah," 1078. The relevance of this, Kselman rightly noted has been demonstrated by Dominique Barthélemy, *Les Devanciers d'Aquila* (VTSup 10, Leiden: Brill, 1963), 163–178.
33 K. Elliger et al., *Biblia Hebraica Stuttgartensia* (Stuttgart: Deutsche Bibelgesellschaft, 1997).
34 See Berlin, *Zephaniah*, 24–25 where she underlines among other things, the importance of the MT as a *textus receptus*.

כי ליהוה חטאו	17c. Because they sinned against the Lord
ושפך דמם כעפר	17d. And their blood shall be spilled like dust
ולחמם כגללים	17e. And their muscles, like dung
גם־כספם גם־זהבם לא־יוכל להצילם	18a. Also their silver and gold shall not save them
ביום עברת יהוה	18b. On the day of the Lord's wrath
ובאש קנאתו	18c. And by the fire of the passion/zeal
תאכל כל־הארץ	18d. All the earth shall be consumed
כי־כלה אך־נבהלה	18e. Because, He will completely destroy
יעשה את כל־ישבי הארץ	18f. Making a terrible end of those who dwell in the land

In verse 14a–b the adverb ומהר (and with speed, quickly) could have been attested וממהר (and more quickly in a comparative sense). The term is found in Genesis 18:6a וימהר (and hasten, and hurry, and speed up); Genesis 18a; Exodus 32:9; Isaiah 8:1–3 *"Maher-shalal-hash-baz"* (quick spoil or speedy plunder). This suggests that the word had not only existed in the culture which Zephaniah inherited or grew up in, but that Zephaniah's audience would have understood clearly the implication of his prophecy of YHWH's intervention and sovereignty.

Also in verse 14c–d, קול יום יהוה מר צרח שם גבור (the voice of the Day of YHWH is bitter. It is swifter like a warrior), is attested in MT, but it undergoes modification in other versions and texts. For example, in the MT textual apparatus, which we follow in this study the following reading, is mentioned: קל יום יהוה מרץ וחש מגבר (the Day of the YHWH is swifter than a runner and faster than a warrior). Vlaardinger-broek calls this, a repetition of verse 14a–b.[35] However, it is most likely that the LXX had a problem with the present Hebrew text. The LXX reads φωνὴ ἡμέρας Κυρίου πικκρὰ σκληρά τέτακται δυνατή (the voice of the Day of Lord is bitter and harsh/rough he has arranged/appointed power). The LXX seems to read צרח (roar, war cry) as "harsh/rough," and "there a warrior" (שם גבור) as "he appointed or arranged power."

The *Targums* attest: מן קדם יוי דביה מרר וצוח תמן גבריא מתקטלין קל יומא דעתיד למתי (the voice of the day which is appointed to come from the presence of YHWH, of which there will be bitterness and cries

---

35   See Vlaardingerbroek, *Zephaniah*, 102–103 for further and interesting insights.

of the warriors who are being killed/slaughtered). Sweeney suggests that by "killed/slaughtered here", the *Targum* is making reference to the זבה (sacrifice of v 7).[36] The *Peshitta* reads, קלל דירמה מירא מריר וקשא וישין (the sound/voice of the Day of the Lord is bitter, hard and strong), omitting "there." While the Vulgate attests, *vox diei Domini amara tribulatur ibi fortis* (the voice of the Day of the Lord is bitter, afflicting the strong).

I would rather stay with the *MT* attestation, since these other versions do not really present a compelling ground for modification. Besides, the fact of the basic contextual meaning of the sovereignty of YHWH, the "Chief Judge," the hymnic nature of the expressions, the urgency and the bitter implications of the Day for the disobedient Judean army or the citizens, are still undeniably well captured in these diverse versions and attestations.

In verse 17c, the expression, כי ליהוה חטאו (because they sinned against YHWH), is suspected as an addition. Vlaardingerbroek gives four reasons for this suspicion. First, both metrically and materially disturb the flow between the other parts of the verse 17(v17 a–b, d–e. Second, the context speaks of what will happen on the Day of YHWH, not of the reasons for it. Third, the argumentation for the judgment offered in these words is blank and general (they), after the specific expressions, given in verse 4–6, 8, and 9. Finally, YHWH is referred to in the third person, in the sentence, (ליהוה חטאו = "they have sinned against the Lord), instead of the first person expression (*hiphil* converted perfect, והצרתי = "I will bring distress"), earlier heard in verse 17a.[37]

Moreover from the point of view of Form Criticism, the expression כי ליהוה חטאו (because they have sinned against the Lord), is not only suspected as being an addition, but it raises an awareness of a judgment or judicial context. But commentators have speculated as to what motivated the addition. Vlaardingerbroek suggests it could be that the redactor wants to remind readers of the ingredients of the coming of the Day of YHWH, namely, judgment. It could also be the work of a person who, later wanted to make this specific message more general,

---

36 Sweeney, *Zephaniah*, 74.
37 Vlaardingerbroek, *Zephaniah*, 104.

with the view of making it more pointedly a warning, in the direction of the life of his contemporaries.[38]

This study considers the expression, כי ליהוה חטאו (because they have sinned against the Lord), as part of the overall "judgment" message of Zephaniah. It is part of the call (of all people, particular and general) for repentance from sin, and to embrace divine promises of restoration and the glory of the Lord. It forms a necessary part and parcel, of an invitation to a renewed fellowship with YHWH, as well as of seeking refuge in his name.

Additionally, the LXX translates the following text of the MT of ושפך דמם כעפר ולחמם כגללים ("and their blood" shall be poured like the dust, and their fat like the dung), as καὶ τὸ αἷμα αὐτῶν ὡς χοῦν καὶ τὰς σάρκας αὐτῶν ὡς βόλβιτα (and their blood like soil, and their flesh like dung), which to me does not change the basic meaning of the devastating nature of the Day of YHWH, similarly attested in the *Peshitta* and the *Vulgate* and in the *Targum*.[39]

Finally, verse 18c–d, as indicated in the textual apparatus of the MT, is viewed by some scholars as an addition. The expression ובאש קנאתו תאכל כל־הארץ (and by the fire of the passion, all the earth shall be consumed), is also thought by some to be the work of someone who had experienced the destruction of Jerusalem, and the deportation to Babylon, as disasters for the entire nation, hence, added words about "all the earth" or 'whole land, and all inhabitants.' So, there is a general feeling, that "the whole earth" and "all humans" here represent the work of an editor, who intended to expand an originally limited judgment, to a universal judgment.[40]

Even the expression in verse 18a, גם־כספם גם־זהבם לא־יוכל להצילם (and their silver and gold shall not save/deliver them), Vlaardingerbroek thinks, does not seem to have been the last statement. The expression in 18c–d, "by the fire of the passion, all the earth shall be consumed," for him seems to have crept in from Zephaniah 3:8.[41] But in my own

---

38 Vlaardingerbroek, *Zephaniah*, 104.
39 See Sweeney, *Zephaniah*, 74 for some additional insights.
40 Vlaardingerbroek, *Zephaniah*, 105.
41 Vlaardingerbroek, *Zephaniah*, 105.

judgment, the language of Zephaniah 1:18, reflected in Zephaniah 3:8, does not only demonstrate the unity of the theme and literary structure of the prophecy of Zephaniah, but it particularly reiterates the warning that YHWH, the Sovereign of creation, will judge and bring a terrible end to those who broke the covenant. It is a reminder of the divine call for obedience to YHWH. This brings us to the delimitation of the specific text or unit of Zephaniah 1:14–18.

2.4.3 Literary Structure and the Delimitation of Zephaniah 1:14–18

The centrality of the notion of the Day of YHWH in the prophecy of Zephaniah is unquestionable. This theme runs through the earlier discussed two major structures, namely, judgment upon all nations and upon Judah (1:2–2:15) and joy, salvation and restoration of fortunes (3:1–20), with different sub-units. Zephaniah 1:14–18, is located within the above first major block of the entire literary structure of the book of Zephaniah. Put differently, it is located within the larger context of universal judgment upon Judah and other nations (1:1–2:15). Verses 2–6 communicate mostly threats of judgment upon creation and upo Judah. This is followed by the direct announcement of the Day of YHWH (1:7–13), with several first person expressions by YHWH.[42]

Nevertheless, in terms of the syntax, this study agrees with Sweeney, that there is a syntactical marker or break at verse 14. This is marked by Zephaniah's repeated use of the Day of YHWH, earlier heard in verse 7. This, according to him, suggests that verses 7–13, are a separate sub-unit from verses 14–18. The former presents YHWH's oracular statements concerning the Day of YHWH, while the latter is the presentation of Zephaniah's explanation of the significance of the Day of YHWH.[43] Verse 13 ends with a *qal converted perfect*, והיה ("it happened that"), which introduces the following consequences of those who have not sought YHWH nor consulted Him (v 6): "their wealth shall be plundered, and their house shall be laid waste. They shall build

---

42 Sweeney, *Zephaniah*, 75.
43 Sweeney, *Zephaniah*, 75.

houses, not dwell in them; plant vineyards but not drink their wine" (v 13). It is from here, that the sub-unit of verses 14–18, begins with its literary integrity.

In verses 14–18, there is a change of person, which serves as one of the literary markers. Here, Zephaniah clearly, uses the third person to make reference to YHWH, beginning with, קָרוֹב יוֹם־יהוה הגדול (near is the great Day of the Lord). It is at this point, that Zephaniah recalls and repeats the expression, "be silent the Day of YHWH is near" (v 7). The Day of YHWH is uniquely repeated twice in this verse, to strengthen the central theme of the entire prophecy (vv 14a and b). This is followed by a list of sayings and attributes, which characterize this Day of YHWH (speed, bitter voice, like the roaring of the warrior, wrath, distress, darkness and black cloud) in verse 14b–16c.

In other words, verses 14–16 are mostly threats, while verses 17–18 express the nature of these threats and punishment. These verses are densely poetic and hymnic in form and rotate around a common theme of יום יהוה (the Day of YHWH). The unit of Zephaniah 1:14–18, is flooded with linguistic features.[44] These features include metaphors, similes, allusions, personifications, alliterations and paronomasias.[45] The כי clause in verse 18c, earlier disputed by some to be an addition, rather functions here metaphorically to highlight the reason for the complete devastation of the inhabitants of the land, who do not seek nor trust in YHWH.

Evidently, verses 14–18, as earlier hinted, are not unconnected with the preceding verses of threats of judgment upon creation and Judah (vv 2–6) and with the announcement of the Day of YHWH, which includes a caution for silence (vv 7–13). Verses 7–13 and 14–18 build on verses 2–6, since those who are to be punished are also those to be sacrificed. This is followed by Zephaniah 2:1–3. This passage (2:1–3),

---

44 See Patterson, *Nahum, Habakkuk, and Zephaniah*, 281–292 for a detailed discussion of the literary features of Zephaniah especially our unit of study (1:14–18).

45 Paronomasia is explained in Soulen, *Hand Book of Biblical Criticism*, 135, as "a play on words, a pun; and in a more technical sense, it is the reoccurrence of the same word, or word stem in close proximity." This is very common in Zephaniah especially in chapter 1: 15–16, which will be discussed in detail in chapter three.

looks back to Zephaniah 1:7–13, 14–18. It does not only re-emphasize the need to seek YHWH, but the Day of YHWH motif is further stressed. Invariably, since the central theme the Day of YHWH dominates the entire unit of verses 14–18, the following verse-by-verse exegesis will further facilitate a thorough discernment of the preaching of Zephaniah, concerning the Day of YHWH.

2.4.4 An Exegetical Analysis of Zephaniah 1:14–18

In this pericope, or in this entire particular rhetorical unit (1:14–18), Zephaniah stresses the significance or the consequences of the Day of YHWH. The prophet picks up and increases the intensity of the motif of the Day of the Lord, earlier heard in verse 7. Zephaniah preaches in a highly poetic fashion, and warns against the conditions which will exist on the arrival of the Day of YHWH. This Day some have interpreted as particular (fall of Jerusalem in 586 B.C.E.), while others see it in the light of the events of 70 C.E., and there are some who see it as referring to the universal and final eschatological fulfillment, as we find in the book of Joel 2:28–32.[46]

Put simply, it could be read as a universal judgment on humans and creation (vv 2–3). Starting from verses 4–10, it is clear that Judah and Jerusalem are, if not the main, at least a target audience here. Yet, it has a great universal implication as well. This is true, since the text is connected to the rest of the material of the three chapters of the book of Zephaniah.

This position, is well captured by Adele Berlin, who has reminded us that if we accept the definition of the Day of the Lord, as referring to a momentous historical event, which the prophets seek to interpret "theologically," and if we date Zephaniah's prophecy to the time of the religious reforms of King Josiah, then, the over-arching momentous event is the deterioration of the mighty Assyrian empire, after the death of Ashurbanipal in 627 B.C.E. There was also the uncertainty of what

---

46 Patterson, *Zephaniah*, 320.

the next dominant empire would be.[47] In other words, this pericope (1:14–18) is not referring to a day in the sense of one week, short or long term or several months and weeks. Rather, it is the "theological" Day of YHWH's intervention in human history and affairs, in all its ramifications.

2.4.4.1 Near is the Day of the Lord (קרוב יום־יהוה, v 14)

Zephaniah begins the description of the significance of this Day of the Lord with how "near" and "great" this Day is, or will be. He uses the masculine singular infinitive adjective קרוב (near). This sense of temporal nearness is also seen in Deuteronomy 32:35 ("for the day of their ruin is close") and in other prophetic literature like Isaiah 13:6, ("for the Day of Yahweh is near") and verse 22 which says "for its doom is about to come, and its days will not last long." Similar expressions are also found in other prophetic texts (Ezek 7:7; Joel 1:15; 2:1; 3:14 and Obad 15).

This, in my own judgment, underlines the imminence or urgency of the coming of the Day of YHWH.[48] This is to a certain level in line with Sweeney who also insightfully suggests that the use of this adjective, not only plays the role of presenting a concern for the urgency or imminence of the coming of the Day of YHWH, but it establishes the relationships or links to the preceding materials of Zephaniah (1:7), and to the *Dodekapropheton* as a whole, which deals with the motif of the Day of YHWH, in order to alert the people to a God who punishes and restores.[49] The facts of these relationships or rapport will be discussed in great detail, in Chapter Five.

However, whereas Zephaniah 1:7 somehow expresses or identifies the participants in the sacrifice, as YHWH's consecrated guest, verse 14a is very blunt and direct about the threatening nature of the Day of

47   Berlin, *Zephaniah*, 92.
48   See Vlaardingerbroek, *Zephaniah*, 105 for similar position by other scholars.
49   Sweeney, *Zephaniah*, 97. See also Savoca, *Abddia-Naum, Abacuc-Sofonia*, 159. Here Savoca affirms that *"è vicino il grande giorno del signore"* of verse 14 is the taking up of that earlier heard in verse 7 when he said; *"viene ora ripreso e puntualizzato l'annunzio del v.17: l'imminenza del "giorno di JHWH."*

YHWH. Following our earlier discussions, יום־יהוה (the Day of the Lord) in verse 14a, is a reiteration of verse 7. Although Zephaniah did not state how close the Day was, he was certainly being influenced by the socio-historical *Sitz-im-Leben* of his time, with a huge theological implication of God's intervention in human affairs.

Zephaniah meant in a renewed way, YHWH's sovereignty, judgment, covenant and restoration of fortunes. He was aware of the earlier traditions, especially of his predecessors and contemporary prophets earlier discussed. Zephaniah added, modified and pronounced his prophecy to suit his listening audience which will be uniquely presented in the course of this exegesis. This is to say that verse 14a is thematically and theologically connected with the rest of the book of Zephaniah, and with the entire prophetic literature, especially the Twelve Minor Prophets.

Furthermore, it is suggested that the adjective הגדול (great), in verse 14a adds, heightens and intensifies the nature of the coming Day of YHWH. It underscores the all-inclusive and particularly eschatological character of the Day of YHWH. This adjective is prevalent in prophetic literature, for example, it is found in Joel 2:11.

Similarly, the use of מהר (speed, swiftly) suggests Zephaniah's familiarity with the language of earlier prophets, like Isaiah 5:26–30 and 8:1–3. He reminds the people of the need for their preparedness, for this rapid coming of the Day of YHWH. Zephaniah proceeded in verse 14c–d to describe the Day as the time when the voice of the Lord will be bitter (מר) and a Day in which the warrior will roar or cry (צרח).

The use of the adjective, "bitter" and *qal participle* (צרח) here creates some interpretative and translational difficulties for exegetes and commentators, as mentioned earlier in the textual-critical section of this study.[50] Intrestingly, the adjective "bitter" is found in earlier prophets, like Amos 8:10, suggesting still, Zephaniah's familiarity with the language of his predecessors. Similarly, Robert observes that although צרח (cry) may sound ambiguous here, in Isaiah 42:13, it designates the

---

50 See Vlaardingerbroek, *Zephaniah*, 107 where these verses, adjective מר and qal participle צרח or their syntactical or hermeneutical roles are extensively debated.

screaming or the battle cry of the warrior, who has worked himself up into a killing rage.

Moreover, Roberts stresses that if its usage is acceptable in this sense, then, the roaring warrior in this context is presumably part of the enemy combatants.[51] However, based on the socio-historical context of Zephaniah's prophecy, I would suggest that the cry here could either be that of the military combatants invading the land or those defending it. It clearly suggests that the Day of YHWH will not be a happy Day, for the unrepentant inhabitants of Jerusalem and Judah, but a Day of Judgment and accountability.[52]

2.4.4.2 Further Characterization of Day of YHWH (vv 15–16)

This Day of YHWH, Day of judgment and accountability, is futher but colorfully described by Zephaniah in verses 15–16, in a uniquely repetitive or anaphoric manner.[53] Some of these words contain some note-worthy elements of a paronomasia, as follows:[54]

יום עברה היום ההוא	15a. A day of wrath is that day
יום צרה ומצוקה	15b. A day of distress and tribulations

51 Robert, *Nahum, Habakkuk and Zephaniah*, 183–184.

52 See also Sweeney, *Zephaniah*, 98 for the explanation or possible interpretation of these verses.

53 However, Soulen, in *The Handbook of Biblical Criticism*, 7 describes anaphora as the use of a word as grammatical substitutes for a preceding word or group of words. In rhetoric, anaphora denotes the repeated use of the initial word or words of two or more clauses, lines or strophes in a sequence, usually for poetic or rhetorical effect.

54 In addition to the above explanation given by Soulen, David E. Aune, in *The Westminster Dictionary of New Testament & Early Christian Literature & Rhetoric* (Louisville: Westminster John Knox Press, 2003) 337 also notes that *paronomasia* is from the Greek word meaning "play upon words which sound alike," and it involves the use of two or more words in relatively brief context that are either very similar in form, or make use of different meanings of the same word. Aune observes that this literary device is not only found in the OT but also in the NT. A famous example is Matt 16:18; "and I tell you, you are Peter [πέτρος], and on this rock [πέτρα], I will build my church."

יום שאה ומשואה	15c. A day of ruin and devastation
יום חשך ואפלה	15d. A day of darkness and gloom
יום ענן וערפל	15e. A day of black cloud and heavy cloud
יום שופר ותרועה	16a. A day of trumpet blast and battle cry
על הערים הבצרות	16b. Against fortified cities
ועל הפנות הגבהות	16c. And against exalted towers

Observing this passage, Sweeney rightly and perfectly suggests that Zephaniah 1:15–16 does not only describe the Day of YHWH in anaphoric line but employs a series of eight paired strophic or lexically paired expressions. The first six statements, which employ a basic construct formation of the noun יום (day), together with either one or a pair of nouns that characterize the threatening nature of the day, and the final two statements, he stresses, relate to the objects against which the Day of YHWH is directed.[55]

Similarly, Széles describes these verses as painted by Zephaniah with dismal colors. According to her, they point to the seriousness of the judgment which will be developed further in the following detailed exegesis.[56]

2.4.4.2.1 Day of Wrath (יום עברה היום ההוא, v 15a)

This is the first of the eight paired strophe statements (15a–16c), with six construct nominal sentences ("a day of wrath is that day"), particularly in verse 15a–15e. Sweeney however, notes that this expression יום עברה היום ההוא, sets the theme for the following five nominal expressions, by pointing to the wrathful and threatening nature of the day. In contrast to the rest of the five statements (15b–e), which employ pairs of nouns in the construct formulation to characterize the nature of the day, verse 15a employs only a noun, "wrath" (עברה/ebrâ), both to set the basic theme and to accommodate the following phrase היום ההוא (that day), which stands as the implied completion of the succeeding five statements.[57]

---

55 Sweeney, *Zephaniah*, 98.
56 Széles, *Wrath and Mercy*, 87.
57 Sweeney, *Zephaniah*, 99.

Vlaardingerbroek, with his exegetical interest in Zephaniah 1:15–16, observes that the word (עברה/*ebrâ*) only occurs in poetic and prophetic texts, in addition to a few places where it means pride, arrogance (Prov 21:24; Isa 16:6; Jer 48:30).[58] There are also other contexts in the OT where עברה/*ebrâ*, is associated with the Day of the wrath of YHWH, or related themes (Isa 9:18; 13:9; Ezek 7: 19; 22:21; Lam 2:2).[59]

However, the picture depicted here by Zephaniah, in my own judgment, is that of the devastating nature of the coming Day of YHWH, upon the disobedient people, as is emphatically expressed with the phrase (היום ההוא), as the subject of verse 15a.[60] In other words, this idea of characterization of the Day of YHWH as a day of fierce judgment or "wrath" is traced back to the prophecy of Amos and other prophets, but Zephaniah characterizes this Day in a uniquely poetic and ironic manner, using his own terminology.

2.4.4.2.2 Day of Distress and Tribulation (יום צרה ומצוקה, v 15b)

Verse 15b, the second of the eight series of statements (a day of distress and tribulation) is linked to the preceding verse 15a, by employing the two nouns, צרה/*sârâ* and מצוק/*mṣûqâ* which demonstrate the effect or the consequences of the Day of YHWH, on those who disobeyed or broke the covenant.[61] Inherent in צרה/*sârâ,* according Vlaardingerbroek is the notion of narrowness, tightness, which is translated as *dies angustiae* in the Vulgate.[62] It occurs frequently in the Hebrew Bible and in the prophetic literature (e. g, Isaiah 30:6; Jeremiah 30:7 and Daniel 12:1

---

58 Vlaardingerbroek, *Zephaniah*, 108.

59 Sweeney, *Zephaniah,* 99.

60 In the Vulgate's translation of verse 15a, *Dies irae dies illa*, forms the beginning of the Medieval Hymn for funeral Mass, which was sometimes attributed to Thomas of Celano (1200-1270). See Savoca, *Abdia-Naum, Abacuc-Sofonia*, 159 and P. Haupt, "The Prototype of the Dies Irael," *JBL* 38 (1919):142–151. See also Vlaardingerbroek, *Zephaniah*, 103–104 and G. Sauer, "עֶבְרָה *ebrâ*, Wrath," *TLOT* 2: 835–36, where the theological and other various usages of the term "wrath" are studied in detail.

61 See also *BDB,* 865; where צָרָה entered as straits, distress, travail, to name but a few.

62 Vlaardingerbroek, *Zephaniah*, 108.

and Obad 14). Vlaardingerbroek further notes the occurances of מצוק/
mĕsûqâ, in the Psalms and Wisdom Literature (25:17; 107:6, 13, 28;
Job 15:24).

Like מצוק, which occurs six times and means "anguish" (translated
in the Vulgate as *tribulationis*) is akin in meaning and significance to
צרה (distress). The Day of YHWH will be a day on which there will be
no escape for sinners from the anger of the Lord.[63] This alliterative
pattern of describing the devastating effect of the Day of YHWH continues in verse 15c.

2.4.4.2.3 Day of Ruin and Devastation/Desolation (יום שאה ומשואה v 15c)

In verse 15c, the effects of the wrath, the distress and the tribulations
already heard in verse 15a–b are intensified. This time will be a "day of
ruin and devastation/desolation" (שאה/*šō'â* and משואה/*mĕšô'â*). Sweeney
affirms that this strophe continues the sequence of the preceding two
strophes, by pointing to the complete destruction as the consequence
or aftermath of divine wrath and human distress.[64] According to
Sweeney the two terms, (שאה/*šō'â* and שואה/*šō'â*), are from the same
root, and seem to mean both "misfortune" (Isa 47:11; Ps 35:8) and
"thunderstorm" (Ezek 38), but also "rubble" (Job 30:14) and "desolate
land" (Job 30:3; 38:27).[65]

Sweeney also notes that the root of these words, שאה/*šō'â* and שואה/
šō'ā, is utilized today in "holocaust" to describe the tragedy of the ex-
termination of millions of Jews during the Second World War.[66] In

---

63   Vlaardingerbroek, *Zephaniah*, 108.
64   Sweeney, *Zephaniah*, 99.
65   Sweeney, *Zephaniah*, 99 and Vlaardingerbroek, *Zephaniah*, 108.
66   Sweeney, *Zephaniah*, 99. On Thursday, February 11, 2010 I had the privilege of
     visiting this holocaust museum in the Holy Land, Israel. This word, "shoah" as
     suggested by Sweeney, is found in the narrative contained in the "Angelicum-
     Berrie Fellows Interreligious Study Trip to Israel February 5–13, 2010." The
     narrative is as follows, "our visit to the Yad Vashem museum will present the
     story of the *shoah*, the Holocaust, from a unique Jewish perspective, emphasing
     the experiences of the individual victims through original artifacts, survivor tes-
     timonies and personal possessions."

other words, all kinds of misfortune, ruin and devastation await the disobedient people on the Day of YHWH.

2.4.4.2.4 Day of Darkness and Gloom (יום חשך ואפלה, v15d)

Zephaniah insists that the Day of YHWH is not only characterized by wrath (15a), distress and tribulations (15b), ruin and devastation (15c), but also with darkness and gloom (חשך/*hōšek* and אפלה/*'ăpēlă* 15d). This notion of darkness was earlier seen in Amos 5:18–20, and in an earlier prophetic tradition than Zephaniah. Even the expression in verses 15d–e, brings to our mind the language of Deuteronomy 4 on advantages of fidelity to the Lord (Deut 4:1–8), God's manifestations (vv 9–14), the danger of idolatry (vv 15–24), promise of God's fidelity (vv 25–31) as well as proofs of God's love (vv 32–40).

Similarly, Vlaardingerbroek notes that the portrayal of the Day of YHWH, in these languages, also resonates the exodus motif (Exod 1:22). The two nouns are more or less synonymous (darkness/gloom), he stresses. However, חשך/*hōšek*, according to him occurs much more frequently than אפלה/*'ăpēlă*, and was probably the more common. Both words are used here literally as well as figuratively.[67] These expressions are seen in Joel 2:2 as well as in Isaiah 59:9. Sweeney notices that because Joel is generally considered to be a composition from the late fourth century B.C.E, the text of Joel is apparently dependent on that of Zephaniah.[68]

However, the imagery of darkness is that of misfortune, wrath, distress, desolation, ruin and complete devastation. In the tradition of the Holy War, "darkness" is physical darkness. It is the opposite of light,

---

67 Vlaardingerbroek, *Zephaniah*, 109.
68 Sweeney, *Zephaniah*, 100. However, Patterson, in his *Nahum, Habakkuk, Zephaniah*, 321 notices the following closeness between Joel 2:1–11 and Zephaniah 1:14–18: the Day of the Lord is near, Zephaniah 1:14//Joel 2:1; It is a great day in Zephaniah 1:14//Joel 2:11; a day of darkness and gloom in Zephaniah 1:15//Joel 2:2; a day of clouds and blackness in Zephaniah 1:15//Joel 2:2; a day of sounding trumpet in Zeph 1:16//Joel 2:1; all the inhabitants of the earth in Zeph 1:18//Joel 2:1. Although the dating of Joel is debated, it is important to keep in mind the common theme of the Day of YHWH that runs through the *Dodekapropheton*, to which Joel and Zephaniah belong.

life and every good thing. Vlaardingerbroek puts it well when he writes "If light means life and God is called "my light" in Psalm 27:1, and we can only see light or really live in the light of God (Ps 36:10), the meaning of darkness becomes clear. It is not so much God's absence as his wrath, a wrath in which there is no life (Ps 3:5)."[69] Hence, after the wrath and darkness comes restoration and salvation. In my opinion, "darkness" represents misfortunes and the turning away form God as manifested in the words of Jesus, the light of the world "I am the light of the world; anyone who follows me will not be walking in dark, but will have the light of life' (John 8:12).[70]

2.4.4.2.5 Day of Cloud and Black Cloud (יום ענן וערפל, v 15e)

The expressions or the nouns in verse 15e, ענן/*ānān and* ערפל/*ărāpel* are very close to the one on "darkness," in the preceding line (v 15d). Vlaardingerbroek suggests again, that for the parallel use of ענן/*ānān and* ערפל/*ărāpel*, it is clear that the latter here also means 'dark or cloudiness.'[71] Practically, both are conditions where there is no sun, resulting not merely in danger to health, but actually in rendering impossible any biological life.[72] But like ערפל/*ărāpel* it has a poetic flavor (Job 22:13; 38:9), and is used further, especially in a more or less 'numinous' sense, in connection with YHWH's dwelling or appearance (Exod 20:21; Deut 4:11; 1 Kgs 8:12; Ps 18:10).[73] Sweeney confirms this when he remarks that the language and imagery of darkness in the present text of Zephaniah appear frequently in the theophanic reports that attempt to depict the presence of YHWH (Exod 19:16; 20:18; Deut 4:11; 5:22; 1 Kgs 8:12; Nah 1:3; Ps 97:2; 2 Chr 6:1).[74]

Most striking for Sweeney are, 1 Kgs 8:12 and 2 Chr 6:1 in particular. Both relate a portion from Solomon's speech at the dedication of the Temple in Jerusalem in which he recounts the imagery of YHWH,

---

69   Vlaardingerbroek, *Zephaniah*, 109.
70   Cf. John 1:4–13; 12:46; Exod 13:22; Isa 42:6 and Zech 14:8ff.
71   Vlaardingerbroek, *Zephaniah,* 109.
72   Széles, *Mercy and Wrath*, 87.
73   Vlaardingerbroek, *Zephaniah*, 109.
74   Sweeney, *Zephaniah*, 100.

surrounded by darkness, thus "then Solomon said, 'YHWH has said that he would dwell in thick darkness (בערפל). I have built you an exalted house, a place for you to dwell forever and ever." He concludes that based on Psalm 97:2 and these other relevant passages cited above, the representation of darkness in Zephaniah's prophecy of the Day of YHWH, draws on the imagery of YHWH's presence in the Holy of Holies in Jerusalem Temple, and thereby aids in establishing the ironic character of the event.[75]

However, these symbolic and ironic descriptions, in my own judgment, represent the misfortunes, the threats of judgments and the miserable nature of the Day of YHWH, upon those who do not keep the covenant. Having described the devastating nature of the Day of YHWH in such discussed anaphoric manner, Zephaniah, once again turns to the socio-political realm of the nature of this Day of YHWH, in the following verse 16.

2.4.4.3 Day of Trumpet Blast and War Cry (יום שׁופר ותרועה, v 16a)

In the sixth strophe (v16a), Zephaniah describes the Day of YHWH with parallel words of שׁופר/ *šôpâ* and תרועה/*tērû'â* (trumpet blast and battle cry). The two terms occur in connection with war and cult. The שׁופר/*šôpâr* (ram's horn) was used in the ancient days in a battle for the purpose of alerting the city.[76] In terms of שׁופר/*šôpâr* connection with war, Vlaardingerbroek cites Judges 7:20, 1 Samuel 13:3 and 2 Samuel 20:22, as some of the examples. With regard to its relationship to the cult, he cites Leviticus 25:9 (announcement of the year on the great Day of Atonement) and Exodus 19:16 (theophany) as other examples of the connection of תרועה/*tērû'â* with war.[77]

---

75 Sweeney, *Zephaniah*, 100.

76 Berlin, *Zephaniah*, 90.

77 See von Rad, *Holy War in Ancient Israel*, 48–49. Here an overview of the tradition and the significance of commencement of the battle with a war cry (תרועה) is presented in detail. I think, von Rad is right, when he concludes that, "this overview makes clear that Yahweh's intervention in the form of confusing divine terror was an indispensable element of the tradition (Lev 26:37

Moreover, 1 Samuel 4:5 (shouting on account of victory) and Jeremiah 4:19; 49:2 (cries of war) have been suggested as additional instances where these terms have been utilized in the context of a war. Vlaardingebroek also suggests its connection with cult, by citing 2 Samuel 6:15 (in the context of procession) and Numbers 29:1 (in the opening of a festival). But in the book of Joshua 6:5; 20, שׁופר/šôpār and תרועה/tērû'â occur together in the contexts of a procession as well as a military campaign.[78]

Nevertheless, שׁופר/šôpār (ram's horn) occurs in other prophetic literature and seems to refer specifically to the blast of the enemy in preparation for attack (Amos 3:6; Hos 5:8). I believe that the significance of these terms, include the fact that the Day of the YHWH with its judgment will arrive like enemy military battalion, storming the city with wrathful (15a), distressful and devastating effects (15b–c), no matter how exalted and fortified the cities and towers of the targets (disobedient people) might be. Nothing surpasses the power of YHWH's judgment and intervention. He is the Sovereign of all creation.

2.4.4.3.1 Fortified Cities and Towers (על הערים הבצרות ועל הפנות, v16b–c)

From the Day of trumpet blast and war cry (v 16a), Zephaniah addresses the effects of YHWH's Day on "fortified cities and against exalted towers" (v 16b–c). Zephaniah, no doubt, was familiar with his environments. Many cities in the eighth and seventh centuries were fortified. This explains the importance of this expression in many texts of the Hebrew Bible (Hos 8:14; Neh 9:25; 2 Chr 32:1; 33:14 and Zeph 3:6).

---

cf 2 Chr 20:21–22= invasion of Edom through songs to the Lord). What happened was that in the panic created by Yahweh, the battle order of the enemy and often also the camp came into such confusion that sometimes the enemies destroyed one another. Without question it was the intention of the narrator to attribute the causation of victory to Yahweh alone."

78 See Vlaardingerbroek, *Zephaniah*, 110 for detailed discussion of these terms and their usages in the Hebrew Bible, as well as Sweeney, *Zephaniah*, 111. See also Amos 2:2.

In fact, Sweeney notices that the term, "fortified cities" appears in the narrative concerning Sennacherib's threats against the fortified cities of Judah, during their attack against Judah in 701 B.C.E (2 Kgs 19:25; Isa 37:26).[79] The expressions "fortified cities and exalted towers," also give us an impression of an impenetrable fence or building of a proud city, surrounded with high fence and exalted towers, to protect the proud leaders.

Vlaardingerbroek insightfully observes that עַל (against), means more in this context than just the violence of the Day of YHWH, which is directed against the cities that have been fortified, and towers that were exalted up on high. It brings to an end those false securities that proud people thought they had.[80]

In other words, the general picture painted in this context is similar to that story of the capture of the city of Jericho, in Joshua 6. Here we can recall that this was an event in which the trumpet blast and the echoes of shouting caused the collapse of the massive security walls of Jericho. One wonders how the citizens of Judah felt at listening to this prophecy. Importantly, the story of Joshua once took place as a demonstration of God's power and intervention to save His people. A similar message is stressed by Zephaniah in his own time, for his contemporaries. But that of Zephaniah, ironically, and at first sight, will bring a terrible end to these people who worship false gods as well as to those who are arrogant. Yet, this judgment, in the prophecy of Zephaniah, anticipates the salvation that awaits the remnant (Zeph 3:14–20).

The theological significance of this verse includes the fact that on judgment day, no one will find shelter elsewhere, except in God. Those who seek protection and fortification in human shelter and lack confidence and trust in God (Zeph 1:12; 3:2), are deceiving themselves (Isa 2:15). Before God, there is no missile shield. There are no military jet fighters or defensive battle ships that can withstand the sovereignty of YHWH on His Day of Judgment and intervention.

However, a linguistic comparative and tabular presentation of the earlier discussed poetic characterization of the Day of YHWH (vv 15a–16c)

79   See Sweeney, *Zephaniah*, 101, where this observation is made in detail.
80   Vlaardingerbroek, *Zephaniah*, 110.

in the following passages is imperative. It will serve a few purposes. It serves to heighten the colorful, inspiring beauty of the prophecy of Zephaniah. It also demonstrates its universal relevance to all cultures. It underlines Zephaniah's poetic consistency with the styles of the prophetic traditions, discussed earlier in this Chapter.

A Poetic Characterization of the Day of YHWH in Different Languages (Zeph 1:15–16)

Efik	English	French	German	Greek	Hebrew	Italian	Latin
15a.Usen Ifuresit edi usen oro	A day of wrath is that day	Ce jour est un jour de courroux	Ein Tag des Zornes ist jener Tag	ἡμέρα ὀργῆς ἡ ἡμέρα ἐκείνη	יום עברה היום ההוא	Giorno di'ira quel giorno	Dies irae dies illa
b.Usen ukut ye nnaneyin	A day of distress and tribulation	Un jour de détresse et d'angoisse	Ein Tag der Bedrängnis und der Not	ἡμέρα θλίψεως καὶ ἀνάγκης	יום צרה ומצוקה	Giorno di angoscia e di afflizione	Dies tribulationis et angustiae
c.Usen Nwure ye nsobo	A day of ruin and devastation	Un jour de devastate on et de ravage	Ein Tag des Krachens und Dröhnens	ἡμέρα ἀωρίας καὶ ἀφανισμοῦ	יום שאה ומשואה	Giorno di rovina e di sterminio	Dies calamitatis et miseriae
d.Usen ekim ye okoneyo	A day of darkness and gloom	Un jour de de ténèbres et d'obscurité	Ein Tag voll Finsternis und Dunkel	ἡμέρα σκότους καὶ γνόφου	יום חשך ואפלה	Giorno di tenebre e di caligine	Dies tenebrarum et caliginis
e.Usen obubit enyong ye ata ekim	A day of black cloud and heavy cloud	Un jour de nuée et de brouillards	Ein Tag der Wolken und der Unwetter	ἡμέρα νεφέλης καὶ ὁμίχλης	יום ענן וערפל	Giorno di nubi e di oscurità	Dies nebulae et turbinis
16aUsen ukorowo ye mkpo ekong	A day of trumpet blast and battle cry	Un jour (où retentironti) le cor et la clameur	Ein Tag des Trompeten-geschmetters und des Kriegslärms	ἡμέρα σάλπιγγος καὶ κραυγῆς	יום שופר ותרועה	Giorno di squilli di tromba e d'allarme	Dies tubae et clangoris
b.Eke ewnanade Ye mme obio *oko* ibibene	Against fortified cities	Contre les villes fortes	Wider die festen Städte	ἐπὶ τὰς πόλεις τὰς ὀχυρὰς	על הערים הבצרות	Sulle fortezze	Super civitates munitas
c.Ye mme edikong tower	And against exalted towers	Et contre les tours élevées	Und wider die hochragenden Zinnen	καὶ ἐπὶ τὰς γωνίας τὰς ὑψηλάς	ועל הפנות גבהות	E sulle torri d'angolo	Et super angulos excelsos

2.4.4.4 Distress to the people (צרר לאדם, v 17)

Following this colorful and third person description of the Day of YHWH (vv 15–16), as well as the first person description of what YHWH will do to those who distrust Him, verse 17 proceeds to present the horrible things which await those who put their trust in fortified cities and defensive towers, instead of in YHWH.[81] Here, Zephaniah continues with his unique terminology. He uses the verb צרר (distress). This verb has been linguistically noticed by many commentators and exegetes to be *hiphil perfect* here, which could be translated as "harassing somebody, or throwing into panic, or squeezing a man into a tight corner."[82] YHWH judges the way he sees fit. He can bring distress (צרר) to those people who disobeyed Him (והצרתי לאדם).

Széles describes this verse in a very simple and down-to-earth manner. She believes that here the effortlessness or the helplessness of man is described. YHWH compresses man's chest so that he can no longer breathe. And where there is no breath, there is no life. In such a situation people would panic, and look for a way and means of escape. They are left useless and helpless to walk like blind people (והלכו כעורים).[83] In fact, verses 17–18 not only provide a detailed portrayal of the consequences of the Day of YHWH's wrath for those who have sinned against the Lord, but the statement of verse 17ab (I will bring distress to the people and they shall walk like the blind) demonstrates that the verse is to be read as a first person stament by YHWH similar to those found in Zephaniah 1:2–4, 8–9.[84]

---

81 Some scholars have argued that, it appears verse 17 was written to convey a statement by YHWH, based on the consistent identification of first person statements throughout the rest of Zephaniah as those by YHWH, whereas third person statements are either those of the prophet or the narrator of the of the book. See Sweeney, *Zephaniah*, 102 for these concerns.

82 Széles, *Mercy and Wrath*, 88; Vlaardingerbroek, *Zephaniah*, 111.

83 Széles, *Wrath and Mercy*, 88.

84 For further discussion on this see Irsigler, *Gottesgericht*, 429; Vlaardingerbroek, *Zephaniah*, 104; Ben Zvi, *Zephaniah*, 128–130; Roberts, *Zephaniah*, 183–185; Berlin *Zephaniah*, 90–91.

In other words, verse 17a is connected with verse 17b, to emphasize the effects of distrusting YHWH. A similar expression is also found in Deuteronomy 28:29, where people who walk about like the blind are found. Distressed people or people who are in panic do not know what to do. They walk around (הלך), drive or travel all over the place, blindly and in desperation without proper focus. But I believe it may also represent the ethical behavior of a person or group of persons who distrust the Lord.

Furthermore, the use of אדם (people) in this verse is also under contention, whether it means a single man, as an individual or "humanity" as an indication of the universal concerns of this text.[85] Some have chosen to be neutral as to whether אדם (people), in this passage implies that the judgment is limited to Judah and to Jerusalem, or that it concerns the whole world.[86] I consistently see an implication of universal judgment, including Judah and Jerusalem, in this passage which is not unconnected with verses 1–3, and with the overall book of the Prophet Zephaniah.[87]

Verse 17c (כי ליהוה חטאו), which is disputed as an addition, has already been discussed in the textual critical section of this study.[88] It is highly significant to the entire theology of Zephaniah that sin against YHWH is punishable, while the repentant shall be restored or redeemed. In fact, sin according to Arbuckle, "is a personal affront to Yahweh and not merely the transgression of an eternal order."[89]

---

85 See Sweeney, *Zephaniah*, 102 for these views.

86 See Vlaardingerbroek, *Zephaniah*, 111 for such neutrality.

87 Berlin in her *Zephaniah*, 90 affirms this reading when she wrote: "Hebrew ʾdm means "human beings" and is often used to distinguish humans from non-humans. Its usage is somewhat strange here. I see it as refocusing the picture on the human inhabitants after having focused on the cities and their architectural features. Many commentators see here a universal destruction (ʾdm = humankind), an interpretation supported by verse 18 "the entire earth" and by the universality of the destruction, in the beginning of the chapter, which I am in agreement with.

88 Robert, *Nahum, Habakkuk and Zephaniah*, 184–185 has vigorously argued against reading this text as a gloss, by stressing that the reason for this judgment on the Day of YHWH is because, the people have sinned against YHWH.

89 Arbuckle, "Zephaniah," 718.

Sweeney also suggests that verse 17c (כי ליהוה חטאו), points to the overall conceptualization of the Day of YHWH, as a day of sacrifice (v 7), since sacrifice in the Judaic religion facilitates maintenance of moral order in society.[90] Sinners were seen as disrupting the peace and order of the world, hence the need for sacrifice for purification.[91] This interpretation is opposed to that of Maria Széles, who rather interprets the situation of verse 17d–e, as referring to the slaughter we read in verse 7. According to her, "in this verse, it is Yahweh himself, who is speaking and who is conveying the judgment he intends to execute. This is then, "the day of the Lord's sacrifice," the time of slaughter, to which verse 7 had referred."[92]

Although Széles might have overstretched the meaning of verse 7, YHWH's Day of Judgment will be very serious, such that the situation of verse 17d–e will take place.[93] Here, in verse 17d–e we have the expression, ושפך דמם כעפר ולחמם כגללים (and their blood shall be spilled like dust, and their fat, like dung). This verse has some interpretative problems, some of which have already been discussed.

---

90 A similar argument is recently suggested by Rabbi Jack Bemporad in *The Inner Journey: Views from the Jewish Tradition* (ed. J. Bemporad, Sandpoint; ID: Morning Light Press, 2007), xxix. He stresses that "religious ritual was created to foster closeness with God. But ritual without ethics is fruitless and ultimately idolatrous, since unethical behavior avows subservience to self-centered desires."

91 See Sweeney, *Zephaniah*, 103, for details.

92 Széles, *Mercy and Wrath*, 88.

93 Vlaardingerbroek, in his *Zephaniah*, 83–84 makes an interesting observation here that verse 7 b is simply telling us what will happen on the Day of YHWH and why the Day of YHWH is near. The preparations for the זבח to be held have been made. Here, Vlaardingerbroek, says, we must not so much think of ambiguity in the sense that Judah might think they would sit as guest(s) at YHWH's banquet. But the context does not permit this idea. It is cultic language that is used here. But זֶבַח for him, can mean, "slaughter" (Isa 34:6; Jer 4:6, 10), just as in the Day of YHWH. But Ezekiel 39:17 is without any connotation and ambiguity (in connection with the English word "victim" like in a motor accident), is not ritualistic. That is to say the reference to the verb זבח can also mean ordinary non-ritual "slaughter." The reference made in verse 7a and the mention of "guest' refers to the victim and the festival meal. See also Arbuckle, "Zephaniah," 718.

But Sweeney thinks that the Hebrew Text of this verse (17d–e) contributes to this problem, due to its graphic display of the disembowelment of the victims of YHWH's judgment.[94] But according to Berlin, the expression, "splattered like dust," translated literally, "poured out," (read in my translation as "spilled"), is an unusual expression, since in normal circumstances blood would be poured out like water and not like dust. For example, we read in Psalm 79:3, "around Jerusalem they have shed blood like water, leaving no one to bury them."[95]

The strangeness of the translation of ושפך דמם כעפר as "and their blood shall be spilled like dust" is also picked up by Vlaardingerbroek. Having sampled opinions of scholars, Vlaardingerbroek wonders whether עפר (dust), really has to refer to something moist, in order to convey the meaning of the analogy of pouring it out like blood.[96] However, the idea, in my judgment, is that of carelessness or worthlessness of which the unrepented victims of the Day of YHWH are being handled. It is meant to challenge sinners to convert and to re-establish fellowship with the Lord. It has both physical and spiritual dimensions.

Verse 17e ולחמם כגללים (and their muscles, like dung), possesses further translational or hermeneutical difficulties.[97] The full meaning of the noun לחם, translated differently ("muscles," "flesh," "intestine"), is clouded in uncertainty (cf Job 20:23).[98] Whatever the full meaning of the noun, it seems to refer to the body tissue, parallel to the body fluid indicated by "blood."[99]

Similarly, the noun גלל (dung), presents translational difficulties for earlier translators, as reflected in different versions, discussed in the textual-critical section of this study. In spite of these grammatical diffi-

---

94   Sweeney, *Zephaniah*, 103.
95   For details of this brilliant observation, see Berlin, *Zephaniah*, 91.
96   See Vlaardingerbroek, *Zephaniah*, 112.
97   See Vlaardingerbroek, *Zephaniah* 113 for different scholarly interpretations, some of which are very insightful.
98   I translate it as "muscles" to underline nothingness of human strength, power (of all kinds), energy, and good health, without YHWH the sovereign of creation. This embraces also the significance of the sharing of the root meaning of the word with that of "food, eat, or fight." See also, Sweeney, *Zephaniah*, 103.
99   Berlin, *Zephaniah*, 91.

culties, the basic theological meaning of verse 17 is not far-fetched. It includes the fact that on the Day of YHWH, material goods shall be doomed to destruction. Those Judeans, who disobeyed YHWH and who rather trusted in their exalted towers (v 16c) and "muscles," (biological, economic, political and military v 17e), would become worthless, like dust and dung. The Day of YHWH would be devastating; money and material wealth shall not save the disobedient victims.

2.4.4.5 Additional Consequences of יום יהוה (v 18)

Zephaniah, in verse 18a–f continues the portrayal of the devastating effects of the Day of YHWH. It is here, that Sweeney also comes in with his suggestions. He points out at the initial גם (also) of verse 18, which is syntactically linked with the preceding verse 17.[100] In verse 18, it is not only the destruction and devastation of the idolatrous common citizens of Judah that is referred to, but their top politicians, their wealthy merchants and the aristocrats are also under judgment. The entire universe is also under judgment (v 18 f). Not even their silver and gold would be able to save them (18 a).

2.4.4.5.1 Worthlessness of כסף וזהב (v 18a)

The expression, גם־כספם גם־זהבם לא־יוכל להצילם (also their silver and gold shall not save them), is identically found in another prophetic text (Ezek 7:19). In fact, some believe the Prophet Ezekiel may have borrowed it from his predecessor Zephaniah.[101] Patterson summarizes the entire verse 18, as a reiteration of the two prominent themes of self-indulgent greed and godless wealth. For Patterson, it also portrays the judgment of all people and nations. He sees the former (v 18a), as signifying the wealthy who heaped up their riches at the expense of their fellow citizens, in pursuit of their selfish material gains. They would soon come to a horrific end, according to Patterson and no amount of

---

100 Sweeney, *Zephaniah*, 103–104. For comments on this see Irsigler, *Gottesgericht*, 417–430; Vlaardingerbroek, *Zephaniah*, 113.
101 Berlin, *Zephaniah*, 91.

silver and gold (כסף וזהב) could buy off the destructive nature of the Day of YHWH.[102]

Robert, reflecting on this very verse 18a, sees it as a situation against an enemy with very little human feeling and emotion, such that the hidden treasures of silver and gold would not buy safety for the conquered Judeans. It is not that the enemy is not interested in money (Isa 13:17), since they could plunder the Judean's wealth (Zeph 1:13). But, Robert's suggestion is that the enemies could take money, although they would not necessarily spare the lives of those who lead them to the location of the money.[103] From the point of view of Sweeney, verse 18a simply presents an imagery of wealth that had long appeared in Zephaniah 1:11, 13, including mention of those who dress up in foreign attire, and fill up the house of their masters with violence and deceit (Zeph 1:8–9).[104]

Then the themes of apostasy are highlighted and the abuse of wealth runs through the entire initial chapter of the Book of Zephaniah. Verse 18a simply points to the culmination of a scenario whereby those collaborators with the Assyrian colonial masters who borrow their attire (culture, economic or political gains and assimilation), would be brought to judgment, on the Day of YHWH. Therefore, for Sweeney, verse 18a focuses on the wealth and riches of those collaborators with their foreign oppressors. They would become the targets of YHWH's punishment and wrath, on His Day.[105]

Nevertheless, I find Vlaardingerbroek's contribution with regard to verse 18a much more comprehensive. He does not just stop at capturing and plundering, as suggested by Robert. Nor does it focus only on the rich collaborators with the Assyrian and foreign cultures.

---

102 Patterson, *Nahum, Habakkuk, Zephaniah*, 325.
103 Robert, *Nahum, Habakkuk and Zephaniah*, 185.
104 For more insights into the reading of those "who dress up in foreign attire," and "leap over the threshold" (Zeph 1:8–9) see, Arbuckle, "Zephaniah," 719. Here, foreign attire refers to as idolatrous customs. While leaping over the threshold could refer to either of the following: (1) to a pagan superstition (2) to rapacious coutiers hastening to cross the threshold of the King's palace (3) to those who are nearest the king's throne, and who are condemned for the injustice of their administration and (4) to those who make arrogant entry into the Temple.
105 Sweeney, *Zephaniah*, 104.

The comment of verse 18a, גם־כספם גם־זהבם לא־יוכל להצילם
(also their silver and gold shall not save them), has a general thrust,
according to him. It affects both the rich and the poor. No disobedient
person shall escape the imminent judgment and accountability, on the
Day of YHWH's Wrath.[106] This brings us to verse 18b.

2.4.4.5.2 Day of YHWH's Wrath (ביום עברת יהוה, v 18b)

Zephaniah, in verse 18b, no doubts recalls, "יום עברה היום ההוא (a
day of wrath is that day)," earlier preached in verse 15a. Similar expressions are found in the Book of Lamentation 1:12 and 2:22. Here it
reads, "ביום חרון אפו (on the day of his wrath)," and "בום אף־יהוה (on
the day of the wrath of the YHWH),' underlining the centrality of the
judgment of YHWH, earlier taken for granted. These, we have already
discussed, but Vlaardingerbroek at this point, reiterates and draws our
attention once again, to the fact that prior to Amos 5:18, the Day of
YHWH was seen positively as a day of vengeance and salvation. It was
seen positively as a day that YHWH had fought battles for His special
people. It was a day that YHWH directed His divine wrath against
Israel's enemies (Isa 34:8; 61:2; Jer 46:10). But, the darkness introduced by Amos has continued to be reintepreted by generations after
him, including Zephaniah. Amos' notion of "darkness" is Zephaniah's
notion of universal "wrath," upon the entire land.[107]

2.4.4.5.3 Universal Consumption (תאכל כל הארץ vv18c–f)

As earlier indicated in the critical section of this study, there are scholars who feel that this expression "by the fire of the passion, all the earth
shall be consumed" (ובאש קנאתו תאכל כל הארץ) in verse 8c–f is an
addition, probably brought in from Zephaniah 3:8. Wilhelm Rudolph
also believes that verse 18c–f is a gloss, from the Babylonian exile redactor, on the grounds that they imply no other thing, but a total
destruction of the land and the inhabitants. For him, this contradicts
the earlier verses in the compositional unit, which suggests that only a

106 Vlaardingerbroek, *Zephaniah*, 112.
107 Vlaardingerbroek, *Zephaniah*, 113.

few groups would be punished. Rudolph refers to those who worship Baal and swear falsely to strange gods (vv 4–5), who turn their back on the Lord, (vv 6, 12). He is refers to the disobedient people, who have no trust in the Lord. He also thought that judgment was meant for the political officers in Judah (vv 8–9), as well as for the wealthy and for corrupt tradesmen (vv 10–11).[108]

Robert on the other hand, argues that if Rudolph's arguments are to hold or if these verses had existed independently of the present compositional unit, then the universal judgment found in 1:2–3 is wanting. For Robert, it is only Zephaniah's reworking of 1:14–18, into the larger compositional unit that has focused on the judgment on Judah and Jerusalem. These traces of that original universal outlook, he argues, now function to underscore how thoroughgoing the judgment would be.[109]

However, I agree with Sweeney and others that the messages of punishment in the theology of Zephaniah are not restricted to an individual, Judah or Jerusalem, but have as well universal implications, that run through the entire text of Zephaniah.[110] The language of verse 18 reflects the unity of the theme and literary structure of Zephaniah. It reiterates the warning that YHWH is the sovereign of all nations, peoples and creation and cultures (Zeph 1:2–3). YHWH will judge and bring to a terrible end those who break the covenant and disobeyed the call to obedience and to the worship of YHWH alone. It also implies that since YHWH created peoples of all times and cultures, YHWH has the power to punish, destroy, and also to restore the repentant (2:1–3).

In fact, at no time shall YHWH completely give up His mercy. He will restore the fortune of His people (3:14–20). This last point which also foreshadows the more explicit teaching of the NT (Mtt 5:3; 5; 11:5; Luke 1:52–53; 4:18 and 6:20), shall be discussed in detail in Chapter Three.

108 Wilhelm Rudolph, *Micha – Nahum – Habakuk – Zephanja* (KAT 13/3; Gütersloh: Gütersloher Verlagshaus Gerd Mohn, 1975), 270.
109 Robert, *Nahum, Habakkuk and Zephaniah*, 185.
110 Patterson, *Nahum, Habakkuk, Zephaniah*, 325; Sweeney, *Zephaniah*, 104–105.

2.5 A Summary Reflection on Chapter Two

Our attention in this chapter focused on an exegetical study of the unit of Zephaniah 1:14–18. This is a unit (1:14–18) widely considered by scholars to contain the *ipsissima verba,* of Zephaniah, on יום יהוה (the Day of YHWH). It is a day of judgment, wrath, punishment and call for repentance, of the arrogant, idolaters and of those who distrust the Lord.

While examining the structure of this short text, it is evident that there have been as many structures as there are Zephaniah's scholars. This does not, of course, diminish the relevance of the traditional tri-partite structure, of threats to Judah (1:2–2:3), threats to nations (2:4–3:8), salvation and divine promises (3:9–20). Based on the focus of this work, on the unity and theological reading of Zephaniah, with the obvious common themes of "the Day of YHWH," universal judgment (1:2–2:15), and hope of a reversal of fortunes (3:1–20), this study proposed broadly two major divisions with five sub units each. The literary unit of 1:14–18, located within the first major literary block and solidly connected to the text that comes before and with that which follows, helps demonstrate the centrality of the message of Zephaniah.

In Zephaniah 1:14–18, based on his knowledge of earlier traditions, this late pre-exilic prophet preached and amplified creatively the significances and consequences of the Day of YHWH, with particular and universal implication. Zephaniah saw himself as YHWH's instrument. He understood YHWH, as the God who participates in human history. The exegesis of Zephaniah 1:14–18 brings out Zephaniah as the Prophets who sees the Day of YHWH as the Day when YHWH would intervene in human activities. It is a Day of YHWH's intervention and sovereignty. There would be judgment upon nations, Judah and Jerusalem due to their sins of idolatry, syncretism and due to the pride of self-sufficiency of their rulers and their disobedience to YHWH (1:2–2:3).

Zephaniah not only relates his preaching to the entire OT and to the other books of the Twelve Minor Prophets, but also to the overall texts of Zephaniah 1–3. This is made clear in several nouns, verbs and concepts borrowed and shared by Zephaniah with these other texts. Earlier motifs, heard in verses 2–3 (universal creation, human and animal), and in verses 4–6 (Judah and wealthy class) and particularly in verses 7–13 (the day of sacrifice in v 7), are found reflected in the rhetorical unit of 1:14–18. This unit, which is Zephaniah's hymnal and poetic-alliterative style of preaching the arrival of the Day of YHWH, not only contrast him with Amos, Joel and other prophets, but highlights the uniqueness and modification of his pattern of language, as expressed in the earlier discussed pair of nominal sentences (vv 15–16).

It was underlined that the "day" in Amos 5:18, was a day of darkness, but Zephaniah nuanced it as a day of wrath. Zephaniah 1:14–18, as we saw is closely paralleled to Joel 2. Details and specifics of Zephaniah's relationship to other OT texts and to the prophetic literature, in terms of language, theological themes, to name but a few, are well spelt out in a summary form in Chapter Five of this work.

Although a further comparative analysis of Zephaniah's Day of YHWH with other OT texts will be discussed as this study progresses, it is imperative to underline the lessons learnt from the prophecy of Zephaniah1:14–18. These lessons include the fact that YHWH intervenes in human activities, in various ways (1:7). YHWH is the Sovereign of creation, of animal and human (vv 2–3). YHWH judges and punishes (vv 8–13). His judgment is swift (v 14) and devastating (v 15). It penetrates barriers and fortification of all kinds of towers (v 16) and renders non-repented people worthless (v 17). YHWH's judgment reaches to the ends of the earth. It affects the poor, as well as the rich (v 18; 2:4–15), regardless of culture and background. As for those who seek the Lord (2:1–3), there is always a hope, a light at the end of the tunnel, a restoration of fortunes and a joy of salvation (Zeph 3:1–20).

Chapter Three

The Restoration of Fortunes (בְּשׁוּב אֶת־שְׁבוּת) and the Joy of Salvation in Zephaniah 3:14–20

In the previous Chapter we attempted a presentation of an overview of the general structure of Zephaniah. We also engaged in a detailed exegetical analysis of the literary unit of 1:14–18, the *ipsissima verba,* of Zephaniah, on יוֹם יהוה (the Day of YHWH). In this Chapter, we shall discuss the theology of the restoration of fortunes (3:14–20).

I will translate, delimit and make an exegesis of Zephaniah 1:14–18, within the overall context of the three chapters of the book of Zephaniah. The poetic and literary features that characterize the texts will be discussed. All these will serve to illumine the theological themes of hope, restoration and reassurances of God's mercy and love, which run through the unit of Zephaniah 3:14–20.

Moreover, it will demonstrate that the motif of the judgment on the Day of YHWH, in 1:14–18, is not disconnected from the rest of the prophetic literature, particularly the Twelve and most especially the preceding texts (1:1–13) and the following texts (2:1–15; 3:1–20), of the Prophet Zephaniah. This Chapter aims at affirming that the wrath, the judgment and the devastation heard in Zephaniah 1:14–18, are reversible to the joy and the salvation in Zephaniah 3:14–20. The meaning and significance of the restoration of fortunes (בְּשׁוּב אֶת־שְׁבוּת, v 20), will be thoroughly discussed.

We shall also demonstrate how the bitter cry, anguish and distress of Zephaniah 1:14–18 would have been reversed by the joyful cheers and salvific song of the restoration of fortunes by YHWH (3:14–20). This will strongly suggest the fact that human persons can face anything, as long as they know or believe it will not last forever, and hope that something better will happen and their fortunes be restored by a merciful and loving God.

3.1 An Exegetical Study of Zephaniah 3:14–20

The literary composition and function of this unit have been inten-sively debated. There are some who believe that this closing unit of Zephaniah, which contains instruction concerning the Day of YHWH, is a late redaction. For them it is a post-exilic redaction because it con-tains the story of the universal restoration and the destruction of Babylon, a call to rejoice at the return of the exiled. In their opinion, a pre-exilic or an exilic text would not narrate a post-exilic condition of the remnant and their return from captivity.[1]

But Sweeney argues that these features are not enough to draw a conclusion, that Zephaniah 3:14–20 is post-exilic. Scholars, he cau-tions, must not limit exile only to that of the Babylonian. Ancient Israel and Judah were also confronted with the hard reality of the Assyrian hegemony and imperialism. The point of restoration of Jerusa-lem and the remnants must be considered in relation to King Josiah's reforms, when the opportunity for such restoration seems to have ar-rived. This, for Sweeney, is the present socio-historical *Sitz-im-Leben*, within which this text functions as an exhortation and promising ma-terial for such a restoration.[2]

In his canonical debate on the shape of Zephaniah, Childs seems at the end of his argument to have arrived at a similar conclusion as Sweeney's. Childs rightly insists that "there are several indications, that the materials comprising the book have undergone a period of devel-opment before reaching its final form."[3] For him, the entire text of Zephaniah, progresses compositionally from the original forms of threat (3:1–8) oracles against foreign nations (2:4–15), to the promise of a restoration of the faithful remnants (3:9–13).

---

1   See Nogalski, *Literary Precursors,* 201–204 for detail lists of some of the scholars who hold onto these views. As we noted in the earlier chapter, even Ben Zvi, in his *Book of Zephaniah,* 348–358 believes that the entire fifty three verses of Zephaniah, are post-exilic or post-monarchical materials.
2   Sweeney, *Zephaniah,* 196–97.
3   Childs, *Introduction to the OT,* 459.

Besides this traditional arrangement of threat before promise, there are other indications of editorial activity in the text, which argue against disjointed reading of the text of Zephaniah 3:9–20, as merely post-exilic.[4] For Childs, different stages of the book bear the stamps of both pre-exilic and post-exilic redactions. What is important is its theological theme, and the line between the historical and eschatological reading of the Day of YHWH, in Zephaniah, which is a fine one to walk, as previously remarked

This is true because, once the message focuses on the eschatological intervention of God on His Day of reckoning; it belongs to the logic of prophetic theology to include within this event, both the judgment against Israel and the nations. And if one begins with a theology of God in terms of his eschatological work, the move to include the oracles of promise as an essential part of the selfsame event follows easily.[5] The point I want to make is that even though the text may have undergone several redactional processes in history, there is no contradiction in the unity and eschatological message of the Day of YHWH, which runs through Zephaniah and the *Dodekapropheton*. This theme of the Day of YHWH, includes a word of judgment (1–2), and the promise of the restoration of fortunes directed against Israel and the nations (3:1–20). In fact, the following translation, textual, structural and exegetical analysis will help shed more light, on the restorative and salvific significance of the unit of Zephaniah 3:14–20.

3.1.1 Translation and Textual Critical Study of Zephaniah 3:14–20

In Zephaniah 3:9–13 YHWH reassures Israel thus; "I will make the peoples… the remnant of Israel shall do no wrong…" This is followed by the materials of Zephaniah 14a–17d, which serve as the prophet's response to this divine reassurance, heard in the immediately preceding verses (3:9–13). This is followed by YHWH's power to provoke a

---

4   See Childs, *Introduction to the OT*, 459 for a detailed exposition of his canonical debate on the formation of the the text of Zephaniah.
5   Childs, *Introduction to the OT*, 460.

positive and joyous response, when the people's fortunes would be restored (vv 18a–20f). The full text of this unit is as follows:

רני בת־ציון	14a. Shout for joy O daughter of Zion
הריעו ישראל	14b. Cry aloud O Israel
שמחי ועלזי בכל־לב בת ירושלם	14b. Rejoice; exult with all your hearts, O Daughter of Zion
הסיר יהוה משפטיך	15a. The Lord has annulled your judgment
פנה איבך	15b. He has turned away your enemy
מלך ישראל יהוה בקרבך	15c. King of Israel is the Lord among you!
לא־תיראי רע עוד	15d. You have nothing to fear anymore
ביום ההוא יאמר לירושלם	16a. On that day, this shall be said to Jerusalem
אל־תיראי ציון	16b. Do not be afraid, O Zion!
אל־ירפו ידיך	16c. Let not your hand fall limp/relax
יהוה אלהיך בקרבך	17a. The Lord your God is in your midst
גבור יושיע	17b. The warrior, a savior
ישיש עליך בשמחה	17c. He will rejoice over you with happy song
יחריש באהבתו	17d. He will renew you by his love
יגיל עליך ברנה	17e. He will dance with shouts of joy for you
נוגי ממועד	18a. As in those days of festivals
אספתי ממך היו	18b. I will take away from you, there are
משאת עליה חרפה	18c. Woe, over which you endured mockery
הנני עשה את־כל־מעניך בעת ההיא	19a. At that time, I will make end of all who afflicted you
והושעתי את־הצלעה והנדחה אקבץ	19b. I will rescue the lame sheep, and gather the strayed
ושמתים לתהלה ולשם	19c. I will exchange, rather, for fame and renown
בכל־הארץ בשתם	19d. With their shame, in all the earth
בעת ההיא אביא אתכם	20a. At that time I will bring you [home]
ובעת קבצי אתכם	20b. And at that time, I will gather you
כי־אתן אתכם לשם	20c. For I will make your name known
ולתהלה בכל עמי הארץ	20d. I will make you famous among all peoples of the earth
בשובי את־שבותיכם לעיניכם	20e. When I will restore your fortunes before their eyes
אמר יהוה	20f. Says the Lord

As in the preceding unit of 1:14–18, a pause for important critical remarks on the above unit of summons for jubilation and restoration

154

of fortunes is imperative. Such remarks, among other things, will help reconcile versions, textual, translational and linguistic problems. It shall further assist in highlighting the possible clearest meaning and significance of this prophetic text of hope, mercy and the glory of the Lord. For instance, verses 14–15 contain four imperatives, namely, רני (shout for joy), ריע (cry aloud), שׂמחי (rejoice), and ועלזי (and exult). These imperatives, which summon the people to rejoice, with reasons, have some textual problems. The MT in verse 14a attests, רני בת־ציון (shout for joy O daughter of Zion).

But Sweeney rightly observes that in the *Targum*, כנשתא דציאן ("O Synagogue of Zion") is rather attested. In the LXX, we have χαῖρε σφοδρα, θύγατερ Σιων (rejoice exceedingly, O daughter of Zion).[6] While Jerome, in the *Vulgate* translates it as "*lauda filia Sion iubilate Israhel*," very close to the MT.

Interestingly, הריעו ישׂראל (Cry aloud O Israel), verse in 14b, attested in MT, is rather translated as Ιερουσαλημ in the LXX, which I believe points to Zion as the dwelling place of YHWH. Similar expressions are found in many other places in the Hebrew Bible, which will be further discussed in the exegetical unit.

Furthermore, verse 15 poses some interpretative problems for commentators and witnesses. For example, the sentence הסיר יהוה משׁפטיך (the Lord has annulled your judgment), in verse 15a is translated in the LXX as "περεῖλεν κύριος τὰ ἀδικήματα σου" (the Lord has cast away your crime/wrong doing). Similar to the attestation of the MT, the *Vulgate* attests, *abstulit Dominus iudicium tuum* (the Lord has annulled your judgment).

Evidently, and from the textual apparatus in the MT, the problem has to do with the noun masculine plural construct, מִשְׁפָּטַיִך (your judgment). Some commentators believe this is not a very good parallel to איבך (your enemy). They argue that since the parallelism of the passage demands a word for a person to balance the noun "enemy," one should rather read "your judges or rulers (מִשְׁפְּטַיִך).[7]

6   Sweeney, *Zephaniah*, 193.
7   See Patterson, *Nahum, Habakkuk, Zephaniah*, 381.

In other words, the reading of the MT apparatus, namely, מִשְׁפָּטֶיךְ, (your opponents), is a vocalization which is believed by some to have been suggested by Wellhausen, on the basis of the text of Job 9:15, or of Psalm 109 (לְמִשְׁפָּטִי = with my judge).[8] As a result of this problematic plural noun construct "your judgment of," some have appealed to the alternative readings in the LXX, *Peshitta* and *Targum*.[9] The *Targum* for instance attests, "false judges" (דַּיָּנֵי שִׁקְרָא). With the appeal to these other manuscripts, the MT apparatus indicates that some Mss, LXX, *Peshitta*, and *Targum* would like it read in the plural. That is, the plural אֹיְבָיִךְ could be read in place of the singular אֹיְבֵךְ.[10]

Additionally, in verse 15c, we read: מֶלֶךְ יִשְׂרָאֵל יהוה בְּקִרְבֵּךְ (the King of Israel is the Lord among you). Based on the LXX tradition (βασιλεύσει), and with reference to Micah 4:7 (וּמָלַךְ יהוה = and the Lord will reign), the MT apparatus suggests an alternate reading, יִמְלֹךְ (will reign), in place of מֶלֶךְ יִשְׂרָאֵל (the King of Israel).[11] With regard to the expression, לֹא־תִירְאִי רַע עוֹד (you have nothing to fear anymore), in 15d, the LXX translated it as, οὐκ ὄψῃ κακὰ οὐκέτι (you shall no longer see evil).

Here, the LXX uses second person singular, future indicative middle of ὁράω, "to see," in place of the MT ירא (to fear). The Peshitta's translation is similar to that of the LXX, "you will not see evil again." The *Vulgate* translation, *"non timebis malum ultra,"* is close to MT. Despite these diverse attestations, the basic meaning, in my own opinion, does not change, since "to see evil no more," could mean "to no more experience evil." Just as, the English, expression, "I am hungry," is trans-

---

8 See the comments in Vlaardingerbroek, *Zephaniah*, 207.

9 For further analytical insight, see Ben Zvi, *Book of Zephaniah*, 240.

10 See Vlaardingerbroek, *Zephaniah*, 207 for further comments.

11 Vlaardingerbroek, *Zephaniah*, 207 makes an interesting comment here that the alternative readings "YHWH is King," and "the King of Israel," might not have been only a gloss on "the king of Israel, but also an attempt to avoid the misunderstanding that there was a mention of the Davidic ruler here. Nevertheless, it should not be horribly strange that just as a number of texts, including the LXX, and the *Peshitta*, do have "Israel," in a situation where a promise of restoration, under the kingship of YHWH, and Israel, the bearer of the covenant and the promise, should not be mentioned. It should not really be strange.

lated into Italian with the same basic meaning as, *"ho fame,"* (literary, "I have hunger,").

Verses 16–17 with its optimistic tone, has few textual problems or adjustments. Vlaardingerbroek suggests that the phrase in 16a, ביום ההוא (on that day), need not point to the return to a point of view, in one's own time, although a promise of deliverance cannot ignore the misery from which it promises deliverance.[12] The remaining sentence in verse 16a, as attested in MT, reads; "this shall be said to Jerusalem" the LXX attests, "the Lord shall say to Jerusalem," (ἐρεῖ κύριος τῇ Ἰερουσαλημ). But the Vulgate's *"in die illa dicetur Hierusalem"* keeps close to the MT.

The role of the expression in verse 17a–b, יהוה אלהיך בקרבך גבור יושיע (the Lord your God is in your midst, the warrior, a savior), is similar to the role of the expression in verse 15c, "the King of Israel is the Lord among you/in your midst." But the noticeable difference here is, that גבור יושיע (warrior/savior, v 17b), stands instead of, מלך ישראל (the king of Israel, v 15c). Moreover, the MT has a disjunctive accent between בקרבך (in your midst) and גבור יושיע (a warrior, savior).[13]

Verse 17d, in my translation, "יחריש באהבתו (He will renew over you with his love), has for a very long time been very problematic, as indicated in the MT textual apparatus. Literally, the attestation in MT reads, "he will plough/silence you with his love." But the LXX and *Peshitta* read it as, καὶ καινιεῖ σε ἐν τῇ ἀγαπήσει αὐτου (he will renew you with his love). The *Vulgate* supports the MT as usual and reads *silebit* (חריש) *in delectione tua* (silence over your wrong doing). The main problem is in the reading of the word, יחריש (plough/silence), which is rather read as יחדיש (new or renew) in LXX and *Peshitta*. What a difference, replacing of "*Resh-* ר with *Daleth-* ד could make! The *Targum* and *Vulgate* interpret יחריש, as referring to YHWH's "silence" or forgiveness of the sins of the people.

Although a further analysis of this will be made in the exegetical section, as the work progresses, the basic meaning of the text, (silence, renew with love or plough), suggests divine judgment and the mercy of

---

12 Vlaardingerbroek, *Zephaniah*, 210.
13 See Ben Zvi, *Book of Zephaniah*, 247.

YHWH, upon those who repent and turn back to Him. It demonstrates the ability of YHWH, to restore and protect His people, to whom He is always present in their midst (v 17a).

Again verse 18 seems to have created some hermeneutical difficulties for ancient versions, including the LXX, the *Vulgate*, the *Targum* and the *Peshitta*. All of them seem to translate this verse differently, or with slight omissions and additions, from the MT. The latter literally has "those who were grieved from the appointed time, I have gathered upon you to overcome your burden." This is where we meet the *lectio difficillior* in the MT.

Interestingly, the LXX and the *Targum* translate it, follow or add to verse 17e, "ὡς ἐν ἡμέρᾳ ἑορτῆς (as in the day of festivals), then continues in verse 18, "καὶ συνάξω τοὺς συντετριμμένους οὐαί, τίς ἔλαβεν ἐπ᾽ αὐτὴν ὀνειδισμόν (I will gather those who are broken into pieces, and your woes upon reproach I will take). The Vulgate reads, *nugas qui a lege recesserant congregabo quia ex te erant, ut non ultra habeas super eis opprobrium.*[14] However, based on the context of this unit, namely YHWH's restoration of the fortunes of his people, the basic meaning of the verse is that YHWH's restoring the fame and the dignity of his covenanted people, Israel and anyone who trusts in him.[15]

---

14 See Vlaardingerbroek, *Zephaniah*, 211 for further comments on this translation of Jerome.

15 See also Ben Zvi, *Book of Zephaniah*, 253–54, who from my judgment, offers interesting suggestions that since it is hard to come to a consensus as to the interpretation of the text, especially of those ancient versions, a possible reading of Zephaniah 18, may be based on the following: (1) נוגי is a *niphal* participle from יגה, which could be translated as, "those who grieved, who are afflicted" (Lam 1:4); (2) מועד may mean "festival" (Lam 1:4); (3) therefore, the combination of נוגי מועד, may mean, "those who are afflicted because they are deprived of the festivals." (4) אספתי, may mean "I (YHWH) have gathered" (Ezek 11:17); (5) ממך היו, may mean, "they were from you." (6) משאת, could mean "sign or signal"(Jer 6:1); (7) עליה, could be referring to "upon Jerusalem" (Cant 1:2); (8) חרפה, could also mean "a reproach, a mockery" (Ezek 22:4). Ben Zvi, concludes that, "the entire verse may be understood as saying: "those who are afflicted because they are deprived of the festivals, I (YHWH) have gathered, they were from you, (they were) a sign on her, (they were) a (source of) mockery."

In verse 19a, the MT attests, הנני עשׂה את־כל־מעהיך בעת ההיא (At that time,/behold I will make an end of all who afflicted you). The *LXX* reads ἰδοὺ ἐγὼ ποιῶ ἐν σοὶ ἕνεκεν σοῦ τῷ καιρῷ ἐκείνῳ λέγει κύριος (behold, I am working/making in you for your sake in that time, says the Lord). The Vulgate reads, *ecce ego interficiam omnes qui adflixerunt te in tempore illo* (behold I am interfering or doing away with all those who afflict you at that time), which is very close to the MT and *Targum*. It is suggested that perhaps the כלה (an end) should have been inserted after "to make" (עשׂה).

However, the dilemma is whether one should rather take the reading, כלה את in place of את־כל. It is clear in the above variant translations that the LXX seems to have read, אתך למעניך (in you/ for your sake), instead of את־כל־מעניך (all who afflict you). This basic sense of YHWH, defending and restoring the fortunes of his people, evident in the MT versions runs through all the variant translations.

Again in verse 19d, the MT attests, בכל־הארץ בשׁתם (with their shame, in all the earth), which when read together with the preceding verse 19c would be " I will make into fame and renown all those whose shame is in the land, or those who have been made to experience shame in the land." Even, the MT went as far as contemplating whether, בשׁתם (their shame), is a mistaken scribal gloss of בשׁובי את־שׁבותיכם (restoring their fortunes) in verse 20e.

However, the fundamental meaning and the overall demonstration of YHWH's sovereignty over His creation everywhere, and restoring their fortunes runs through this verse. This is to say that verse 20, plays an important function in the literary context of the entire unit. Many ancient versions (LXX, *Vulgate, Targum* and *Peshitta*) confirm and translate the MT's בכל־הארץ as, ἐν πάσῃ τῇ γῇ (in all the earth); *in omni terra* (in all the earth/land), respectively.

In other words, in verse 20e, we encounter an expression which this study considers important, and its detailed critical-analysis long overdue; בשׁובי את־שׁבותיכם לעיניכם (when I will restore your fortunes before their eyes). The LXX translates the, MT's בשׁובי את־שׁבותיכם, as, ἐν τῷ ἐπιστρέφειν με τὴν αἰμαλωσίαν ὑμῶν (in my turning or returning our host of captivity), using the infinitive presence of ἐπιστρέφω (to turn).

Similarly the *Vulgate* attests, *cum convertero captivitatem vestram co-ram occulis vestris, dicit Dominus* (when I restore or convert your fortunes in the presence of all their eyes, says the Lord). Additionally, the MT apparatus indicates an alternative vocalization of שְׁבוּתֵיכֶם as שְׁבוּתֵיכֶם, which Vlaardingerbroek's studies have observed, to be unnecessary.[16] Although the full literary contextual and exegetical study and significance of שׁוּב/*šûb* שְׁבוּת/*š^ebût*, or שׁבית *(qere)* and שְׁבוּת *(ketiv)* in Zephaniah (2:7; 3:20), will be investigated in the appropriate unit, a few observations are imperative here. It is generally agreed that the above expression, has been extensively studied by scholars.[17]

Besides, it is known to be frequently used in the Hebrew Bible.[18] Ben Zvi notices that the pairs of *qere-ketiv (yod vs. waw)* are relatively common, and some suggest that they are traceable to the Herodian era. The LXX and other ancient versions render the pairs as captivity or exile (Zeph 2:7; 3:20e). He also notices that traditional interpreters like Ibn Ezra, Radak, Abrabanel and Calvin interpreted it with particular reference to "coming back" from the Babylonian exile. But they did not deduce from their interpretation, a post-exilic text. According to

16   For further comments on this, see Vlaardingerbroek, *Zephaniah*, 219.

17   Some of these studies include; E. Preuschen, "Die Bedeutung von שׁבות שׁוב im Alten Testament," *ZAW* 15 (1895): 1–74; W. L. Dietrich, *שׁוב שׁבות*, *Die Endzeitliche Wiederherstellung bei den Propheten*, (BZAW 40; 1925); E. Baumann, "שׁבות שׁוב, eine exegetische Untersunchung," *ZAW* 47 (1929): 17–44; Riekele Borger, "שׁוב שׁבו/ית" *ZAW* 66 (1954): 315–16; William L. Holladay, *The Root Šûbh in the Old Testament: With Particular References to Its Usages in Covenantal Contexts* (Leiden: E. J. Brill, 1958); John M. Bracke, "šûb š^ebût: A Reappraisal," *ZAW* 97 (1985): 233–244 and J. A. Soggin, "שׁוב Šûb, to return," in *TLOT* 3:1312–1317.

18   Vlaardingerbroek, *Zephaniah,* 134–135; list the following frequency of occurrences of שׁבית and שְׁבוּת (to include: שׁבית (Num 21:29; Ezek 16:53, twice); שְׁבוּת: Deut 30:3; Jer 30:3, 18; 31:23; 32:44; 33:7, 11; 48:47; Ezek 29:14; Hos 6:11; Amos 9:14; Zeph 3:20; Ps 14:7; 53:7. The *Ketiv* שׁבית, *Qere* שְׁבוּת: Jer 29:14; 49:39; Ezek 16:53 (3×); 39:25; Job 42:10; Lam *Ketiv* שְׁבוּת, *Qere* שׁבית: Zeph 2:7; Ps 85:2 and Ps 126:4. However, Vlaardingerbroek suggests that though the interchangeable reading of Ketiv and *Qere* or *Qere* and *Ketiv* in the MT is not quite clear, he believes that the meanings of both are synonymous.

them, for a prophecy to be fulfilled even in the Babylonian exile was congruent with a dating in the days of Josiah and Zephaniah's authorship.[19]

However, a detailed discussion of modern approaches to the pairs as captivity and as signification of restoration of fortunes, whose fundamental characteristics include YHWH's reversal of the judgment, or the fortunes of his people, will be carried out in the exegetical section of this unit (3:14–20).

But an identification of the literary unit and delimitation of Zephaniah 3:14–20 will not only facilitate the exegesis that follows, but also will highlight the relationship of the unit with the texts that precede and follow, as well as help to highlight the relationship of the entire Book of Zephaniah with the rest of the Twelve Minor Prophets.

3.1.2 Literary Structure and Delimitation of Zephaniah 3:14–20

Zephaniah 3:14–20 is hugely an essential part of the theme or the theology of the Day of YHWH, which dominates the entire three chapters. Whether seen from the point of view of the familiar tri-partite eschatological divisions of judgment/threats against Judah and Jerusalem (1:2–2:3), threats against nations (2:4–3:8) and divine promises (3:9–20), or from the two macro-structures, with five sub-units each, adopted by this study, our sub-literary unit (3:14–20), is located within the major section of joy, salvation and restoration or reversal of fortunes (3:1–20). In fact, the disagreement among scholars on the macro-structure of the Book of Zephaniah is perceived or carried over into the micro-structure of the contextual units of Zephaniah.

For example, Széles in 1987 classified Zephaniah 3:9–20, as prophecies of universal salvation, which was anticipated by the threat and judgment heard in Zephaniah 2:4–3:8. But she went on to split the pericope of Zephaniah 3:9–20, into the Lord's promise (vv 9–13), Zion's joy of having the Lord in their midst (vv 14–17), and the realization of

---

19   Ben Zvi, *Book of Zephaniah*, 161.

the day of grace (vv 18–20). Among her reasons and observations for giving this unit a unique literary integrity she includes the fact that this unit noticeably, is a handiwork of a late redactor.

The unit has the features or the characteristics of exilic and a post-exilic eschatology. In this unit, YHWH anthropomorphically, is a Judge, Army Commander, Bridegroom and Shepherd (vv 15, 17 and 19). The hymnic joy of verse 14 is repeated in verse 17. Verse 18 seems to be corrupted, though the sub-unit of 18–20 expresses the theme of the Day of grace.[20]

Széles was followed by James Nogalski, in the debate on the literary structure and context of 3:14–20. He sees Zephaniah 3:14–17, as being proximately preceded by 3:9–13. Verse 9f asserts that the utterly destructive judgment on the nations proclaimed in 3:8 is indeed not the end, but a judgment of purification.[21] This positive qualification continues down to verse 17. Zephaniah 3:11–13 contains an address by YHWH to Jerusalem, concerning the purification of Zion. In verse 11, YHWH will remove the proud and the arrogant. He will leave within them a poor and humble remnant (v 12). This remnant shall do no wrong (v 13). According to Nogalski verses 11–13 re-echo the preceding verse 9.[22]

The function of 3:14–17, Nogalski interestingly notes, is to serve as a prophetic response to the divine pronouncement in the preceding verses 9–13. Nogalski notices a chiastic thematic structure in verses 14–17. Following the translation arrangement presented in this study, the joy of the daughter of Zion as a result of YHWH's annulment of their judgment (14a–15a), parallels the joy of YHWH over Israel (v 17c). The presence of YHWH in their midst (v 15c) parallels the Warrior and Savior (v 17b). Finally, the call not to fear (v 15d) chiastically parallels Zion's admonition not to fear (v 16b).[23]

On the other hand, the sub-unit of 3:18–20, presupposes YHWH as a speaker. Verse 18a and 19a are integrally related, since YHWH

---

20   See Széles, *Wrath and Mercy*, 106–113.
21   Nogalski, *Literary Precursors*, 202.
22   Nogalski, *Literary Precursors*, 203.
23   See Nogalski, *Literary Precursors*, 203 for his unique chiastic presentation.

speaks and addresses a devastated community of Zion (vv 14a–b; 16b). Zephaniah 3:19b is closely linked with 19a and should be regarded as part of the same speech, even though there is no direct mention of Zion. As noticed earlier, verse 18bc is problematic with its change of address and treatment of Zion in the third person, unlike the preceding second person's address (v 18a), and YHWH's promise of restoration to the people (v 20).[24] Nogalski ends with a suspicion of redactional activities at the end of the book of Zephaniah, based on the changes and movements in persons, syntax and mood of addresses.

Similarly, Vlaardingerbroek picks up from where Nogalski stopped. He believes that a redactor must have reworked this unit since different parts, like verses 14, 16–18 and 20 are reminiscences of the time after the exile. The broader unit of Zephaniah 3:9–20, of which the unit of 3:14–20 is part, is clearly demarcated with a transition, from the message of doom (v 8) to the prophecy of salvation and restoration (v 9). Units also exist within this broader unit of 3:9–20, with several noticeable thematic and linguistic markers. Some of them include a shift in person, change of focus, mood and import.

Vlaardingerbroek went on to divide the structure of the prophecy of salvation (3:9–20) into five smaller units.[25] They include: 1) promise of conversion of the dispersed Judeans (vv 9–10); 2) promise of rescue for a remnant in Judah and Jerusalem (vv 11–13), linked to verse 3:1–8, just as 2:1–3 is linkable with 1:2–18; 3) summons to jubilation for Jerusalem on account of the coming glory (vv 14–15); 4) promise of glory for Jerusalem and return for the dispersed (vv 16–18) and finally, 5) the promise of restoration and return (vv 19–20).[26]

Sweeney has also extensively discussed the literary structure and context of Zephaniah 3:14–20. A summary of his study is sufficient here.[27] Zephaniah 3:14–20 for him, constitutes the third basic sub-unit of the prophet's exhortative speech (vv 1–20), containing YHWH's plans to establish Jerusalem as the center of his creation. It is the prophet's ex-

---

24   Nogalski, *Literary Precursors*, 201.
25   Vlaardingerbroek, *Zephaniah*, 192–93.
26   Vlaardingerbroek, *Zephaniah*, 194.
27   See Sweeney, *Zephaniah*, 194–197, for details.

hortative address through which Zephaniah communicates YHWH's oracles of reassurance of the restoration of Jerusalem. In the preceding verses 14–20 are two sub-units, which relate the reasons for Jerusalem's punishment (vv 1–4), and YHWH's plan to prompt the nations to recognize the importance of Jerusalem (vv 5–13).[28] Sweeney insists that the structure of 3:14–20 is based on the genre of a hymn or a psalm of praise, including reasons for the praise.

Like Nogalski and others, Sweeney notices that verse 14 begins this praise with the second person feminine singular imperative verbs, such as, ועלזי/שׂמחי/רני (shout for joy, rejoice, exult) and one masculine plural imperative הריע (cry aloud). Sweeney also notices the uniqueness of this unit with different mood and addresses; "on that day" (v 16a–17e) by the prophets, and "as in those days" (vv 18–20) by YHWH. These and other markers combine to give integrity to the unit of 3:14–20.[29]

What is interesting in the above structural and contextual analysis is not only the recognition of changes in moods, addresses, persons and hymnic genre, but the central message of hope and salvation, that runs through Zephaniah 3:14–20, earlier anticipated by the threat and judgment heard in the preceding chapters. The same fundamental message is underlined by the structural proposal made by this study.

The hymn of joy of the restored people (3:18–20) is preceded by YHWH's determination to punish the rulers and leaders in Judah. And the "misfortune oracle" (הוי), earlier heard in Zephaniah 2:5, is repeated in Zephaniah 3:1–5. Verse 6 begins uniquely and forcefully with a *hiphil* perfect verb, first person singular, הכרתי (I cut/wiped out), and paints a picture of doom to the non-repented people (vv 6–8). While verses 9–13 present the picture of YHWH purifying, punishing and leaving behind the humble remnant. This is followed by the joy of the restored Israel (vv 14–18) and the promise of restoration (vv 19–20).

Therefore, Zephaniah 3:14–20 is not only an independent literary unit of the message of joy of salvation and restoration of the remnants,

---

28   Sweeney, *Zephaniah*, 194.
29   Sweeney, *Zephaniah*, 196.

but it is connected with the preceding chapters of Zephaniah, and with the rest of the Twelve Minor Prophets, especially with Haggai.[30]

The following detailed exegesis of 3:14–20, will help to further highlight the fact that the doom and judgment heard in 1:14–18, was not the end. It was rather, an anticipation of the joy, salvation and restoration of the fortunes of YHWH's people (3:14–20).

3.1.3 An Exegesis of Zephaniah 3:14–20

Some portions of the text of Zephaniah 3:14–20 posed interpretative and translational problems to ancient scribes and commentators. This is evident in the discussions and the clarifications made on the above textual critical section of this Chapter. The preceding structural and contextual analysis of 3:14–20 also revealed the shifts in person, change of focus, mood, addresses and import in this unit. Its genre, a hymn or psalm of praise, with other linguistic and literary markers, combined to give a literary integrity to the unit.[31]

Zephaniah 3:14–20, though treated here as a literary unit, is linked with texts that preceded and followed, since the overall literary context of his prophecy was meant to inform the readers, in his unique way, of the coming of the Day of YHWH. This is a day of judgment (1:14–18), and restoration of fortunes (3:14–20). Although Zephaniah's prophecy undoubtedly is influenced by the earlier traditions of the prophet, a further verse-by-verse exegesis of the unit under investigation (3:14–20), will help highlight Zephaniah's theology of the Day of YHWH, especially those elements of hope and restoration, since YHWH is always in the midst of His remnant people (3:12–18).

---

30 Although this will be discussed in Chapter Five, see Nogalski, *Literary Precursor*, 209. Here he notes already that, "Zephaniah 3:18–20 serves several functions: an interpretation within Zephaniah, an introduction to the book of Haggai, and a connective link to other passages within the Book of the Twelve, most notably to the corpus of Deuteronomistic history."

31 See, Stuhlmueller, *Amos, Hosea, Micah, Nahum, Zephaniah, Habakkuk*, 105. Here, this unit as a Psalm of praise is stressed. And it reminds us of the many jubilant lines in Isa 40–55, particularly chapters 40–48.

It will illumine and underline those particular ways by which Zephaniah communicated his prophetic message, bearing his own life situation in mind. This will bring a renewed insight into the relationship, or to the functioning of the unit of Zephaniah 3:14–20 in the Book of Zephaniah, in the prophetic literature and within the overall contexts of other OT literature, especially Psalm 126 and the Deuteronomistic History. This will be developed in full, in Chapter Five.

3.1.3.1 Zion is called to Praise YHWH (רני בת־ציון, v 14ab)

Zephaniah begins this section of his prophecy of hope and restoration (3:14–20), by enthusiastically and optimistically calling people to put those sorrows and threats heard in the previous chapter behind them, and be filled with joy and exultation (v 14). In fact, Savoca is right to have also observed that from here begins the hymn of joy of the glorious vision of the New Zion (*"da qui inizia l'inno di esultanza per la radiosa vision della nuova Sion"*).[32] Zephaniah does this emphatically by the use of the following four verbs, namely, ועלזי/שמחי/רני (shout for joy, rejoice, exult) and הריע (cry aloud). The root of the first verb, רנן/rnn "to rejoice, shout for joy," can also occur outside the OT.[33]

But the verb form, as used here in Zephaniah 3:14, is attested about 53 times in the OT: *qal* 19 times (Isa 9 times), *piel* 28 times (Pss 21 times and Isa 4 times), *pual* 1 time (Isa 16:10 "to be jubilant"). We also have the *hiphil* form about 5 times (Ps 65:9 and Job 29:13), causatively "to cause to rejoice" or "to rejoice," in Deuteronomy 32:43, in Psalms 32:11 and 81:2. Most of the occurrences are found about 25 times in the Psalms and about 8 times in Isaiah 40–46. Similarly, the substantive form, רנה/rinnâ, occurs about 33 times in the Psalms and 7 times in Isaiah 40–66.[34]

Again, Vlaardingerbroek also confirms that רנן/rnn in *qal* and *piel* forms, usually mean "raise shouts of rejoicing," mostly in a religious or cultic

---

32 Savoca, *Abdia-Naum, Abacuc-Sofonia*, 175.

33 See R. Ficker, "רנן rnn to rejoice," *TLOT* 3: 1240–1243 for a detailed study of this root and various usages, both in and outside the OT.

34 Ficker, "רנן," 1240.

setting, and the meaning "to shout for joy," as in Zephaniah 3:14, is dominant in the verb, rather than in the substantive. The latter רנה/*rinnâ* (subst) in fact may also denote other forms of cry, including lament.[35]

It is also noticeable that the LXX renders *rnn* in different ways, including, ἀγαλλιάμαι (2 Sam 1:20; 1 Chr 16:31; Isa 12:6; 25:9; 29:19), as "to rejoice exceedingly, to exult."[36] Also in the NT, the ἀγαλλιάω (rejoice, exult, be glad) is attested about 11 times, and the noun, ἀγαλλίασις (rejoicing, gladness) about 5 times. A. Weiser also stresses that these words, both in the LXX and in NT, just like in the OT, have a religious sense. They designate the joy and exultation over the salvation which God has given and promised his people, in the NT "through Jesus."[37]

In Zephaniah 3:14, רני (רנן/*rnn*) "to rejoice, shout for joy," a singular feminine imperative, is addressed to בת־ציון (daughter of Zion, *MT*), and θύγατερ Ιερουσαλημ (daughter of Jerusalem, *LXX*). In fact, the meaning of the the phrase, "daughter of Zion" (בת־ציון) has dominated biblical exegesis in recent past.[38] W. F. Stinespring had once understood this phrase as an appositional genitive. From the point of view of Stinespring, the two nouns בת and ציון should not be read as if they have that possessive relationship typical of a Hebrew construct phrase.

For him, since the phrase is in apposition it should be translated as "daughter Zion," and not as "daughter of Zion." According to him,

---

35 This is the form found, for example in Psalm 126. See also Vlaardingerbroek, *Zephaniah*, 208 and Sweeney, *Zephaniah,* 197 where further break-down and detailed occurrences of this verb is listed thus: *Piel* form (Pss 5:12; 67:5; 90:14; 92:5; 98:4; 149:5; 132:9; 145:7; 132:16; 51:16; 59:17; 33:31; 20:6; 63:8; 89:13; 95:1; 84:3; 96:12 etc. This *piel* form also occurs in some prophetic texts (Jer 31:12; 51:48; Isa 26:19; 35:2; 52:8), all of which have cultic association as suggested earlier by Vlaardingerbroek. The *qal* form, Sweeney also insists appears only once in the Psalms (Ps 35:27), but more frequently in the Prophetic Literature, (Jer 31:7; Isa 12:6; 24:14; 54:1; 44:23; 49:13; 42:11; 35:6; 61:7; Zech 2:14).

36 Johan Lust, E. Eynikel and K. Hauspie, *Greek-English Lexicon of the Septuagint* (revised ed. Stuttgart: Deutche Bibelgesellschaft, 2003), 2. See also the verb, Χαίρω "to rejoice, to be glad," (Gen 45:16; Zeph 3:14), *idem*, 658.

37 A. Weiser, "ἀγαλλιάω *agalliaō* rejoice, exult, be glad," *EDNT* 1:7–8.

38 See Michael H. Floyd, "Welcome Back, Daughter of Zion!," *CBQ* 70 (2008): 484–504 for some of these opinions on the phrase.

this phrase does not metaphorically imagine Zion as a mother. Zion does not have a daughter, rather Zion is a daughter. In other words, "daughter" here should not be read in a familial sense but in the sense of endearment or respect we have for a young woman. Hence, for him it would be more suitable to idiomatically read the phrase as "Maid Zion," "Lady Zion," or "Dear Zion."[39]

Aloysius Fitzgerald also argued that since the Western Semetic capital cities were typically characterized as divine consorts of the national god, the phrase בת־ציון should be interpreted in this light. Fitzgerald thinks that this reflects a concept of Jerusalem as YHWH's wife.

In his view, this concept is generally related to the prophetic metaphorical description of the convenant as a marriage relationship, and more specifically to the prophetic metaphorical comparison of religious fidelity with adultery and harlotry.[40]

Many others, like Adele Berlin and Magnar Kartveit, seem to agree more with Stinespring.[41] But, I agree with Floyd that the significance of this phrase should be taken beyond the level of grammatical appositioning and mythological discussion to a theological level with a search for its significance for us today.[42]

Jon D. Levenson in my own judgment is on this theological direction. He gives an interesting insight into the meaning, theology and history of Zion traditions. The first point deserves a brief elaboration here. The four uses of the term Zion in the Bible include: Zion as a fortress in Jerusalem during the period before David captured the city from the Jebusites, and then changed the name from "the stronghold of Zion," to "the City of David," (2 Sam 5:7, 9). This is most likely the

---

39   See W.F. Stinespring, "No Daughter of Zion: A Study of the Appositional Genitive in Hebrew Grammer," *Encounter* 26 (1965): 133–141 cited in Floyd, "Welcome Back," 484.

40   For more details see Aloysius Fitzgerald, "The Mythological Background for the Presentation of Jerusalem as Queen and False Worship as Adultery in the OT," *CBQ* 34 (1972): 403–16 cited in Floyd, "Welcome Back," 485.

41   See Berlin, *Lamentation: A Commentary* (OTL; Louisville/London: Westminster John Knox, 2002), 10–12; Magnar Kartveit, "Daughter of Zion," *Theology and Life* 27 (2004): 25–41.

42   See Floyd's conclusion of his twenty page article "Welcome Back," 505.

South-East section of Jerusalem, later expanded by successors of David to the North-West, where Solomon built the temple for YHWH that came to be known as "Mount Zion," (Ps 78:68–69). From here, Zion came to designate the Temple. And by the process of metonymy,[43] "Zion" came to refer to "Jerusalem," ("fair Zion" Lam 2:6–8), a personification of the great Temple City. Levenson rightly observes that it was from here that Zion, the Temple City came to be metonymically used, to refer to the people Israel and not just the City (Isa 51:16; Zech 2:11).[44]

Levenson makes it easier for us to decipher if in Zephaniah 3:14, and in dealing with the personification of the city or the people of the city, Israel is represented as a single female figure. This female figure personification is well discussed by Elaine R. Follis, in her work on "the daughter of Zion," which represents the city of Jerusalem.[45]

Follis describes בת־ציון (daughter of Zion), as the poetic personification of the city of Jerusalem and her inhabitants. This expression occurs 26 times in the OT, all in poetic contexts. Its symbolic origin is traceable to the nationalistic traditions of Judah, epitomized by its capital city.[46] This city is personified as daughter, partially because such a practice was common in Hebrew language (Tyre in Ps 45:13, Babylon in Ps 137:8 and Tarshish in Isa 23:10).[47] Reasons behind this are not clear;

---

43 Soulen, *Biblical Criticism,* 113 explains "metonymy" that suit the context of our study, as "a figure of speech in which a word is substituted for the thing it is intended to suggest." For example in the book of Revelation, terms such as "head" or "crown," are pseudocryptic substitutes for Caesar (Rev 13:3), mount Zion for Jerusalem, heaven for God, and the bottomless pit for hell.

44 See Jon D. Levenson, "Zion Traditions; Meaning; theology and traditions connected with the term," in ABD 6:198–1102 for details of this study.

45 See Vlaardingbroek, *Zephaniah,* 208.

46 See also Raymond E. Brown, *The Birth of the Messiah: A Commentary on the Infancy Narratives in the Gospels of Matthew and Luke* (Anchor Bible Reference Library; New York: Doubleday, 1993), 320–321 for additional insights into the "daughter of Zion in the Old Testament."

47 See Vlaardingbroek, *Zephaniah,* 208 also for other comparative expressions such as; יושבת ציון, (Isa 12:6; Micah 1:13); cities of Judah, cities of Jerusalem (Isa 40:9); "fair Judah" (Lam 2:2; 5; "the daughter of my people," (Jer 4:11; 8:11–23; 9:6; 14:17; Lam 2:11; 3:48; 4:3, 6, 10).

perhaps cities were thought of as daughters, and subordinate offspring of a nation as a whole. Or the Hebrew predisposition to use feminine nouns for abstract or collective concepts may be at work here.[48]

Follis further speculates that while sons were thought to represent the adventuresome spirit of a society, constantly pressing beyond established boundaries of the community, female children are associated with stability, and with nurturing of the community at its very center. While the expression is not used to refer to the Hebrew people when they were wandering in the desert, it is seen to be used to refer to them as settled people. Although these speculations cannot be fully confirmed, Follis rightly observes that half of the occurrences of "Daughter of Zion," imagery in the OT including Zephaniah 3:14, reflects, joy, favor, and exaltation.[49]

However, it is worth noting that Floyd has, from a socio-cultural perspective, argued that the figure personification of בת ציון, refers not only to the female inhabitants of Jerusalem and in extension, the entire citizenry, but also to the leadership roles of women and mothers, with their capacity to celebrate or share their sorrows.[50]

The implication of this, according to him is that if the people of Jerusalem are collectively represented as one of Zion's daughters, Jerusalem resumes not only the position of the mother, but it also indicates a people who had been generationally removed.[51]

Using the text of Zephaniah 3, Floyd suggests that in Zephaniah 3:14–20 it is Jerusalem "the daughter of Zion," who, as the subsequent generation of Jerusalem's inhabitants, is being urged to rejoice (vv 14–15) over the prospect that she (they) will someday constitute the New Jerusalem (vv 16–18).[52]

---

48   Elaine R. Follis, "Zion Daughter of," *ABD* 6: 1103.

49   Follis, "Zion Daughter of," 1103.

50   Floyd, "Welcome Back," 502.

51   Floyd, "Welcome Back," 502.

52   See Floyd, "Welcome Back," 502–504 for the rest of his opinions. However, on the wall of the Hagia Maria Sion Abbey in Jerusalem (according to Christian tradition Jesus celebrated the last supper here, Acts 1:13; 2:1–13) where I visited along with the Angelicum-Berrie Fellows interreligious study trip on Tusday, February 9, 2010, is written this prophecy of Zephaniah "Rejoice, Daughter of

The significance of this expression, I would agree, is theologically clear from the context of this unit, that Zephaniah is inviting Jerusalem as a whole (men and women) and the remnant people in particular, after the physical, spiritual and all kinds of destructions, to shout for joy over the reversal of their fortunes, from threats and judgment and destruction to a rebuilding, renewal and restoration to salvation. Floyd, I would also suggest, will need to guard against the danger of exclusivism, since the mercy and love of YHWH is not restricted to a particular culture, nationality or geographical area. It is rather, universal.

Similarly, the next verb, הריעו (cry aloud) from the *hiphil* root רוע, (masculine plural) is directed to the collective addressee, Israel. Here Israel is being considered with regard to its individual citizens.[53] The people of Jerusalem, "Israel" in this context is parallel to "daughter of Zion/Jerusalem."[54]

Moreover, it is further pointed out by Vlaardingerbroek that, רוע (only *hiphil*) has more nuances than רנן. Among other things, it denotes a variety of loud cries in battle (both of the victor and the van-

---

Zion, Shout, Daughter of Jerusalem." The tradition has it taught after the destruction of Jerusalem in 70 CE, the original upper room was destroyed and rebuilt as a "synagogue-church" by Judeo-Christian after the return from exile, and named the "Church of the Apostles," or the "Mother of all Churches." In the year 383 CE, the Byzantines built a church on Mt. Zion north of the Judeo-Christian Church with pillars brought from the house of Caiaphas. This church was later transformed into the Basilica of Hagia Sion in 415 by Bishop John II of Jerusalem. The Flagellation at the centre of the Basilica was venerated by pilgrims as the place where Mary, the mother of Jesus, had lived and died. When the Hagia Sion was destroyed in 1099 it was rebuilt again by the crusaders, combining the churches of the Apostles and the church of the pillars and named it "St. Mary of Mount Zion' or the Dormition Church of Mount Zion. "Dormition" signifies to sleep or to die. Interesting to this study is the Mosaic pavement on the floor of this church designed by Fr. Maruitus Gisler, a Benedictine Monk. It has three rings representing the Holy Trinity. The Second and third carry the names of the major and minor prophets (where Zephaniah belongs) is symbolically linked by the four Evagelists to the Twelve Apostles, who like torches, carried the Word of God to the ends of the earth.

53   Patterson, *Nahum, Habakkuk, Zephaniah,* 381.
54   Berlin, *Zephaniah,* 143.

quished). It is much less a religious or cultic word, than רנן (shout for joy).[55] Its meaning in this context, I would agree with Sweeney, is religious and theological, since YHWH has promised to turn away Israel's enemies and restore their fortunes. These restored remnants were to possess the religious qualities of humility, lowliness and the seeking of the refuge in the name of YHWH (3:12–14). Nevertheless, it is the promise of YHWH, which has caused these cries and shouts for joy.[56]

The verb שׂמחי (rejoice) is feminine. It depicts joy, dancing and clapping. It is a manifestation of an intrinsic happiness and joy directed towards the "daughters of Jerusalem." It has a religious meaning (Judg 16:23; 2 Sam 6:12; Hos 9:1–4).[57] On the other hand the verb עלז (to exult, 14b), indicates the utterance of triumphant exclamations, in and outside the cult (Pss 28:7; 68:5; Hab 3:18).

These four verbs רני/שׂמחי/ועליזי and הריע, point at the future and positive scene of YHWH's blessing which will necessitate unending joy and exultation. The reason for this joy and exultation will be further analysed in the following verse 15.

3.1.3.2 Annulment of Judgment (סור משׁפטים, v 15)

Furthermore, in verse 15 it is heard that the Lord has annulled the judgment of the people (הסיר יהוה משׁפטיך, v 15a). He has turned away their enemy (פנה איבך, 15b) and they should not fear any longer (לא־תיראי רע עוד, v 15d). This verse 15a–d highlights the reason for the joy expressed in the preceding verse 14. The verb סור (to turn), is a

55   Vlaardingerbroek, *Zephaniah*, 208. See also Sweeney, *Zephaniah*, 197 where he confirms that "although the verb appears in a number of Psalms that praise YHWH (Pss 47:2; 66:1; 81:2; 95:1, 2; 98:4, 6; 100:1; cf 41:12) and in narratives that relate such contexts (1 Sam 4:5; Ezra 3;11, 13), it appears to be quite at home in narratives and other texts that depict battle and triumph over enemies (e.g., Josh 6:5, 10, 16, 20; Judge 7:21; 1 Sam 17:52; Isa 42:13; 2 Chr 13:12, 15; Num 10:7, 9; Hos 5:8; Joel 2:1; Jer 50:15)."

56   Sweeney, *Zephaniah*, 197.

57   See Sweeney, *Zephaniah*, 198 where he notices that, the verb שׂמח depicts religious rejoicing in Pss 21:2; 32:11; 9:3; 48:12; 1 Sam 2:1; Joel 2:23. See also Zech 9:9.

hiphil root, which indicates the removal of the source of stress (v 15a).[58] Theologically, it points to the action of YHWH (towards), for, or on behalf of, a person or a group of persons. For example in *qal* form, YHWH himself can withdraw from a person as stated in relation to Samson (Judg 16:20) and Saul (1 Sam 18:12; 28:15f). But in *hiphil* form, as in Zephaniah 3:15, and in other historical and prophetic books, YHWH is in action. He acts against or on behalf of Israel/Judah.[59]

This verb has no specific equivalent in the LXX. Instead, the verb περιαιρέω (to cast away), is sometimes used in its place. In our context, the verb parallels פנה, a *piel*, which emphasizes the situation of being sent or turned away (v 15b). The objects of these verbs are, מִשְׁפָּט (judgment), and אֹיֵב (enemy). Patterson compares this scene with that of a court setting where YHWH, the judge has overturned the sentences against His people, freed them as well as sent away their enemies. He thinks this interpretation will be the best solution to the critical conjecture discussed earlier, in the text-critical section of this work.[60]

Patterson further notices that Zephaniah has previously brought up the themes of judgment and justice (2:3; 3:5, 8), and so, their presence in verse 15 should not be seen as a surprise. YHWH has served as witness against the entire universe. He is the overall judge of the universe and Sovereign of creation (3:8), and Jerusalem's Righteous Judge (3:5). He will rescue those who obey Him and keep His commandments (2:3). YHWH will preserve and restore the remnant, while Israel's collective enemies or adversaries shall be cast away.[61]

---

58   For a detailed study of the verb סור, see S. Schwertner, "סוּר *sûr* to deviate," *TLOT* 2: 796–97. Here Schwertner observes that the root of this verb is traceable to Phonician- "yi" (to remove), Akkadian sarâ (to circle, to dance). It occurs as a verb 299 times (*qal* 159 times, *hiphil*, 134 times, *hophal* 5 times and *Piel* about 1 time in the Hebrew Bible. As adjective it occurs about 3 times (Isa 49:21; Jer 2:21; 17:13). The basic meaning of the verb "to turn aside from the direction one has set on is found in 1 Sam 6:12. Its semantic scale reaches from "to go away" "to stay overnight." Four connotations developed from the basic meaning, 1) "to deviate (Judg 14:8; Exod 32:8); 2)"to abandon" (1 Sam 15:6; Num 12:10); 3) "to avoid," (Lam 4:15) and (4) "to turn to," (Gen 19:2; Judg 20:8).

59   S. Schwertner, "סוּר *sûr* to deviate," *TLOT* 2:796–97.

60   Patterson, *Nahum, Habakkuk, Zephaniah*, 381.

61   Patterson, *Nahum, Habakkuk, Zephaniah*, 382.

Sweeney seems to have arrived at a similar conclusion with Patterson, of a single or collective enemy to Israel. He argues that the assertion, that YHWH "has turned away your enemy," provides a parallel, especially since prophetic texts presuppose YHWH's actions to rise up against a foreign enemy and to execute judgment against those who disobey in Israel (e.g., Isa 5).[62]

In the case of Zephaniah 3:15, the removal of the enemy coincides with the removal of judgment against Israel. The attempt to emend or conjecture the singular אֹיְבֵךְ, "your enemy," to read the plural, as in the Murabba'at Mss, LXX and *Peshitta*, is not necessary. Socio-historically, Assyria and Babylon were the major agents of Israel's and Judah's oppression throughout the eighth century and late pre-exilic period (seventh century). This of course, Sweeney argues, was the time of Josiah's reign and Zephaniah's prophecy. YHWH was perceived to be acting to restore Jerusalem and Israel, by "turning away their enemy," (15b).[63]

Verse 15c affirms the possibility of turning Israel's enemy away as well as annulling their judgment because, "the King of Israel, YHWH is in your midst." In the ancient society, the image of the human king present in the city, usually conveyed a sense of security. In this context, it is used metaphorically, to depict YHWH's protection of Jerusalem and his remnant people from all harm.[64] A further implication is that when God is recognized as King (1sa 44:6), pride and disobedience and the worship of false gods, are cast away and God's protection is present.[65]

In fact, the expression YHWH is "in your midst," was already heard in Zephaniah 3:1, 3, 5, 11–12, 15, and will be heard again in verse 17a. Its meaning is debatable as well. According to Széles, this expression means, "that God himself has conquered all the opposition of those who kept him distant from his people. It was because of them He had brought charges and pronounced judgment through his prophet. These charges included their adherence to foreign cult (1:5), their alienation

---

62   See Sweeney, *Zephaniah*, 198–199.
63   Sweeney, *Zephaniah*, 199.
64   Sweeney, *Zephaniah*, 199.
65   Berlin, *Zephaniah*, 143.

from YHWH (1:6), their indifference (1:12), shamelessness, refracto-riness, rebelliousness (3:1) and sins of faithless officials (1:8; 3:3–4)."[66]

Although no single simple answer can be given to these questions, it is my opinion based on the context of this study, that YHWH judges, calls for repentance, restores and saves his people, with his presence in their midst. As Savoca, rightly suggests, it highlights the cancellation of all past faults and assurance of protection of the repenting people, against anything that would cause fear and sadness. He originally, wrote, "Anzitutto, la cancellazione di tutti i capi d'accusa, cioè di tutte le colpe passate (Ger 31, 31.34), come anche di tutto ciò che può causare paura e tristezza."[67]

In fact, the rapport between judgment, the call to repentance and eventual salvation becomes clearer when the text is read as a whole, which this study insists upon. In Zephaniah 2:1–3 we read:

> Gather together, gather together, nations without shame, before you are dis-persed like chaff which disappears in a day; before Yahweh's burning anger over-takes you (before the Day of Yahweh's anger overakes you). Seek Yahweh, all you humble of the earth, who obey his commands. Seek uprightness, seek humility: you may perhaps find shelter on the Day of Yahwh's anger.

This passage is a clear prophetic invitation to repentance and conver-sion, so as to be saved (3:9–20), otherwise they would be "dispersed like chaff" (2:1). The passage also addresses the remnant of the nation (2:2), since they are the humble or the meek of the land that have kept the precepts of the Lord and seek refuge in YHWH alone.[68] This humble of the land will be heard again in Zephaniah 3:11–13. In the OT the "poor" or "humble," due to material condition, were considered to rely on Yahweh and on his providence, keeping the rules. This was in con-trast to the "rich" (Zeph 1:10–13) with silver and gold (Zeph 1:18) who were proud and disobedient to YHWH. They were the oppressors of the poor. In this way the term took on religious meaning that could

---

66 Széles, *Wrath and Mercy*, 111.
67 Savoca, *Abdia-Naum, Abacuc-Sofonia*, 175. That is to say, "cancellation of all past charges and all that cause fear and sadness."
68 See Feinberg, *The Minor Prophets*, 226 for details.

be stretched on inexhaustively.[69] In other words, in Zephaniah there is this close rapport between repentance, covenant renewal and salvation, especially by the presence of the remnant concept.[70]

With the Lord's close and renewed relationship with the remnant Israel, confidence and trust are rebuilt. Those who trust in YHWH must no longer fear (לא־תיראי רע עוד, v 15d). This reassurance formula, "do not fear," is common in salvation oracles, which promise deliverance from adversity or future security (Gen 15:1; 35:17; 1 Sam 22:23; Isa 7:4–9; 37:6–7; Job 5:21–22).[71] Even in this context, when the text has been read differently, "do no longer fear," "shall no longer see evil," as discussed earlier, the basic theological meaning does not change, since YHWH has now provided or renewed his love, fellowship and divine security upon Israel and his entire creation.

3.1.3.3 No More Fear, O Zion! (לא־תיראי ציון, v16)

Moreover, the expression in verse 16a–c, namely, "On that Day, this shall be said to Jerusalem, do not be afraid, O Zion let not your hand fall limp/relax," is not unconnected from the preceding verses, and its theological message. Zephaniah 3:16a–c parallels Zephaniah 14a–c ("shout for joy O daughter of Zion cry aloud, O Israel, rejoice and exult with all your hearts, O daughter of Zion,"), antithetically.[72] It is an invitation to rejoice and not to fear, since YHWH, their God and Champion is already in their midst.[73] This is confirmed by Sweeney, who also notices that "verse 16 introduces a block of material in verses 16–20, that elaborates on the prophet's preceding statement in

---

69 See Abruckle, "Zephaniah," 719.

70 In fact, this aspect of close rapport between repentance and salvation in Zephaniah is well illustrated in Greg King, "The Day of the Lord," 22–31. He compellingly demonstrates that the Day of YHWH is a day of judgment, covenant renewal, call to repentance, and a day of salvation.

71 Sweeney, *Zephaniah*, 200.

72 See Soulen, *Biblical Criticism*, 134 where antithetical parallelism is described as a "parallelism of thought in which the second line is posed as a contrast to the first."

73 See Vlaardingerbroek, *Zephaniah*, 210.

verse 15, concerning the basis for his summons to praise, earlier heard in verse 14."[74]

The formula ביום ההוא (on that day), in verse 16a has been a major point of contention. There are those (e.g., Ben Zvi, Vlaardingerbroek), who believe that this formula is a sign that this section of Zephaniah is the work of post-monarchical or post-exilic redactors. Their conclusion is mostly based on the fact that there are passages in pre-exilic prophetic literature, introduced by this formula, which could be taken to be pointing to the future salvation (eschatological).

Vlaardingerbroek, as mentioned earlier, believes that the expression ביום ההוא (on that day), means, returning to a viewpoint in one's own era. He argues that even a promise of deliverance can hardly ignore the misery from which it promises deliverance.[75] But Sweeney is of the view that the expression ביום ההוא (on that day), is not a perfect indication of the work of a late redactor. Zephaniah instead was preaching to his contemporaries within the context of Josiah's reformation. Hence the formula, ביום ההוא (on that day), does not point to an eschatological future. The expression, according to Sweeney, merely indicates a future time and not an eschatological event.[76] In other words, it is historical not eschatological.

Although Sweeney does not clearly define "eschatology" (broadly or strictly), he is right, that the formula may not always give a secure sign of later redaction. For example, the formula appears in Amos 9:11 and in Obadiah 8, in different contexts. In Amos it may point to the restoration, while in Obadiah it points to the destruction of Edom.[77] Sweeney, I believe runs short of recognizing how difficult it is to clearly and theologically demarcate the historical from the eschatological, as mentioned in the introductory section of this work.

This argument, in my opinion parallels also the argument whether the judgment in Zephaniah is particular or universal. This study em-

74   Sweeney, *Zephaniah*, 200.
75   Vlaardingerbroek, *Zephaniah*, 210.
76   Sweeney, *Zephaniah*, 200–201.
77   Kenneth H. Curffey, "Remnant, Redactor, and Biblical Theologian: A Comparative Study of Coherence in Micah and the Twelve," in *Reading and Hearing the Book of the Twelve*, 206.

braces both. The formula ביום ההוא (on that day), may also refer to both, depending on the context in which the formula is used. In Zephaniah, the expression might be historical, but foreshadows the eschatological. This is best expressed by the already cited observation of VangGermeren, that the Lord's acts of judgment take place in the history of redemption and each of these acts foreshadows the eschatological judgment.[78] In other words, the line between the historical and eschatological, as earlier noted, is often very fine and difficult to discern, especially in Zephaniah's prophecy.[79]

The underlining factor in Zephaniah 3:16, is that this situation requires a new approach to life. On that Day (ביום ההו אם), it shall be said to Jerusalem and the people, do not be afraid O Zion (אל־תיראי ציון). And Jerusalem, "let not your hand fall limp / relax or slack (אל־ירפו ידיך). This latter expression is idiomatic with a basic root meaning "to be slack." It is believed that it could be used in different ways in the Bible, depending on the context in which it occurs, but mostly to express the need for courage and action.[80]

As a verb, it is used in an idiomatic way with "hands." It can also be used in the sense of expressing an alleviation of divine judgment (2 Sam 24:16; 1 Chr 21:15). It is used in the sense of abandoning one another (Josh 10:6) and several other times it is used for the losing of one's courage or of being discouraged and to refer to other adversities (2 Sam 4:1; 2 Chr 15:7; Jer 38:4).[81] But as to the former expression (אל־תיראי ציון) "do not be afraid Zion," Savoca in line with Sweeney affirms that this is an ancient biblical phrase used to encourage the people against loss of hope, and to trust in YHWH, the God of their fathers, in the walls of Zion who always leads them victoriously through all kinds of adversities with love and happiness."[82]

78   See Vanggermeren, *Interpreting the Prophetic Word*, 175–176
79   Merril, *Kingdom of Priests*, 457–458.
80   Patterson, *Zephaniah*, 382; Sweeney, *Zephaniah*, 201.
81   Patterson, *Zephaniah*, 382.
82   Savoca, *Abdia-Naum, Abacuc-Sofonia*, 175. He originally writes *"È l'antica frequente frase biblica di incoraggiamento a non perdere mai la fiducia, per un motive solidissimo: fra mura di Sion c'è il dio dei suoi padre, un condittiero sempre vittorioso contro qualsiasi avversario.*

In other instances, as in Zephaniah 3: 16, the discouragement could turn to fear (Neh 6:9; Ezek 21:7; Isa 13:7–8; Jer 6:24–25; 50:43; Ezek 7:17–18), which often leads to the prophetic message of fearlessness (Isa 13:7–8; Jer 6:24–25; 50:43; Ezek 7:17–18). Zephaniah is calling the people to act, to be courageous and not to be afraid, for YHWH is always with them (v 17a).[83]

3.1.3.4 A Reassurances of the Warrior/ Savior (גבור יושיע, v 17)

Verse 17 continues from what has just been heard, the prophecy of salvation. For instance 17a–b, יהוה אלהיך בקרבך (The Lord your God is in your midst) is a repetition of what has been heard in verse 15c ("the King of Israel is the Lord among you/in your midst,"). But the noticeable difference here is, that גבור יושיע (warrior/savior v 17b) stands, instead of מלך ישראל (the king of Israel v 15c).[84] In other words, verse 15c emphasizes YHWH's role as King, while verse 17a–b, stresses YHWH's role as a saving hero.[85] In its intensive form of expression, גבור, denotes a strong or mighty person who carries out, or has carried out certain actions, and may surpass others in doing such actions. It denotes YHWH as our war hero and the Mighty One (Isa 10:21; 42:13; Ps 24:8).[86]

Historically, Sweeney observes that some interpreters might be very uncomfortable with the military and battle connotation of this verse within the context of salvation and peace. But he would want to remind readers of the socio-historical context of this prophecy, namely the seventh century B.C.E., and the downfall of the Assyrian empire.

---

83 See also Széles, *Mercy and Wrath*, 112 where the root verb, רפי is interpreted as "to languish, be despondent, and be exhausted."

84 J. Kühlewein, "גבר gbr to be superior," in *TLOT* 1: 299–302; has given a detailed study of the root meaning of גבר and its occurrences to include: (1) "to be superior, strong," (2) though it occurs about 25 times in the OT, all semantic nuances of the *qal* are related to the basic meaning of "to be/become superior or strong," (3) and it intensive form is very close to the meaning of the root, "strong" (1 Sam 14:52), mighty hunter (Prov 30:30) and war hero (Josh 6:2ff).

85 Sweeney, *Zephaniah*, 202.

86 Vlaardingerbroek, *Zephaniah*, 213.

Judah and the rest of the ancient Near East were known for military conflicts and confrontation. Assyria controlled Judah by military might. The former was later conquered by the Babylonians.[87]

So, by גבור (warrior/savior) in this context, Zephaniah refers to the power of YHWH to perform acts of deliverance and restoration of fortunes and salvation. He wants to emphasize that God is a real Savior in contrast to idols, wooden images and human military might, which cannot save (Isa 45:20). The reading of the text of verse 17c, "He will rejoice over you with happy song" (ישיש עליך בשמחה), re-echoes the reading in verse 14, on the rejoicing of Jerusalem. Words of the same roots (שמח and רנן) are used.

The root שיש and שוש, (to exult) usually occurs in poetic or prophetic text. It is construed with the prepositions ב (in) or ל (to), to mean "to rejoice over." Therefore, anthropomorphically, it is YHWH who is rejoicing over Jerusalem and his creation. Moreover, this is not the only place in the Bible where God celebrates. The joy of God is also mentioned in other prophetic texts (Isa 9:16; 62:5; 65:19; Jer 32:41) and in the Psalms (Ps 104:31).[88]

Verse 17d "יחריש באהבתו" ("He will renew you by his love"), as earlier mentioned in the text critical section, has given room to different interpretations. Ben Zvi for example groups the possible meanings of חרש (be silent) into three categories. First, the love of God "will be too tender and strong for expression." Second, God will be at rest (lit. be silent) or satisfied. Third, חרש (be silent) as meaning "God will be silent concerning the sins of the people."[89] Ben Zvi observes further that the analysis of *hiphil* verbal forms from the root חרש (be silent) in the OT shows that many of them actually convey the meaning of refraining from reacting to the deeds of someone else (Gen 34:5; Num 30:5; 1 Sam 10:27; Hab 1:13; Ps 50:21).[90]

But Sweeney comes up with a historical reading because of the difficulties of settling with one meaning (such as "plough," "devise," "engrave," and "renew"). He suggests that the root חרש be examined meta-

---

87 Sweeney, *Zephaniah*, 202–203.
88 See Vlaardingerbroek, *Zephaniah*, 214.
89 Ben Zvi, *Book of Zephaniah*, 251.
90 Ben Zvi, *Book of Zephaniah*, 251–252.

phorically. As a metaphor for ploughing, its function is seen in different contexts. For example in Hosea 10:11 "Judah must plough, Jacob must harrow himself." This is meaningful in the context in which YHWH calls for Judah and Israel to take action by acting righteously, and in conformity to the will of God.

This ethical usage is clearer in Hosea 10:13, "you have ploughed wickedness; you have reaped injustice." It is also evident in Job 4:8, "as I have seen, those who plow iniquity and sow trouble reap the same." And Psalm 129:3 uses it as an expression of oppression, "the ploughers ploughed upon my back, they made furrows long."[91]

However, none of these in my own judgment has the monopoly of a satisfactory explanation of this verse. Ben Zvi makes an interesting remark, close to what I think. For him, if one considers verses 16–17 as containing a positive response to an implied entreaty made by the people to God, asking YHWH to deliver and save them from the hands of their enemies and from the present misfortunes, then the meaning of יחריש באהבתו (He will renew over you by his love), becomes clear.[92] The basic meaning of the text, (silence, renew with love or plough), in my judgment, and as earlier argued in the text critical section, should be derived, when the text is read contextually. In our context, it points at the judgment and mercy of YHWH, upon those who repent. It demonstrates the ability of YHWH, to restore and protect his people, for YHWH is always in their midst (v 17a). He will bring them joy. He will dance with shouts of joy (v 17e), as in those days of the festivals (v 18a).

3.1.3.5 YHWH Gathers Away the Woes (אסף יהוה היו, v 18)

Zephaniah 3:18, is a continuation of verse 17e, where the expression "He will dance with shouts of joy for you" (יגיל עליך ברנה), presents undoubtedly, an atmosphere and the experience of great joy. This section of the prophecy (vv 18–20) with its first person expression, presupposes YHWH as a speaker. Verse 18, "as in those days of festivals,

---

91 See Sweeney, *Zephaniah*, 202–203 for a detailed historical analysis of this concept.

92 Ben Zvi, *Book of Zephaniah*, 251.

I will take away from you the woe, over which you endured mockery"
(נוגי ממועד אספתי ממך היו משאת עליה חרפה), many believe is one of
the most difficult expressions in the book of Zephaniah. It has created
many difficulties for commentators.

And not a single one of them has a final say with regard to the
translation, as we saw earlier in the text critical section.[93] There are
those who suggest that the verse is a commentary on the previous verses
or on the following reading. Others under the influence of the LXX,
translate it "as on a day of festival," and join it to the previous verse.[94]

Sweeney who objects to this translation, notices that the major part
of the problem is posed by the expression "נוגי ממועד," which is generally taken to be referring to the cultic celebration due to the word
מועד ("festival or appointed time"). In other words, should the word
be translated, "festival" or "appointed time" has been a major point of
contention.[95]

His contention is that if נוגי, conveys the sense of suffering or oppression, and it is a *niphal* participle derived from יגה (to suffer), then
when this is added to מועד, with its unusual preposition מן (from) to
read the text "those who were aggrieved/thrust out from the festival,"
little sense would be made out of the entire meaning of the text, bearing in mind, the following expression, אספתי ממך (I have gathered
from you).[96]

The following verb, היו (*qal* perfect 3mp of היי = to be/become),
evidently has posed many difficulties. Sweeney suggests that the verse
should be read "those who have suffered from the appointed time when
I punished/gathered from you were…" He thinks this way, if אספתי ממך
is taken to mean "I punished you," or "I have gathered you." Also if
אסך, as in Zephaniah 1:2, 3; 3:8, presupposes YHWH's actions to punish, destroy and to remove those who are subject to divine judgment,
Sweeney, therefore concludes that verse 18, was meant to rationalize

---

93 See Ben Zvi, *Book of Zephaniah*, 253–54; Patterson, *Zephaniah*, 385–86;
    Roberts, *Zephaniah*, 219; Vlaardingerborek, *Zephaniah*, 215–216 and Sweeney,
    Zephaniah, 203–205.
94 Széles, *Mercy and Wrath*, 113.
95 Sweeney, *Zephaniah*, 204.
96 Sweeney, *Zephaniah*, 204.

YHWH's punishment, or to purge Jerusalem and Judah in terms and imageries, like the ones found in Zephaniah 1, whereby YHWH is not responsible for Judah's suffering, but the nation itself is responsible by its act of disobedience.[97]

When we compare this to the argument earlier made by Ben Zvi and others, it is hard to jump to a one-sided conclusion. But, in my judgment based on the context of this prophecy, and the unity of the entire work of Zephaniah YHWH's restoration of the fortunes of his people, it is easy to decipher the basic meaning of this text. It underscores the fact that at the appointed time, YHWH is or will be the one who protects and restores the dignity of Jerusalem, Judah and his entire creation, from the power of hostile nations, enemies and all kinds of difficulties. He will protect them from mockery, intrusion, exploitation and deprivation of their freedom, including the right and freedom to worship YHWH. It is neither by might, fortified cities and walls, nor by silver and gold (1:14–18), that salvation is obtained, but by the mighty power of YHWH.

3.1.3.6 YHWH Puts to an End the Oppressors
(עשׂה את־כל־מעניך, v 19)

Verses 19–20 advance with the narration of YHWH's acts and its consequences, leading to the final restoration of Zion and the people. Within this sub-unit, are also found the repeated use of the temporal formula בעת ההיא (at that time). Sweeney observes that some scholars have used the presence of this formula to draw their conclusion that verses 19–20, are not only an addition but an eschatological text or unit, both of which he has consistently refuted. He believes that "at that time," may refer to the future, as well as to the early Assyrian activities in Israel, hence the text is not referring singly to the Babylonian exile.[98]

But my position remains the same as on the discussion on verse 16a, that it points to both the historical and to the eschatological events,

---

97 See Sweeney, *Zephaniah*, 204–205 and Irsigler, *Gottesgericht*, 6–11 for a detailed argument.
98 Sweeney, *Zephaniah*, 206.

since the Lord's acts of judgment take place within the frame-work of the history of redemption.

Furthermore, the text of Zephaniah 3:19–20 is linked closely to the preceding verses 16–18, with the use of this phrase ("at that time"). That is to say, there is the presence of the temporal clauses בעת ההיא (at that time), in verses 19 and 20. Verse 20 opens with בעת ההיא, while verse 19 does not open with בעת ההיא plus the imperfect.[99] Patterson insists that the construction of verse 19a הנני עשה את־כל־מעהיך (behold/ I will make an end of all who afflicted you), especially, הנני plus a participle in the future, lays emphasis on the certainty of the Lord's action.[100] The main hermeneutical difficulty we face in this verse, is that of the immediacy of עשה (make/"deal with"). Since מְעַנַּיִךְ means "those who afflicted you," עשה then should point to punishment or judgment.[101] It is suggested that perhaps the כלה (an end), should have been inserted after "to make" (עשה).

The dilemma we saw was whether one should rather read, כלה את in place of את־כל. It is clear in the above variant translations that the LXX seems to have read אֹתָךְ לְמַעֲנֵךְ (in your/for your sake), instead of אֶת־כָּל־מְעַנַּיִךְ (all who afflict you). Additionally, Patterson also notices that, the verb עשה (make), followed by the particle, את alternatively is often interpreted in the sense of "to deal with," (cf. Jer 21:2; Ezek 22:14; 23:25, 29). In Zephaniah 1:18 we heard the prophet uses עשה to prophesy the speedy end of the world in the Day of YHWH, underscoring the effectiveness of God's power and sovereignty.[102] Although, some may still see the texts as vague, I believe the basic sense of YHWH defending, and restoring the fortunes of his people underlines the context of these expressions.[103]

---

99 Ben Zvi, *Book of Zephaniah*, 255. Other texts that use this formula, like in verse 20 include Isa 18:7; Jer 3:17; 4:11; Amos 9:1 and Zeph 3:16.

100 Patterson, *Nahum, Habakkuk, Zephaniah*, 386.

101 Ben Zvi, *Book of Zephaniah*, 255.

102 Patterson, *Nahum, Habakkuk, Zephaniah*, 386.

103 Ben Zvi, *Book of Zephaniah*, 256, still believes that the text is vague concerning what YHWH will do with the afflicted. On the contrary, the text is not vague about what YHWH will do with the lame and the stray (הצלעה והנדחה).

184

Still on this Day of YHWH, the lame (והנדחה) would be rescued and the strayed (הצלעה), gathered (v 19b). Ben Zvi and others argue for the post-monarchic nature of this text, since Zephaniah 3:19 depends on Micah 4:6.[104] On the contrary, Sweeney maintains his socio-historical setting, and dates the text to the time of Josiah's reform in the seventh century B.C.E, since he believes that it is Micah 4:6 that depends on Zephaniah 3:19.[105] Important to this study is the obvious meaning of the passage that YHWH is there to support the lame. YHWH would strengthen the weak. He would rescue them from hopeless situation of all kinds, including their socio-historical difficulties.

This restoring work of YHWH continues in verse 19 c–d. In verse 19d, it is true that the MT attests, בכל־הארץ בשתם (With their shame, in all the earth), which when read together with the preceding verse 19c as follows, ושמתים לתהלה ולשם (I will exchange, rather, for fame and renown) becomes: "I will make into fame and renown all those whose shame is in the land, or those who have been made to experience shame in the land." The reading, adopted by this study, falls into the following second proposal suggested by Ben Zvi. This is in addition to studies made in the text critical section.

Ben Zvi in his own part has once again observes that there are two main ways of reading the text of Zephaniah 3:19c–d. The first, is to read it as written, ושמתים לתהלה ולשם בכל־הארץ בשתם, drop off the definitive article, ה (the) from ארץ (earth). The reading will then be, "I will get them praise and fame in every land where they have been put to shame." This is the traditional way of reading the text.

The second approach is to consider, בשתם as the object of the verb "ושמתים" either by considering the final *mem* as enclitic that points towards בשת (their shame) or drop it out completely, so that the text reads, "I will change their shame into praise and renown in all the earth."[106] Even the MT, as we saw earlier, went as far as contemplating whether, בשתם (their shame) is a mistaken scribal gloss of

104 For details see Ben Zvi, *Book of Zephaniah*, 256–257.
105 See Sweeney, *Zephaniah*, 206–207.
106 Ben Zvi, *Book of Zephaniah*, 259.

בשובי את־שבותיכם (restoring their fortunes), in verse 20e, which I think, will be an over-reading of the significance of this passage.

However, the fundamental meaning of this text includes an overall demonstration of YHWH's sovereignty over His creation everywhere. It emphasizes the ever consistent presence of God in the midst of His people. It also signifies YHWH's restoring of their fortunes after the profound sufferings. These include the alleviation of all their humiliation and shameful experiences of exiles and deprivations of all kinds (v 18), which the Lord would soon reverse (v 20).

3.1.3.7 YHWH Restores the Fortunes (שוב את־שבות, v 20)

Zephaniah 3:20 had long been anticipated by the unit of 1:14–18, already discussed. It represents hope, or the fact that "there is light at the end of the tunnel." It indicates at the reversal of fortunes of the people of Jerusalem, their return from exile with its universal salvific restoration. Sweeney rightly draws our attention to the repetitive or thematic linkage of verse 20 to the preceding unit and verses, particularly verse 19a–d, which reads, namely, "at that time, I will make an end of all who afflicted you, for their shame, in all the earth." In other words, there is a close similarity or connection between Zephaniah 3:19 and the following verse 20.

For instance, in verse 20a–f we read "and at that time, I will bring you [home], and I will make your name known, I will make you famous among all the peoples of the earth, when I will restore your fortunes before their eyes, says the Lord." Here, the addressee is decorated with אתכם, which has a second person masculine plural pronominal suffix. On the contrary, verse 19 is characterized with the third person singular feminine. Although the issue of shame is not stressed in verse 20, the restoration of the exiles and the reversal of misfortunes to fortunes are emphasized.[107] It is this positive expectation unit of Zephaniah filled with promises, that usually prompts the debate, whether this last verse is post-exilic, redacted to avoid the ambiguity

---

107 Sweeney, *Zephaniah*, 207.

of verse 19, or not. This point has already been addressed, repeatedly, in this study.[108]

Interestingly, some scholars have emended and translated verse 19a as, בעת היטבי ("in the time when I do good [to you]."[109] This might be due to the influence of the LXX translation, ὅταν καλῶς ὑμῖν ποιήσω (when I will do good/well to you), which Patterson thought is unwarranted and out of context.[110] But, I beg to differ with Patterson, since the entire context of Zephaniah 3:14–20, is clearly quite positive. It is the opposite of the wrath and judgments earlier heard in Zephaniah 1:14–18. Nothing will be better than YHWH bringing the exiled "home," from foreign land and restoring their fortune from wrath, and darkness (1:14–18), to light, and well-being at home (3:20a).

In addition, an interesting observation has also been rightly brought to bear on verses 19a and 20b. In verse 19a, there is no *waw* (ו) prefixed to בעת (at that time), as opposed to verse 20b, which has a *waw*, as follows [ו] בעת קבצי אתכם (and at that time, I will gather you).[111] Remarkably, the use of בעת (at that time), with an infinitive construct, first person singular, rather than with a verb to express a temporal clause may be explained on the analogy of similarly formed nominal clauses, used as genitive in Genesis 2:17 and in Jeremiah 2:7.

For example, in the following manner, "at that time of my gathering you" becomes "at that time (when) I gather you." The LXX translates with aorist subjunctive middle as, καὶ ἐν τῷ καιρῷ ὅταν εἰσδέξωμαι ὑμᾶς (at that time when I might have welcomed or received you). But, looking at its eschatological context and with the use of imperfects like, אביא "I will bring" (v 20a) and אתן "I will give/make," (v 20c), it makes sense to translate "gather" with the imperfect קבץ (I will gather), as adopted in this study, and as suggested in the MT textual apparatus.[112]

---

108 Nogalski, *Literary Precursors*, 203.

109 See John M. P. Smith, *A Critical and Exegetical Commentary on Zephaniah and Nahum* (ICC; Edinburg: T. & T. Clark, 1911), 263.

110 Patterson, *Nahum, Habakkuk, Zephaniah*, 387.

111 Some scholars call this, "explicative." For a detailed study of this, see R. J. Williams, *Syntax* (2nd ed., Toronto: University of Toronto, 1972), 71.

112 See Patterson, *Nahum, Habakkuk, Zephaniah*, 388 for a slightly different opinion.

The function of the כִּי in the following statement, כִּי־אֶתֵּן אֶתְכֶם לְשֵׁם (for I will make your name known), in verse 20c has also met with diverse opinions. Some prefer to take it as assertive (for, surely) while some prefer to take it as causative (because). Sweeney, for instance, thinks that it is assertive, since it follows an infinitive construct in the preceding verse 20b, and that it conveys emphasis rather than causation. Its function is to emphasize YHWH's promise to grant renown or make the name of his people famous among the people of the whole earth.[113] As an emphatic כִּי (kî) it stresses explicitly the fulfillment of the promises made in the preceding chapters and verses, that roots back to the covenant traditions. This is an event which was already occurring and will continue to occur, namely YHWH rescuing his people from the hands of their enemies and oppressors and making them famous (v 20d).[114]

In addition, Széles brought in a cherishing insight, to the reading of the "name" in verse 20c–d. She observes that שֵׁם (name), could be appreciated as the inner "I" and its "stamp." Name declares, expresses, and defines its bearer since *"Nomen est omen,"* (a name is a sign). She stresses that a new name points to a new personality.[115]

Széles's, statement left this way, in my judgment, might be too general and fallacious. But it is explainable that within this context or for the ancient biblical Israel, name and name-changing was highly significant. A new name, such as in the case of Abram to Abraham, points to a new theological personality and being. Israel will be given (נתן) a new name. Their socio-political and religious misfortunes shall be restored to good fortunes (v 20e).

Verse 20e actually brings us to this important expression, long anticipated, בְּשׁוּבִי אֶת־שְׁבוּתֵיכֶם לְעֵינֵיכֶם (when I will restore your fortunes before their eyes), rather translated by the LXX as, "in my turning or returning our host of captivity," (ἐν τῷ ἐπιστρέφειν με τὴν αἰχμαλωσίαν ὑμῶν). It is not only the summary of YHWH's work in the

---

113 Sweeney, *Zephaniah*, 208.
114 See Patterson, *Nahum Habakkuk, Zephaniah*, 388; Vlaadingerbroek, *Zephaniah*, 218–219.
115 Széles, *Wrath and Mercy*, 114.

immediate preceding literary unit (3:1–20), but the joy that had long been anticipated by the preceding two chapters of the Book of Zephaniah.

In fact, the entire phrase, שבות/šᵉbût שוב/šûb, is very important in the in the OT studies. It is also very problematic. Scholars, including E. Preuschen, W.L. Dietrich, E. Baumann, Riekele Borger, William L. Holladay, John M. Bracke and J.A. Soggin, as earlier noted, have in the past engaged in the search for its meaning and significance. A further brief and quick reflection on some of these studies, will definitely shed light on the theological significance and meaning of שבות/šᵉbût שוב/šûb, in Zephaniah 3:20, as used in this particular work.

Bracke commendably, notices that some of these past studies and investigations have been done mainly from an etymological perspective and with reference to a change of loyalty on the part of Israel or God. For instance, he cites Preuschen who focused on its etymological analysis, and traced the root of šᵉbût, to šbh.

Influenced by his native language *"in die Gefangenschaft führen,"* Preuschen suggested that the phrase be translated as "turn the captivity," or "to lead into captivity." In other words, he does not prefer the word *"Elend"* (misery or misfortune).[116] In Job 42:10 we read ויהוה שב את־שבית שבות איוב (the Lord restored Job's fortunes). But Preuschen thinks it was here in the book of Job that the phrase, "turn the captivity," took on another meaning, namely "turn the misfortune."[117]

Baumann on the other hand studied Psalms 126:4; 85:2 and Ezekiel 16:53 and came out with a conclusion that the root verb of šᵉbût, is šbh. He looks at the phrase שבות/šᵉbût שוב/šûb from an ethical-judicial perspective, rather than from a socio-historical or geographical view point. The phrase for him would then mean "do away with the sentence of imprisonment," instead, of Preuschen's "turn the captivity."[118]

Additionally, Bracke's summary of Dietrich's contribution is appealing to this study. He observes that Dietrich, while concerned with

---

116 Bracke, "šûb šᵉbût," 233.

117 See Preuschen, "Die Bedeutung von שוב שבות," 72 cited in Bracke, "šûb šᵉbût," 233.

118 Baumann, "שוב שבות," 29 cited in Bracke, "šûb šᵉbût," 234.

etymological issues, prefers to begin his investigation of שבות/*šᵉbût* שוב/*šûb* from the perspective of the OT. He sees שבות/*šᵉbût* שוב/*šûb* as a technical term whose origin is eschatological and prophetic. This technical term indicates the hope for a return to an earlier, more prosperous time. It was lately that the phrase took on an exilic connotation. He believes, contrary to Preuschen and Baumann, that Diertrich's etymological analysis of *šᵉbût* is right. For Diertrich, *šᵉbût* was originally derived from *šûb,* meaning "render a restoration (*wiederherstellen* [*wie einst*]). But the phrase *šᵉbût*, got mixed up with the noun, *šᵉbît* derived from *šûb* during the post-exilic era literature, when Israel became dominantly concerned with events of restoration from exile. This accounts for the *ketiv* and *qere* variants in the MT.[119]

Most of these earlier studies on the phrase restricted its meaning to etymological analysis, which is increasingly unsatisfactory to our study of Zephaniah 1:14–18; 3:14–20. In fact, the arbitrary mixing of various occurences of *ketiv* and *qere* variants in the MT, has let Borger to conclude rightly that an etymological solution to the phrase is not sufficient, and in my opinion it may not lead to clearer understanding of Zephaniah's theology.

Bracke commendably discusses Borgers's concerns which center on the extreme difficulties in interpreting the multiplicity of the *ketiv* and *qere* variants or choosing one over the other. For instance, "*šbwt*, Bracke observes, occurs seventeen times without *qᵉrê*. While *šbyt* occurs two times without *qᵉrê*, *šbwt* occurs four times as the *qᵉrê* of *šbyt*, and *šbyt* occurs seven times as the *qᵉrê* of *šbw*t."[120]

Similarly, William M. Holladay in his monograph, *The Root Šûbh in the Old Testament: With Particular References to Its Usages in Covenantal Contexts,* engages in the etymological and lexical analyses of the verb, *Šûbh,* stressing as well its implication of YHWH's covenant relationship with Israel.[121] Citing the Prophet Jeremiah 8:4 which states

---

119 See Dietrich, שוב שבות, 30–36 as cited in Bracke, "*šûb šᵉbût,*" 234.

120 See Borger, "שוב שבו/ית," 315–316 as cited in Bracke, "*šûb šᵉbû,*" 235.

121 For interesting details see, Holladay, *Šûbh in the Old Testament,* 1–159, where the study includes: the basic data of the etymological root of the verb in cognate languages, in ancient versions' its lexical analysis and covenanted usages by the

as follows: וְאֵלֵיהֶם כֹּה אָמַר יְהוָה הֲיִפְּלוּ יְלֹא יָקוּמוּ אִם־יָשׁוּב וְלֹא יָשׁוּב
(you say to them; thus says YHWH, if someone/they fall, do they not get up again? If they turn aside/stray, do they not turn back?), Holladay extensively points out the ambiguities inherent in the use of שׁוּב, in this statement. Here, Jeremiah is using שׁוּב, to embrace both physical motion and religious relation.[122]

Additionally, in prophetic literature, שׁוּב according to Holladay is understood as expressing the change of loyalty on the part of Israel or God.[123] But Holladay's views are strongly criticized by many, including Bracke, who particularly assumes that the study of the etymology of a word is all about its history, rather than its proper theological meaning and significance.[124]

Bracke basically believes that despite the preceding extensive etymological study of the phrase, שְׁבוּת/šᵉbût שׁוּב/šûb, its meaning is problematic. Thus he decided to take the literary contextual approach. With

eight century prophets, like, Amos, Hosea, Isaiah and Micah. Its usages are also identified in the Pentateuch, Deuteronomistic passages, in Jeremiah, Zephaniah's contemporary. For the postexilic prophetic literature, Holladay cites Ezekiel, Deutero-Isaiah, Zechariah, Trito-Isaiah, Malachi, Joel and Jonah. Its occurrences in the Psalms, Job, proverbs, Lamentation, Nehemiah, and Daniel and other synonymous verbs of motion, are also studied by Holladay.

122 Holladay, *Šûbh in the Old Testament,* 1–2. Similarly, A. J. Soggin, "שׁוּב Šûb, to return," in *TLOT* 3:1312–1317 engages in a detail and insightful analysis of the root of the verb, שׁוּב Šûb, which according to him is attested in several Semitic languages, but absent in a few like, the Akkadian and Phoenician. Like Holladay, Soggin also gives a detail statistical breakdown of the verb in various stems (qal, *hiphil, hophal polael* etc) in the Hebrew Bible. Acknowledging the detail study of Holladay, Soggin affirms the complexity and the ambiguity inherent in this verb of movement. For him, the theological use of the figurative meaning of this verb, שׁוּב Šûb, encompasses to a lesser degree apostasy from God (Num 14:43), and turning away from evil (1 Kgs 8:35), as well as primarily, repentance and return to God (Deut 30:2). Soggin delightfully draws our attention to the LXX translation of the verb, שׁוּב Šûb, as *strephein.* See also, E. Würthwein, "μετανοέω," in *TDNT* 4:975–1008; G. Betram, "στρέφω," *TDNT* 7:714–729 and Hans-Joachim Kraus, *Pslams 60–150: A Continental Commentary* (Minneapolis: Fortress Press, 1993), 448.

123 See Holladay, *Šûbh in the Old Testament,* 117–157.

124 Bracke, "*šûb šᵉbût,*" 236.

this approach he demonstrates that the phrase identifies a model of restoration whose primary characteristic is God's reversal of his judgment, which of course brings out the sense of restoration of fortunes, used in our text (Zeph 3:20e).[125]

Bracke does this so well by his investigation of the concept or the phrase in the OT, especially in Jeremiah, Zephaniah's contemporary.[126] He notices that the greatest concentration of occurrences of the phrase is found in Jeremiah 29–33, where the phrase is used eight times, mostly referring to YHWH's reversal of his judgments.[127] Other texts of the OT, including, Deuteronomy 30:3, Amos 9:14–15; Psalms 14; 53; 85:1–3; Lamentation 2:14; Job 42:10 and especially Zephaniah, all portray God's reversal of his judgment.[128]

Moreover, from Bracke's perspective, Zephaniah chapter 1, announces YHWH's intent to devastate Jerusalem for the sin of the people, while Zephaniah 2:5–7, which ends with the promise of שבות/$š^ebût$ שוב/$šûb$ (restoration of fortunes), portray the time when the remnant of Judah will re-possess the seacoast, once occupied by her enemies.

Zephaniah 3:14–20 calls Israel to rejoice because the Lord has taken away judgments against her. This is followed by the judgment of Israel's enemies and her return to the land (3:20).[129] In other words, the phrase שבות/$š^ebût$ שוב/$šûb$, is used to identify a model of restoration, and YHWH's fulfillment of His promises of restoring the fortune and the well-being of his people.

In sum, in modern scholarship two main approaches have been identified in interpreting this concept. They are that of the "return from captivity" and that of the "reversal of fortunes."[130] Although the "restoration of fortune," implies a conception of a lot of well-being, Ben Zvi rightly thinks that it does not necessarily imply either captivity in gen-

---

125 Bracke, "šûb š^ebût," 233.
126 Bracke, however, in 1983 wrote his doctoral dissertation on Jeremiah; "The Coherence and Theology of Jeremiah (PhD diss., Richmond, VA: Union Theological Seminary, 1983).
127 See Bracke, "šûb š^ebût," 236–239 for an extensive insight.
128 See Bracke, "šûb š^ebût," 239–243 for details.
129 Bracke, "šûb š^ebût," 242.
130 Ben Zvi, Book of Zephaniah, 162.

eral or the Babylonian exile in particular. But it is clear that the "reversal of fortune," implies that there has been a misfortune and a judgment. Also, one can safely say that for Israel, the events of the exile were a significant misfortune.[131] Zephaniah 3:20e, in my judgment, represents a general reversal of the fortunes of Israel, including the horrible events of the exile.

The features of these restored conditions of Israel in the prophetic literature,[132] and particularly in Zephaniah, are well outlined by Mowinckel.[133]

They include: the political and national deliverance of Israel (Isa 9:3; 10:27; 14:25; 52:2; Jer 30:8; Ezek 34:27), the restoration of the dynasty and the kingdom of David (Isa 11:13ff; Jer 3:18; 31: 27; 33:7; Ezek 37:15–22; Hos 2:2ff; 3:5; Obad 18; Zech 7:13; 9:10–13; 10:5ff; 11:4–17; 13:7–9; Isa 4:2; 7:10–17; Jer 17:25; Mic 4:8; 5:1–3; Zech 9:9ff).[134] It also embraces the reunion of the two kingdoms (Isa 11:13ff; Jer 3:18; Ezek 37:15–22; Obad 18), the destruction of the enemy powers (Isa 13–23; Jer 46–51; Ezek 25–32 and Zeph 2), as well as the return of the Diaspora (Isa 43: 5ff; 48:20; 49:17ff; 52:8–11; 56:7; 57:13; 60:4–8; Jer 3:18 and Zeph 3:19–20).[135] In other words, YHWH will restore the total well-being of those who trust in him. This divine restoration highlights the sovereignty and the universality of YHWH. It also highlights his salvific power, as he had promised (Zeph 3:20).

131 Ben Zvi, *Book of Zephaniah,* 163.
132 Besides Zephaniah 1:4–6; 3:11–20, the religious and moral restoration of the people including judgment on the traitors, is evident in the following prophetic texts: Isa 1:18–31; 2:20; 3:11–23; 4:3–6; 17:8; 27:9; 29:20; 33:22; Ezek 14:1–11; 22:36–38; 34:17–22; Jer 33:8; Mic 5:9–13; Zech 13:2–6; Mal 2:10–13.
133 Mowinckel, *He That Cometh,* 146–147.
134 Mowinckel, *He That Cometh,* 146.
135 See Mowinckel, 146. Here, besides peace among the nations, (Isa 2:4) and the fertility of the land, people and cattle (Isa 49:20; Joel 4:20), the restoration of Jerusalem as the political and religious capital of the world (Isa 49: 16–19) also fall within the limits of the restored conditions of Israel.

3.2 A Summary Reflection on Chapter Three

Chapter Three concentrated on the exegesis and on the theology of Zephaniah 3:14–20. We saw that the joy of salvation and restoration long anticipated by the wrath and judgment in the unit of Zephaniah 1:14–18, are fulfilled in the unit of Zephaniah 3:14–20. The uniquely poetic, literary and linguistic features of Zephaniah 3:14–20 bring to light the creativity of this prophet, as distinct from the prophets before and after him, which will become clearer by the time we have discussed Chapters Four and Five. Its genre has also been identified as a hymn or psalm of praise. These literary features functioned not in isolation from the rest of the texts of Zephaniah and the Twelve.

The foregoing detailed verse-by-verse exegetical study of Zephaniah 3:14–20, highlights unequivocally that the judgment and doom heard in 1:14–18, was never the end, but an anticipation, or a foreshadowing of the joy, salvation and reversal of fortune, summated in the discussed phrase, שְׁבוּת/ *šᵉbût* שׁוּב/*šûb* (v 20e). This phrase theologically embraces captivity, general well-being and the entire judgments with the reversal of misfortunes. These reversables include bad name, mockery, and exile, denial of liberty, promotion of fundamental human right and freedom of worship, for the people. It also involves the political and national deliverance of Israel, the restoration of the dynasty and the kingdom of Israel, the unification of the two kingdoms, the defeat of the enemies, return from captivity, joy, peace, as well as moral, spiritual and religious restoration of Israel. This is true, since among other things, the religious qualities of the remnant to be restored include humility, lowliness, seeking refuge in the the Lord. It is contingent upon rejection of pride (1:16; 2:10, 15; 3:11) and placing of absolute trust and hope in YHWH alone, the sovereign of all creation.

This message foreshadows the more explicit teaching of the NT (Matt 5; 11:5 and Luke 1:26–53; 4:18). Zephaniah's theology of the Day of YHWH is fulfilled or alluded to in the Christian theology of hope, continued by the apostles (Acts 1:6) and especially by St. Paul (1: Thess 4:13–18; 1 Cor 5:5; Phil 1:6). Zephaniah's theology of hope, suggests that a believing person can face or endure hardship in as much

194

as he or she is convinced that it will not last forever, with the hope that something greater will happen when their fortunes shall be restored.

In fact, the prophets, including Zephaniah, as described by David P. Reid were pastors. They helped Israel to put language on its experiences, that is, they helped to reinterpret Israel's reality. They were Israel's creative, living, challenging and actualizing memory.[136] Zephaniah not only adapted past traditions, but he arose to the occasion of creatively actualizing these past traditions, discussed in Chapter Four of this thesis.

Therefore, an investigation into the usage of the concept of יום יהוה (the Day of the Lord) in the prophetic tradition, especially in Amos 5:18–20 and in the rest of the Twelve Minor Prophets, in the next Chapter will serve to shed more light on, and facilitates a better understanding of, the discussed concept of the Day of YHWH in the prophet Zephaniah. It will help create the setting for a comparative overview of Zephaniah with the other prophets. In other words, it will help us appreciate and adapt better the pastoral dividends of the specific creativity of the prophecy of Zephaniah.

---

136 Reid, *What Are They Saying About the Prophets?*, 33.

Chapter Four

A Study of the Day of YHWH Traditions in the Old Testament and in the Traditions of the Minor Prophets Other than Zephaniah

In the last Chapter we investigated the theology of the restoration of fortunes and the salvation of the poor remnant, who seek refuge in YHWH (3:14–20). This we noted was long foreshadowed in the pericope of judgment and call for repentance (1:14–18). In this Chapter we shall examine the various traditions of the Day of YHWH in the relevant passages of the Old Testament (antecedent scriptural motifs), particularly in the prophetic traditions, of the Minor Prophets, other than Zephaniah.

This will enable us appreciate better the adaptation, modification and the level of specific acts of contextualization made by Zephaniah, in his proclamation of the message of יום יהוה (the Day of YHWH). The scope of our investigation as mentioned earlier will be limited to relevant passages in the prophetic books of Amos, Hosea, Micah, and in the remaining books of the Twelve Minor Prophets (Joel, Obadiah, Jonah, Nahum, Habakkuk, Haggai, Zechariah and Malachi). But a strong emphasis will be laid on the centrality of the themes of the Day of the Lord and restoration of fortunes in the Book of the Twelve.

4.1 Antecedent Scriptural Motifs in the OT

Although there is a fundamental agreement among scholars that Amos 5:18–20, is one of the most ancient sources of the phrase, יום יהוה (the Day of YHWH), thematic and verbal allusions to other OT motifs, especially, details of Israel's salvation history, reveal an intimate familiarity of the prophets with antecedent scriptures.[1]

In other words, the implications of YHWH's covenant relationship with His people (Exod 20:22–23:33), later innovated by the deuteronomistic historians (Deut–2Kgs), and the priestly writers (Lev17–26) are familiar to the prophets.[2] But in response to Israel's disobedience and the violation of YHWH's divine initiative, the prophets, YHWH's messengers, announced judgment upon Israel and other nations. The prophets, including Zephaniah, anticipated YHWH's judgment on Israel. These prophetic pronouncements are traceable to other OT texts. A typical example of this is the implementation of the curses and threats, evident in Leviticus 26:14–39 and in Deuteronomy 28:15–68. For the limited scope of this chapter, we shall begin the study of these prophetic traditions, with Amos, the first of the classical prophets[3] and the first prophet with a book in his name, where the concept of the Day of YHWH was first specifically heard.[4]

4.2 The Day of YHWH Tradition in the Prophet Amos

Several scholars, as we have already illustrated, believe that the concept of the Day of YHWH was first heard in the text of the prophet Amos. Hans M. Barstad is one of those who argue for the ancient and em-

1   Robert B. Chisholm, Jr., "Theology of the Minor Prophets," in *A Biblical Theology of the Old Testament* (ed. Roy B. Zuck; Chicago: Moody Press, 1991), 399.

2   See Chisholm Jr., "Theology of the Minor Prophets," 399–403 for an impressive theological exposition of this divine initiative with His people.

3   See Wcela, *Prophets,* 11–12 for the distinction between "primitive prophets" and the "classical prophets." Here he basically describes the primitive prophets as those we have the description of what they did and stories about how they lived and said, but without a collection of the words they spoke in the name of Yahweh. On the other hand the "classical prophets" indicates those whose words were spoken in the name of Yahweh and have been handed. See also Reid, *What Are They Saying about the Prophets?*, 8–12.

4   See Stuhlmueller, *Amos, Hosea, Micah, Nahum, Zephaniah, Habakkuk,* 9.

phatic rootedness of the "Day of YHWH," in the Prophet Amos (עמוס).[5]
He describes Amos 5:18–20 as "one of the most intriguing passages in
the prophetic message of Amos."[6] It is a passage located within the
wider context of Amos' cultic polemics (Amos 5: 1–17, 18–20 and 21–
27) that has left an impressive landmark, on the sand of the history of
research.[7]

5   The meaning of this word, עמוס is not completely known. In the *BDB*, its root
    meaning is traced to the verb, עמס an infinitive absolute, which means "load,"
    and "carry." These could further imply the loading of a load on someone (Gen
    44:13; Neh 13:15) or the actual carrying of the load (Zech 12:3; Isa 46:1). If it
    is seen theophorically, as an abbreviation of עמסיה which was a common
    name in Judah, the meaning would then be; "YHWH's load" or "YHWH car-
    ries the load of the person." That is to say, YHWH supports the individual.
    However, the meaning is not completely known, neither do we know the rea-
    son, his parents named him Amos. See also, John L. McKenzie, *Dictionary of the
    Bible* (New York: Touchstone Book, 1995), 27–28, for further insights.
6   Hans M. Barstad, *The Religious Polemics of Amos: Studies in the Preaching of Am
    2, 7B–8; 4, 1–1 3; 5: 1–2 7; 6; 4–7, 8, 14* (VTSup 34; Leiden, The Nether-
    lands: Brill, 1984), 89.
7   Early research on this subject include: P. Volz, "Die radikale Ablehnung der
    Kultreligion durch die altestamentlichen Propheten," *ZSTh* 14 (1937): 63–85;
    Ernst Würthwein, "Amos 5: 21–27," *ThLZ* 72 (1947): 143–52; A. Bentzen,
    "The Ritual Background of Amos 1:2–2:16," *Oudtestamentische Studien* 8 (1950):
    85–99 ; Arvid S. Kapelrud, *Studia Theologica* 4 (1951): 5–12; idem., "God As
    Destroyer in the Preaching of Amos and in the Ancient Near East," *JBL* 1 (1952):
    33–38; H. H. Rowley, "Ritual and the Hebrew Prophets," *JSS* 1 (1956): 338–
    60; R. Hetscheke, *Die Stellung der vorexilitishchen Schriftpropheten zum Kultus*
    (BZAW 75; Berlin: 1957); M. J. Buss, "The Meaning of "Cult" and Interpreta-
    tion of the Old Testament," *JBR* 32 (1964): 317–25; Kapelrud, "The Role of
    Cult in Old Israel," in *The Bible in Modern Scholarship* (ed., J. Philip Hyatt,
    Nashville, NY: Abingdon Press, 1965) 44–56; Georges Farr, "The Language of
    Amos, Popular Or Cultic?," *VT* 16 (1966): 312–24; M. Sekine, "Das Problem
    der Kultpolemik bei den Propheten," *EvTh* 28 (1968): 605–609; Larry J. Rec-
    tor, "Israel's Rejected Worship: An Exegesis of Amos 5," *ResQ* 21 (1978): 161–
    175; Barstad, *The Religious Polemics of Amos* (1984); and Meir Weiss, "Con-
    cerning Amos' Repudiation of The Cult," in *Pomegranates and Golden Bells:
    Studies in Biblical, Jewish, and Near Eastern Ritual, Law, and Literature in Honor
    of Jacob Milgrom* (ed., D. P. Wright, D. N. Freeman and A. Hurvitz; Winona
    Lake, IN: Eisenbrauns, 1995), 199–214 .

Shalom M. Paul also observes that the words of Amos 5:18–20, where the concept of the Day of YHWH is located, is followed by another pericope accenting the words of the Lord (vv 21–27). They are connected by a common ideological denominator.[8] It is a denominator of abuse of justice and popular belief in election theology, common as well in the time of Amos, which deserves a brief elaboration here.

Amos, preached in the eighth century, during the reigns of Jeroboam II (788–747 B.C.E.) in the north and Uzziah in the south (785–733 B.C.E.).[9] It was a time of political equilibrium. Israel, at this time reached its pinnacle of material, political power and economic prosperity, expanding its territory northward and southwards at the expense of Hamath and Damascus, restoring Davidic border in Syria (2 Kgs 14:23–29). Assyria was weak and Syria was in decline to the commercial and military advantages of Israel.[10]

8   Shalom M. Paul, *Amos: A Commentary on the Book of Amos* (ed., Frank Moore Cross; Philadelphia: Fortress Press, 1991), 182.

9   James, L. Mays, "Words about the Words of Amos," *Interpretation* 13 (1959): 263; J. D. Smart, "Amos," (*IDB* 1; Nashville: Abingdon Press, 1962), 118; Hans Walter Wolff, *Joel and Amos: A Commentary* (trans., Waldemar Janzen, S. D. McBride and C. A. Muenchow, Jr.; Philadelphia: Fortress Press, 1977), 89; Shalom M. Paul, *Amos: A Commentary on the Book of Amos* (ed., Frank Moore Cross.Minneapolis: Fortress Press, 1991), 1. Here Shalom is right by stating that "chronology is very complicated subject, and the dates given by historians for the various regnal variance years are often at variance." His suggestion that the following be consulted for different chronological opinions is recommended: H. Tadmor, "Chronology," *EM* 4:261–62 (Heb,); J. Bright, *A History of Israel* (3rd ed.; Philadelphia: Westminster, 1981), 470–71; J. M. Miller and J. H. Hayes, *A History of Ancient Israel and Judah* (Philadelphia: Westminster, 1986) 296; and J. A. Brinkman, "Appendix: Mesopotamian Chronology of the History Period," in A. Leo Oppenheim, *Ancient Mesopotamia: Portrait of a Dead Civilization,* (Chicago: The University Press, 1964), 347. See also Jörg Jeremias, *The Book of Amos: A Commentary* (OTL; Louisville, KY: Westminster John Knox Press, 1998), 1–2; Michael D. Coogan, *The Old Testament,* 307–309. I find Coogan's "Chronological Table of Rulers," 530–533, very useful.

10 Abraham J. Heschel, *The Prophets* (New York: Haperennial, 1995), 33. See also 2 Kings 14:23–15:7 and 2 Chronicles 26 for further information. See also Coogan, *Old Testament,* 307–309.

Consequently, wealth and pride prevailed in the land (Amos 6:4). With the emergent wealth, there was an unfortunate corresponding emergence of idle banqueting, feasting and consuming of rich food by the rich class (6:4–6), to the detriment of the poor class. Women of the ruling, and rich class (פרות הבשׁן), encouraged their husbands to ignore the אביונים, the דלים, and the ענוים (4:1; 2:7; 8:4). Marketers and merchants were dishonest in order to increase their prosperity, often giving small measures and charging inflated prices (8:5). Bribery and corruption, expropriation, and fraud became the order of the day even in the law courts (5:5–12).[11]

The wealthy and the powerful minority oppressed and marginalized the majority poor (2:6). There was a yawning gap between the rich and the poor people.[12] For example, the poor were often sold for a pair of sandals, by the rich (2:6; 8:6). Yet religious zeal was at an all time peak. Despite elaborated and decorated ceremonies, rich offerings, festival gatherings and sweet melodies (5:21–23), the absence of justice, righteousness and ethical standards made religion mere formal observances. The message of Amos 5:18–20 is not isolated from this overall setting of social injustices and hypocritical practice of faith. In addition, his poetic talents, courage, interest in international affairs (1:3–2:5; 9:7), experiences and Amos' acquaintance with life, furnished the linguistic vessels in which he transported his message of the Day of YHWH.[13]

11   Heschel, *Prophets*, 33.
12   See Roland de Vaux, *Ancient Israel: Its Life and Institutions* (Grand Rapids, MI: Erdmann Publishing, 1997) 135–38 and Coogan, *Old Testament*, 309 where the eighth century B.C.E. stratified society is said to have been different from the pre-Monarchy homogenous society. The later was characterized by solidarity and oneness; while the former is noted for making distinctions between the rich and the poor. Archaeologically, Ivories have been discovered to have been used in the eighth century Samaria. Also the excavation of Tell erl-Farah (Tirzah) shows evidence of social revolution that had taken place. While the houses of the pre-Monarchy period were discovered to have been built in a uniform, homogeneous manner, those of the eighth century were constructed in different shapes, styles and sizes, to differentiated between the wealthy and the poor.
13   James Limburg, *Hosea–Micah*. Interpretation (ed. James Luther Mays; Atlanta: John Knox Press, 1988), 82–83.

Beside these injustices and abuses of wealth, the people of Israel saw in Jeroboam's military successes an act of YHWH's benevolence or protection of a special people (2 Kgs 14:25–27). In fact, prior to the emergence of the Prophet Amos, they were already consumed with the belief that they were chosen and destined by YHWH for greater things, especially political preeminence. They were destined to be instrumental in demonstrating to the nations the superiority of YHWH, Israel's God, over all the other gods of the nations.[14] YHWH had just shown his pleasure in Israel and had manifested his power in recent days by subduing Damascus, her foe. So, Amos preached to a community of Israel so proud of their military strength and confident that in the future, the Day the Lord will manifest Himself in Israel's destruction and humiliation of all the rest of their enemies.

The popular conception of the Day of YHWH, was therefore, that of a great day of battle on which YHWH would place Himself at the head of the armies of Israel and lead them to crush their enemies.[15] This popular belief was based on the covenant traditions by which Israel regarded herself, as a special people, chosen by YHWH. But this privilege was abused by their discussed acts of idolatry, injustices and acts of exploitation of the poor and the less privileged people, including men, women and children.

In fact, justice of the highest level was denied to some classes of society. There were also all kinds of abuses of cultic practices and power, which we mentioned above. Following this backdrop of abuse of freedom and benevolence of God, Amos changed salvation history to judgment history. Amos stresses that the Day of the Lord will be a day of punishment not a day of victory as earlier understood by the community of Israel. Amos challenged the existent situation of social injustices of his time. He reversed the existent popular conception of the Day of YHWH as a day of light to that of darkness.

---

14   Smith, "Day of Yahweh," 511.
15   Smith, "Day of Yahweh," 512.

The following prophetic oracle of Amos 5:18–20, is worth citing in full here:[16]

הוי המתאוים את־יום יהוה	18a	Misfortunes![17] for you who desire the Day of YHWH
למה־זה לכם יום יהוה	18b	What is this Day of YHWH for you?
הוא־חשך ולא־אור	18c	This (Day) shall be darkness, not light
כאשר ינוס איש מפני הארי	19a	It is as a man who escape from the lion
ופגעו הדב	19b	But he is attacked by a bear
ובא הבית	19c	Then coming home
וסמך ידו על־הקיר	19d	And lean his hand on the wall
ונשכו הנחש	19e	But he is bitten by a snake
הלא־חשך יום יהוה ולא־אור	20a	Is not the Day of YHWH darkness and no light?
ואפל ולא־נגה לו	20b	Gloomy and no brightness?

16 The translations are mine.

17 I translate הוֹי (misfortune-a noun) an interjection for few reasons. First, it seems to covey better all the woes of a contemporary audience. Also the following synonyms of "misfortunes" from the *Rogets's 21st Century Thesaurus In Dictionary Form* (ed., The Princeton Language Institute, Barbara Ann Kipfer; New York: The Philip Life Group, 1999), in my judgment might help modern readers towards a better understanding of Amos' message of doom: bad luck; disaster; accident; adversity; affliction, annoyance, anxiety, bad break, bad news, blow; burden, calamity, casualty, cataclysm, catastrophe, contretemps, cross, crunch, debacle, hardship, harm, inconvenience, misadventure, mischance, misery, reverse, trouble etc. Second, scholars do not agree on the original *Sitz im Leben* of this form. Some trace it to wisdom tradition while others trace it to the funeral laments. For instance Erhard Gersternberger in his article, "The Woe-Oracle of the Prophets," *JBL* 81(1962): 249–63 argues that the woe article came from the wise men's reflection about the vicissitude of life in the world. For him it is a wisdom saying. While Claus Westermann, in his work, *Basic Forms of Prophetic Speech* (trans., H.C. White; Philadelphia: The Westminster Press, 1967), 190–94, sees it a curse form. While R.J. Clifford, in "The Use of Hôy in the Prophets," *CBQ* 28 (1966): 458–464, traces it to the lament over the dead. Also, G. Wanke in his "ʼōy und hôy," *ZAW* 78 (1966): 215–18 argues that "ʼōy" is cry of dread, perils and lament, while "hôy" is lament for dead. I do not think the meaning should be confined to these distinctions as "woes" can take any form of "misfortune" or its synonyms.

Reaction to this widely discussed passage, by scholars, including Smith who confirms that it is in the hands of Amos that the popular conception of the Day of YHWH underwent a transformation. Instead of being the day of Israel's glorification at the expense of her enemies, it now became the day of her humiliation, and chastisement at the hands of YHWH. It was a complete reversal of all the hopes which Israel has so long centered on this day.[18]

Smith concludes his observation on the above passage by suggesting that while formulating his doctrine of יום יהוה (the Day of YHWH), Amos did not break away completely from the past. He made use of some of the extant elements of popular belief namely, the thought that YHWH would personally manifest himself in judgment which will occur in a specific day. The thought was also that this day would be a day of battle, to be accompanied by wonderful phenomena on earth and in the heavens. It would include judgment and punishment upon Israel and its enemies. But Amos's radical reversal brought challenging discomfort upon Israel.[19]

On this changing message of Amos, James Luther Mays affirms that Amos is known for taking the central themes in Israel's faith and turning them against his audience (Amos 3:1–2; 5:4–6; and 9:7).[20] Amos knew the decision of YHWH, contested the piety of his hearers and warned against the disastrous outcome of their piety (Amos 5:18–20).[21] The coming reversal of salvation history (2:9–11), the election (3:1–2), culticism (5:4–6) and the Exodus (9:7), was the complete opposite of the expectation of Israel. Northern Israel anticipated to their disappointment, the "soon arrival" of the Day of the Lord, in which the Lord would intervene against the nation's enemies and lead it to greater glory (Amos 5:18).[22]

---

18 Smith, "Day of Yahweh," 513.
19 Smith, "Day of Yahweh," 515.
20 James L. Mays, *Amos: A Commentary* (OTL; Philadelphia: The Westminster Press, 1969), 103. See also Shalom, *Amos: A Commentary* (Minneapolis: Fortress Press, 1991), 185.
21 Mays, *Amos*, 103.
22 Chisholm Jr, "A Theology of the Minor Prophets," 406.

Similarly, Barstad re-affirms that the woe utterance contained in Amos 5:18–20, is a pronouncement of doom (misfortunes) for those who desire this Day of YHWH.[23] In verse 18a, for instance, the Prophet Amos begins with the interjection of "misfortunes" (הוֹי) followed by an absolute participle which describes the conduct which attracts the lamentation. Such an absolute participle without an interjection of misfortune (הוֹי) was earlier heard in Amos 5:7 and with the interjection further up, in the text of Amos 6:1.[24]

This sort of woe-cry or "cry of misfortune," pronounced over a living audience, according to Mays, is found only in the prophetic literature. The prophet, Mays stresses, plays the role of denouncing or lamenting the death of his audience in his preaching, since the prophet would know in advance the punishment decreed by YHWH, that commensurate the dire consequences of the audience's conduct.[25]

In verse 18a, the *hithpael* participle הַמִּתְאַוִּים ("you who desired") the Day of the Lord, strongly suggests against those who object that Amos's audience had no pre-conception of this concept. Hans Walter Wolff also affirmingly calls attention to the fact that Amos evidently grapples with this expression. Also, the fact that this is repeated thrice (5:18a, 18b, and 20), clearly shows it to be the point of contention in this oracle."[26] Verses 18b and 20a present questions that challenge further interpretation of the message of Amos. In verse 18b, Amos directly confronts his audience, with this rhetorical question, "לָמָּה־זֶּה לָכֶם יוֹם יְהוָה" (what is this Day of YHWH for you?).

Amos unequivocally states that the Day of YHWH will be characterized by darkness and not light (הוּא־חֹשֶׁךְ וְלֹא־אוֹר). Darkness here symbolizes judgment, while light is a symbol of salvation. Amos em-

---

23   Barstad, *Religious Polemics,* 109.

24   The interjection of misfortune, used to refer to dead was used in 1 Kings 13:30 (הוֹי אָחִי), "misfortune, my brother!" and in Jeremiah 22:18.

25   Mays, *Amos,* 103.

26   Hans Walter Wolff, *Joel and Amos: A Commentary on the Books of the Prophet Joel and Amos,* ed., S. Dean McBride, Jr. (trans., Waldemar Janzen, S. D. McBride, Jr., and C.A. Muenchow; Philadelphia: Fortress Press, 1977), 255. And outside prophetic texts the phrase appears only once in Lamentation 2:22, (בְּיוֹם אַף־יְהוָה) "on the day of the wrath of the Lord."

phasizes the calamity and doom in store for Israel. It will be a time of inescapable judgment (5:19) that will culminate in exile (5:27).[27]

The motif of darkness, literally (8:9) and figuratively (9:1) becomes vivid part of the description of the Day of YHWH in the prophetic literature (Isa 13:10; Ezek 30:3; Joel 2:1–2; Zeph 1:15).[28] Moreover, such an antithetical-rhetorical structuring is common in Amos' prophetic messages (5:4–5; 14, 20; 8:11; 9:4). Again, by repeating הלא־חשך יום יהוה ולא־אור ("Is not the Day of YHWH darkness and no light") in verse 20a, Amos not only stresses the importance of this message for his audience, but he effectively and masterfully creates an *inclusio.*[29]

In verse 19a-e, Amos resorts to his usual repertoire of linguistic and metaphorical expressions (2:13; 3:12; 6:12; and 9:9), to convey his message. The Day of YHWH for Amos, is compared to the situation of a man who escapes from the lion (הארי), but only to end up been attacked by a bear (הדב). It is compared to the situation of a man who comes home to lean his hand on the supposedly safe walls of his house, but only to find himself been bitten by a snake (הנחש). In fact, an encounter with these deadly creatures is never a pleasant one (1 Sam 17:34, 36–37; 2 Kgs 2:24; Hos 13:7–8; Prov 28:15 and Num 21:6). Sometimes it leads to a catastrophe and death.

By these, the Prophet Amos wants to metaphorically reminds Israel that misfortunes can occur when least expected. Relying on the laurel of momentary success, like in the case of Jeroboam II (2kgs 14:23–29), who crushed Damascus, could be an illusion. In other words, even if Israel had escaped death from the hands of its enemies during previous

---

27 Chisholm Jr., "Theology of the Minor Prophet," 406.

28 Shalom, *Amos*, 185.

29 Richard N. Soulen and R. Kendall Soulen, in *Handbook of Biblical Criticism*, 85–86 describes rightly an *"Inclusio,"* as (from Lat: shutting off, confinement) "a technical term for a passage of scripture in which the opening phrase or idea is repeated, paraphrased, or otherwise returned to at the close (also called a cyclic or ring composition) such as Ps 1; 4:1a –3b; 8; 21; Amos 1:3–5, 6–8, 9–15; Ezek 25:3–7, 8–11, 12–17; Jer 3:1–4:4." I agree with Soulen that "the presence of the inclusion can aid the critic in determining the limits of an idea or tradition, particularly in the analysis of material that is composite in nature such as the prophetic literature."

battles, deliverance would not really come since they lapsed back to injustices, expropriation, fraud and the practice of unrighteousness (Amos 5:21–27). The coming of יום יהוה (the Day of YHWH) will be as deadly as an encounter of someone with הארי, הדב, and הנחש (lion, bear and snake). In verse 20a–b, Amos employs an *inclusio*, which began in verse 18a–c, with negative notes of darkness and no light. But a synonymous parallelism[30] is employed by Amos by repeating in an intensive way ואפל ולא־נגה לו (gloomy and no brightness), to stress the misfortunes of the Day of YHWH.

Therefore, in verses 18–20, Amos as usual confronts the fundamental theme of Israel's faith, election, exodus, and salvation history and turns it against the community of Israel (3:2; 9:7; 2:9–11). It is worth emphasizing also that though the Day of YHWH appeared for the first time in the prophecy of Amos, it was already a familiar concept in the community of Amos's audience (Isa 9:3; Hos 2:2; Ps 137:7; Ezek 30:9; Amos 5:18a, b, and 20a). Amos was addressing his contemporary. He was actually referring to specific events in the immediate future, especially the fall of the Northern Kingdom of Israel in 722 B.C.E., approximately 40 years after the prophecy of Amos.[31] Amos knew that man's injustices bring God's justice and judgment (Amos 5:1–27), on the Day of the Lord.

But the significance of this concept in Amos, has also been subjected to various kinds of scrutiny. Even though this study maintains that Amos' audience believed that YHWH would act in a battle on their behalf on the "Day of the YHWH," some scholars, particularly

---

30 For a detailed treatment of parallelism, see, James L. Kugel, *The Idea of Biblical Poetry: Parallelism and Its History* (Baltimore: John Hopkins University Press, 1981), 1–58; Adele Berlin, "Parallelism," *ABD* 5: 155–162. Here Berlin, my professor, who taught me Biblical Hebrew Poetry in the Fall of 2007, at the Catholic University of America, Washington D.C., treats in admirable detail, parallelism, types and categories, parallel word pairs and linguistic models. In synonymous parallelism, she stresses with an example with Ps 112:1 that the same sense is expressed, but in a different way. See also Berlin, "On Reading Biblical Poetry: The Role of Metaphor," *Congress Volume Cambridge 1995* (ed. J.A. Emerton; VTSup; Leden: Brill, 1997); Luis Alonso Schökel, *A Manuel of Hebrew Poetics* (Rome: Editrice Pontificio Istituto Biblico, 2000), esp., 48–68; and Soulen, *Biblical Criticism,* 133–134.

31 Chisholm, Jr., "Theology of the Minor Prophets," 406.

Meir Weiss thinks that the Day of the Lord was not a familiar concept in the audience of Amos. For him, the Israelite understood by "day" not primarily a calendrically fixed span of time; rather, a "day" was defined in terms of events, interruptions and outcomes which occurred within that span of time, a neutral reference to a general course of events determined by YHWH.[32]

Additionally, the view that יום יהוה (the Day of YHWH) was not a definite term in any biblical period is advanced by some Jewish exegetes, beginning from the time of the Aramaic Targum.[33] Hoffmann observes that T. Jonathan, for instance, never translates *(targumized)* the phrase יום יהוה (the Day of YHWH), which would have been expected, had he believed it to be a definite term, since we find the LXX in its part, has *"septuaginized"* it as ἡ ἡμέρα τοῦ θεοῦ. Hoffmann insists that Rashi, Ibn Ezra, Maimonides and others including Weiss failed to take it as a definite term.[34]

However, for Amos if God is coming in judgment on his day (5:18–20) against his people, it is to redress the injustices, the abuse of power,

---

32   See Wolff, *Joel and Amos*, 255 for his argument against Weiss's position.

33   Yair Hoffmann, "Day of the Lord," 39. Soulen, *Biblical Criticism*, 187 clarifies the word *Targum*, (which I find very useful for non experts who may lay hand on this work), as meaning "translation" or "interpretation." This "refers specifically to Aramaic versions of the OT. In rabbinic literature the word may refer simply to the Aramiac portions, even single words of the Bible, as found in Ezra, Nehemiah, and Daniel. The Targum arose out of the synagogal practice of accompanying the reading of the Hebrew text with an Aramiac translation (*Targum*) for the benefit of Aramaic-speaking Jews. The translation, however, was provided with interpretative additions, making the Targum an expanded paraphrase of the original. No single Targum, therefore, existed; rather, numerous targumic traditions arose on the various books of the OT, except those listed previously. The most authoritative (esp. for Orthodox Jews) is *Targum Onkelos*, a version of the Palestinian Targum developed by Babylonian Jews. A reportedly Palestinian Targum of the Pentateuch containing a tradition, going back possibly to the first century C.E. was discovered by A. Diez Macho in the Vatican Library in 1956, called *Neofiti* I. Pesudo-Jonathan is the name of another Babylonian Targum, also of the Pentateuch alone." See also the earlier article of Robert P. Gorden, "Targums" in *The Oxford Companion of the Bible*, eds., Bruce M. Metzger and Michael D. Coogan (New York: Oxford University Press, 1993), 754–55.

34   Hoffmann, "Day of the Lord," 39.

wealth, cult, religious mediocrity, class distinctions and all the interrelationship of all things in creation which makes the universe an enduring and functioning entity. This judgment calls for justice that touches the lives of man and woman in relationships with his or her neighbors, including the alien, the orphan and the widow.[35] This judgment on the day of the Lord, calls for justice *(misphat)* that surges like water, and rightouesnss *(sedeqah)* like an unfailing stream (5:23–24). It is from this tradition that Zephaniah adapted his prophecy of the Day of YHWH. He would do the same with the following tradition of Hosea.

4.3 The Day of YHWH Traditions in the Prophet Hosea

Most of the motifs discussed as the foundation of the prophecy of Amos are applicable to Hosea and Micah, as well. Hosea like Amos preached in the Northern Kingdom of Israel in the middle of the eighth century (about 750 B.C.E) to a nation that was moving towards its ruin (1:1).[36] This was also a time when Israel was threatened by the Assyrian empire which was expanding westward. The king of Israel became a vassal of Assyria in 732 B.C.E., and the kingdom was brought to an end with the surrendering of Samaria in 722 B.C.E., to Assyria.

This period witnessed confusion and succession of kings, one after another. In fact, after the death of King Jeroboam II in 746 B.C.E., and the coming to an end of the first Assyrian colonialism[37] of Israel

---

35   Reid, *What Are They Saying About the Prophets*, 78.

36   See McKenzie, "Hosea," in *Dictionary of the Bible*, esp., 372 where it is suggested that, the name הושע is probably an abbreviation of "Yahweh saves."

37   Although this is a modern term, the distinction of Edward Said, *Culture and Imperialism* (New York: Vintage Books, 1993), 9 helps to explain the meaning the usage here, within the context of eighth and seventh centuries B.C.E. Israel/Judah. For Said, the term, "imperialism" means the practice, the theory, and the attitudes of dominating metropolitan center, ruling a distance territory; "colonialism," which is almost a consequence of imperialism, is the implanting of settlements on the distance territory. Israel and Judah had lived under the influence foreign dominations, including Assyria and Babylon.

in 732 B.C.E., about five kings fought and battle ambitiously for the throne.

This political battle was succeeded by the sixth one, Hoshea (732–722 B.C.E.).[38] But by then, it was a period of great instability and uncertainty. Law and order were nothing to write home about, with a resulting insecurity of lives and properties of the citizens (4:1f; 7:1). In spite, of these ugly social, political and moral life situations, Hosea's time and culture was blessed with a unique form of expression, communicating values which would come to enrich his prophecy.

John J. Collins has rightly observed that the attractiveness of Hosea's prophecy comes from his use of metaphor and symbol, drawn from human relationships, to drive home his message of hope, judgment and restoration. Hosea's metaphor of marriage (God's relationship with Israel), is prominent in his message of hope and restoration.[39]

Here, God chose Israel and brought her into an outstanding and a special relationship with Himself. But while in this state of marriage relationship with Gomer (Israel), she committed harlotry (turning towards other gods). By this very act Israel broke her covenant with God (Hos 1). In verses 3–5, we see the outcome of this marriage in the first child, a son, named Jezreel.[40] Jehu (842–814 B.C.E.) we know, became

38   See the "Chronological Table of Rulers," in *The New Oxford Annotated Bible: New Revised Standard Version with Apocrypha* (ed. Michael D. Coogan et al., Oxford: Oxford University Press, 2001), 530–31 for the list of these kings, which include: Zechariah (747 B.C.E.), Shallum (747 B.C.E.), Menahem (747–737 B.C.E.), Pekahia (737–735 B.C.E.) and Pekah (735–732 B.C.E.).

39   Collins, "Hosea," in *The Catholic Study Bible: New American Bible* (ed. Donald Senior et al.; New York: Oxford University Press, 1990), 354–361. But there is a diversity of opinions as to the interpretation of Hosea's usage of harlotry imagery which is beyond the scope of this work. Although some think that Gomer was not just an ordinary prostitute, but a cult prostitute devoted to the worship of pagan gods, we stress in this study the familiarity of Hosea's audience to the tradition complexes as well as the experience of infidelity in marriage to drive home the message of Israel's unfaithfulness to the covenant traditions noted earlier. That is to say God's relationship with Israel.

40   See McKenzie, *Dictionary of the Bible*, 245–246 where Jezreel is said to have been corruptly called "Esdraelon" in Greek. Jezreel means "God's sows." Its geographical significance is also extensively discussed, but the theological significance of this term will be seen as this study progresses.

the instrument of God to execute His judgment upon the house of Ahab (873–852 B.C.E.). Jeroboam II, who ruled then, was of Jehu's house and who abused the prosperity of that time as well as departed from YHWH.

Hosea attacked the apostasy, using the symbolism of the fertility cult. He condemned the departure of Israel from YHWH, to follow other gods. This act, for Hosea, was a violation of the covenant. This resulted in the loss of fertility, which swept through Israel. In Hosea, this marriage produced other children, significantly called, לא רחמה (no more pity) and לא עמי (not my people), to express the love of God and the relationship between Israel and God. It also reminded Israel that YHWH was about to punish them (Hos 1:6–9).[41]

James D. Nogalski, has recently made an impressive study of the text of Hosea in his effort to identify those elements relating to יום יהוה (the Day of YHWH).[42] He dwells on Hosea 2 as one of the units that makes use of the marriage metaphor, noted earlier to convey his prophetic message of judgment and restoration.

He argues that although Hosea presents a metaphorical role of YHWH, as the husband to Israel (Hos 1), this role of personification parallels the role played by the personified Lady Zion, in other prophetic texts (Isa 60; Jer 30:12–17; Ezek 22; Mic 7:8–13; Zeph 3:14–19). Hosea 2, Nogalski insists, reflects these contexts.[43]

---

41 See a very clear and pastoral discussion of "Hosea and the Love of God," in Wcela, *The Prophets,* 29–44.

42 Nogalski's studies will be summarized here due to the scope of this work. But see, James D. Nogalski, "The Day (s) of YHWH in the Book of the Twelve," SBL *1999 Seminar Papers: One Hundred and Thirty-Fifth Annual Meeting, November 20–23, 1999* (SBL 38; Atlanta, GA: Scholars Press, 1999), 622–626.

43 Nogalski, "Day(s) of YHWH," 623. Here, he also cites several studies on the background of the concept of Lady wisdom to include: Aloysius Fitzgerald, "The Mythological Background for the Presentation of Jerusalem as Queen and False Worship as Adultery in the OT," 403–416; Mark E. Biddle, "The Figure of Lady Jerusalem: Identification, Deification and Personification of cities in the Ancient Near East," in *The Biblical Canon in Comparative Perspective* (ed. B.Batto et al.; Lewiston, NY: Mellen Press, 1991), 173–94; Julie Galambush, *Jerusalem in the Book of Ezekiel: The City as Yahweh's Wife* (SBLDS 130; Atlanta, GA: Scholars Press, 1992) and John J. Schimitt, "The Motherhood of God and Zion as Mother," *RB* 92 (1995): 557–569.

Nogalski continues to note that "Day" appears eight times in Hosea chapter 2 (2:2, 5, 15, 17 (2xs), 18, 20, 23), but only in four instances (vv 2, 18, 20 and 23) does יום refer explicitly to a period of divine intervention with a futuristic implication.[44] Verse 2 refers to a future time when Israel and Judah will be reunited under one king, hence a time of political restoration. Verses 18, 20 and 23 on the other hand, refer to future intervention using the formula ביום ההוא ("on that Day"). Verses 18–19, in particular, anticipate a restoration of the relationship between YHWH and Israel ביום ההוא ("on that Day"). This results in YHWH's intervention, who says; "I shall banish the names of the Baals from her lips and their name will be mentioned no more." This quotation contrasts the future restoration ביום ההוא ("on that Day") with את־ימי הבעלים (the day of Baals), in verse 15.[45]

Verses 23–25 focus on the promise that has intra-textual connections with a provision of additional thematic aspect. YHWH's response ביום ההוא ("on that Day") will touch the sky which responds to the earth (23b), the earth responds to new grain, wine and oil and they shall respond to Jezreel (vv 23c–24). In these verses, as in Amos and in other contexts within Hosea, there is a reversal of judgment. Elements from nature, removed earlier by YHWH, are restored (vv 10–11). While the reference to Jezreel in verse 24b, not only refers back to the name of the first son, but it also introduces word play in verse 25.[46]

Verse 25 reverses all the judgment symbolized in the name of all the three children (לא־עמי / לא רחמה/יזרעאל), "Jazreel," (the Lord sows), "Lo-ruhamah" (no more pity), and "Lo-ammi" not my people.[47] Nogalski, brilliantly calls attention to these word plays thus: "I will sow (זרע) her for myself in the land, and I will have compassion (רחם) on her who had not obtained compassion (לא־רחמה), and I will say to those who were not my people (אל־עמי), you are my people."[48] Although Nogalski's

44   Nogalski, "Day(s) of YHWH," 623.
45   Nogalski, "Day (s) of YHWH," 624.
46   Nogalski, "Day(s) of YHWH," 624.
47   See Wcela, *The Prophets,* 32, for further analysis of the significance of "Lo-ruhama" and "Lo-ammi."
48   Nogalski, "Day(s) of YHWH," 624. See also the explanation of this in Wcela, *The Prophets,* 32–35.

word play may not be convincing to some, the message of Hosea 2, on YHWH's judgment, intervention and restoration "on that Day," is very compelling and points to Zephaniah's message of hope and restoration and fulfillment of God's promises (Zeph 3:1–20), discussed in the preceding chapters and shall be strengthened in the following one.

Lindblom had also observed these compelling elements in Hosea's prophecy. During the early stage of Hosea's prophecy, there was the hope after a period of chastisement and trial bringing about national repentance and conversion, which a new age would follow. This was an age rich in happiness and blessing of every kind (3:5).[49] But this was temporary. Hosea, convinced that conversion was not imminent lamented the ugly situation. This is well captured in the following passage (4:1–3):

> Israelites, hear what Yahweh says, for Yahweh indicts the citizens of the country: there is no loyalty, no faithful love, no knowledge of God in the country, only perjury and lying, murder, theft, adultery and violence, bloodshed. This is why the country is in mourning... Even the fish in the sea will disappear.[50]

This passage and the entire text of Hosea 4, serves as an introduction to the rest of the book and contains a summary of the prophet's message of YHWH's choice and love for Israel. It also represents, as Zephaniah would, a call for Israel's repentance to turn away from Baalism and to seek YHWH. It points clearly at YHWH's intervention, punishment and restoration.[51]

49 Lindblom, *Prophecy*, 355.

50 Other passages which demonstrate Hosea's decrying of Israel's behavior with indications of YHWH's punishment include Hosea 5:7; 6:16; 8:8–14; 9:2–17; 10:5–10; 11:5–6; 13:3 and 14:1. See also Nogalski, "Day (s) of YHWH," 625 where he discusses Hosea 9 with its five references to יוֹם (9:5[2xs], 9:7[2xs], 9:9), but only three refer to days of divine intervention (9:7 "days of punishment" = ימי הפקדה) and "days of retribution/acquittal" = ימי השלם and "the days of Gibeah" = בימי הגבעה in 9:9. Hence, 9:7–9 anticipates a period in the near future when YHWH will intervene in judgment against Israel, based on traditions especially from Judges 19–21.

51 See A. Valunlier Hunter, *Seek the Lord !: A Study of the Meaning and Function of the Exhortations in Amos, Hosea, Isaiah, Micah and Zephaniah* (Baltimore, MD: St. Mary's Seminary & University, 1982) esp., 123–175, where Hunter identifies arguments relevant to our study. This includes the fact that, Prophet Hosea

We can safely conclude that Hosea's understanding of the future, like his contemporary Amos, was shaped by his familiarity with cultural concepts, the traditions of exodus, wilderness wandering and entrance into the Promised Land. It also bore elements of the covenant, made in the desert at Sinai, which we have already discussed.

In fact similar motifs, terms and thematic concepts of judgment, punishment and restoration traditions of יום יהוה (the Day of YHWH), are found in both Micah and Isaiah[52] who preached in Judah in the same eighth century, as Amos and Hosea did in the section of Samaria.

4.4 The Day of YHWH Tradition in the Prophet Micah

The Prophet Micah,[53] from Moresheth in Judah, was a contemporary of Isaiah, who preached in the eighth century B.C.E. Micah as a book, is said to have gone through several redactional processes of pre-exilic

---

went beyond merely announcing judgment upon Israel to announcing salvation as well. Hosea seems to have perceived that the coming judgment was a necessary pre-fix for Israel's salvation. Hunter did a thorough analysis of Hosea 2:2–4; 4:15; 6:6; 10:12; 12:7 and 14:2–4 in his effort to convince us that exhortation in contemporary Israel played a role in the prophecy. In other words, traditions and the values to which Hosea's audience were familiar with influenced his prophetic message. He concludes from the analysis of those texts that, Hosea does not intend to provide a last minute escape from judgment by calling his contemporaries to repentance. Rather, Hosea is more interested in showing the people how their lack of repentance in the past has brought them to the present moment. While exhortations are present in his prophecy and do set forth what YHWH wants of His people, there is no indication that the judgment can be averted by a response of the people now. But Hosea also believes that beyond the judgment, YHWH has salvation in store for His people. Hunter's conclusion anticipated the themes of judgment, restoration of fortunes that are central to this study, on the Prophet Zephaniah.

52 The Day of YHWH in Isaiah will be discussed in Chapter Five.

53 See also McKenzie, "Micah," in *Dictionary of the Bible*, 572 for an interesting entry of the root meaning of the Hebrew name מיכה an abbreviation of מכיהו meaning, "who is like Yahweh."

texts (1–3; 6 and part of chapter 7), while Micah 4 and 5 would have been added after the Exile in Babylon.[54]

But this study approaches Micah's theophany, which is like Amos' יום יהוה (Day of YHWH), as a unified or coherent theological message of call to repentance (Mic 6), judgment (Mic 2), and restoration (Mic 4–5),[55] themes also found in the prophets already discussed. It seems that a similar motivation, which had propelled Amos to announce the Day of YHWH, prompted Micah especially in his condemnation of social injustice. Micah in chapter 2:1–5, specifically attacks the crimes of the society in the following words:

> Disaster for those who plot evil, who lie in bed planning mischief! No sooner is it dawn than they do it, since they have the power to do so. Seizing the fields that they covet, they take over houses as well, owner and house they seize alike,

---

54 Jasen, in his *Ethical Dimensions*, 129 thinks that, "he (Micah) may have been to the prophetic ministry before 721, since Samaria is referred to as still standing (1:5), and he must have continued at least till 701, since 1:8–16 seems to have an invasion of Sennacherib's siege of Jerusalem." But Jensen cites Hans Walter Wolff, *Micah the Prophet* (Philadelphia: Fortress, 1981), 3 where Wolff bases his position of the inscription of the book (1:1, which lists Jotham, Ahaz, and Hezekiah as the kings in whose days he prophesied), and argues that, Micah appeared on the scene at the very latest in 734 and was active at least until 728. But Wolff, Jensen stresses, also identifies Sennacherib's siege as the occasion for 4:14 (5:1), which would therefore, have to be dated (701).

55 For details see the work of Kenneth H. Cuffey, "Remnant, Redactor, and Biblical Theologian: A Comparative Study of Coherence in Micah and the Twelve," in *Reading and Hearing the Book of the Twelve* (ed. James D. Nogalski and Marvin A. Sweeney, Symposium Series15; Atlanta: SBL, 2000), 185–208. Here Cuffey argues that in the past modern critical scholarship would take pleasure in dissecting and reassembling biblical especially prophetic texts, hence seeing discontinuity in the text. But recently there is a welcoming approach to the texts as it stand- canonical reading or the final form of the text. He proceeds to identify coherence in the Twelve, especially in the Book of Micah (structural, thematic, internal, external coherence within sections, coherence of perspective, and coherence in the Twelve etc). With regard to coherence in theme, he stresses that Micah had a theological intent in the final form as the book stands. Micah desires to communicate something about the Lord as the God who (punishes yet) restores. The remnant is the focus of God's restoring work.

the man himself as well as his inheritance… Because of this, you will have no one to measure out a share in Yahweh's community.[56]

In fact, like the prophets discussed already, Micah sees Israel's misbehavior against the backdrop of YHWH's grace to her, which we noted in the covenant complexes. They were also presumptuous of the election theology. Israel committed these crimes without excuses. Micah 3 noted rightly some of these expressions of presumption on the part of people, thus: "Isn't Yahweh among us?' they say, 'no disaster is going to overtake us" (Mic 3: 9–12).[57] He, like Amos, would not relent in calling for accountability, on the Day of YHWH. This is well expressed in YHWH's legal suit against His people in Micah 6 as follows:

> Now listen to what Yahweh says: 'Stand up, state your case to the mountains and let the hills hear what you have to say! Listen mountains to the case as Yahweh puts it, give ear, you foundations of the earth, for Yahweh has a case against his people and he will argue it with Israel. My people what have I done to you, how have I made you tired of me? Answer me! For I brought you out of Egypt…for you know Yahweh's saving justice.

This passage demonstrates, among other things, the fact that Israel owes everything to the love and grace of YHWH. It looks back at YHWH's salvific actions. It also points at Micah's theology of hope for the poor, whom he calls YHWH's true people. When he realized the seriousness

---

56   See Jensen *Ethical Dimensions*, 130, Here he presents the material in Micah as (1) punishment of Israel's sins (judgment, social evils, and present leaders in chapters 1–3), (2) the new Israel (the people and the future king in 4 and 4:14–5:14) and (3) admonitions and threats and (6:1–7:7) then, finally (4) future mercy (7:8–20).

57   See Bright, *Covenant and Promises*, 117, where he thinks Micah's theology allowed no room whatever for such presumption of complacency as the official theology may have tended to create in the minds of the chosen people. See also, Mark E. Biddle, "Israel" and "Jacob" in the Book of Micah: Micah in the Context of the Twelve," in *Reading and Hearing the Book of the Twelve* (ed. James D. Nogalski and Marvin A Sweeney. Symposium Series 15; Atlanta: SBL, 2000), 146–165 where Biddle discusses in detail the implication of the use of "Jacob," and "Israel," in Micah 3, *vis-á-vis* the Book of the Twelve.

of this moral decadence and injustices, Micah proclaimed that judgment and destruction were unavoidable.

Samaria would be destroyed by a horrible earthquake. Jerusalem with its temple would be laid in ruins. The land would be conquered by enemies and the population deported into a foreign country. Thus the end would come upon Israel (Mic 1:1–7; 10–16; 2:4; 3:12; 4:9–13), but the remnant would be restored.[58]

Bright also confirms that Micah, still contains an abundant promise of the yet farther future, based on the Zion-David traditions.[59] This promise of restoration, like in Isaiah, is reiterated in Micah 4:1–3 thus:

> But in days to come Yahweh's Temple Mountain will tower above mountains, rise higher than the hills. Then the peoples will stream to it, then many nations will come and say, 'Come, we will go up to Yahweh's mountain, to the Temple of the God of Jacob, so that he may teach us his ways and we may walk in his paths; for the Law issues from Zion and Yahweh's word from Jerusalem.' He will judge between many peoples and arbitrate between mighty nations. They will hammer their swords into ploughshares and their spears into bill-hooks. Nations will not lift sword against nation or ever again be trained to make war.

Finally, although, the phrase or the construct form, יום יהוה (the Day of YHWH) is not prominent in the Book of Micah, "Micah's theophany, however, besides resembling that of Isaiah, is also like Amos's Day of the Lord."[60] YHWH in His Day would manifest Himself in acts of

58 See Lindblom, *Prophecy*, 365 and Bright, *Covenant and Promises*, 114–18 for an additional in-put on this subject.

59 Hunter, who in his *Seek the Lord*, 244–59 work on the exhortatory implication of Micah 6:8 concludes that, this verse is a summary of YHWH's time-honored requirements. Yet, Micah's poignant wording has made this verse one of the best known from the prophetic books, used today as a call for repentance. But Hunter believes (to the disapproval of this study), that "a future salvation based on repentance seems to be beyond the scope of this verse and chapter 6 of Micah. It seems to me it is not enough to judge Micah based on a single verse. The context of his message and the traditional backdrops of covenant traditions as suggested by Bright must be brought into consideration, while interpreting Micah and other eighth century prophets.

60 John J. Collins, "Daniel and the Minor Prophets," in *The Catholic Study Bible* (ed. Donald Senior et al., New York: Oxford University Press, 1990), 371.

judgment, justice, and restoration of the remnant, as illustrated in the above passages.

4.5 The Day of YHWH Tradition in the Prophet Joel

The Prophecy of Joel historically, is considered a late post-exilic text (400 B.C.E.).[61] By the time of Joel, any disaster could have been interpreted as "the Day of YHWH." In Joel 1–2 for instance, we read of the Day of YHWH befalling Israel. We also hear of the divine judgment against Israel's enemies, as well as some great cosmic events (Joel 3–4).

In fact, Joel, as summarized by Nogalski, "contains eleven יום (day) texts, that refer specifically to divine intervention and use a significant variety of phrases. For example, the day (1:15), the day of YHWH (1:15; 2:1; 2:11; 3:4; 4:14) and the day of darkness and gloom (2:2). Other phrases noted by Nogalski are, the day of clouds and thick darkness (2:2), in those days (3:2, 4:1), and on that day (4:18).[62] The nature of these references brings out the depth of the theological message of Joel. It is a message of judgment, a call for repentance, judgment on the colonialists and oppressors of Judah. It is above all, a message of judgment, restoration and salvation. This is clearer when we critically examine some relevant passages of the text of Joel, beginning from Joel 1:1–15.

These verses begin with the laments over the ruins of the country, calling the elders, priests and the citizens to listen (שמעו־זאת הזקנים). These laments presume the guilt of the people, leading to the first explicit mention of יום יהוה (the Day of YHWH), in Joel (1:15). This passage describes the surprising nature of the in-coming attack on, and devastation of the land.[63] Some scholars have also noticed that because

---

61 Interestingly, Joel is from the Hebrew word, יואל meaning, and "Yahweh is El." For more detail, see Mckenzie, *Dictionary of the Bible*, "Joel," 442.

62 Nogalski, "The Day(s) of YHWH," 626.

63 Nogalski, "The Day(s) of YHWH," 627.

Joel is generally considered to be he compostion from the late fourth century BCE that cites extensively form earlier biblical literature, the text of Joel is most likely dependent on that of Zephaniah, since the motifs of the statement of the imminent Day of YHWH employs the same language and imagery as in Zephaniah 1:7, 14, 15–16.[64]

The text that follows, particularly Joel 2:1–11, describes the nature of this day as an invading locust, representing a devastating army to any country. Several imageries are used here (2:2). The victims in this case are not the crops, but citizens of the land. Joel 2: 3–11 is very close to the texts of Amos and Hosea. Verses 2–17 call for the repentance and emphasis the eventual promise of YHWH's intervention and mercy, on behalf of Judah. Verse 12 for example, in this sentence, "turn back to me with all your hearts, fasting, weeping and mourning" (שבו עדי בכל־ לבבכם), demands a return to YHWH.

The following verse 13 is worth quoting in full:

וקרעו לבבכם	Tear/rend your hearts
ואל ־ בגדיכם	and not your garments
ושובו אל ־יהוה אלהיכם	and turn back to YHWH your God
כי־חנרן ורחום הוא	because he is gracious and compassionate
ארך אפים ורב ־חסד	slow to anger rich/much in kindness
ונחם על הרעה	and sorry/relent upon inflicting misery.[65]

This text goes back to the covenant tradition already discussed (Exd 34:6). In Joel, there is no certainty that God will relent or turn back and leave a blessing behind; nobody knows (v 14). But with the prayers of the priests (vv 16–17), heard, YHWH, out of his mercy, is able to restore them peace and joy (vv 19–26), as well as plenty of food and hope. That the people shall never be humiliated again, is re-assured in this expression, for (ואני יהוה אלהיכם) "I am YHWH your God" (v 27).

In addition, the outpouring of the spirit of YHWH, in Joel 3 is contingent upon the repentance, expected of the people in the above passage (Joel 2). The description of this great and terrible Day of YHWH

---

64 See Irsigler, *Gottesgericht*, 106–107; Wolff, *Joel and Amos*, 10–12, 43–44; Sweeney, *Zephaniah*, 100.

65 The Hebrew text is consistently from MT, while this translation is mine.

(vv 3–5), resembles what we heard in Zephaniah 1:14–15. It is a universal-eschatological event. During this event everyone who calls upon the name of the Lord will be saved (v 5). And as we saw when we discussed Zephaniah 3:14–20, in Chapter Three, Joel 4, continues with this language of restoration of fortunes and salvation to the people.

Joel 4:1 uses the phrase, בימים ההמה (in those days) and ובעת ההיא (and at that time), when (אשר אשוב את ־שבית יהודה וירושלם) "I will restore the fortunes of Judah and Jerusalem." This, Nogalski notices is not unconnected from the preceding chapter 3:1–5. The divine intervention of 4: 1–21, Nogalski stesses, continues the message of the restoration of Judah and Jerusalem as well as that of the punishment of the recalcitrant nations.[66]

Finally, the motif of the "Day of YHWH," in the Prophet Joel, in my opinion, is well captured by Rendtorff, when he wrote that Joel shows that the Day of the Lord can be experienced under quite different circumstances of threat and judgment, escape and repentance, individual and universal restoration or salvation).[67] This takes us to the traditions, in Obadiah, Jonah, Nahum and Habakkuk.

4.6 The Traditions in the Prophets Obadiah, Jonah, Nahum and Habakkuk

The prophetic message of Obadiah concerning the Day of YHWH, as mentioned earlier, belongs to the sixth and fifth centuries in Israel's history. It follows the traditions of the eighth century prophets. In Obadiah, like in the rest of the Twelve, the theological theme of יום יהוה (the Day of YHWH) dominates the text.[68]

---

66 Nogalski, "The Day (s) of YHWH," 629.
67 See Rendtorff, "How to Read the Book of the Twelve," 80.
68 See McKenzie, "Obadiah," in *Dictionary of the Bible*, 624 where the Hebrew word, עבדיה is translated into English as "servant of Yahweh."

But this time, this day is mostly focused on Edom or Esau, Judah's enemy.[69] Rendtorff, having studied this prophet, stresses that central in the prophecy of Obadiah, is the fact that the Lord has come to punish Edom/Esau, because of all his misdeeds against his brother, Jacob/Judah."[70]

Moreover, the word יום (day) appears in this shortest prophetic book of Obadiah, about 12 times. The construct phrase, יום יהוה (the Day of YHWH), is found only once *(hapax)* in Obadiah 15. But a close reading of the prophecy, at least starting from verse 8, with the phrase, ביום ההוא (on that day), to יום יהוה (the Day of YHWH), in verse 15, leaves no doubt that the "day (s)" here in Obadiah, are related to the same theological message of the Day of the Lord, in other prophetic books.

This lends some credibility to the arguments of A. Joseph Everson and members of his school, discussed earlier in Chapter One of this study, that other terms and motifs could refer to יום יהוה (the Day of YHWH), which could lie in the past or in the future.[71]

However, Obadiah 1:1–7 introduce the Lord's announcement on the destruction of Edom. This is followed by verse 8, which ushers in this judgment with the phrase ביום ההוא (in/on that day), on Esau "because of the violence done to Jacob," (v 10). The poetic, repetitive and parallelistic intensity of the following verses 11–15, with its inherent theological implication and description of the nature of the Day of YHWH, in Obadiah is worth citing here in full as follows:

> On that Day, when you stood aloof while strangers carried off his riches, while foreigners passed through his gate, and cast lots for Jerusalem. Do not gloat over the children of Judah on that day of their ruin. Do not play the braggart on the day of distress. Do not enter my people's gate on their day of calamity. Do not, you especially, feast your eyes on their suffering on their day of calamity. Do not touch their possessions on their day of calamity. Do not wait at the crossroads to

69   See Rolf Rendtorff, "Alas for the Day! The "Day of the Lord" in the Book of the Twelve," in *God in the Fray: A Tribute to Walter Brueggemann* (ed., Tod Linafelt and Timothy K. Beal; Minneapolis: Fortress, 1998), 192–193.
70   Rendtorff, "Alas for the Day!" 193.
71   See Nogalski, "The Day(s) of YHWH," 635.

annihilate their fugitives. Do not hand over their survivors on the day of distress. For the day of Yahweh is near for all the nations...

This passage evidently is referring to Edom's violence on Jacob or to the gloating over Judah's distress. It warns Edom, who had stood idle and celebrated Judah's collapse. Edom shall in turn like Judah, be punished on the Day of YHWH. All the other nations shall be punished, as well. Nogalski, on this particularly thinks that unlike verse 8, verses 11–15 allude to the destruction of Jerusalem as the day of divine intervention while warning Edom on the Day of YHWH for all nations.[72] The implication is that the Day of YHWH, in Obadiah has both individual and universal dimensions. The prophet does not restrict the events of the Day of YHWH to a restricted, limited or exclusive geographical environment.

In other words, when the Day of the Lord is explicitly mentioned in verse 15, it refers to all nations thus, (כי־קרוב יום ־יהוה על־כל־הגוים) "for the Day YHWH is near for all the nations."[73] Still, in relation to the Twelve, particularly to the book of Joel, the expectation that on Mount Zion "there shall be those who escape or survive/recover (פליטה), in verse 17, re-echoes Joel 3:5. But the uniqueness in Joel is that the remnant will consist of believers from all the nations, who call upon the name of YHWH. This is contrary to the prophecy of Obadiah, where only the house of Judah or the house of Joseph shall rule over their enemies from Mount Zion. In other words, in Obadiah, there will be no survivor of the house of Esau.[74] However, the expression in verse 21, ליהוה המלוכה (for sovereignty is to YHWH), suggests that the Day belongs to YHWH, and it is the Lord who rules everyone regardless of nationality.

---

72 Nogalski, "The Day(s) of YHWH," 636.
73 See Rendtorff, Alas for the Day!" 193. See also Piergorgio Beretta, ed., ספר תרי עשר (*Libro di Dodici Profeti*), *I Profeti Minori: Osea, Gioele, Amos, Abdia, Giona, Michea, Naum, Abacuc, Sofonia, Aggeo, Zecharia, Malachia, Ebraico, Greco, Latino, Italiano*(Milano: San Paolo,1997), 134 where it is translated as "Perché è vicino il giorno de Signore contro tutte le nazioni."
74 See Rendtorff, "How to Read the Book of the Twelve," 82.

On the other hand, the Book of Jonah presents its uniqueness in the prophetic literature.[75] Jonah's uniqueness, according to James Nogalski, extends to both the form and the context, since no other prophetic book so extensively consists of prophetic narrative. It is also unique, since no other prophetic writing so consistently portrays foreigners, positively at the expense of the prophet around, to whom the story revolves.[76]

In other words, some commentators see Jonah as anti-prophet and his message a fable or parable, with the backdrop of the history of Assyrian corrupt and excessive colonial practices. We may recall that Jonah was composed most likely in the post-exilic period, quite close to the time of Joel and Obadiah. But while Obadiah seems to suggest that salvation is for Judah only, Jonah stresses salvation for all nations. Although the Day of YHWH is not explicitly mentioned anywhere in the Book of Jonah, the implicitness of this theological concept and the importance of Jonah, in the history of Israel's salvation and of the entire world, cannot be underestimated.[77]

Paul Murray, an Irish Dominican from Northern Ireland, in his simple and readable spiritual-theological masterpiece, *A Journey with Jonah: the Spirituality of Bewilderment*, presents, in my own opinion, presents a poetic, powerful and concise outline of the theological story in Jonah. He insightfully captures well Jonah's Day of YHWH's restoration of his people in this little book.

The Book of Jonah, Murray stresses, opens with Jonah rejecting God's explicit command to preach to the Gentiles of Nineveh, the an-

---

75 The meaning of Jonah is not clear. But some say the Hebrew word יוֹנָה means, "dove."

76 Nogalski, *Redactional Processes in the Book of The Twelve* (BZAW 218; Berlin: de Gruyter, 1993), 248.

77 Scholars have noticed that the episode in the belly of the fish is full of humor but with high theological significance in the NT. Jesus uses this theological story in a very profound way. In Matthew 12:38–42; 16: 1–4; Luke 11: 29–32 signs of Jonah are explicitly quoted, and Judgment Day invoked. Jonah's stay in the belly of the fish is interpreted as prefigure of Jesus in the womb of Virgin Mary, and Jonah is often used as a symbol of resurrection in Christian art. His stay in the Fish's belly is the netherworld. His rescue is the resurrection. In OT, YHWH gives and takes life. YHWH is the sovereign of creation. See, further summary of this in Collins, "Daniel and the Minor Prophets," 370.

cient capital of the Assyrian Empire on the eastern bank of the Tigris River, as a result of sin and corruption (Jonah 1). But Jonah's rejection extended his flight in the opposite western direction of Tarshish, by the next moving ship. Jonah, while sailing, was cast into the sea by the gentile sailors, when the vehicle was threatened by a mysterious wave in an extraordinary manner.[78]

Jonah was preyed upon by a fish. He remained in the belly of the fish for three days, undigested, praying in anguish, until the fish vomited him back to the land (Jonah 2). Jonah now picked himself up with a repentant spirit and obedience to YHWH. He proceeded to preach to the sinful Assyrian-Ninevites. Since mercy is the final work of God, Jonah's preaching was finally instrumental to YHWH's mercy and restoration of the repentant Ninevites (Jonah 3).

Ironically, Jonah was unhappy about God's mercy and forgiveness, generously extended to the people of Nineveh, to the extent that he wished himself dead. But when the tree made by YHWH, which had given Jonah temporary shelter withered, he realized that YHWH, to whom we are called to obey, and to whom mercy belongs, can show kindness to whom He wills and when He wishes, regardless of nationality, race or color (Jonah 4).[79]

This theological story continues, but, when Jonah turned back to YHWH, he was restored back to the earth. The theological implication of this is that Israel, in the study of all the prophets, on יום יהוה (the Day of YHWH), would be restored back to Mount Zion. In Jonah particularly, this restoration extends to all nations and cultures, especially to those who repent.

---

78 Paul Murray, *A Journey with Jonah: The Spirituality of Bewilderment* (Blackrock, Dublin: The Columbia Press, 2000), 10–11. It is also worth noting that Nineveh appears for the first time in Genesis 10: 11–12 in the description of Assyria. It became the ancient capital of the Assyrian Empire during the reign of Sennacherib (2 Kgs 19: 36; Isa 37:37). But it was destroyed by the Medes and Persians in 612 B.C.E. For further insight on Nineveh see, Daniel E. Fleming, "Nineveh," in *Oxford Companion to the Bible* (ed. Bruce M. Metzger, and Michael D. Coogan. New York: Oxford University Press, 1993), 557; John L. McKenzie, *Dictionary of the Bible* (New York: A Touchstone Book, 1995), 616.

79 Murray, *A Journey with Jonah*, 11.

In Nahum, the Day of YHWH is that of judgment and punishment and a show of wrath upon Nineveh (1: 1–2). Unlike in Jonah, Nineveh is not presented as a repentant city, as one that faces YHWH's anger and vengeful wrath, since the Lord, the sovereign of all creation takes vengeance on his enemy (נקם יהוה לצביו). This goes back to the Exodus tradition where God is a warrior (Exod 15:3), which is not unconnected with the very foundation or the development of the concept of the Day of YHWH. The wrath of YHWH in these verses expresses the justice of God.

However, Nahum 1:3ff re-invoked the expression ארך אפים ("the Lord is slow to anger) found earlier in Joel 2:13. YHWH is full of great forbearance (וגדול ־כח). Yet in verse 7, Nahum also expresses the Goodness and the safetiness of YHWH to the righteous people, in the following sentence, טוב יהוה למעוז יום צרה וידע חסי בו ('the Lord is good for a place of safety in the day of distress for those who know Him and seek refuge in Him"). In verses 9–14 the prophet presents the defeats of the Assyrian. In the beginning of Nahum 2, Judah is delivered, followed by complete destruction and judgment on Nineveh. So we can say that for Nahum, the Day of YHWH is the Day of His vengeance and a Day of consolation.[80]

This image of God's relationship with his people, on his Day is continued in Habakkuk. In Habakkuk, it is presented in a reflexive or introspective manner. It is that of theodicy, or of righteousness and faith, which preoccupies the Prophet Habakkuk. The language resembles that of Job. Unlike the Assyrians in Nahum, it is the Chaldeans and perhaps, the Judean collaborators, who are been addressed as the unjust in Habakkuk (1:1–16). For the prophet, it is only faith and righteousness that would help the faithful ones. Salvation in Habakkuk requires time and great patience (Hab 2).

Worthy of note is that the language of Habakkuk has been linked with the apocalyptic literature, as well as with that of St. Paul (Rom 1:17; Gal 3:11). But according to Collins, in Paul it is "simply the trust

---

80   See McKenzie, "Nahum," in *Dictionary of the Bible*, 602 where it is noted that the very Hebrew word, נחום is probably "a shortened form of Nahumiah", [meaning] "Yahweh comforts'"

in God which enables one to wait for the future, closer to hope than to faith in the traditional Christian sense."[81] In Habakkuk 3, especially verses 8–15, we have a classic and a poetic presentation of YHWH as a mighty warrior, which I would like to present thus:

> Yahweh, are you enraged with the rivers, are you angry with the sea, that you should mount your charges, your rescuing chariots? You uncover your bow, and give the string its fill of arrows. You drench the soils with torrents; the mountains see you and tremble, great floods sweep by, the abyss roars aloud, lifting high its waves…with your horses you trampled through the sea, through the surging abyss!

This is not unconnected with the long traditions of the Day of YHWH in the OT, discussed above. It is the Day of God's past activities to salvage Israel from all kinds of troubles and enemies. Habakkuk expected this day of distress (יום צרה), to be the Day of God's theophany, against those who would come to attack Israel, presumably the Babylonians, as well as those insiders who collaborated or assisted their oppressive colonial domination, hence he says, "calmly I wait the day of anguish which is dawing on the people now attacking us," (Hab 3:16). This Day of the manifestation of YHWH would make Israel rejoice in their God, and would make them exult in God their savior (vv 17–19).

4.7 The Traditions of the Day of YHWH in the Prophets Haggai, Zechariah and Malachi

These prophetic traditions of the Day of YHWH are continued in Haggai, Zechariah and Malachi, in their own ways and times. Haggai (חגי)[82] and Zechariah (זכריה) are known to have been very active in the rebuild-

---

81   Collins, "Daniel and the Minor Prophets," 375.
82   The meaning of the name is not completely certain. But some scholars have suggested that it means "feast" or "festal one" because he was born on a feast day. See, McKenzie, "Haggai," in the *Dictionary of the Bible,* 331; Feinberg, *The Minor Prophets,* 237.

ing of the Jerusalem temple in 520 B.C.E. This was around the second year of Darius' reign.[83] Themes of restoration and fulfillment of promise, which are not unrelated to the Day of YHWH, run through these books. Haggai for example, contends that the full national renewal cannot take place until the temple destroyed by the Babylonians is rebuilt. Although the rebuilding of the temple was stopped (Ezra 3:8–4:24), Haggai believes that it is now the time to try again.[84] Haggai preaches that God deserves honor (1:1–15), God is the one who promises greater glory for the new temple (2:1–9), and God purifies, He renews the people (2:10–19), as well as the covenant with David (2:20–23).[85] For Haggai, YHWH works in His day, as in earlier times, since God continues to warn, to explain, to manifest and to heal.

Zechariah on the other hand depicts God as the one who is jealous in Zion and as the shepherd of Israel in His Day. Zechariah shows and defends how God deals with Israel (1:1–6). The fact that the people have repented (1:6), points to a new era in the history of Israel. YHWH is once again protective and jealous of Jerusalem. Then, Zechariah continues with visions that the defeat, misfortunes of Israel will be restored (1:7–6:15), by the person God calls "my servant the branch," (3:8, 10) and David's heir (6:12–13).[86] So, for Zechariah like earlier prophets, YHWH, warns, punishes, heals and restores the people and the city in His day.

On the other hand, the Prophet Malachi (מלאכי)[87] expresses the cost of renewal and explains how the barriers to restoration may be

---

83   Zechariah on the other hand means, "Yahweh remembers." See, Feinberg, *The Minor Prophets*, 273; McKenzie, "Zechariah," in *Dictionary of the Bible*, 948.

84   House, "The Character of God in the Book of the Twelve," *in Reading and Hearing the Book of the Twelve,* 141.

85   House, "The Character of God,"141.

86   House, "The Character of God,' 142.

87   Some commentators think that מלאכי is not a proper name but means "my messenger," taken from Mal 3:1 which says הנני שלח מלאכי ("behold, I am sending my messenger"), to designate the one through whom this word of the Lord was given. See, Collins, "Daniel and the Minor Prophets," 383; McKenzie, "Malachi," in *Dictionary of the Bible*, 537; Coogan, "Malachi, the Book of," in *The Oxford Companion of the Bible*, 484–485.

removed.[88] It is in this last book of the Twelve, especially in the last chapter, that the construct phrase יום יהוה (the Day of YHWH), is once again mentioned in full (3: 23).[89] In Collins' division of the book of the prophet Malachi, there are six oracles (1:2–5; 1:6–2:9; 2:10–16; 2:17–3:5; 3:6–12; 3:13–21 and the appendix (3:22–24). The Day of YHWH, is located in the sixth oracle of this last chapter (Mal 3:13–21).[90]

Firstly, the announcement of the messenger is heard in Malachi 3:1, "Behold, I am sending my messenger to clear the way before me…" But this day is unbearable "who will be able to resist the day of his coming," (v 2). The question here, ומי מכלכל את יום (who can bear/endure/resist the day?) reechoes Joel 2:11, ונורא מאד ומי יכילנו (very terrible, who can endure it?). According to Rendtorff, the question also presumed, "when the Day of the Lord is near."[91] The description of this day carries the emblem of the traditional characteristics of the Day of YHWH of judgment and scrutiny. Verses 3–5 describe then what YHWH will do on arrival on that day which is worth quoting here in full:

> He will take his seat as refiner and purifier; he will purify the sons of Levi and refine them like gold and silver, so that they can make the offering to Yahweh with uprightness. The offering of Judah and Jerusalem will then be acceptable to Yahweh as in former days, as in the years of old. I am coming to put you on trial and I shall be ready witness against sorcerers, adulterers, perjurers, and against those who oppress the wage-earner, the widow and the orphan, and who rob the foreigner of his rights and do not respect me, says Yahweh Sabaoth.

This passage with various linguistic characteristics of parallelism and metaphors, narrates what YHWH will do, no doubt forms an *inclusio* to the description or the circumstances of abuse of cultic practices and cases of injustices earlier underlined in Amos 5. This indicates not only continuity and a rapport, but in my own opinion, it is an adaptation and modification of this tradition from an earlier prophet, an exercise that Zephaniah took seriously.

---

88 House, "The Character of God," 142–144.
89 Rendtorff, "Alas for the Day!", 195.
90 Collins, "Daniel and the Minor Prophets," 383. There may be as many divisions as there are scholars.
91 Rendtorff, "How to Read the Book of the Twelve," 85.

However, Prophet Malachi's use of the messenger formula adds to the uniqueness of this book. In verses 16–17, God will write down the list of those who fear him, who will be God's special possession or property (סגלה) on the Day the Lord would prepare (ליום אשר אני עשה). These verses run as follows in full:

> On that day when I act, says Yahweh Saboath, they will be my most prized possession, and I shall spare them in the way a man spares the son who serves him. Then once again you will see the difference between the upright person and the wicked one, between the one who serves God and the one who does not serve him.

The Day will come, glowing like an oven and the evil doers would be completely destroyed (vv 18–19). Those who fear the Lord will be rewarded on this Day. They would come out with joy leaping like calves from the stall (v 20). They would, on this Day trample on the wicked who becomes nothing but ashes on the feet of the righteous (v 21). The content of the last pages of the prophetic literature are also remarkable (vv 22–24), which says:

> Remember the Law of my servant Moses to whom at Horeb I prescribed decrees and rulings for all Israel. Look, I shall send you the prophet Elijah before the great and awesome Day of YHWH come. He will reconcile parents to their children and children to their parent, to forestall my putting the country under the curse of destruction.

This passage presents a good conclusion to this section of the study of the theme of the theology of the Day of YHWH in the prophetic traditions, which was continuously being modified among prophets of different times, particularly the Twelve Minor Prophets, than the above passage (Mal 3:22–24). Some scholars have also identified the messenger motif of Malachi 3:1 with Elijah in the above passage (vv 22–23). It is argued that the mention of Moses alongside Elijah here, was meant to reconnect the Prophets (נביאים) with the Torah (תורה) and with the Writings (כתובים), which is also a remincient of Joel 2:31–32.[92] It rein-

---

92   See J. Blenkinsopp, *Prophecy and Canon: A Contribution to the Study of Jewish Origins* (Notre Dame, IN: University of Notre Dame Press, 1977), 120–123, cited in Rendtorff, "How to Read the Book of the Twelve," 86.

forces the Law of Moses, "remember the law of my servant Moses …"
(v 22), alongside the theme of judgment, repentance and restoration of
fortunes.[93] This brings us to the summary of scholarly opinions on the
centrality of the theme of the Day of YHWH in the Twelve Minor
Prophets.

4.8 The Day of YHWH in the Twelve: A Synthesis of Scholarly Opinions

It is clear from the above studies that the Day of YHWH traditions
(judgment, punishment, repentance, the glory of the Lord and restoration of fortunes), run explicitly or implicitly through the Twelve Minor Prophets. It is from these traditions that Zephaniah built on his
prophecy of the Day of YHWH, enabling Israel of his time to look
back on its past, make a choice in the present while anticipating its
future.

Recent scholarship, some of which we have seen already realizes the
need to study biblical texts, especially the Minor Prophets, as a unified
whole with a unified theological theme. It challenges the modern critical approach for sometimes dissecting and reassembling the books of
the prophets. The need for this unity-approach of the text, including
the text of Zephaniah, has also won tremendous consensus of opinion,
among scholars.[94]

93   See Collins, "Daniel and the Minor Prophets," 385.
94   For some of these opinions see Nogalski and Sweeney, "preface," *Reading and
     Hearing the Book of the Twelve,* vii–viii. Here our attention is drawn to the
     following studies made already towards this direction: Karl Budde, "Eine folgen-
     schwere Redaktion des Zwölfprophetenbuchs," *ZAW* 39 (1921): 218–229;
     Roland Emerson Wolfe, "The Editing of the Book of the Twelve," *ZAW* 53
     (1935): 90–129; Peter Weimer, "Obadja: Eine redaktionskritische Analyse,"
     BN 27 (1985): 35–99; Erich Bosshard-Nepustil, "Beobachtungen zum Zwölf-
     prophetenbuch," *BN* 40 (1987): 30–62; Paul R. House, *The Unity of the Twelve*
     (Bible and Literature Series 27; JSOTSup 97; Sheffield: Amond Press, 1990);

David L. Petersen, who argues for the unity of the Twelve, from the point of view of scribal practice, size, order, catchwords, chronology and other literary features, also identifies the presence of a common theme of the Day of YHWH as a rallying point for the Twelve.

So, as Isaiah focuses on Zion, Jeremiah on the rhetoric of lament, Ezekiel on the Glory of YHWH (כבוד יהוה), so are the Minor Prophets on the theme of the Day of YHWH.[95] Rolff Rendtorff also argues for the significant unifying presence of the concept of the Day of YHWH in the Book of the Twelve. He lines up with those who have

Erich Bosshard-Nepustil and Reinhold Gregor Kratz, "Maleachi im Zwölfprophetenbuch," *BN* 52 (1990): 27–46; Odil Hannes Steck, *Der Abschluss der Prophetie im Alten Testament: Ein Versuch zur Frage der Vorgeschichte des Kanons* (BTS 17; Neukirchen-Vluyn: Nerkirchener, 1991); Terence Collins, *The Mantle of Elijah: The Redaction Criticism of the Prophetical Books* (Biblical Seminar 20; Sheffield: JSOT Press, 1993), 59–87; James Nogalski, *Literary Precursors to the Book of the Twelve* (BZAW 217; Berlin and New York: de Gruyter, 1993), idem, *Redactional Processes in the Book of the Twelve* (BZAW 218; Berlin and New York: de Gruyter, 1993); R.J. Coggins, "The Minor Prophets – One Book or Twelve?" in *Crossing the Boundaries: Essays in Biblical Interpretation in Honour of Michael D. Goulder* (ed. S.E. Porter, P. Joyce, and D.E. Orton; Biblical Interpretation Series 8; Leiden: Bill, 1994), 57–68; Barry Alan Jones, *The Formation of the Twelve: A Study of Text and Canon* (SBLDS 149; Atlanta: Scholar Press, 1995); John Barton, "The Canonical Meaning of the Book of the Twelve," in *After the Exile* (ed. J. Barton and D. J. Remer; Macon, GA: Mercer University Press, 1996); James W. Watts and Paul R. House, eds., *Forming Prophetic Literature: Essays on Isaiah and the Twelve in Honour of John D. W. Watts* (JSOTSup 235; Sheffield: Sheffield Academic Press, 1996); Erich Bosshard-Nepustil, *Rezeptionen von Jesaja 1–39 im Zwölfprophetenbuch* (OBO 154; Fribourg, Switzerland: Universitätverlag; Göttingen: Vandenhoeck & Reprecht, 1997); Burkhard M. Zapff, *Redaktionsgeschichtliche Studien zum Michabuch im Kontext des Dodekapropheton* (BZAW 256; Berlin and New York: de Gruyter, 1997); Aaron Schart, *Die Entstehung des Zwölfprophetenbuchs* (BZAW 260; Berlin and New York: de Gruyter, 1998); Marvin A. Sweeney, et al., *The Book of the Twelve Prophets* (2 vols.; Berit Olam; Collegeville; MI: Liturgical Press, 2000). Others are: Rolf Rendtorff, "How to Read the Book of the Twelve as a Theological unity," in *Reading and Hearing the Book of the Twelve* (ed. James D. Nogalski and Marvin Sweeney; Symposium Series 15; Atlanta: SBL, 2000), 75–90.

95 David L. Petersen, "A Book of the Twelve," in *Reading and Hearing the Book of the Twelve*, 1–10.

suggested that we should refrain from restricting the concept to simply those texts which the specific construct form, יום יהוה (the Day of YHWH) strictly occurs.[96]

In other words, scholars have generally agreed that the theme of (the Day of YHWH (יום יהוה) is the most striking and prominent theme in the Book of the Twelve Minor Prophets. According to Aaron Schart, no other prophetic literature contains as many passages about this day, which are at the same time central for the overall structure, than the Twelve.[97] In those texts which we have studied, the Day of the Lord is more than just a phrase. It is a moment when YHWH will act as the Lord of history (judges, punishes sinners, restores and brings salvation to Israel). The day is ambiguous. It can offer woe or weal, depending on the historic circumstances.[98]

4.9 A Summary Reflection on Chapter Four

The theme of the Day of the Lord was first explicitly heard in Amos 5:18–20. He reversed it from the popular "covenant" day of light to darkness. He changed salvation history to judgment history. Hosea and his other contemporary prophets of the eighth century used it effectively in their messages of judgment, punishment, repentance and restoration of the fortunes of the faithful to YHWH. They underlined the manner of YHWH's relationship with his people. Hosea particu-

---

96 Rendtorff, "How to Read the Book of the Twelve as a Theological Unity," 75–87. See also, Nogalski, "The "Day(s) of YHWH," 617.

97 Aaron Schart, "Reconstructing the Redaction History of the Twelve Prophets: Problems and Models," in *Reading and Hearing the Book of the Twelve*, 40–41.

98 John J. Collins, in "Daniel and the Minor Prophets," 352–354 has rightly observed that, "the Book of the Twelve is a collection of prophetic oracles over a period of about 300 years." It is therefore, necessary to keep in mind the different historical circumstances/contexts in which these prophecies proclaimed (pre-exilic, exilic and post-exilic periods), since they are not arranged in a chronological order. It is a reflection on the past and a lesson for the future.

larly used metaphors and symbols of human relationships, to drive home his message of hope, and of the call for repentance, judgment and restoration (Hosea 2).

Prophet Micah's theophany and message of judgment (Micah 2:1–5) is similar to that of Amos. Micah underlines YHWH's legal suit against Israel (Micah 6). For Micah, although the end will come upon Israel (I: 1–7, 10–16; 2:4; 3:12; 4:9–13), the remnant will be restored and nations shall know no more wars (Micah 4:1–3)

Prophet Joel employs the imagery of an invading locust to describe the judgment aspect of this Day of YHWH (Joel 2). But before then he calls for repentance with the hope of restoration and salvation (1:13–20). Obadiah focuses on the destruction of Edom, Israel's enemy. The Day of YHWH, for Obadiah is a day when Judah, from Zion shall rule over its enemies. This day unquestionably belongs to the sovereignty of YHWH (v 21).

This sovereignty is stressed in Jonah. In the book of Jonah, YHWH extends His mercy, generosity, forgiveness and salvation to people of all cultures, and nations, including the Ninevites. For Nahum, the Day of YHWH is that of judgment and punishment and a show of wrath upon Nineveh (1: 1–2). Unlike in Jonah, in Nahum, Nineveh is not presented as a repentant city, as one that faces YHWH's anger and vengeful wrath, since the Lord takes vengeance on his enemy (נקם יהוה לצביו).

Nahum 1:3ff re-invokes the expression ארך אפים ("the Lord is slow to anger) found earlier in Joel 2:13. YHWH is also full of great forbearance (וגול וגדל ־כח). Yet in verse 7, as we saw, Nahum also stresses the goodness of the righteous, טוב יהוה למעוז יום צרה וידע חסי בו ("the Lord is good for a place of safety in the day of distress for those who know Him and seek refuge in Him"). In verses 9–14 the prophet presents the defeats of the Assyrian. In Nahum 2, Judah is delivered, followed by complete destruction and judgment on Nineveh. So we can say that for Nahum, the Day of YHWH is the day of His vengeance and a day of consolation.

In Habakkuk, Babylon shall be judged and the righteous vindicated (Hab 2), since YHWH is a mighty warrior (3:8–17). The theme of the Day of YHWH continues to grow in Haggai, Zechariah and in Prophet

Malachi (Mal 3:22–24) who emphasized the fulfillment of promise and renewal.

These prophets motivate us not only to trust in God alone, rather than in military might and reckless alliances, but also train us in the present, to look beyond the past and embrace the future with faith, hope and love for "that Day of the Lord," when YHWH would come again, in mercy, peace, joy and blessing to restore the fortunes of His people under His righteous reign. Zephaniah builds on traditions which enable us to continuously seek meaning in history through faith.

In other words the theme of יום יהוה (the Day of YHWH), preached by Zephaniah, first heard in Amos 5:18–20, runs through the entire Twelve Minor Prophets, with profound theological modifications. Each of the prophets discussed in this thesis, adapted the theme with the help of various linguistic and creative styles, to address the social, political, religious and theological situations of his time, including Zephaniah.

In the following chapter we shall compare the concept of the Day of the Lord in Zephaniah with these OT and prophetic traditions, especially with Amos, since it is the first of the classical prophets where this notion was first heard. By doing this, we hope to demonstrate, among other things, the relationship of Zephaniah 1:14–20; 3:14–20, with the entire three chapters of the book of Zephaniah. We also intend, to specifically highlight the creative contextualization and the uniqueness of Zephaniah, in handling the concept and his unique theology of the Day of YHWH.

Chapter Five

The Day of YHWH in Zephaniah and in Other Traditions: A Comparative Synthesis and Theological Values of 1:14–18 and 3:14–20

In the preceding chapter we examined the Day of YHWH in the prophetic traditions, especially in the tradition of the Twelve Minor Prophets, where the concept of יום יהוה (the Day of the Lord) not only remain central, but is being constantly re-interpreted within each particular prophetic historical context.

In this chapter, we will draw up a comparative synthesis of this theological concept in Zephaniah with other texts. We will discuss the similarities and the differences of the usage of this concept in the theology of Zephaniah and other prophets discussed, especially in Amos, where this concept was first heard in terms of darkness and not light.

The concept of the Day of YHWH in Isaiah, Jeremiah and Ezekiel shall also be briefly sketched. Those elements of modification and adaptation by Zephaniah from the OT passages and from the other Prophets, particularly Amos will be highlighted. We will also highlight the theological significance of these contacts or the centrality of the theme of the Day of YHWH, in the Twelve and in other OT texts.

In order to do this we will begin by stressing that units of our study (Zeph 1:14–18; 3:14–20) are not only related with the entire three chapters of the prophecy of Zephaniah as highlighted earlier, but its thematic and literary relationship with *Dodekapropheton* (Hosea–Malachi), the Major Prophets (Isaiah, Jeremiah and Ezekiel), the Deuteronomistic History (Deut–2Kgs) and with Psalm 126, shall be emphasized. In other words, the themes of these two units are central not only to the entire text of Zephaniah, but also to the entire Twelve Minor Prophets.

A comparative study of Zephaniah with Amos, as a case study shall be demonstrated. This will be followed by a detailed discussion of the theological and religious relevance of Zephaniah 1:14–18 and 3:14–20 in Chapter Six.

5.1 Relationship of Zeph1:14–18 and 3:14–20 with *Dodekapropheton*

We have argued in the preceding section that Zephaniah 1:14–18 and 3:14–20 cannot be completely discussed, without reference to the rest of the Book. A similar case could be made for the place or relationship of our units with the body of the Twelve Minor Prophets. This reaffirms our earlier assertion that recently, OT exegetes have realized more and more the need to discuss the Book of the Twelve as a unit, to which Zephaniah belongs, rather than as isolated or fragmentary entities.[1]

Recently, Michael Weigl adopted a similar position in his studies on "Current Research on the Book of Nahum: Exegetical Methodologies in Turmoil." Weigl accurately observes the recent shift or revival of impulses among students of Nahum. They believe that this short prophetic book of the oppressed cannot be fully interpreted in isolation, only within the larger context of the Twelve.[2] Weigl's remarks, and its implications, in my opinion, are not restricted to Nahum. The same is true of the Book of the Prophet Zephaniah, especially our two *pericopae* (1:14–18 and 3:14–20), in relation to the Twelve.

In fact, that scholars consistently insist on the relationship of Zephaniah with other prophetic books is further reflected in the title

---

1   For interesting clues for reading or conceptualizing the Twelve as one Book see, Sweeney, "Sequence and Interpretation in the Book of the Twelve," in *Reading and Hearing the Book of the Twelve* (ed., James D. Nogalski and Marvin S. Sweeney. Symposium Series 15; SBL; Atlanta: 2000), 49–64.

2   Weigl, "Current Research on the Book of Nahum: Exegetical Methodologies in Turmoil?" *CR* 9 (2001): 95.

of the work of Sweeney, "Zephaniah: A Paradigm for the Study of the Prophetic Books." By this, Sweeney is suggesting that Zephaniah's relationship is not only limited to the Twelve, but to the prophetic books as a whole. It generally reflects the traditional and common post-exilic and Jewish community understanding of the process of world history, in relation to the experiences of Israel and Judah. These experiences are nothing less than the fact that judgment against Israel and Judah would be followed by universal judgment against nations. But this will be followed by the universal restoration and recognition of YHWH, as the sovereign King of the entire universe.[3]

Moreover, that the Book of the Twelve, including Zephaniah's texts, are generally glued together or interrelated has been supported with several arguments. These are usually based, among other things on the superscription, the general structure, catchwords, arrangement of the books, and on the common theme of the Day of YHWH, that runs through the Twelve Minor Prophets.

With regard to the superscription, scholars generally argue that in Zephaniah 1:1, "the word of the Lord which was addressed to Zephaniah, son of Cushi, son of Gadaliah, son of Amariah, son of Hezekiah, in the days of Josiah son of Ammon," is historically related with our texts. Similar titles, they argue, are found in the other Books of the Twelve since this is the characteristic style of the growth of the prophetic books.

Heinrich Ewald, for instance, had long made a proposition of a three- stage process of the historical collection or growth of the Twelve, based on his study of the unity element, particularly the superscription.

First, he grouped and dated Joel, Amos, Hosea, Micah, Nahum and Zephaniah as belonging to the historical setting of the seventh century. Second, he grouped Obadiah, Jonah, Habakkuk, Haggai, and Zechariah 1–8 in one family, as also belonging to the post-exilic era. Finally, he maintained that Zechariah 9–14 and Malachi were added in the time of Nehemiah.[4]

---

3   Sweeney, "Zephaniah: A Paradigm," 119ff.
4   Heinrich Ewald, *Die Propheten des Alten Bundes erklärt* (Göttingen: Vandenhoeck & Ruprecht,[2] 1868), 74–82 cited in Nogalski, *Literary Precursors*, 4–5.

In other words, since similar titles are found in most of the *Dodeka-propheton*, including Zephaniah, one gets the impression not only of the unity of the Twelve, but also of that which it intends to unfold, namely, the common history of prophecy.[5]

Advancing the argument further, for the unity of the Twelve from the point of view of a common history, Paul R. House thinks that the implied history of Israel parallels the tripartite formula of sin, punishment, and restoration. That is to say, the Books of Hosea, Joel, Amos Obadiah, Jonah and Micah, going by his grouping, have the common sub-theme of the sin of Israel. While the Books of Nahum, Habakkuk, and Zephaniah discuss the punishment for that sin, the Books of Haggai, Zechariah, and Malachi treat the restoration of Israel within the nations.[6]

Paul House's theory, influenced by his fundamental view of the Book of Zephaniah as a prophetic drama is not universally acceptable.[7] It has been challenged and confronted with many criticisms. For example, on this note, Aaron Schart sharply remarked that although House's

---

5   B.A. Jones, *The Formation of the Book of the Twelve: A Study in Text and Canon* (SBLDS 149; Atlanta: Scholars Press, 1995), 129–169; Aaron Schart, *Die Entstehung des Zwölfprophetenbuchs: Neubearbeitungen von Amos von Rahmen Schriftenübergreifender Redaktionsprozesse* (BZAW 260; Berlin: de Gruyter, 1998), 290. For further redactional explanation based on the superscription as a point of reference for unity see Ibid. 5–8.

6   Paul R. House, *The Unity of the Twelve* (JSOTSup 77; Sheffield Academic Press, 1990), 63–109.

7   In 1988 Paul R. House published the work: *A Prophetic Drama* (JSOTSup 69; Sheffield: Almond Press, 1988) where as the title suggests, discusses Zephaniah's prophecy as a drama which features the characters of YHWH and the prophet. But he was criticized by some scholars. Upper most in my mind is Vlaardingerbroek, *Zephaniah*, 9. Here Vlaardingerbroek observes disapprovingly that House's sole basis, for his position which includes some utterances of YHWH and the prophetic speech in the first person is not convincing. Also, that it does not make clear the movement from judgment to grace. For Vlaardingerbroek, it is not very clear if there is a "plot" here. Moreover, the juxtaposition of judgment and grace is not just a drama, but has a theological implication. And I agree with Vlaardingerbroek. Zephaniah's prophecy is not a drama, in the ordinary sense of the word, but a theological message of hope, repentance and salvation.

description of the global structure of the Twelve contains many insights into the intertextual relationships among the different writings, his scheme of sin-punishment-restoration seems not only unconvincing, but imprecise.[8]

Part of the argument against House's theory is that each of these divisions of his proposed scheme cannot be restricted just to those books associated with the particular component. For example, in the Book of Malachi, which House presumes treats restoration, there is more accusation in it than even in the Book of Joel. Therefore, it is difficult to strictly limit the role of Joel, to discussing the sin of Israel, or to confine Malachi to the function of discussing the restoration of the fortunes of Israel.[9] In other words, these themes of sin, punishment and restoration overlap in each of the Books of the Minor Prophets. They are theologically connected with one another.

Besides the argument from the phenomenon of superscription which provoked the debate on the common history of Israel, scholars have also identified *Stichwortverkettung* (catchword chain) phenomenon, to argue for Zephaniah's relationship with the Twelve. Some believe that certain books were joined together due to the comparable material that stood next to the beginning of one book, and the ending of another. For example, that Amos follows Joel may be justified by the expression; "The Lord roars from Zion and utters his voice from Jerusalem." This statement occurs both at the end of Joel (4:16), and near the beginning of Amos (1:2). This closeness, however, may be that the writer or redactor intentionally placed these works together. Similar closeness is found between Habakkuk 2:20 and Zephaniah 1:7, especially with the use of silence (הם) to admonish the people before YHWH. This closeness was long noticed by F. Delitzsch in 1851, who had observed that "the ending of a writing and the beginning of the adjacent one often share significant vocabulary."[10] Some of these significant endings in-

---

8   Schart, "Reconstructing the Redaction History of the Twelve Prophets: Problems and Models," in *Reading and Hearing the Book of the Twelve*, 39.

9   Schart, "Reconstructing the Redaction History," 39.

10   F. Delitzsch, "Wann weissagte Obadja?" *Zeitschrift für die gesamte Lutherische Theologie und Kirche* 12 (1851): 92–93 cited by Schart, "Reconstructing the Redaction History," 35.

clude: Hosea 14:2// Joel 2; Joel 4:16 //Amos 1:2; Amos 9:12//Obadiah 19; Obadiah 1//Jonah (as messenger to the nations); Jonah 4:2//Micah 7:18–19 //Nahum 1:2–3; Nahum 1:1//Habakkuk 1:1 (מַשָּׂא)."[11]

But others who disagree with this phenomenon include B.A. Jones and Ben Zvi. Both of them doubt that *stichwörter* can provide evidence for the redactional unity. Their problem is that shared vocabulary does exist between writings that do not stand adjacent. Obadiah, for example, could have easily followed Joel 4:19 (where Edom is mentioned) as in Amos 9:12. This is true, especially since the decisive term "Edom" in Amos 9:12, is not found in the Hebrew *Vorlage* of the *LXX*.[12] But Nogalski, cited often in this work, insists on the relevance of the catchword to demonstrate not only the redactional linking, but the unity of Zephaniah and the rest of the Twelve.

Nogalski sees Zephaniah 3:18–20 as serving serveral functions. These include the role for an interpretation of Zephaniah as part of the Twelve. Zephaniah, for instance, introduces the book of Haggai and links it to other passages within the book of the Twelve, and most notably to the Deuteromonistic corpus. Zephaniah 3:19 quotes Micah 4:6–7 since the later would have been dependent upon it.[13] Additionally, Nogalski notices the word "time" (עת) which connects Zephaniah 3:20a–b with Haggai 1: 2, 4.[14] In Zephaniah, for example we read as follows:

בעת ההיא אביא אתכם	20a. At that *time* I will bring you [home]
ובעת קבצי אתכם	20b. And at that time, I will gather you
כי־אתן אתכם לשם	20c. For I will make your name known
ולתהלה בכל עמי הארץ	20d. I will make you famous among all people of the earth
בשובי את־שבותיכם לעיניכם	20e. When I will restore your fortunes before their eyes
אמר יהוה	20f. Says the Lord

11   Schart, "Reconstructing the Redaction History," 35.
12   Jones, *Formation of the Book of the Twelve*, 175–191 as discussed in Schart, "Reconstructing the Redaction History," 36.
13   Nogalski, *Literary Precursors*, 209.
14   Nogalski, *Literary Precursors*, 214.

While in Haggai 1:2 we read:

כה אמר יהוה צבאות לאמר	Thus says the Lord of Host,
העם הזה אמרו	these people says,
לא עת־בא	'the *time* has not yet come,
עת־בית יהוה להבנות	for rebuilding the house of the Lord,

Nogalski wants to draw our attention to the contrasting negative element in Haggai as compared to Zephaniah 3:18–20. For him the possible explanation would be that the promise of Zephaniah's text is fulfilled with regard to the gathering of the remnant, which presumably includes the returnees from the exile, and those living in the immediate vicinity of Jerusalem. On the other hand, Haggai 1:2ff portrays a situation in which the exiles have obviously returned and have gathered at the site of the ruin of the devastated temple.[15]

Nogalski thinks that this is a marvelous example of literary juxtaposition between the expectation of an immediate grand salvific act and the state of Jerusalem, prior to the building of the temple. Moreover, he stresses that this expectation of salvation is further accentuated by the fact that Zephaniah 3:20 draws specifically (or reflects) the promise of Joel, "for behold in those days and at that time, when I restore the fortunes of Judah and Jerusalem, I will gather all the nations" (Joel 4:1).

Nogalski concludes his lengthy observation on the relationship between Zephaniah, and Haggai through the presence of the catchword "time," by accepting that the two texts cited above imply different explanations as to why this glory has not come. For Haggai, Jerusalem is in a desolate situation because the people are not concerned with rebuilding the temple. On the other hand, Zephaniah 3:20 which reflects a post-exilic composition after the temple had been long rebuilt, is concerned with the glory of Jerusalem, which still lies in the future.

That is to say that it is only by unification of the people of YHWH, the remnant and the dispersed, that YHWH will truly glorify Zion. In this manner Nogalski concludes that Zephaniah 3:18ff introduces Haggai, but also looks beyond Haggai.[16]

---

15   Nogalski, *Literary Precursors*, 215.
16   Nogalski, *Literary Precursors*, 215.

However, it is remarkable that prior to this, Nogalski had also noticed the important functions of the Habakkuk-Zephaniah connection. Zephaniah 1:2–2:3, which centers on judgment against Judah, Jerusalem, nations and universe is linked with or has shaped the theme of Nahum (judgment on Assyria) and with Habakkuk (judgment on Babylon). The function of this is to highlight the announcement of judgment against a specific group of people, within the literary frame of universal judgment in the Book of the Twelve.

Also all three chapters of Zephaniah, Nogalski suggests, are not unrelated to Joel's portrayal of universal judgment, which plays a role in outlining YHWH's design and control over all events and nations within the Book of the Twelve.[17]

Besides the global literary structure, features and catchwords which link Zephaniah 1:14–18 and 3:14–20 to the *Dodekapropheton*, scholars have also observed a common theme of the Day of YHWH, the presence of a God who punishes and restores in Zephaniah and in the Twelve, supports their close relationship.

Additionally, T. Collins argues that "the principal themes of the whole book are those of covenant-election, fidelity and infidelity, fertility and infertility, turning and returning, the justice of God and mercy of God, the kingship of God, and the place of his dwelling (Temple / Mt. Zion)."[18] Collins' suggestion is regarded by others as being too complex, especially when he tries to justify his unity or relational argument. Collins does this by his illustration with passages dealing with the temple in the books of Hosea, Joel, Micah and Zephaniah. Hosea, he stresses, accuses the temple of northern Israel of idolatry, because a calf is worshiped there, while Joel's call to repentance points to the fact that true worship of YHWH

---

17 Nogalski, *Literary Precursors*, 193–200. See also, Idem "Joel's as "Literary Anchor" for the Book of the Twelve," in *Reading and Hearing the Book of the Twelve*, 91–109 where he refreshingly discusses the Book of the Twelve, the dovetailing genre from Hosea to Joel and Amos, the recurring theme of fertility language in Joel, the theodicy in Joel with an interesting table of parallel elements or language shared by Zephaniah, Joel and Amos.

18 T. Collins, *The Mantle of Elijah: The Redaction Criticism of the Prophetical Books* (The Biblical Seminar 20; Sheffield: JOST Press, 1993), 65 cited in Aaron Schart, "Reconstructing the Redaction History," 39.

is taking place in Jerusalem. According to Collins it is not until Micah 3:12 that the temple on Mount Zion is condemned. But this is followed by the prophecy that Mount Zion would be restored as the center of worship, Torah and peace. This topic, he thinks, is further explored by Zephaniah 3:9–20, setting the stage for the Prophets Haggai, Zechariah and Malachi.[19]

But in my judgment, although Collins' suggestion is complex, it still points to the fact of Zephaniah's relationship with the other books of the Twelve, particularly through a common theme, of the Day of YHWH (Hos 9:5; Joel 3:4; Amos 5:18–20; Obad 15; Mic 2:4; Hab 3:16; Hag 2:23; Zech 14:1; Mal 4:1 and Zephaniah 1–3). This theme of יום יהוה (the Day of YHWH) integrates basic topics into one scenario. It is a day on which YHWH will act as the Lord of history and the sovereign of creation and the universe.

Evidently, the foregoing discussion demonstrates among other things the reliability of Zephaniah on past history and the need to contextualize the faith. It shows that our units of discussion (Zeph 1:14–18 and 3:14–20) and the entire text of Zephaniah are related to the rest of the Twelve. This is true in terms of redactional history, global structure, catchwords, other literary features and common theology of the Day of the Lord (judgment, punishment and restoration of fortunes).[20] That this theme was shared and repeatedly preached by each of these prophets demonstrates the importance of their message or theme, and challenges us today on the essentials as we preach in our times in various cultural contexts.

---

19 For more details of Collins' position see, Schart, "Reconstructing the Redaction History," 39–40.

20 See also Berlin, *Zephaniah*, 15–16 for a good comparative synthesis of "Zephaniah and Prophetic Literature," especially the Twelve Minor Prophets. Also the parallel and comparative table between Joel and the Twelve in Nogalski, "Joel as 'Literary Anchor' for the Book of the Twelve," in the *Reading and Hearing of the Book of the Twelve*, 106, is very informative.

5.2 The Relationship of Zephaniah 1:14–18 and 3:14–20 with Other Prophetic Books

Besides Zephaniah's relatedness to the rest of the Minor Prophets, his language is also close to that of the Major Prophets (Isaiah, Jeremiah and Ezekiel).[21] These prophets emphasized trust in God and worship of YHWH alone. What Amos and Hosea did in Israel (North) in the the eighth century, Isaiah and Micah were busy doing the same in the South (Judah). They laid the foundation for the message of the Day of YHWH that Zephaniah came to build on.[22] Affirming this, Childs observes that "Zephaniah's words have blended with other prophetic voices (First and Second Isaiah and Amos), which have been used in fashioning a prophetic compendium."[23]

Before discussing יום יהוה (the Day of YHWH) in Isaiah and its relationship with Zephaniah, I want to acknowledge briefly that the literary structure and composition-history of the book of Isaiah has

---

21 See Berlin, *Zephaniah*,15–16 where she lists some of these similarities, particularly those of Zephaniah, Jeremiah and Ezekiel: Zeph 1:2 "I will utterly sweep,"// Jer 8:13 " I shall put an end of them"; Zeph 1:7 "The Lord has prepared a sacrifice,"// Jer 46:10"for the Lord Sabaoth is holding a sacrificial feast,"; Zeph 1:12 "Congealing on their dregs"//Jer 48:11 "he settle on his lees,"; Zeph 1:13 "They shall build houses but not live in them; they shall plant vineyards but not drink their wine," // Jer 29:5–7 "Build houses settle down; plant gardens and eat what they produce…since on its welfare yours depends,"; Zeph 1:18 "neither their silver nor their gold will be able to save them on the day of the wrath of the Lord,"// Ezek 7:19 "They will throw their silver away in the streets and their gold they will regard as a pollution; neither their silver nor their gold will be able to save them on the day of YHWH's fury"; Zeph 3:17 "He rejoices over you with gladness," //Jer 32:41 "my joy lie in them and in doing them good, and I shall plant them firmly in this country, with all my here and soul." Stress is laid on Jeremiah and Ezekiel here, since Isaiah which no doubt had influence on Zephaniah has already been discussed in the preceding chapters.

22 See McKenzie, "Isaiah," in *Dictionary of the Bible,* 397 for treatment of this prophet, especially the root meaning of the Hebrew word, ישעיה meaning "Yahweh is salvation."

23 Childs, *Introduction to the OT,* 462.

been the focal point of intense higher critical debate, which unfortunately lies beyond the scope of this work.

Apart from the Psalms, Isaiah is the longest book in the Bible. Its three major divisions, First Isaiah (1–39), Deutero-Isaiah (40–55) and Trito-Isaiah (56–66), are literary and theological products of several centuries (742–500 B.C. E.).[24]

It is also virtually accepted among most scholars that these three major divisions represent stages in the history of Israel. First, is the eighth century kingship of Ahaz and Hezekiah and their attempt to preserve the Davidic dynasty (735–687/6 B.C.E.). Second, the destruction of dynasty and city and the shocking experience of the exile (587–539 B.C.E.) and third, is the time of the early post-exilic age (537–500 B.C.E.).[25]

Rooted in the covenant tradition complexes, and the failure of the people to keep their covenant with YHWH, Isaiah proclaimed judgment as well as God's love, blessing, restoration and salvation to the remnant, on the Day of YHWH. According to Bright, Isaiah's overall theology and eschatological message of hope, was to trust in God and His promises that YHWH will fulfill His ideal for Israel, by purifying his people through judgment and restoring them to a new covenantal relationship, in which God's people should orientate its policies upon

---

24   However, just as we did with Amos and Hosea, we intend here to identify the concept of the Day of the YHWH (judgment and restoration/hope) in relevant Isaianic passages, its usage in the overall theology of Isaiah, so as to prepare the ground for its adaptation by subsequent prophets, especially Zephaniah. But See, Carroll Stuhlmueller, "The Major Prophets, Baruch, and Lamentations," in *The Catholic Study Bible* (ed. Donald Senior et al.; New York: Oxford University Press, 1990) esp. 287–304; Chisholm, Jr., "Theology of Isaiah," in *A Biblical Theology of the Old Testament* (ed. Roy B. Zuck., Chicago: Moody Press, 1991), 309–40; Christopher R. Seitz, "Isaiah, Book of (First Isaiah)" *ABD* 3: 488; William I. Millar, "Isaiah 24–27 (Little Apocalypse)," *ABD* 3: 488–90; Richard J. Clifford, "Second Isaiah," *ABD* 3: 490–501; Seitz, "Third Isaiah," 501–506 for a concise study of the theology, history of research and the problems of method regarding the literary composition or redactional processes of Isaiah.

25   Stuhlmueller, "Major Prophets," 287 and Chisholm, Jr. "Isaiah," 305–306.

God and his promises and place its trust in them rather than in political cleverness and military alliances. YHWH will re-establish Jerusalem (Zion) as the center of His worldwide kingdom and reconcile once hostile nations to Himself, on the Day of the Lord.[26]

Although Meir Weiss follows a different line of thought with regard to the popular existence of the concept of the Day of YHWH in the Israelite community, he acknowledges at least that Prophets influenced one another. Amos, for example, had some kind of general influence on Isaiah, *vis-à-vis* the expression, יום יהוה (the Day of YHWH). Even though Amos' usages are not strictly followed by Isaiah the adaptation of Amos' motifs and phraseology is evident in Isaiah. Amos may have provided Isaiah with the material from which he modified his theology of the Day of YHWH (Isa 2 and 13).[27] In Isaiah 2, we find the major elements of Isaiah's prophecy of judgment on the Day of YHWH. In verses 10–16 we read as follows:

> Go into the rock; hide in the dust, in terror of Yahweh, at the brilliance of his majesty, when he arises to make the earth quake. Human pride will lower its eyes, human arrogance will be humbled, and Yahweh alone will be exalted, on that day. That will be a day for Yahweh Saboath, for all who are majestic and haughty, for all who are proud, to be brought low…for all the ships of Tarshish and for everything held precious.

In this passage, Isaiah calls Israel and humankind to realize that the Day of the Lord is a day of reckoning and judgment. This day is com-

---

26 Bright, *Covenant and Promises*, 95.

27 See Weiss, "the "Day of the Lord," esp. 48–60 plus his attached tables for further details and passages on Weiss' study on Amos-Isaiah relationship *vis-à-vis*, the Day of YHWH. Weiss as we had noted earlier believes that both Amos' and Isaiah's prophecies deal with the Lord making Himself manifest to the world, and with the subsequent after effects, especially regarding the powerful and terrorizing impact of that *mysterium tremendum* on man. So for him, the Day of YHWH stops at being theophanic and Isaiah adopted these theophanic expressions from Amos in the message of YHWH's manifestation. But this study has always held that the Day of YHWH in Amos, Hosea and Isaiah is much more than theophanic, but eschatological in the broader sense already noted, of judgment, punishment and hope for restoration or salvation rooted in the patriarchal promises, and discussed covenant tradition complexes.

ing for those who put their trust in human power, in a fortified city, in military strength and in precious things. In other words, even if they go into the rock or bury themselves in the ground, nobody will escape the judgment on the Day of the Lord (v 10). The haughty look or behavior shall be brought low (עיני גבהות אדם שפל). The human arrogance shall be humbled (ושח רום אנשים). Here in verse 11, it is evident that Isaiah is employing antithetic parallelism in order to make his point. The haughty look or behavior of man parallels the resulting, lowly stage of the arrogance. In other words, the proud take the risk of being brought humbled (גבהות // שפל) and (ושח רום), but YHWH alone shall be exalted on that Day (ביום ההוא).

In verse 12, the prophet intensified the message of the preceding verse with reasons, "for that will be the Day of YHWH Sabaoth" (כי יום ליהוה צבאות). Weiss draws our attention again to the facts that these verses, re-echo Amos 5:18–20.[28] Verses 17–21 repeat the preceding call and judgment (vv 10–16), in clear terms, worth quoting in full as follows:

> Human pride will be humbled, human arrogance brought low, and Yahweh alone will be exalted, on that Day. When the idols all disappear, they will go into the caverns of the rocks and into the fissures of the earth in terror of Yahweh, at the brilliance of his majesty, when he arises to make the earth quake. That day, people will fling to moles and bats the silver idols and golden idols which have been made for them to worship… when he arises to make the earth quake.

The Day of the Lord is not only mentioned in verses 11–12, 17 and 20, but, as Lindblom suggested, Isaiah speaks not only of Israel, but the whole of mankind. The scene of YHWH's judgment is the whole earth.[29] What provokes YHWH's judgment is the pride of human beings, which is depicted by linguistic or poetic style of parallelism and metaphors taken from nature. Isaiah mentions the cedars of Lebanon and the oaks of Bashan (v 13). He also stresses the facts of the self-sufficiency of human culture and self preservation, like the high

28   Weiss, "the "Day of the Lord," 49.
29   Lindblom, *Prophecy*, 365.

mountains (v 14), the towers, the ship of Tarshish and precious things (vv 15–16).

Isaiah further mentions idolatry as a behavior which militates against worshipping YHWH alone and His divinity. The universal character of Isaiah's message of YHWH's judgment is based on his faith in the sublimity of YHWH as God of the universe, and the conviction that whoever disobeyed the will of YHWH would be brought to an inescapable judgment, on that Day (ביום ההוא).[30]

In Isaiah 3: 13ff, YHWH is about to bring judgment on the people as well as on the elders and princes of his people because of the injustices and violation that pervade the culture. It is also due to the deviance of the leaders who have refused to listen to his voice, telling them not to go to war but to trust in YHWH. This is best illustrated in the Book of Immanuel (Isaiah 7–12) and its historical backdrop.

A few years after Isaiah had begun his career, during the reigns of Ahaz and Hezekiah (735–687 B. C. E.), a coalition of military forces from Syria and Israel was formed to fight Assyria and its threats against Judah (Syro-Ephramite War). The leaders of these coalition parties were Rezin, King of Aram and Pekah son of Remaliah, King of Israel (Isaiah 7:1). Rezin of Syria and Pekah of Israel had wished Judah would join them to wage war against Assyria. Judah thought it was a risky venture to do so. This prompted the coalition armies of Syria and Israel to wage war against Judah, with the aim of forcing Judah to be part of their movement to resist Assyrian threats, under Tiglath-Pileser III (745–727 B.C.E.). They moved to depose Ahaz and replace him with the "son of Tabeel," (vv 1–2).

The survival and prosperity of the legitimate royal line was threatened, and the promises of God to David were under skepticism. Ahaz and the people of Judah were naturally afraid. The house of David was informed in the following sentence, "Aram has halted in Ephraimite territory' at this, his heart and his people's heart shook like forest trees shaking in the wind" (v 2). Ahaz was terrified. He sent tribute to the

---

30   Lindblom, *Prophecy*, 366.

Assyrian King and became his vassal and implored his support (2 Kgs 16:7–9), to the disapproval of Isaiah.[31]

Isaiah challenged and opposed Ahaz's movement with all his prophetic zeal and power. Meeting the king at the Lord's command, he says: "Lord, Yahweh says this: this will not happen, it will never occur, for the head of Aram is Damascus, and the head of Damascus is Razon; …the head of Israel is Samaria, if you will not take your stand on me, you will not stand firm," (vv 7–9). In other words, Isaiah commanded the Judean King to keep calm and not to be afraid!

Isaiah worked very hard to convince the king and the people that the course he had counseled them was indeed the way that YHWH expected the nation to follow. He gave to Ahaz the sign of the three children. Their names are significant bearers of God's positive message to Judah (cf Isa 7: 3, 14 and 8: 1ff), namely, שאר ישוב (*Shear-jashub* = "remnant restored or will return,"), *Immanuel,* עמנו אל ("God is with us,"), and מהר שלל חש בז (*Maher-shalal-hash-baz* = "quick spoil or speedy plunder"). Stuhlmueller, is right to observe that Immanuel (7:14) provides the key to 8: 5–10. That is, *Shear-jashub* (7:3) provides the key to the reading of 10:19–32; 11:10–16. While *Maher-shalal-hash-baz* (8:1), provides key to the interpretation of 10:1–6.[32]

This historic landmark provides the historical backdrop for the message of Isaiah, namely, that if the king and his people would have faith and hold firm, the danger will soon be a thing of the past. This is well expressed in the following, אם לא תאמינו כי לא תאמנו = "unless you believe, you will not be firm," (7:9b).[33]

Although we have examined Amos and some other prophets, whose ideas on this subject of the Day of YHWH, are reflected in Isaiah, I agree with Lindblom that Isaiah's teaching contains some unique ideas, with an idea of immense significance for later thought, namely the idea of the remnant. In other words, Prophet Isaiah taught that the

---

31   See also Coogan, *Old Testament*, 336–337 for a good summary of the Syro-Ephramite War and the siege of Jerusalem.

32   Stuhlmueller, "Major Prophets," 292.

33   See Bright, *Covenant and Promises*, 96–100 for an impressive study of this subject.

nation would be demolished, but a remnant or a small minority would survive. They will turn to YHWH.[34]

Isaiah 13–23 continues the oracles against the nations. The prophecy of the Day of YHWH (Isa 13) is expressed in the language typical of Isaiah's prophecies in general. The Day of YHWH in Isaiah 13 is similar to those of Isaiah 2, noted above. Isaiah 13 takes up again, the motifs of nearness (vv 6–8), mercilessness, wrath, anger and darkness (vv 9–14), which we saw in Amos. Verses 6–9 are also worth quoting here in full:

> How for the Day of Yahweh is near, coming like devastation from Shaddai. This is why all hands fall limp, why all the men are losing heart; they are panic-stricken, seized with pains and convulsions; they writhe like a woman in labour, they look at one another appalled, with feverish faces. Look, the Day of Yahweh is coming, merciless, with wrath and burning anger, to reduce the country to a desert and root out the sinners from it.

These motifs illustrated in this passage will reoccur in subsequent prophetic messages, especially, Zephaniah. Nations will be judged on the Day of YHWH and the remnant of the house of Judah will remain. This remnant, in Isaiah is that object of faith, a future reality and an element in Isaianic conception of the new age. This remnant, when that Day comes, will no longer lean upon the threatening nations. They will depend upon YHWH, the Holy One of Israel (1:20). The restoration day will be nothing but the Day of YHWH Sabaoth, a day of "crown of splendor and a proud diadem for the remnant of His people" (28:5), which owes its existence to the Zeal and Love of YHWH for His people (37:32).[35]

Even though this day belongs to the future, it has already begun to take shape in the little flock of the prophets, who responded to his words, and appreciated the need to express and put their faith in YHWH. Nevertheless, Isaiah's primary thought was the destruction of the nation. His message was shaped by the tradition of YHWH's choice of Mount Zion and his promise of dynasty to David.

---

34 Lindblom, *Prophecy*, 367.
35 Lindblom, *Prophecy*, 368–69.

It dominated his preaching and influenced his notion of the Day of YHWH from beginning to end. But the condition for a positive experience of this day was repentance for everyone, Judah and other nations alike: "wash, make yourselves clean. Take your wrong doings out of my sight. Cease doing evil.[36] Learn to do good, search for justice, discipline the violent, be just to the orphan, and plead for the widow…" (1:16).[37] These admonitions were followed with hope, and with YHWH's Days of restoration for the obedient and faithful remnant.

Isaiah's theology of the Day of YHWH could be summarized in the following words, namely, that the Day of YHWH will come when YHWH will fulfill his love and manifest Himself to His people, by calling them to repentance and purifying them through His judgment pronouncements, and restoring them back to a renewed covenant relationship (Isa 2:2–4; 11:1–10; 16:5 and 32:1–8). This is the Day when the Lord will establish Jerusalem as the center of his worldwide kingdom and reconcile to Himself once again the hostile nations. Isaiah 2:2–4 is worth stating in full as follows:

> It will happen in the final days that the mountain of Yahweh's house will rise higher than the mountains and tower above the heights. Then all the nations will stream to it, many people will come to it and say, 'come, let us go up to the

---

36 See Joseph Jensen, *Ethical Dimensions of the Prophets* (Collegeville, MI: Liturgical Press, 2006), 111–128 for a good summary of the ethical teaching in Prophet Isaiah: the sources of his ethical teaching, wisdom and ethical teaching in Isaiah, pride as the capital sin some positive aspects and its application; "to abandon the arms race involves a willingness to trust others, and that may involve some risk. Undoubtedly, Ahaz thought that what Isaiah demanded of him involved risk, but by refusing to accept a risk some might call idealism, but… it is what Isaiah will call faith," in our relationship with YHWH *vis-à-vis* His Days.

37 See Hunter, *Seek the Lord!*, 176–243, where he presents a thorough study of exhortation passages in Isaiah (1:18–20; 7:3–9; 28:11–12; 28:16; 30:15) including Isa 1:16–17, calling for repentance. But Hunter acknowledged with a list of scholars who have argued in the past whether these Isaiah passages called for repentance from Israel or not. I agree with Hunter that these passages call for repentance in the part of Judah. In other words, these exhortatory passages are not unconnected from the theology of the Day of YHWH in Isaiah. They are all connected to the judgment situation.

mountain of Yahweh, to the house of the God of Jacob that he may teach us his ways so that we may walk in his path.' For the Law will issue from Zion and the word of Yahweh from Jerusalem. Then he will judge between the nations and arbitrate between many peoples. They will hammer their swords into ploughshares and their spears into sickles. Nation will not lift sword against nation, no longer will they learn how to make war.

This Day of course, is extended further and re-interpreted in Christian theology in Christ, "Today in the town of David a Savior has been born to you; he is Christ the Lord," (Luke 2:11).

In fact, just as the prophetic thoughts of Amos and Hosea were adapted by subsequent prophets, Isaiah's ideas were shared by Micah, his contemporary. They were further developed by Jeremiah, Zephaniah and in the prophecy during the exile.[38] Feinberg, reflecting on how Zephaniah adapted his theology from past prophetic traditions, said "he has affinities in his prophecy with the message of the earlier prophets. Similar expressions are found between Isaiah and Zephaniah and even more between Jeremiah and Zephaniah."[39]

On the other hand, Jeremiah and Ezekiel, according to their superscription preached during or shortly after Zephaniah. Hence, this thought of judgment on the Day of the Lord and on Israel's restoration to YHWH's favor, did not end with the preaching of Zephaniah. For example in Jeremiah 17:1–18 we continue to read the following words:

Heal me, Yahweh, and I shall be healed, save me, and I shall be saved, for you are my praise. Look, they keep saying to me, 'where is Yahweh's word? Let it

38 Though the scope of this work may not permit a lengthy discussion of Jeremiah and Ezekiel, the Day of YHWH is well expressed in Jeremiah 46 and Ezekiel 30 as a day of victory for YHWH and vengeance against enemy nations. Jer 46:10–11 for instance says;"For this is the Day of Lord Yahweh Sabaoth, a day of vengeance when he takes revenge on his foes: the sword will devour until gorged, until drunk with their blood, for Yahweh Sabaoth is holding a sacrificial feast in the land of the north, on the River Euphrates." And Ezekiel during the exile repeated; "The Lord Yahweh says this: Howl; Disaster day! For the day is near, the day of Yahweh is near; it will be a day dark with cloud, a time of doom for the nations" (vv 2–3).

39 Feinberg, *The Minor Prophets*, 222.

come true then!' Yet I have never urged you to send disaster, I never desired the fatal day, this you know; what came from my lips was not concealed from you. Do not be a terror to me, you, my refuge in time of disaster. Let my persecutors be confounded, not me, let them, not me, be terrified. On them bring the day of disaster, destroy them, and destroy them twice over!

This passage indicates that Jeremiah, a contemporary of Zephaniah, also grasped the significance of the day of disaster, and Judah's worship of other gods that provoked it. Jeremiah sounded an alarm against it. He preached repentance as the only way to escape the impending calamity, although he did not call it explicitly "the Day of YHWH," as Amos had done in the north and Zephaniah in the south. Jeremiah 46:3–12 shares a similar theme and language with Zephaniah, "For this is the Day of the Lord Yahweh Sabaoth, a day of vengeance, when he takes revenge on his foes, the sword will devour until gorged, until drunk with their blood, for the Lord Yahweh Sabaoth is holding a sacrificial feast in the land of the north, on the River Euphrates" (Jer 46:10; Zeph 1:7). Like Zephaniah, the sins he condemned include; idolatry, sun-worship, human sacrifices, superstitious multiplication of sacrifices and offerings to Baals, blind trust in the inviolability of Jerusalem Temple, disobedience, the failure to keep the covenant and lack of trust in the sovereignty of YHWH (Jer 2:13; 7:4–19; 11:13; 15:4; Zeph 1:4–7, 12–13; 3:1–5). In his discussion of the reign of Josiah during which we have also situated Zephaniah's prophectic activities, Wright recently observes that:

Active during the reign of Josiah, the prophet Jeremiah never tired of likening the Lord God to life-giving water, while equating Baal and Asherach, the local deities to rainfall and fertility, with dryness and death. This was a powerful image of Israel, whose historic identity was grounded in a desert experience. "my people have forsaken me, the fountain of living waters" (Jer 2:13), Jeremiah declared as God's spokesman, setting the record straight that even the powerful spring at Dan, in Baal's home territory, fell under the sovereignty of the Lord."[40]

However, although like in Zephaniah the thought of judgment, vengeance, and the call to obedience and Israel's restoration to YHWH's

40 Wright, *Greatness, Grace and Glory*, 103.

favor was emphasized by Jeremiah and Ezekiel, the Day of YHWH is given a larger place in Ezekiel than in Jeremiah. Smith, suggests that this is so, given the fact that Jeremiah sought to reform the nation, and to avert the impending disaster in the late pre-exilic period, while Ezekiel, a prophet of exile (post 586 B.C.E.), concerned himself mainly with the future of his people.[41]

Like the pre-prophetic presentation, Ezekiel conceives of the Day of YHWH, as a day of battle in which YHWH inflicts punishment upon Israel due to her sins (Ezek 7:15–27). Like Zephaniah he preached the nearness of the Lord which is also well articulated in the following passage:

> The end is coming for the four corners of the country. This is the end of you; I shall unleash my anger on you, and judge you as your conduct deserves and call you to account for all your loathsome practices....I shall show neither pity nor mercy, but shall repay you for your conduct and the loathsome practices in which you persist... Now is the day, your turn has come, it has come, it appears, the scepter has blossomed, pride is at its peak....the trumpet sounds, all is ready, but one goes into battle, since my fury rests on all alike (Ezek 7:2–10).

This passage, which Berlin earlier alluded to, is very similar to Zephaniah 1:14–18. Like Zephaniah, Ezekiel sees the judgment as national, as well as an individual responsibility (Ezek 11:17–21). In Ezekiel, the Day of YHWH is mainly the time when YHWH will take vengeance upon his foes. Israel's enemies will be subdued, before the latter could attain the place necessary for her as YHWH's representative on earth.[42] In fact, Zephaniah's sense of judgment, hope, call to obedience, faithfulness to the covenant, worship of one God, recognition of His sovereignty and restoration was not only shared by Isaiah, Jeremiah and Ezekiel, but also by the Deuteronomistic Historians.

---

41   Smith, "Day of Yahweh," 520.
42   Smith, "Day of Yahweh," 522.

5.3 Relationship of Zephaniah 1:14–18; 3:14–20 with Deuteronomistic History

Several commentators have pointed out the link or relationship between DH and the book of Zephaniah, particularly the units under study. Uppermost in my mind, are the contributions of Nogalski, Berlin, Vlaardingerbroek and Christopher Begg.[43]

Nogalski highlights the fundamental layers behind the process of the compilation of the Twelve, and links Zephaniah to what he calls the "Deuteronomistic corpus." This presupposes the theological aim of Deuteronomistic writers (Deut–2Kgs), to explain the tragic events of the 722 B.C.E. and the collapse of Judah (586/7 B.C.E.). Similar preoccupation, Nogalski believes, characterizes the preaching of the prophets including Zephaniah. They all emphasized repentance, obedience to the laws, worship of the Lord alone, and faithfulness to covenant promises.[44]

Zephaniah, he proposes, reached its present form through the two processes of redaction, namely, the Deuteronomistic corpus (Hosea, Amos, Micah, and Zephaniah) and the expanded corpus (Joel, Obadiah, Nahum, Habakkuk, Haggai, Zechariah 1–8, and Malachi). The Deuteronomistic corpus is the product of the Deuteronomistic Historian, who attempted to explain in a single work, reasons for the destruction of Israel, the Northern Kingdom, including disobedience and their refusal to repent. The same would happen to Jerusalem if they did not listen to the teachings of the prophets.

---

43 Christopher Begg who lectures presently in the area of OT, especially on DH, at the Catholic University of America in Washington DC, has in his work; "The Non-mention of Zephaniah, Nahum, and Habakkuk in the Deuteronomistic History," *BN* 38/39 (1987): 19–25, raised stimulating and thought-provoking questions with regard to themes in the later pre-exilic prophets, especially, Zephaniah that shall be taken up in the course of this study.

44 Nogalski, *Literary Precursors*, 176.

Nogalski attempts to substantiate his argument for a shared "Deuteronomistic corpus" with the following four elements: (1) there is a similar superscription, (2) substantial portion of Hosea mentions the practice of baalism as the main cause of the demise of Israel (Hos 2:1ff; 8:14; 9:1–6), (3) Micah applies this lesson of Samaria and Israel as warning to Jerusalem and Judah against its own destruction if it does not change its behavior and worship YHWH alone, a theme that pervades DH, and (4) the continuous polemic in Micah 6 suggests that the warning was not heeded, hence, the Book of Zephaniah provides the conclusion of this Deuteronomistic corpus, with the depiction of the destruction of unrepentant Judah.[45]

This Deuteronomistic corpus, Nogalski continues, underwent a further redaction, or expansion when its writing received promises of eschatological salvation with a particularly strong Jerusalem orientation (Amos 9:11, 14–15; Mic 2:12f; 4:1ff; 7:8ff and Zeph 3:9ff). This promise reflects exilic and post exilic layers. In other words, the expansion of the writings to include Joel, Obadiah, Nahum, Habakkuk, Haggai, Zechariah 1–8 and Malachi contributed to the diminishing of the Deuteronomistic corpus.[46]

A similar position was demonstrated in 1994 by Adele Berlin. She observed that there were a number of links between Zephaniah and the Book of Deuteronomy, as well as with DH, especially 2 Kings. Berlin, in my judgment, is much more precise and more articulate. For her, Zephaniah shared the same socio-historical settings as Hezekiah and his grandson Josiah. Such similar socio-historical settings with themes are found in the Book of Deuteronomy.

It presents a picture of a wealthy Jerusalem, which may have resulted from migration from the north, following the destruction of the Israel in 722 B.C.E., as well as the time of political equilibrium and Judean prosperity in the seventh century, due to the collapse of the Assyrian empire.[47]

---

45   Nogalski, *Literary Precursors*, 176.
46   See Nogalski, *Literary Precursors*, 176–178.
47   Berlin, *Zephaniah*, 14.

She went on to observe that like the Deuteronomic theology, Zephaniah's theology is strongly in opposition to all forms of syncretistic behavior. Like Deuteronomic writings, the book of Zephaniah presents idolatry as the reason for the loss of the land and the exile of the people. Berlin rightly notices that the description of syncretism in Zephaniah 1 is very similar to that in 2 Kings 23, with its echoes in the parenetic chapter of Deuteronomy 4, especially verses 17–19.[48]

Berlin sees the Deutronomic introduction of the idea of the ban on the Canaanites as quite fitting to the reading of Zephaniah 2. The latter, she thought, plays on the view of the world in Genesis 10. She identifies a common theme among Zephaniah 2:7; 3:20, Deuteronomy 30:3, Jeremiah and other prophets, through the phrase שבות/šᵉbût שוב/šûb ("restore fortunes, return to captivity").[49] Berlin further sees similarities between the languages used in Zephaniah 3:19–20 and Deuteronomy 30:3–4, such as "the strayed I will gather in" and "restore your fortunes." She compares the "fame and renown…in all the earth," (Zeph 3:19) with Deuteronomy 26:19.[50]

Vlaardingerbroek also draws attention to what he calls the 'frustration formula' which exists both in Zephaniah and Deuteronomy. For example, "though they build houses, they will not inhabit them; though they plant vineyards, they will not drink wine from them" (Zeph 1:13), resembles Deuteronomy 28:30ff, especially verse 30; "You will build a house, but not live in it. You will plant a vineyard, but not enjoy its fruits." Vlaardingerbroek observes that in Zephaniah, the style is prophetic, apodictic, while in Deuteronomy, it is homiletic, evident from its extensive elaborations and from the context.[51]

There are also the similarities between the "distress and tribulations," (Zeph 1:15b); "darkness and gloom," (v 5d), the 'cloud and heavy clouds or thick darkness' (v 15e) and those of the Deuteronomy 4:11; 28:53, 55, 57).

---

48 Berlin, *Zephaniah*, 14.
49 Berlin, *Zephaniah*, 14–15.
50 Berlin, *Zephaniah*, 15.
51 Vlaardingerbroek, *Zephaniah*, 22.

Here again the prophetic announcements in the prophet Zephaniah are very short. The homiletic in Deuteronomy sounds like an admonition in many words.[52] In other words, for Vlaardingerbreok, there is a profound relationship between the text of Zephaniah and those of Deuteronomy. They have the same pattern of thought, but a slightly different view of the place of the people of God in history and future. One still expects 'salvation' (Zeph) after conversion while the other sees an imminent end (Deut). However, in the prophetic preaching of judgment, as well as in the preaching of Deuteronomy, we face a view of the history of Israel which deviates from an earlier one. The old view, according to Vlaardingerbroek is illustrated by the book of the Judges through Kings, patterned to address apostasy, repentance, and restoration. The new perspective is eschatological due to the bitter historical experiences.

Both the prophetic preaching in Zephaniah and optimistic deuteronomistic-levitical movement each travelled its path, but the final form of Zephaniah shares the views of deuteronomistic historians.[53] But in spite of these close thematic and structural links between Zephaniah, especially our units (1:14–18 and 3:14–20) and DH, Begg made some interesting observations which have to do with the non-mention of Zephaniah in the DH. First of all, Begg observes that since the superscription dates the Book of Zephaniah to the "days of Josiah," (1:1), one of the Judean Kings, described in 2 Kings 22:1–23, 30, Zephaniah

---

52 Vlaardingerbroek, *Zephaniah*, 23. Further examples cited by Vlaardingerbroek include: Zeph 1:18 with Deut 32:21f; Zeph 3:5 with Deut 32:4; Zeph 3:17 with Deut 28:63; 30:9; Zeph 3:19 with Deut 26:19.

53 Vlaardingerbroek, *Zephaniah*, 24. However, the Deuteronomistic Historian's views and interest centers on stressing Israel's special relationship between God and His people. They see the events of 722 B.C.E., and 586/7 B.C.E., as a result of disobedience. They recognize that God is at work in history. He is a God who continuously challenges any moral decline, with threats, warnings, punishment and destruction, if these warnings fall on deaf ears. They understand this as divine retribution. Its theology like Zephaniah emphasizes among other things, worship of YHWH alone, the land and Zion as the dwelling place of YHWH as well as the universalism of the saving grace of YHWH (1Kgs 8:41–43).

258

could have been mentioned in the latter's book. But this was not the case.[54]

Second, in that account, Begg notices, the Deuteronomist does associate Josiah with the various prophetic figures, like Huldah, wife of Shallum (2 Kgs 22:13–20) and with other "prophets" who took part in the king's covenant making (2 Kgs 23:3). Begg rightly thinks it is thought-provoking that the Deuteronomist does give a substantial segment of his work to Josiah and does incorporate "prophets" into that presentation, but fails to utilize the figure of Josiah's prophet, Zephaniah, in this connection.[55] Third, these questions are relevant since many commentators including Nogalski, Vlaadingerbroek and K. Seybold, believe that a reasonable part of the final form of Zephaniah was redacted by the Deutronomistic writers.[56]

In his attempt to respond to the above questions, Begg takes as his departing point the presupposition that Zephaniah's prophecy reflects pre-Josianic reforms and that Zephaniah's prophetic message was part of that reform. Begg draws attention to the feature of the Deuteronomist's presentation of Josiah's thirty-one year (2 Kgs 22:1) reign, which concerns events of a single year, that is, his eighteenth regnal (2 Kgs 22:3) year; the year of the reform. In other words, for almost more than a decade, the Deuteronomist had nothing to report about the reign of Josiah, although he summarizes the final days, death and burial in 2 Kings 23: 29–30.[57]

In his effort to push for an explanation for the non-mention of Zephaniah in the DH, in spite of their close thematic relationship as discussed, Begg draws our attention again to the narrative of the reign of Josiah, in 2 Chronicles. Unlike the Deuteronomists, the Chronicler narrates an extensive reform activity undertaken by Josiah in his eighth year of rule (2 Chr 34:3–7), as well as presenting a far more detailed

---

54 Begg, "Non-Mention of Zephaniah," 20.
55 See Begg, "Non-Mention of Zephaniah," 20.
56 See K. Seybold, *Satirische Prophetie*. Studein Zum Buch Zefanja (SBD 120; Stuttgart: Katholishches Bibelwerk, 1985), 83–93 cited in Begg, "Non-Mention of Zephaniah," 21.
57 Begg, "Non-Mention of Zephaniah," 21.

account of Josiah's death (2 Chr 35:20–25).[58] Begg initiates a comparison between the narrative of Josiah's reign in the Books of Kings and in the Chronicles. In Kings, it is the finding of the Book of the Law in the Temple which is highlighted as the driving force of Josiah's reformation. It is recorded in the Chronicles that Josiah even embarked on a reformation activity before he ever came in contact with the Book of the Law. This disparity and points of focus rather illumine the principal interest of the Deuteronomist, namely, shedding light on Josiah's eighteenth regnal year and on the finding of the Book of the Law in that same year in particular, as the most important moment in Josiah's long reign. This is why he passes over the doings of King Josiah which the Chronicles preserves.[59]

Similarly, although the themes of the Book of Zephaniah run through the DH, the principal preoccupation of the Deuteronomist was "to maintain the status of the discovered law book as the sole and sufficient stimulus to Josiah's reform activity that the Deuteronomist passes over Zephaniah."[60] Additionally, Begg observes that the Deuteronomist consistently presents Josiah as a good leader who was in control of events, starting from his sending of Shaphan to the Temple (2 Kgs 22:3), to his advancing to challenge Neco of Egypt (2 Kgs 23:29).

Begg again observes that this is contrary to the Book of Zephaniah, which, apart from the superscription, has hardly mentioned the name of any Judean King. Zephaniah only preaches generally about the misbehavior of the Judean Kings (Zeph 1:8–9; 3:3–4), giving the impression that the leaders of Judah at the time of Josiah were irresponsible. The Deuteronomists, Begg suggests, may have found such representation threatening to the image of the masterful and responsible Josiah.[61]

Moreover, in Zephaniah, "priests and prophets" (3:4), as well as various categories of civil officials (1:8; 3:3), Begg notices, appear as corrupt beyond repair, fit only for destruction. While on the contrary, 2 Kings 22–23, presents the leadership circles, priests and prophets

---

58 Begg, "Non-Mention of Zephaniah," 21.
59 Begg, "Non-Mention of Zephaniah," 21–22.
60 Begg, "Non-Mention of Zephaniah," 22.
61 Begg, "Non-Mention of Zephaniah," 22.

(2 Kgs 23:3) in a positive way as individuals and groups who supported Josiah in the reforms effort. This suggests that the Deuteronomists probably found that Zephaniah's prophecy conflicted a little if not drastically, with his own picture of Josiah's reign.[62]

However, in the light of the above discussion, the point I am making here is that Zephaniah shares among other things, some theological themes and socio-historical tradition with DH, even though his name and other prophets like Jeremiah, Nahum and Habakkuk are not explicitly mentioned in the DH. This sharing and contextualization done by various prophetic traditions affirms the importance of the message which they attempted to communicate. Zephaniah's language and theme are also shared with the psalms, especially Psalm 126.

5.4 Zephaniah 1:14–18; 3:14–20 and Psalm 126

It has also been observed that since psalms, wisdom literature, and prophetic speeches are all forms of elevated speech or poetry, it is not surprising that they share some common language. It is this common and shared language, genre, socio-historical context and theological themes between Zephaniah and Psalm 126, that this segment of our study once again seeks to focus on.[63]

In fact, the importance of Psalms especially Psalm 126, for Judaism and Christianity cannot be overemphasized. Like the concept of the Day of YHWH, they had long formed a very important element in both the corporate and private religious life of the Hebrew and

---

62 See Begg, "Non-Mention of Zephaniah," 22–23 for details, particularly Begg's caution that none of these reasons should be taken in isolation to explain why Zephaniah is absent in DH.

63 Berlin, *Zephaniah*, 16. According to Berlin, "Zephaniah uses terms or phrases which are relatively common in Psalms and Wisdom Literature. For example, echoes of phrase like; "the humble of the land," (2:3; 3:12) are heard in Psalms 10, 22, 25, 34, 37, 69, 76, and 147.

Christian communities.[64] The Psalms, especially Psalm 126, like the unit of Zephaniah under study, express poetically in songs the foundation of the hope of the Israelites as well as their love, trust and confidence in YHWH, their God of the covenant and sovereign of all creation.[65]

Psalm 126, like the concept of the Day of YHWH in Zephaniah, shares the theme of divine salvific interaction in human history. Merlin Aloma, for instance, calls Psalm 126, an outstanding Psalm in which the poet expresses a joyful confidence in the fulfillment of the salvation and the final restoration that YHWH brings to the people of the covenant, at the end of the ages.[66] Walter Beyerlin acknowledges it as "one of the outstanding texts in the Psalter. In form and content it is a little masterpiece."[67]

Just like Zephaniah 1:14–18, particularly 3:14–20, Psalm 126 is characterized by repetition, brevity, and often uses a form of a staircase parallelism in which a phrase from one line is repeated as a building block in the next line, as follows:

1a. When YHWH restored the fortunes of Zion,	בשוב יהוה את שיבת ציון
1b. We were like those who were dreaming,	היינו כחלמים
2a. Then our mouth was filled with laughter,	אז ימלא שחוק פינו
2b. And our tongue with ringing/joyful shouts,	ולשוננו רנה

---

64   Brevard S. Childs, *Introduction to the Old Testament*, 508.

65   In chapter 3 we underlined recent scholarly opinions which held that Zephaniah 3:14–20 shares the characteristics of the hymn or psalm, especially of the call to praise YHWH during the temple liturgical celebration. For details characteristic of praise and lament in Psalm see, Claus Westermann, *Praise and Lament in the Psalm* (Trans., Keith R. Crim and Richard N. Soulen; Atlanta: John Knox Press 1981). Also for types and general grouping of Psalms, see James Limburg, "Psalms, Book of," *ABD* 5: 522–536. Here, the "Songs of Ascents" or "Pilgrimage Psalms" (120–134) are said to have been used by those "going up" to Jerusalem for one of the regular festivals (Deut 16:16–17).

66   Merling Aloma, "The Psalms of the "Blessed Hope": comment on Psalm 126," in *To Understand the Scriptures; Essays in Honor of William H. Shea* (Berrien Springs; MI: Institute of Archaeology, Andres University, 1997), 46.

67   Walter Beyerlin, *We are Like Dreamers: Studies in Psalm 126* (trans., Dinah Livingstone; Edinburg: T & T Clark, 1982), 1.

2c. Then the nations would say,	אז יאמרו בגוים
2d. YHWH has done great things with them,	הגדיל יהוה לעשות עם אלה
3a. YHWH has done great things for us,	הגדלֿ יהוה לעשות עמנו
3b. We were glad,	היינו שנמחים
4a. Restore O YHWH our fortunes (captives),	שובה יהוה את (שבותנו)שביתנו
4b. Like the channels of water in Negev,	כאפיקים בנגב
5a. The ones who sow in tears,	הזרעים בדמעה
5b. Will reap with ringing/joyful shouts,	ברנה יקצרו
6a. The ones who go forth weeping,	הלוך ילך ובכה
6b. And carrying seeds for sowing,	נשא משך הזרע
6c. Will return with rings/joyful shouts,	בא יבֿרא ברנה
6d. Carrying their sheaves,[68]	נשא אלמתיו

A side-by-side comparative view of this passage with the texts of Zephaniah 1:14–18 and particularly 3:14–20, discloses not only their shared poetic features, but also the language and theme of "restoration of fortunes of Zion by YHWH" (בשוב יהוה את שיבת ציון). For example, Zephaniah 3:14a–b, "Shout for joy, O daughter of Zion, cry aloud, O Israel, rejoice, exult with all your heart, O daughter of Zion," parallel Psalm 126:1–2b, 5b, and verse 6c. God's saving deeds in the past are not only recalled in Psalm 26:1–3, but the phrase of "restoration of fortunes (v 4) resembles the language of the Zephaniah "when I will restore your fortunes before their eyes" (Zeph 3:20e).

Additionally, the language of the "greatness" of the Lord in Zephaniah 1:14 "near is the great day of the Lord," is also noticed in Psalm 126:2d–3a "YHWH has done great things with them/for us." The language of reassurances in Psalm 126:5–6, is also reflected in Zephaniah 3:14–20. In other words, the language of joy, greatness and restoration of fortunes of Zion are shared by Zephaniah and Psalm 126.

Like that of Zephaniah, the socio-historical context of Psalm 126 is debatable. Mitchell Dahood argues that if the Psalm is a hymn, then its context must be a festival of YHWH.[69] Hans-Joachim Kraus thinks that the historical context of verses 1–3, is that of exile. The events of

---

68 The Translation and arrangement are mine.
69 Mitchell Dahood, *Psalms III: 101–150* (AB 17A; Garden City, NY: Doubleday, 1970), 217–221.

the return of the exiles are the great prophetically announced change of fortune, which Israel experiences in amazement.[70] It is a also argued that to elucidate verses 4–6, with its tone for help, a later period just as in the case of Zephaniah 3:14–20 must be posited, and in the case of Psalm 126, a period of disappointment and disillusionment. H. Schmidt for instance, expressely holds that the Psalm dates a few years after the return from exile.[71] The *Sitz-im-Leben* of these returnees from exile is well painted by Michael D. Coogan in the following words:

> The community of Judea was divided, and Jerusalem was in shambles. The reconstruction of the Temple would take several decades, and that of the city nearly a century. There were struggles over leadership, and tensions existed both between the returnees and those who had not gone into exile but remained in Judah and between the returnees and other neighboring peoples.[72]

Thematically, the gradual change from bitterness, wrath, darkness and from the devastating judgment (Zeph 1:14–18), to joy, hope, restoration or reversal of fortunes and salvation of Zephaniah 3:14–20), are also shared by Psalm 126. Verses 1–3 looked back to YHWH's great deeds and recalled the glorious good fortune of former time. The poet laments in verse 4 over the difficulties and adversities the communities have encountered. This lament comes to meet the comforting promises and reversal of fortunes in verses 5–6. In other words, like Zephaniah, the poet of Psalm 126 takes up the themes of eager expectation and hope. He develops these themes to include suffering as part of the process of final salvation. This comparison could be summarized thus:

---

70   See Hans-Joachim Kraus, *Psalms 60–150: A Continental Commentary* (trans., H.C. Oswald; Minneapolis: Fortress Press, 1993), 448.
71   H. Schimdt, *Die Psalmen* (HAT 1; Tübingen: 1934), 226 cited in Beyerlin, *Dreamers*, 5.
72   Coogan, *The Old Testament*, 419.

The Texts of Zephaniah	Psalm 126
Theme of the restoration of fortunes (2:7; 3:20e) "when I will restore your fortunes before their eyes."	Restoration of fortunes also stressed (vv1a and 4a) "When YHWH restores the fortunes of Zion."
Zeph 14:a–b "shout for joy of daughter of Zion…"	Vv1–2b, 5b, 6c "ringing/joyful shouts."
Zeph1:14 "near is the great day of the Lord."	Vv2d–3a "great things for us."
Language of reassurance (Zeph 3:14–20)	Vv 5–6 also possess language of rassurance
Zephaniah shows themes of suffering (1:14–18) and eager expectation and hope (3:14–20)	Themes of difficulties (vv 4a, 5a, 6a) and hope and joy (5b,6c)
Zephaniah expresses salvation	Also Psalm 126 expresses salvation
Zephaniah especially the text of 3:14–20 us a poetry/a hymn	Psalm 126 is also a poetry or a hymn
Stresses the sovereignty of YHWH	Stresses the sovereignty of YHWH as well
Zephaniah is generally characterized by repetition, brevity and uses forms of staircase parallelism	So also is Psalm 126 where phrases from one line is repeated as a building block in the next line

Finally, the resemblance of Zephaniah to other prophetic traditions, the DH, Psalm 126 and other parts of the Bible discussed, may suggests a familiarity of these materials with later redactors. It underscores the fact that Zephaniah is a part of the whole prophetic message.[73] It also confirms the suggestion earlier made that "if anyone wishes all the secret oracles of the prophets to be given in a brief compendium, let him (or her) read through this brief Zephaniah."[74]

Zephaniah has affinities in his prophecy with the message of earlier prophets. Similar expressions are found between Isaiah and Zephaniah, as well as between Jeremiah, his contemporaries and Zephaniah. But most importantly, it highlights at least the thematic and the theological unity of the text, as well as the theology that these prophets

---

73   Donald, E. Gowan, *Theology of the Prophetic Books: The Death & Resurrection of Israel* (Louisville: Westminster John Knox Press, 1998), 84.

74   See Feinberg, *The Minor Prophets*, 222.

attempted to convey. The true King of Israel is YHWH, as in the Psalms, especially of the enthronement. YHWH punishes, judges, rewards and restores the fortunes of his faithful and obedient people, who persevere in faith. This is a faith that has matured through suffering and learned that tears are seeds sown. Those who endure with faith and hope will reap the harvest with joy. These comparisons also help highlight the differences and similarities between Amos (who bears the earliest prophetic imprint of יהוה יום) and Zephaniah.

5.5 Zephaniah 1:14–18; 3:14–20 and Amos 5:18–20: A Synthesis

What separates Zephaniah 1:14–18 and 3:14–20 from the rest of the prophetic literature, especially Amos 5:18–20, is not difficult to discern from the foregoing discussion. Amos is an eighth-century Prophet who introduced the concept of the Day of YHWH. This motif was picked up by Zephaniah, a late pre-exilic prophet in the seventh-century. Amos came from Judah, but preached in the North, while Zephaniah, whose origin is debatable, preached mostly in the South. Much like the Deuteronomic reform, Zephaniah focused mostly on false worship, while Amos is popularly known as a prophet of social justice, although these themes overlap. Amos spent more time as a spokeperson for the poor than Zephaniah who devoted time to speaking out against those behaviors of Manasseh such as fertility rites in the Temple of Jerusalem (2 Kgs 21:7) and the immolation of his son by fire (2 Kgs 21:6) and all kinds of abominable practices (2 Kgs 21:2). In Amos the concept was rather limited in scope, referring to Israel's impending judgment at the hands of the Assyrian (Amos 5:18–20). In Zephaniah the Day of YHWH is more universal and far-reaching.

Zephaniah spoke of the nearness and swift coming of this Day of Judgment (1:7, 14; 2:2). Zephaniah evidently has his own unique terminology that Amos does not have.[75] Various nations would be involved including Judah, Philistia, Moab, Ammon, Cush, and Assyria. This day also has cosmic and universal dimensions that transcend anything that happened in Zephaniah's day, since "all the earth shall be consumed" (Zeph 1:2–3, 18; 3:8).[76] In other words, Zephaniah is closest to Isaiah 2:6–22 in his depiction of worldwide judgment.

Nevertheless, both Amos and Zephaniah pictured the Day of YHWH, as that of judgment. Both described it as a day of darkness and not light (Amos 5:18, 20; Zeph 1:15). But this is much more described by Zephaniah at length (Zeph 1: 14–18), as the day of wrath, ruin, devastation, trumpet blast against fortified cities and exalted towers. Zephaniah stresses further its eschatological dimension. He preached about the Day of YHWH in a very remarkable creative manner, bearing his own life situation in mind. Rendtorff suggests that the uniqueness of Zephaniah also lies in the fact that "this is the first time in the Book of the Twelve that particular reasons are given why the day of the Lord will come upon Israel. It is the worship of foreign gods that provokes God's wrath so that He now will set out to judge and to punish his people, in particular those responsible for the false worship.[77] Amos and other prophets have all spoken of this day, but Zephaniah alone, who preached more than 100 years after Amos, emphasized more strenuously than all the universality of its judgment while also surprisingly predicting the conversion of the nations and restoration of the fortunes of the remnant (3:14–20).

In other words, Zephaniah encouraged Israel to be obedient. He exhorted them to continue in righteousness and faith and he spoke of the remnant that would form the basis of the restored community.[78]

---

75   Rendtorff, "Alas for the Day!" 194.

76   Zuck, *A Bibical Theology of the OT*, 418.

77   Rendtorff, "Alas for the Day!," 194.

78   For study of this remnant see, Greg King, "The Remnant in Zephaniah," *BSac* 151(Oct–Dec 1994): 414–27. Here Greg explicates two terms used in Zephaniah to communicate the idea of remnant: שְׁאָר which appears only in Zeph 1:4 and שְׁאֵרִית, which is used three times (2:7, 9; 3:13). Also יֶתֶר, appearing only

As in Isaiah, the theme of God's relationship to Zion is more prominent in Zephaniah than in Amos. Because of its corrupt practices and bad leadership the city would be judged and all evildoers would be destroyed (Zeph 1:4–13; 3:1–7). The Lord will then restore the city and the inhabitants with his protection. The Lord "will rejoice over them with happy song" (Zeph 3:17ff). Zephaniah 2:1–3 on "seeking righteousness" resembles the theme of the call to "seek" in Amos 5:14–15. So like Amos, Zephaniah saw YHWH as the sovereign of all creation. He saw YHWH as one who has the strength to control the destiny of his remnant people.[79] In fact, Stuhlmueller has also suggested that "Zephaniah's way of handling offenses enabled prophecy to take its first steps toward the apocalyptic style, more evident in such writings such as Ezekiel 38–39 and fully developed in Daniel 7–12.[80]

For Zephaniah, the Day of YHWH is a day of God's intervention in human affairs.[81] It is a day of YHWH's universal sovereignty, judgment, covenant renewal, reversal of fortunes and salvation.[82] The relational implications between Amos 5:18–20 and Zephaniah 1:14–18; 3:14–20 could as well be synthesized further, in the following table:

in 2:9, and השארתי in 3:12, he suggests should be considered as part of the remnant terminology. He went on to stress the meaning of remnant in relation to judgment since; the former is 'what is left of a community after it undergoes a catastrophe. The characteristics of the remnant include; "people who are fully committed to Yahweh, and people who are righteous and ethical in their interaction with the treatment of others." Additionally, the destiny of this remnant include, God protecting them on the Day of Judgment. They will spread out from their own land and occupy territory that formerly belonged to their enemy, and they will surely enjoy security and peace (3:13), since YHWH is in their midst, they should not fear anything as their fortunes will be restored (3:15–20).

79   For a detailed insight into the destiny of the remnant people of Israel, see Greg, "Remnant," 421–423.

80   Stuhlmueller, *Amos, Hosea, Micah, Nahum, Zehaniah, Habakkuk*, 97.

81   King, "Day of the Lord in Zephaniah," 18–20.

82   King, "Day of the Lord in Zephaniah," 21–31.

A Table of Comparative synthesis of Amos 5:18–20 With Zephaniah's Texts

Amos 5:18–20	Zephaniah 1:14–18; 3:14–20
Prophet Amos grew up in the Tekoa-south	Zephaniah' origin: Cushi/Judah? (1:1)
Amos preached in the North	Zephaniah preached in the south (640–609)
Amos preached in the eighth century (socio-historical context	Zephanizh preached in the seventh century (socio-historical context)
Contemporary of Isaiah, Micah and Hosea	Contemporary of Jeremiah, Habakkuk and Nahum
The concept first heard here	Adopted/modified the Day of YHWH
Aware of covenant traditions and election	Aware of covenant traditions and election
Day of YHWH is darkness, and quite near	The Day of YHWH is darkness, near with speed, wrath, distress, tribulation, ruin, devastation, gloom, black and heavy cloud, trumpet blast and battle cry
Becomes day of judgment. Dances, joy and salvation are not stressed	Day of judgment, punishment, repentance, joy dances and salvation stressed (3:14–20)
Restoration less stressed	Restoration and hope much stressed
Less eschatological, strictly speaking	Towards eschatological, *senso stricto*
Less emphasis on universalism	Universalism much stressed (1:2–3; 18; 3:8)
YHWH is the creator and sovereign	YHWH is the creator and sovereign
Theme of remnant less prominent	Theme of remnant prominent(1:4–6; 2:1–3,4–11; 3:9–20)
YHWH alone implied	YHWH alone implied
Share some themes with DH, but less with Psalm 126	Share themes and elements with DH, Psalm 126
YHWH/Zion relationship less stressed	YHWH/Zion relationship stressed (1:4–13; 3:1–7:3:17)

5.6 A Summary Reflection on Chapter Five

Zephaniah's preaching was founded on the ancient Israel's covenant traditions and on the preaching of earlier prophets. Our units under consideration (1:14–18 and 3:14–20) do not function in isolation. They are literally, structurally, thematically and theologically related to the rest of the Book of Zephaniah, the Twelve Minor Prophets. The language of our texts is also related to Isaiah, Jeremiah and Ezekiel.

Isaiah emphasized trust and hope in God, not in human military might. For Isaiah, YHWH will fulfill His promises, and purify His people through judgment. He will restore them to a new covenanted relationship (Isa 2: 10–16; 7–13). Isaiah stresses that the Day of YHWH will come when YHWH will fulfill His love and manifest Himself to his people by calling them to repentance. YHWH will purify them and restore them back to the renewed covenant relationship (Isa 11:1–10; 16:5; 32:1–8). This is the day when YHWH will re-establish or restore Jerusalem as the centre of His worldwide kingdom. He will once again reconcile hostile nations to Himself and they shall fight wars no more (Isa 2:2–4 cf Micah 4:1–3). This is fulfilled in Christ Jesus "today in the town of David a Saviour has been born; he is Christ the Lord," (Luke 2:11).

Although like Zephaniah, the thoughts of judgment, vengeance and Israel's restoration to YHWH's favor were emphasized by his contemporary, Jeremiah, the day is given a larger place in Ezekiel, the prophet of exile. Moreover, the Twelve, Isaiah, Jeremiah, and Ezekiel, several commentators, including the author of this study, are convinced that, Zephaniah shares among other things, some theological themes and socio-historical traditions with the Deuteronomistic Historians. Its language, literary features, genre and theology are also shared with other prophets, and with the Psalms, especially Psalm 126. Building on Amos and other prophetic and OT traditions Zephaniah gives detailed insights into the day, in a much more creative and expanded way than Amos. Zephaniah stresses the theology of universalism, of the grace of God, sovereignty of YHWH, sin, judgment and punishment. He also stresses YHWH's covenant renewal and reversal of fortunes of the remnants that bring about dances, hope, joy and salvation, which was not the case in other prophets.

This sharing suggests a certain level of Zephaniah's or a late redactor's familiarity with these materials. It also underscores the fact that Zephaniah is a whole and should be read as part of the prophetic message. It highlights the common theme of the Day of YHWH that runs through them. The similarities and differences among them, especially with Prophet Amos, have also been well projected. The significance of these relationships or contacts cannot be over-emphasized.

It demonstrates that the prophets were the conscience of the people of their time. It shows that each of them repeated this particular theme in their own way, in their own time. It is also a testimony to the importance of this particular theme of the Day of YHWH to their people. It shows the reliability of their memory on past traditions, as they live the present while anticipating the future. They searched for meaning in history through faith.

The relevance of this contact also lies in its demonstration of the consistency of the prophet in reminding the people that YHWH is a God of promise to whom appeal could be made on the basis of known fidelity and obedience to the precepts. For Israel there will be a future because Israel's' God was a God of proven fidelity and mercy.

In other words, the prophets were consistent in adapting the message that if the experience of the presence of God grounded the promise of encounter, that encounter could mean salvation or judgment. These levels of theological contacts also show that the prophets of various times, including Zephaniah, were faithful and zealous in reminding their contemporaries that their future depended on how they responded ethically to the demands of the present.[83] They were the conscience of the people. Their persistence on these themes challenges pastors and leaders of religious communities today on the essentials of their ministries. Zephaniah demands from each and every one of us the constant struggle of faith actualization. His theological values especially of the universalism of the grace of God, and a proposal for an appreciation of its ecumenical and interreligious values will be the subject of Chapter Six.

---

83   See Reid, *What Are they Saying About the Prophets?*, 51–52.

Chapter Six

The Theological Values of Zephaniah 1:14–18 and 3:14–20: An Ecumenical-intercultural/Religious Proposal

This chapter focuses on synthesizing the theology of Zephaniah and its contextual relevance. I will also propose its ecumenical and interreligious values for our pluri-religious communities today. This will be done by identifying those common elements that bind the theology of Zephaniah with other religions like African Traditional Religions (ATR), Islam and Christianity. Zephaniah's preaching on the Day of YHWH and its values or relevance to the NT, the Church and the contemporary religious communities especially in Africa are clearly discernable from the preceding studies, thus far.

The theological strands of the Day of YHWH (sin, punishment, worship of YHWH alone, repentance, hope, restoration and universality of God's grace), are shared with the Deuteonomistic Historians and with poets of the Psalms, especially Psalm 126, demonstrating among other things, the importance of the point each of these prophets was attempting to make.[1]

Zephaniah, as a conscience of his people was skillful and creative in adapting the older prophetic traditions to the advantage of his own socio-cultural context. Zephaniah, among other things denounced the

---

1   In the DH there is the idea of special bond between God and his people/covenant (1 Sam 9:16; 2 Sam 7:7ff; 1 Sam 12:22; 1 Kgs 8:16). This people conquered the land the land promised them, because God was with Moses (Deut 31:8; Jos 1:5, 17; Deut 2:26ff). For them like in Zephaniah, YHWH is a righteous judge with steadfast love (1 Kgs 8:3; 1 Sam 12:3, 5). God's Grace is universal (I Kgs 8:60, and one day "all the people of the earth will learn to fear God,"). In other words, DH stresses the theology of exclusive worship of YHWH alone, joy and inclusivity, fidelity to God, the theology of the land, Zion, name and election (Deut 12).

syncreticism of the neighboring nations while vigorously promoting the worship of YHWH alone, universalism of divine favour, contextualization of earlier traditions and monotheism. Much of this has also been embraced directly or indirectly by other religions, and is reflected also in the teachings of Vatican II.[2]

In his commentary on *Dei Verbum* for instance, Roland D. Witherup not only rightly underscores the relationship between Scripture and Tradition (Judeo-Christian Tradition), but also the fact that the Bible (OT and NT) has always remained a common ecumenical ground for dialogue among Christians of diverse denominations and cultural backgrounds.[3]

In other words, issues wrestled with by Prophet Zephaniah during his time, are in some forms the same problems that confront our pluri-religious communities today, particularly Judaism, Christianity, Islam and ATR. Zephaniah's person, his debatable origin or background (Africa or Judah) and the universality of his messages represent the universalism of God's judgment and grace, irrespective of one's nation, cultural background or religion. Zephaniah's theology in my proposal represents a call or model for ecumenical and interreligious dialogue.[4]

---

2   Because of the limited scope of this study for an extensive discussion of this subject, I want to refer readers to the following commentaries and sources on the teachings of Vatican II on Ecumenism; Pontifical Council for Promoting Christian Unity, *Directory for the Application of Principles and Norms on Ecumenism* (Vatican City: Libreria Editrice, 1993); Edaward Idris Cardinal Cassidy, *Ecumenism and Interreligious Dialogue: Unitatis Redintegratio, Nostra Aetate* (Rediscovering of Vatican II; New York: Paulist Press, 2005); Richard R. Gaillardetz, *The Church in the Making: Lumen Gentium, Christ Dominus, Orientalium Ecclesiarium* (Rediscovering of Vatican II; New York: Paulist Press, 2006); Roland D. Witherup, *Scripture: Dei Verbum* (Rediscovering of Vatican II; New York: Paulist Press, 2006); Stephen B. Bevans and Jeffrey Gros, *Evangelization and Relgious Freedom: Ad Gentes, Dignitatis Humanae* (Rediscovering Vatican II; New York: Paulist Press, 2009).

3   Witherup, *Scripture,* 77–102.

4   In addition to the teachings of Vatican II other basic and relevant materials on the meaning, and nature of Ecumenism and Interreligious Dialogue include: Charles Colson and Richard John Neuhaus, eds., *Evangelicals & Catholics: Towards A Common Mission Together* (Nashville: Thomas Nelson, 1995); Jeffrey

6.1 The Theology of Zephaniah 1:14–18 and 3:14–20 in Retrospect: Its Values

Zephaniah, we may recall, in spite of his debatable origin, was God's universal instrument for evangelization. He was rooted in the covenant traditions, with the idea of YHWH as their Warrior and Deliverer (Exod 3:14; 14:14; 15:1–23). He was familiar with the earlier prophetic traditions. Zephaniah proclaimed the theologies of YHWH alone as the sovereign of all creation. He preached the theology of hope, repentance, universalism, judgment, justice and punishment, covenant renewal and restoration of fortunes. These various strands of Zephaniah's message are delivered in a single theological package of the Day of YHWH as earlier mentioned.

Although these theological strands overlap one another, the *pericopae* of Zephaniah 1:14–18 and 3:14–20, demonstrate and highlight YHWH, as the master of all creation, with an unchallenged superiority. YHWH, in Zephaniah is the overall Judge (1:2–3, 7, 14–18, 3:8). Although YHWH is the King of Israel, in the prophecy of Zephaniah, He is also the King of the entire universe. YHWH's reign extends or reaches to the boundaries of all cultures on earth.

In addition, YHWH, in Zephaniah, is the one who punishes the wicked action of human beings (1:8–9, 17; 3:7, 11) and nations (2:4–15; 3:6), especially of those who oppose His people (2:8, 10).[5] The phrase "face of the earth" (Zeph 1:2–3), which is also found in the flood narrative (Gen 6:7; 7:4) highlights YHWH's plan to bring judgment on the entire creation, including animals and human beings.[6]

Gros, Eamon Mcmanus and Ann Riggs, *Introduction to Ecumenism* (New York: Paulist Press, 1998); Walter Kasper, *That they May all be One: The Call to Unity* (New York: Burns & Oates, 2004); Gavin D'Costa, *Christianity and World Religions: Disputed Questions in the Theology of Religions* (West Sussex, United Kingdom: Wiley-Blackwell, 2009).

5   Patterson, *Nahum, Habakkuk, Zephaniah,* 295.

6   See M. DeRoche, "Zephaniah 1:2–3, The Sweeping of Creation," *VT* 30 (1979): 106 where it is argued that the full extent of the judgment is understood only

Zephaniah like the other pre-exilic prophets stresses the covenant tradition earlier highlighted in this study. F.C. Fensham even posited that the whole concept of the Day of the Lord, in the OT should be understood against the background of the covenant curses, or covenant implementation and renewal.[7]

Stressing Zephaniah's covenant theology, he argues that the Day of YHWH may be seen as the day of the Lord's covenant by which he establishes his sovereign Lordship over human beings, either by instituting the covenant or by enforcing the provisions of the covenant.[8]

The prophets, including Zephaniah, preached against sin. They emphasized repentance of Israel, called for hope and optimism in YHWH's restoration of their fortunes. They stood before Yahweh, accusing and warning the people of certain consequences of covenant violation. While there are several other ways of nuancing their proclamation, their overall message, particularly of Zephaniah, could be summarized under three points.

First, the people have sinned by breaking the covenant, hence must repent. Second, if there is no repentance, then judgment, devastation, wrath, misfortunes and exile will follow. Third, beyond the judgment there is hope for reversal of fortunes, and salvation.[9]

With this window of hope, the prophets were to bring God closer to the community and the community closer to God. They were to draw the community to fellowship with God, for the purpose of converting the former. If God had spoken to the community through the

---

when it is realized that "it is the undoing or reversal of fortune." In other words, the original order of creation in Genesis 1:20–24, 27 was fish, birds, animals, and humans. But in Zephaniah it is the opposite. God creates and uncreates. He is the Author of life. He gives and he takes.

7   See F.C. Fensham, "A Possible Origin of the Concept of the Day of the Lord," in *Biblical Essays Die Ou Testamentiese Werkgemeenshap in Suid Afrika-9th Congress* (Potschefstroom Rege Pers Beperk, 1966), 90–97 as cited in King, "Day of the Lord," 26.

8   See O. Palmer Robertson, *The Books of Nahum, Habakkuk, and Zephaniah* (NICOT; Grand Rapids, MI: 1990), 266, cited in King, "Day of the Lord," 27.

9   C. Marvin Pate et al., *The Story of Israel: A Biblical Theology* (ed. Downers Grove; IL: InterVarsity Press, 2004), 93.

prophets, he wanted them to be converted.[10] Zephaniah was committed to these theological roles, particularly of the preaching of conversion that would come to dominate the preaching of Christ and his apostles.

Zephaniah preached the theology of repentance from sin, worship of YHWH alone and hope in the Lord's restoration. His theology exposes the finite nature of human beings. This human condition is vividly described by W. S. Lasor, in the following words:

> He saw that God does not brook haughtiness and that people's only hope lay in recognizing their own frailty. Pride is a problem rooted in human nature, and neither Judah (2:3), Ammon, Moab (v 10), nor Nineveh is exempt. Nineveh is made to epitomize insolence, boasting "I am and there is none else' (v 15). Such rebellion, the declaration of spiritual independence from God, is the most heinous of sins.[11]

Zephaniah preached loudly against several sins that attract YHWH's judgment. These include injustices or lack of social justice. These were of course earlier and mostly heard in Amos 5. But in the time of Zephaniah, some people were still said to have "stepped up the threshold, and filled up the house of their master with violence and deceits" (1:9). Also Jerusalem was polluted and made tyrannical (3:1). While the prophets and priests, on the other hand, became reckless, faithless and violated laws and social order (3:2–4).

The word חמס (violence) used in Zephaniah 1:9 is not unconnected with those words used in Zephaniah 3:1–4 (e.g., rebellious, polluted, reckless, and violated). H. Hagg rightly notices that the context of these words especially, חמס תורה ("violence to the law") in Zephaniah 3:4 points to the wrong-doing and violating of the powerless, to whose disadvantage the religious laws were bent. He added that the socio-ethical aspect of חמס ("violence) stands in the foreground from the very

10   Joseph Agius, "Class Lectures on Amos" (Rome: Pontifical University of St. Thomas Aquinas, March 13, 2009).

11   W. S. Lasor, D. A. Hubbard and F. W. Bush, *Old Testament Survey* (Grand Rapids, MI: Eerdmans, 1982), 437 cited in Patterson, *Nahum, Habakkuk, Zephaniah*, 295.

outset, signifying the arbitrary and autocratic appropriation and expropriation of what belongs to God and to one's neighbors.[12] This act of social injustice was countered by the Lord (3:5), and the pursuit of justice is not restricted to one culture or religion. It is a universal need.

Zephaniah highlighted that human arrogance and injustices will bring judgment on the Day of the Lord (1:14–18), but those who repent and seek the Lord (2:1–3) shall be restored. Zephaniah's theology of hope and salvation guarantees the hope that God will not turn back anyone who repents and surrenders to him. Examples of such people are those who are humble, keep the law, seek righteousness, and humility (2:3). Zephaniah also recommends faith, truthfulness and pursuit of that which is right (3:12–13). Such humble and faithful remnant shall be rewarded by the Lord. YHWH will purify them (3:9–10). YHWH will re-gather and bring many joys (3:13–14). YHWH will calm their fears and turn away their enemies, and rejoices over them with love and happy songs (vv 15–17). He will reverse their woes and misfortunes into good fortunes and well-being before the eyes of their enemies (vv 18–20).

In other words, YHWH's universal Kingship is not only demonstrated through His act of judgment, but also by his redemptive and salvific acts.[13] YHWH is not only a Righteous Lord (3:5) but also a God of love who annuls judgment and turns away enemies of his people (3:15ff). This theological idea is well communicated by D. A. Schneider,

12   H. Hagg, "חָמָס chāmās," in *TDOT* 4: 479. Similar behavior is found in Ezekiel 22:26. And in Jeremiah 22:3, the same socio-ethical oppression of the poor is implied by the root חמס where the subject matter is the brutal exploitation of the helpless aliens or stranger, the orphan, the widow. Also the continuation "shed no innocent blood in this place," Hagg believes "introduces the notion of assault on the life of one's neighbor, which is often designated by חָמָס."

13   See G. Ernest Wright, *God Who Acts: Biblical Theology of Recital* (SBT 8; London: SCM Press, 1958), esp., 59–86 for an interesting presentation of Biblical Theology as the confessional recital of the redemptive act of God, which include saving act that brought the community of Israel into being. See also PBC, *The Bible and Morality: Biblical Roots of Christian Conduct* (Vatican City: Libreria Editrice Vaticana, 2008), 28–29. Here these salvific acts of the God of Israel or the God of Israel is describe as a God who accompanies, liberates, gives and gathers.

who stresses that the book (Zephaniah) persistently portrays the holiness and peace of God. God's holiness appears in the contrasts between Him and the proud sinners: they pretend to rule, but God judges with inexorable power; they hold office, but the Lord gives unfailing justice (3:1–5). God's grace appears chiefly in the two passages (2:1–3; 3:11–20), that offer hope and salvation.[14]

In other words, the religious value of Zephaniah lies in the fact that while he condemns the particular external fault of his day, worship of false gods (1:4–5), the adaptation of foreign customs (1:8), violent and fraudulent behavior (1:11), faulty rituals and false prophecy (3:4), he also condemns the interior causes of these sins, pride and arrogance (1:16; 2:10, 15; 3:11), rebellion and lack of trust in God (1:12; 3:2).

6.2 Zephaniah: Common Elements with Other Religious Communities Today

As earlier noted by Roland D. Witherup, the relevance of the message of Zephaniah, particularly his theology of YHWH alone and His universal sovereignty, forms a common dialogue ground for our pluri-religious communities today. As part of the OT texts, Zephaniah's prophecy demonstrates some commonalities among Judaism, Christianity, Islam, and African Traditional Religions. Judaism, like Islam, as well as ATR for instance, value monotheism. We shall return to Islam and ATR later in this Chapter.

A full blown monotheism in Judaism is located in the Second Isaiah. But it is sufficient to broadly mention that Israel's monotheism went through a long process of emergence. It witnessed Elijah and Elisha's movements (1 Kgs 17–21; 2 Kgs 9–10:36). This was followed by the prophetic messages of the eighth century prophets, (Amos, Hosea, Micah,

---

14   See D.A. Schneider, "Book of Zephaniah," *ISBE* 4:1190–1191, as cited in Patterson, *Nahum, Habakkuk, Zephaniah*, 295.

Isaiah), the reforms of Hezekiah (2 Kgs 18:4,) and Josiah (2 Kgs 22–23). Alongside King Josiah, Zephaniah preached the worship of YHWH alone, with its final breakthrough in exilic and post-exilic Judaism during the time of Deutero-Isaiah.

As suggested earlier by Stuhlmueller, Zephaniah's prophecy affected subsequent ones. Second Isaiah (Isa 40–55) built on these prophetic traditions, particularly of Zephaniah. In Second Isaiah, as in Zephaniah, YHWH as the one Lord is the Lord of history. YHWH is not just the Lord of Israel, but of all lands and nations.[15] This aspect of the prophetic message in the exile was to encourage the Judeans in their current situation to turn a new page, by looking at the new vision of their only one God.[16] The point I want to make is that the significance and resultant effects of Zephaniah's preaching on YHWH alone, remain central to the exilic and to the post-exilic Judaism. They also remain central to the NT theology of universalism and unity of the Church.

6.3 Theological Values of Zephaniah for the NT/the Church

Besides the call to worship YHWH alone *(κύριος)* that creates a common dialogue ground for Judaism and Christianity, other strands of theology stressed by Zephaniah do the same. For example, the hope, reversal of fortunes and salvation, theologically preached by Zephaniah

---

15   See R.N. Whybray, *The Second Isaiah* (New York: T &T Clark, 2003), 45 for a summary of the central message of Deutero-Isaiah. Its essential features are: (1) the exile people are to take heart because their sins have now been expiated and their term of punishment is over (40:1–2), (2) Yahweh is about to come to their aid his people in such a decisive fashion that the whole world will be astonished at this revelation of his glory (vv 3–5) and (3) the guarantee of this message of hope and restoration is the work of Yahweh spoken through the prophet. He is all-powerful, and compared with Him all human activity is ludicrously impotent (vv 6–8).

16   Monotheistic statements in Isaiah are located in the following passages: Isa 43:1–11; 44:6, 8; 45:5–7, 14, 18, 21; 46:9.

through his central concept of the Day of YHWH, is rooted in the faith and future hope of Israel, preached by all the prophets before and after him. Széles affirms that the period conveying YHWH's acts stretched out towards the future. It embraces not only the past and the present, but unites itself with the future as the time when more acts of the Lord would be realized. Israel always knew that its life was in the hand of God, whose might was directed to the issue of calling mankind to be responsible and accountable. YHWH executed justice, which involved the proclamation of judgment and mercy towards Israel and every nation on earth.[17]

John Bright articulated these past-future elements in the message of the prophets, which is re-interpreted or fulfilled in the NT, when he wrote:

> Virtually all of the pre-exilic prophets, albeit by no means in identical ways, looked beyond the judgment they were compelled to announce to a farther future when God would come again to his people in mercy, restore their fortunes, and establish his rule over them in righteousness and peace. This promise of future salvation is one of the most distinctive features in the message of the prophets, and it is this perhaps more than anything else that serves to bind the Old Testament unbreakably with the New in a single canon of Scripture.[18]

This unbreakable relationship between the OT and the NT is also well articulated in the Pontifical Biblical Commission document, *The Jewish People and their Sacred Scriptures in the Christian Bible.* Although it is debatable whether the NT texts do at all interpret Christ events as the fulfillment of the prophecy of Zephaniah, this document specifically highlights that what is written in the Jewish Scriptures must of necessity be fulfilled because it reveals the plan of God which cannot fail to be accomplished in the life, death and resurrection of Christ.[19]

---

17 Széles, *Wrath and Mercy*, 66.

18 Bright, *Covenant and Promise*, 15. See also Pate et al., *The Story of Israel*, 89 where the theological implications of the proclaimed future restoration is affirmed to be of immense value not only to our formulation of biblical theology, but ties the NT fulfillment to the OT, thus solidifying the continuity of biblical theology.

19 The Pontifical Biblical Commission, *The Jewish People and their Sacred Scriptures in the Christian Bible* (Vaticano: Libreria Editrice Vaticana, 2002), 20–21.

The necessity and value of this fulfillment is further and strongly underlined by the document which observes that the clearest expression of such, is found in the words addressed by the Risen Christ to his disciples, in the Gospel of Luke: "These are my words that I spoke to you while I was still with you; that everything written about me in the Law of Moses, the Prophets, and the Psalms must (δει) be fulfilled" (Lk 24:44). The basis of this necessity is affirmed in several passages of the NT (Mtt 16:21; Mk 8:31; Lk 9:22; 17:25; 22:37).[20]

In other words, this document affirms the observation of G. Ernest Wright that "the faith of Israel is fulfilled in Christ. It is Israel which first broke radically with the 'pagan' conception of life and provided the view of history and the characteristic hope on which the NT and the Christian faith so firmly rest."[21] This hope and restoration of fortunes which dominates prophetic literature especially Zephaniah remains valuable to the NT and the Church today.

Stuhlmueller also notices the NT's use of Zephaniah in a number of phrases in the Lukan presentation of the annunciation to Mary, that she was to become the mother of Jesus: "be glad," The Lord is in your midst," "Fear not," "mighty savior (Lk 1:26–38).[22] Zephaniah's teach-

---

20 PBC, *Jewish People*, 21–138. Here the document takes time to discuss various fundamental themes which the OT (particularly Zephaniah) shares with the NT to include: Revelation of God, the wretchedness and dependency of human beings, God the Liberator and Savior (Zeph 3:17b// Lk1:47) the election of Israel (Deut 7:6; Ps 132:13; Amos 3:2; 9:7; Matt 2:6; 15:24), the covenant (Gen 9:8–17; 15:1–21; 17:1–26; Exod 19:4–8; Deut 7:12; 8:18; 2 Kgs 23:1–3; Ps 89:; 132; Jer 31:31–34; Lk 1:72; 1 Col 11:25); the Law (2 Kgs 22–23, Matt 5) ; prayer, cult and Jerusalem temple (Zeph 3:14ff; John 7:14, 28 Mk 12:35; Lk 19:47; Mtt 26:55), divine reproaches and condemnation (Amos, Hos, Isa, Zeph 1–3, Mtt 3:7; Lk 3:7) and divine promises, descendant from Abraham, land, eternal life and salvation (Zeph 3:14–20; Acts 2:38; 13:38–39, Rom 11:17–29) and the universal reign of God (Zeph 1–3; Ps 47; 96; 114; Lk19:11; Mtt 4:17, 23; 9:35; Mtt 16:28; 25:31, 34; Rev 11:15).

21 Wright, *God Who Acts*, 26.

22 Stuhlmueller, *Amos, Hosea, Micah, Nahum, Zephaniah, Habakkuk*, 105. See also Brown, *The Brith of the Messiah*, 323–26. Here although Zephaniah 3:14–17 has been suggested as the Lukan background for 1:28, 30–31 Brown warns against extreme connection of these texts or reading of the Lukan texts as direct fulfillment of the OT.

ing on the hope of the remnant (3:11–20) as mentioned earlier fore-shadows the teaching of the NT (Matt 5:3, 5; Lk 4:18ff). However, this is not to say that the mystery of Christ presented in the NT is completely the fulfillment of the hopes raised by Zephaniah.

Zephaniah's relevance is again well articulated in or alluded to in the recent *Encyclical Letter* of Benedict XVI, *Spe Salvi*. Reiterating the words of St. Paul, *"spe salvi facti sumus"* (in hope we were saved, Rom 8:24), who was familiar with the writings of the prophet, Benedict XVI highlights that in light of the Christian faith (redemption or salvation) is not simply a given. Redemption is offered to us in the sense that we have been given hope, trustworthy hope, by virtue of which we can face our present.[23] The point here is the continuity of this message of hope.

In his several references to NT passages that bear testimony to the overall biblical faith and prophetic hope, Benedict XVI particularly cites 1 Thessalonians 4:13, which we usually read along with Zephaniah 1:14–18, Matthew 25:14–15; 27:45; Mark 15:33 and John 12:31–36, during the advent and funeral eschatological liturgies of the Christian communities.[24] This Day of the Lord passages, especially in St. Paul (1 Thess 4:13–18), is worth illustrating in full:

> We want you to be quite certain, brothers, about those who have fallen asleep, to make sure that you do not grieve for them, as others do who have no hope. We believe that Jesus died and rose again, and that in the same way God will bring with him those who have fallen asleep in Jesus. We can tell you this from the Lord's own teaching, that we who are still alive for the Lord's coming will not have advantage over those who have fallen asleep… then, you should encourage one another.

Evidently, this passage is mostly famous for its description of Jesus' glorious second coming. Paul's basic point here is to affirm that believers who had died with hope in the Lord, will participate in that event of the resurrection (1 Cor 15:50–57).

---

23   Benedict XVI, *Encyclical Letter: Spe Salvi* (Vatican City: Libreria Editrice Vaticana, 2007), 3.
24   Benedict XVI, *Spe Salvi*, 4–5.

In other words, St. Paul in 1 Thessalonians 4:13–18, certainly is not only close to the Jewish apocalyptic writings,[25] but highlights the covenant-rooted future hope, prophesized by Israel's prophets, especially Zephaniah. It affirms in the Christian community the taking on of a new meaning of this theology of hope in Christ: his passion, death and resurrection.[26]

Harrington notices that these Jewish and prophetic traditions continue in Paul. In the First Letter to the Thessalonians 5:1–11, Paul quickly dampened the enthusiasm of this community about the end-time events, by insisting that since the precise time of Christ's return is unknown (Mark 13:32), the proper Christian attitude is constant vigilance (hope) and behavior appropriate to those who seek to obtain "salvation through our Lord Jesus Christ" (5:9). His description of those who will witness the second coming (4:17), suggests that he may well have expected it to happen soon, in his own lifetime and in the immediate future.[27]

Apart from Harrington, other scholars, particularly John Paul Heil, in his "From Remnant to Seed of Hope for Israel: Romans 9:27–29," persuasively demonstrates that the theme of hope pervades Paul's Letter to the Romans. He sees in Romans 9: 27–29, the OT background of the theology of hope in the prophetic literature (Isa 10:22–23 and Hos 2:1).[28] In fact it is also argued, as we saw earlier, that Zephaniah's announcement of the Day of YHWH (1:14–18), through Jerome's Latin Vulgate translation, provided the script for the famous composition of Thomas Celano's, *Dies irae, dies illa* (ca. 1250 A.D), used at funeral liturgies in the Church.[29]

---

25   Daniel J. Harrington, *Meeting St. Paul Today: Understanding the Man, His Mission, and His Message* (Chicago: Loyola Press, 2008), 33.

26   E. Achtemeier, *Nahum–Malachi*, Interpretation (Atlanta: John Knox Press, 1986), 71–73.

27   Harrington, *Meeting St. Paul Today*, 33.

28   John Paul Heil, "From Remnant to Seed of Hope for Israel: Romans 9:27–29," *CBQ* 64 (2002): 703. But see also Heil, *Romans–Paul's Letter of Hope* (AnBib 112; Rome: Biblical Institute Press, 1987), 64–70 for an extensive study of this subject of hope in which Israel shall be saved in Paul's Letter.

29   See Stuhlmueller, *Amos, Hosea, Micah, Nahum, Zephaniah, Habakkuk*, 97.

In addition to this liturgical relevance, of Zephaniah's development of the theme of the Day of YHWH, his emphasis on unity and worhip of YHWH alone is challenging for the Church today. The unity of faith and worhsip stressed by Zephaniah has not yet been fully achieved. This is evident in the prayer of Christ in John 17.

Decrying this situation Jeffrey Gros writes: "We know that Christians do not live in that unity for which Christ prayed, though through common faith, baptism, and Scripture, they share a real, and yet imperfect communion."[30] Historically, he observes that after the mission of Christ, God's self-manifestation, Paul, a man of diverse cultures and symbol of Christian unity, continued the proclamation of the gospel. That there were many communities to which the early Christians belonged is not only evident in the different Gospel narratives, but also in Pauline literature (1 Cor 11–14), and in Acts of the Apostles (Acts 15:2). The latter gives an indication to *Koinonia* as an essential element for the communion of churches of such a diverse cultural background (Acts 2:42). Hence, a common faith, a common worship life, bonds of communion with the apostles, and charity were necessary for the unity of the Christian communities from the beginning.[31]

In other words, although the unity of worship in Zephaniah does not directly imply unity of worship of all Christian denominations, this study proposes that the Christian community today is always challenged to share in common or learn from Zephaniah not only the importance of renewal and monotheism, but also the need constantly to promote unity of worship and renewal of services in her evangelizing mission. This must be realized in the spirit of prayer, mission, ministry, service and dialogue.[32]

Credit must also be given, at least broadly speaking, to the influence of the Bible on ecumenical dialogue of which the text of Zephaniah and other prophetic literature form a significant part. This influence if we may reiterate flourished in the wake of Vatican II's *Dei Verbum*.[33]

---

30   Gros, *Introduction to Ecumenism*, 1.
31   Gros, *Introdcution to Ecumenism*, 10–11.
32   Gros, *Introduction to Ecumenism*, 2.
33   Witherup, *Scripture*, 77.

This document has promoted and encouraged ecumenically organized bible studies around the world, as well as dialogue between the Catholic Church and other denominations, such as Anglicans, Lutherans, Baptist, Methodists, Evangelicals, Orthodox and Pentecostals.[34]

Like Zephaniah who bore the message of hope, justice, judgment, perseverance in the midst of suffering, universalism of salvation and restoration, single-mindedness in the worship of YHWH alone, it is incumbent on the Church today to persevere in her proclamation to bring about the kingdom of God after the example of Jesus, a manifestation of YHWH preached by Zephaniah. This Kingdom is the source of full liberation, justice, restoration of fortunes and salvation for all people of all cultures.[35] In other words, human history finds its true and full meaning in the incarnation of the Word of God, who is the foundation of hope and restorer of human dignity. It is through Christ, the "image of the invisible God, the firstborn of all creation" (Col 1:15), that the human person is redeemed.[36]

Zephaniah 1:14–18 and 3:14–20, encapsulated in the theme of the Day of YHWH provides a theological foundation for the struggle for and defense of the joy of personal dignity. It also promotes fundamental human rights, justice and peace. These are values shared by most world religions. It champions reconciliation with God, rebuilding faith and hope, promotion and the restoration of integral development of people of all cultures. Jesus of Nazareth, God's Messiah, is the concrete historical instance of the union of the divine and the human. This historical union, incarnation, took place in time and space.[37]

34 Witherup, *Scripture*, 78–81.
35 John Paul II, *Encyclical Letter, Redemptoris Missio* (7 December 1990), 15: *AAS* 83 (1991), 263, cited in *Ecclesia in Africa,* 53.
36 *Ecclesia in Africa,* 53,
37 Malina, *New Testament World,* 184.

6.4 Zephaniah: ATR/Culture and Islam

The text of Zephaniah has enormous ecumenical and further interreligious implications, especially for religious communities in Africa. It is true that communal living, family life, respect for elders and all human persons, a deep sense of the sacred, and monolatry are among numerous positive values that characterize African cultures. There are also moments these values are overlooked, especially the sacredness of the Supreme Being, YHWH. This sense of the sacred in particular has to be renewed not only in the spirit of Zephaniah's rejection of Assyrian syncretism, but also in the ecumenical spirit, interreligious and cultural dialogues that have been constantly encouraged by Vatican II.

In *Nostra Aetate,* for instance, it is stated that the Church rejects nothing that is true and holy in the non-Christian religions who "often reflect a ray of that truth which enlightens all men (people)."[38] In the same light, Edward Cassidy points out this document's timely indication of the relationship between the Christian faith in YHWH alone and with other religions, Islam in particular thus:

> Muslims "adore the one God, living and subsisting in Himself, merciful and all-powerful, the Creator of heaven and earth, who has spoken to men; they take pains to submit wholeheartedly even to His inscrutable decrees, just as Abraham, with whom the faith of Islam takes pleasure in linking itself, submitted to God (NA, 3).They revere Jesus as a prophet and honor Mary his virgin mother, to whom they turn at times with devotion. They await the Day of Judgment when God will give each man his due after raising him up, and consequently the prize the moral life while giving worship to God, especially through prayer, almsgiving, and fasting."[39]

Furthermore, the Council qualifies its understanding and recommendation of ecumenism by stressing that while relatively few are in a posi-

---

38 Second Ecumenical Council Declaration on the Relation of the Church to non-Christian Religions, *Nostra Aetate,* 2, (October 28, 1965), in Austin Flannery ed., *Vatican II: The Conciliar and Post Conciliar Documents*, vol. 1, (new rev. ed. Dublin, Ireland: Domincan Publications, 1988).

39 Cassidy, *Ecumenism and Interreligious Dailogue*, 130.

tion to participate actively in the ecumenical process, all are called to contribute to the effort of its actualization.[40]

In Nigeria for instance, the challenges of various religious communities (Islam, African Traditional Religions),[41] especially Christian communities working together without losing Christ, the centre of their faith, is as enormous as those challenges that Zephaniah surmounted in the late pre-exilic period. The monolatrous culture which Zephaniah challenged and successfully dialogued with, in the seventh century B.C.E., makes the prophet's promotion of monotheism ever more relevant in a monolatrous Africa today.

John Mbiti, who has researched African religions extensively, examined cult practices and ideas about God and deities in about 300 African peoples who follow traditional native religions.[42] For most African people and like the prophets of Ancient Israel, God is the origin and sovereign of all creation. God is omniscient, omnipresent, and omnipotent. While it is debatable whether African religion is homogeneous, every ethnic group seems to hold the notion of God as the Supreme Being.[43] Among some groups as in Ancient Israel, God bears

40   Second Vatican II Decree on Ecumenism, *Unitatis Redintegratio,* (21 November, 1964), 5.

41   E. B. Idowu, *African Traditional Religion: A Problem of Definition* (London: SCM Press, 1977), 106. Here Idowu gives a breakdown of the worldviews of African Traditional Religion (ATR) to include: belief in God, belief in divinities, belief in spirits, belief in ancestors, and practice of magic and medicine, each with its own consequent, attendant cult.

42   John S. Mibiti, *African Religions & Philosophy* (New York: Praeger, 1969), idem, *Concept of God in Africa* (New York: Praeger, 1970). His findings are based on data derived from a combination of published fieldwork, and oral testimony. Although some of the data are said to be fragmentary and the reliability of certain sources questionable, the bulk of the information is believed to be accurate and reflects native African thought. In antiquity it is possible that these ideas may have diffused from Egypt and/or Semitic culture into African religions.

43   Mbiti, *African Religions,* 29–38; *Leneamenta: Synod of Bishops Special Assembly for Africa* (Vatican: General Secretariat of the Synod of Bishops Editrice Vaticana, 1990), 63–65.

different names mostly expressed in epithets such as Creator, Almighty, Master of all things, and Giver of light.[44]

The Ashanti of Ghana consider the earth to be second to God in power, being the first of His creations. They personified Him as the fertile, great-breasted goddess, *Asase Yaa*. The Ashanti religion features a pantheon of major and minor divinities through which God manifests himself.[45] The religion of the Yoruba of Nigeria shows similar concepts, and their God, the "Sky God" or Supreme God," is ruler of the whole.[46] Other divinities are God's agents carrying out the functions of the Supreme Being on earth.[47] Prayer is often directed to various divinities, and the venerations of divinities and spirits other than God are found in the religious systems of African peoples like in the folk religion of Ancient Israel.[48] A common belief is that the divinities and spirits are intermediaries between humans and God.[49]

Again, while lesser divinities and spirits are commonly identified with natural phenomena, God is not. God's moral attributes are further expressed as: pity, mercy, kindness, justice, righteousness as found in the prophetic literatures of the ancient Israel.[50] Although I hold that in ATR, the concept of God is not strictly polytheistic; the monolatrous tendencies are there, very strong and they need to be addressed, cognizance of African high moral values.

Stressing the importance and necessity of dialogue and addressing the prevailing and persistent ATR, or monolatrous tendencies, especially in Ikot Ekpene Diocese today, Vincent Nyoyoko makes the following relevant remarks:

---

44 Mbiti, *Concepts of God*, 45.
45 Mbiti, *Concepts of God*, 144–45.
46 E. Bolaji Idowu, *Olódùmarè: God in Yoruba Belief* (London: Longmans, 1962), 21–58.
47 Idowu, *Olódùmarè*, 203.
48 This folk religion of the Ancient Israel is articulately discussed in Dever, *Did God Have a Wife*, 91–195.
49 E. Boloaji Idowu, *African Traditional Religion* (New York: Orbis, 1973), 169–175.
50 Mbiti, *Concepts of God*, 31–42.

These adherents to ATR are not only close relations and friends who in general are willing to engage in dialogue, but many are converts from ATR into Christianity who retain most of their traditional beliefs, thus, there is need to formalize the on-going dialogue in the converts. There are many beliefs in ATR which are similar to those in Christianity. The clarification of these through dialogue could enhance their role as basis for *"preparation evangelica."* …, Vatican Council II, has advocated deeper theological research into each cultural area in order to enable the particular church better achieve its identity, and make its contribution to the universal Church. And attention to ATR (through dialogue) will enhance inculturation, adaptation; promote evangelization and actualization of the Word of God.[51]

This passage invites us to be the Zephaniahs of today. Besides, Zephaniah's prophetic confrontation of the worship of false gods and monolatry culture of his time, his universal theological message, embodied in his person, is also exemplary for our pluri-religious and multi-cultural society today. For example, the superscription (Zeph 1:1) provoked scholarly debate as to his origin, Cushi or Judah. Although, the foregoing opinions as to his origin had its rights, the centrality and the discussed universality of Zephaniah's message, with his person as YHWH's instrument, irrespective of his birth place, remains exemplary for the church in Africa, plagued with linguistic, socio-political, cultural and religious divisions.

6.5 Zephaniah's Relevance for our Times and Cultures Today

Apart from the shores of the Church in Africa, where the theology of Zephaniah is received, today we all live in a world threatened by war, terrorism, nuclear weapons, materialism and relativism. We are constantly confronted with all forms of uncertainties, including natural disasters, like the tsunami of South Asia, the hurricanes and oil spill

51   Vincent Nyoyoko, "Dialogue and Inculturation," in *Reconciliation and Renewal of Services in the Church, Lineamenta for the First Synod of the Catholic Diocese of Ikot Ekpene* (Uyo, Nigeria: Trinity Press, 2002), 117–118.

disaster that devastated the southern part of the United States of America, the recent Aquila and Haitian's earthquakes, poverty, cultural misunderstanding and secularism. If Zephaniah could actualize or adapt the ancient Judaism covenant-based theology of hope and earlier prophetic traditions of social justice, judgment, sin, punishment and salvation, relevant to his contemporaries, his theological message, especially of hope, in times of uncertainties, increasingly challenges our times and *Sitz-im-Leben,* as well.[52]

Zephaniah's theology becomes refreshingly applicable to our times, valuable to individuals and Christian communities, when we recall once again the exhortation the Fathers of the Vatican II that, "at all times the Church carries the responsibility of reading the signs and of interpreting them in the light of the Gospel if it is to carry out its task."[53] This task involves sharing in "the joy and hope, the grief and anguish of the men of our time, especially of those who are poor or afflicted in any way."[54]

This call for contextualization of Zephaniah's theology is affirmed by the Pontifical Biblical Commission. The Commission observes that "the Church receives the Bible as a Word of God, addressed both to itself and to the entire world at the present time…actualization is possible because the richness of meaning contained in the biblical text gives it a value for all time and all cultures."[55] By culture here, we

---

52   Vatican II, *Dogmatic Constitution on Divine Revelation, Dei Verbum,* n.12 (Boston: Daughters of St. Paul, 1965), 10. Here the document among other things stresses that, "the interpreter must investigate what meaning the sacred writer intended to express and actually expressed in particular circumstances by using contemporary literary forms in accordance with the situation of his own time and culture."

53   Vatican II, Pastoral Constitution on the Church in the Modern World: *Gaudium et Spes,* 7 December, 1965, 4, in The Conciliar and Post Conciliar Documents, vol. 1 (ed., Austin Flannery; North Port, NY: Costello Publishing Company, 1998), 905.

54   *Gaudium et Spes,* n. 1.

55   The Pontifical Biblical Commission, *The Interpretation of the Bible in the Church: Address of His Holiness John Paul II and Document of the Pontifical Biblical Commission* (Vatican City: Libreria Editrice Vaticana, 1993), 117–132. See also, Pope John Paul II, *The Encyclical Letter, Redemptoris Missio* (Vatican City: Libreria Editrice Vaticana, 1990), 52.

draw insight from Alfred L. Kreober and Klyde Kluckhohn who once stated that:

> Culture (he said) consists of patterns, explicit and implicit, of and for behavior acquired and transmitted by symbols constituting the distinctive achievement of the human groups, including their embodiments in the artifacts: the essential core of culture consists of traditional (i.e., historically derived and selected) ideas and especially their attached values; cultural system may on the one hand, be considered as products of action, on the other as conditioning influences upon further action.[56]

In other words, culture is a system of symbols relating to and embracing people, things and events that are socially symbolic; or "filling people, things, and events with meaning and value, making them meaningful in such a way that all the members of the given group mutually share, appreciate, and live out that meaning and value in some way."[57] Kathryn Tanner also believes that culture produces a commonality of beliefs, sentiments and presumes common stakes. Culture in this sense even goes beyond the boundary of ethnocentrism. Hence, the distinctiveness of cultural identity therefore, is neither a product of isolation nor a matter of "us" versus "them."[58]

This explanation is affirmed by Robert J. Schreiter, who depicts culture, "as patterned systems (of beliefs, values, rules) in which the various elements are coordinated in such a fashion as to create a unified whole."[59]

56   Alfred L. Kroeber and Klyde Kluckhohn, *A Critical Review of Concepts and Definition* (Papers of the Peabody Museum of American Archaeology and Ethnology, Harvard University 47, n. 1. Cambridge: MA: Peabody Museum, 1952), 51 cited in Bruce J. Malina, *The New Testament World: Insight from Cultural Anthropology* (revised edition, Louisville, KY: Westminster John Knox Press, 1993), 12.

57   See Malina, *New Testament World*, 12 for an expanded insight into the meaning of culture.

58   Kathryn Tanner, *Theories of Culture: A New Agenda for Theology* (Minneapolis: Fortress Press, 1997), 57.

59   Robert J. Schreiter, *The New Catholicity: Theology between the Global and the Local* (Maryknoll, NY: Orbis Books, 2002), 47–48. Recently, contextual theology is also excellently discussed in Stephen B. Bevans, *Models of Contextual Theology: Faith and Culture* (revised and expanded edition. Maryknool, NY:

He also stresses the importance of applying biblical lessons, including the texts of Zephaniah, to every culture, and of interpreting Christ, the New Prophet and the Messiah contextually, to every cultural and life situation. Schreiter's point on inculturation was an endorsement of the teaching of the Synod Fathers who in 1995 stressed the particular importance of evangelization or inculturation, the process by which 'catechesis 'takes flesh' in the various cultures."[60]

Inculturation, the Synod Fathers stressed, includes "the ultimate transformation of authentic cultural values through their intergration in Christianity," as well as "the insertion of Christianity in the various strata of human cultures."[61] Zephaniah's prophecy foreshadows the Good News in Christ; "Just as the 'Word became flesh and dwelt among us" (Jn 1:14), so too the Good News, the Word of Jesus Christ proclaimed to the nations, must take root in the life-situation of the hearers of the Word. Inculturation is precisely this insertion of the Gospel message into cultures."[62]

Therefore, Zephaniah is relevant to all cultures. In Zephaniah, the colorful, aesthetic and poetic description of the Day of YHWH (Zeph 1:14–18; 3:14–20), in the preceding chapters radiates a beauty and provokes a prayerful, hymnic and meditative atmosphere, that is not restricted to one particular culture and language.[63] The problems which confronted Zephaniah and his contemporaries with his response are not only paradigmatic to the church, but remain a huge challenge for society today.

According to our studies, ancient Judah would have suffered massive destruction of its population, land and abuse of their fundamental human rights. Zephaniah brought them hope in the course of their

Orbis Books, 2004); Fernando F. Segovia and Mary Ann Tolberts, eds., *Reading From This Place: Social Location and Biblical Interpretaion*, 2 vols. (Minneapolis: Fortress Press, 1995).

60   See John Paul II, *Apostolic Exhortatiion Catechiest Tradendae* (16 October 1979), 53: AAS 71 (1979), 1319 cited in John Paul II, *Post-Synodal Apostolic Exhortation: Ecclesia in Africa* (Vatican City: Libreria Editrice Vaticana, 1995), 44.

61   John Paul II, *Ecclesia in Africa,* 45.

62   John Paul II, *Ecclesia in Africa*, 45–46.

63   See for instance the comparative table of chapter three.

task of surviving, regaining and rebuilding their rural farming population, as well as its moral social, political and religious structures.[64] Zephaniah also announced his theology of the worship of YHWH alone in the midst of the syncretism of Assyrian collaborators. It was risky to oppose such hegemony, since a prophetic opposition, even of those Judeans who collaborated with the enemies, was usually regarded as punishable opposition to Assyrian imperialism and military might.

Thus, Zephaniah's prophecy challenges us pastorally. It challenges religious communities of Africa to which my home diocese of Ikot Ekpene, in South-South Nigeria forms a part.[65] These pastoral problems range from the need to overcome divisions among various religious and tribal groups, to overcoming poverty and promoting civil self-governing, that would eliminate corruption, and ensure social justice, peace and order.[66] *Ecclesia in Africa* has also rightly articulated these problems to include: increasing poverty, urbanization, international debt, arms trade, refugees and displacement of persons, oppression of women, ethnocentrity, war, tribal tensions, political instability and the violations of fundamental human rights.[67] These are challenges of the work of faith, the endurance of hope and the labor of love (1 Thess 1:1–5).

---

64 Sweeney, *Zephaniah*, 189.

65 If Zephaniah had shared common themes of YHWH alone worship with the Deuteronomistic theologians, promoting, justice and universalism, then his theological trends are more than relevant to Ikot Ekpene Diocese faced not only with challenges of mutual co-existence with churches of other denomination, but managing those aspects of African Traditional Religion that contradicts Christianity and the dignity of the human persons, including women and children. For details of this particular needs and problems See, The Catholic Diocese of Ikot Ekpene, *Reconciliation and Renewal of Services in the Church,* esp. 1–15, 105–110.

66 For a concise insight into the political, social and religious climates of this part of Africa and the hope that modern prophets can bring, especially the church, See, Michael U. Udoekpo, *Corruption in Nigerian Culture: The Liberation Mission of the Church* (Enugu; Nigeria: Snaap Press, 1994), esp, 16–49; Idem, *The Limits of Divided Nation* (Enugu; Nigeria: Snaap Press, 1999), 17–83.

67 See, John Paul II, *Ecclesia in Africa,* 35–38.

6.6 A Summary Reflection on Chapter Six

Zephaniah proclaimed the theology of unity of worship or of YHWH alone as the sovereign of all creation. This element of one God is found in Christianity, Islam and ATR. He preached the theology of hope, faith, universalism, judgment, justice and punishment, covenant renewal and restoration of fortunes. These various aspects of Zephaniah's prophecies are delivered in a single theological package of the Day of YHWH, with the ecumenical and interreligious implications discussed in this thesis.

Although these theological strands overlap one another, our two *pericopae* (Zeph 1:14–18 and 3:14–20) demonstrate and highlight YHWH as the master of all creation, with an unchallenged superiority. YHWH in Zephaniah is the overall judge (1:2–3, 7, 14–18, 3:8).

In Zephaniah, although YHWH is the King of Israel, He is also the King of the Universe. YHWH's reign extends to all the earth and penetrates the fabrics of all cultures. It is the center of all monotheistic religions, particularly Christianity, Islam and Judaism. Mercy would be His final work (3:14–20).

The relevance of Zephaniah to exilic and post-exilic Judaism, Christianity, ATR, Islam and the Church, is reflected in the shared themes of future hope, monotheism between the OT and NT, which binds the two testaments together. The hope in YHWH preached by the prophets and Zephaniah is fulfilled and made anew in Jesus, the Savior and Lord of the Universe. Zephaniah is ever relevant to the Church and people of all cultures, especially African communities.

This is true since the problems addressed by Zephaniah take on new forms in poverty, war, syncretism, divisions, political instability, and threats of nuclear weapons, secularism, relativism and abuse of fundamental human rights of some people and different cultures today, the ecumenical and interreligious relevance of this work is indisputable, especially in the light of the debates that shaped the final form of the teachings of the Vatican II and other ecclesiastical documents.[68]

---

68   Some of these documents already discussed are: *Dei Verbum, Gaudium et Spes, Lumen Gentium, Christus Dominus, Orientalium Ecclesiarum, Ad Gentes,*

However, the church today as well as individual Christians and members of religious communities especially in Africa are challenged to be the "Zephaniahs" of today, and the bearers of the message of hope, unity of worship, faith, peace and justice. The suffering and wrath in the theology of Zephaniah (1:14–18), remain a foreshadowing of the hope, joy, dances and restoration of fortunes that YHWH brings to his humble remnants (3:14–20).

Dignitatis Humanae, Unitatis Redintegratio, Nostra Aetate and the PBC documents, especially *The Interpretation of the Bible in the church* (1993), and *The Jewish People and the Sacred Sciptures in the Christian Bible* (2002) to name, but a few.

General Conclusion

Perhaps it is pertinent to sum up the studies of the six preceding Chapters, by recalling the fact that Zephaniah is a compendium of the prophetic thoughts, on the nature of YHWH's relationship with His people. Zephaniah delivers this key theological message in his prophecy of the Day of YHWH (יום יהוה).[1]

Zephaniah uses this expression more than any other OT Prophet. He uses it primarily when he wants to emphasize the notion of a God who loves, judges, punishes (Zeph 1:14–18) and restores (3:14–20). A God who is always in the midst of His people (Zeph 3:15c; 17e) and a God who involves Himself in human history. For Zephaniah this history is mingled with wrath, hope, faith, endurance, repentance, restoration of fortunes and with God's promises. It is a theological history inseparable from the problem of biblical or prohetic eschatology, since prophets helped Israel to look back creatively on its past, judge the present and anticipate the future.

While discussing the *Status Quaestionis* in Chapter One, we argued that generations of scholars in the past have unsatisfactorily applied several methods and used different approaches in search for the meaning, origin and significance of יום יהוה (the Day of YHWH). As we focused on these past studies, it became evident that prior to the 1950s, scholars were confined to traditio-historical, mythical and cultic-theophanic interpretations of the Day of YHWH. Much more dynamic and synchronic methods were deployed in this regard beginning from the 1980s, but this was not without reference to the earlier historical studies.

---

1   And I think the observation made earlier by Feinberg, in *The Minor Prophets*, 222, is true. He notices that a sixteenth-century writer once indicated that, "if anyone wishes all the secret oracles of the prophets to be given in a brief compendium, let him (or her) read through this brief Zephaniah." Moreover, "similar expressions are found between Isaiah and Zephaniah and even more between Jeremiah and Zephaniah."

This brought us in contact with R. H. Charles and John M. P. Smith, who, for example, traced the origin of the Day of YHWH to the pre-prophetic stage of Israel's history. Hugo Gressmann linked the Day of YHWH to the "popular eschatological belief" among the Israelites. This is when God, mindful of his covenant, will bring His people the promised blessings and prosperity. Sigmund Mowinckel thought the motif was primarily understood within the context of Israel's cultic life of the New Year's Festival, when YHWH was dramatically enthroned as a King.

Ladislav Černy, as we saw, recognized the centrality of this concept in the teachings of the Hebrew Prophets. For Černy, יום יהוה (the Day of YHWH) does not only embrace the basic notion of Hebrew eschatology, it touches on the intellectual, emotional, theological, spiritual, social, ritual, ideological and political dimension of the Hebrew religion. He rejected Mowinckel's cultic-dramatic proposal, borrowed from Canaanite and Babylonian religions. Černy rather suggested that the concept be traced to the day of divine decree.

Gerhard von Rad and his school, in the 1950s basically emphasized the Holy War *(Der heilige Krieg)* motif. He argues persuasively that the origin of the Day of YHWH be traced to the Holy War traditions. For von Rad, although Amos 5:18–20 is usually acknowledged as the earliest written text for the study of the Day of YHWH, there are other texts (Isa 2:12; 13:6, 9; 22:5; 34:8; Jer 46:10; Ezek 7:10; 13:5; 30:3; Joel 1:15; 2:1, 11; 3:4; Obad 15; Zeph 1:7, 8, 14–18; Zech 14:1), from which a contextual setting for the study of the meaning of the Day of YHWH could be drawn.

Studying the passages of Isaiah 13 (poem on Babylon), Isaiah 34 (Oracle against Edom), Ezekiel 7 (Oracle against Egypt) and Joel 2 (locust in Judah), von Rad notices some stimulating similarities in these texts. This is obvious, mostly in the area of their portrayal of the sacral war. Several images which dominate these texts he stresses, suggest that we are dealing with a well-established component part of eschatological tradition. These images include: the call to warriors and military personnel to gather for the levy of YHWH, the sanctification of the army, panic among the enemy forces, sacrifices, and the shedding of blood. Others are; distress, wailing and blowing of the trumpet and changes in the natural order with a consequent total annihilation.

For von Rad, these are images and stereotyped cries by which people were recruited for military services in earlier times. They are cries by which men once went out into battle with YHWH as their "Commander-in-Chief."[2] Gerhard von Rad believes that Zephaniah 1:7–18, is the most important source for a detailed debate on the Day of YHWH. He dwells on the metaphor of "sacrifice" (זבח), which runs through other passages (Isa 36:6; Jer 46:10; and Ezek 34:17) that deal with the Day of YHWH. These texts and metaphors, according to von Rad, depict the context of a Holy War.

Critics of von Rad especially in the 1960s, include Meir Weiss, who thinks that considering the prominent place which the concept of the YHWH as "a man of war" occupies in the entire biblical faith, יום יהוה (the Day of YHWH), as a pure event of war, is far from being the constitutive element in the prophecies of the Day of YHWH. For Weiss there are some prophecies that threaten warlike attacks executed by the Lord, without necessarily alluding to the Day of the Lord. Also among the Day of the Lord texts cited by von Rad, the majority are found in Isaiah 13 and Joel, two prophecies which betray a certain affinity to each other, and which do not belong to the earlier prophecies of the Day of the Lord.

Weiss concluded on an unpopular note that the motif-complex and phraseology of the Day of the Lord is not pre-prophetic, but has actually originated in a phrase coined by Amos in the course of his polemic with his contemporaries, about the manifestation of the Lord. For Weiss, unlike von Rad, the Day of YHWH traditions is traceable to the motif-complex of the theophanic-descriptions. For him it was here that Amos stumbled over the phrase that subsequently came to exert such a huge impact on generations of scholars.

Frank Moore Cross and his student, Patrick Miller, are less critical of von Rad. They believe that von Rad in the first place, was influenced by the School of Alt, which is of the opinion that only individual tribes entered the conquered land or infiltrated it. Cross and Miller attempted

2   This is actually a modern expression, used here metaphorically to portray YHWH within the context of this discussion, as the sovereign of creation, men and women.

a reconciliation of Mowinckel and von Rad. For Cross and Miller, the Day of YHWH is both a day of YHWH's victory in battle and a day of YHWH's royal festival. Cross particularly believes that the cult of Israel is an amalgamation of imagery from the Holy War tradition, with that of the creation-kinship motifs. It is a dramatization of the Exodus and the Conquest.

Cross is convinced that it was YHWH, the heavenly warrior, who masterminded actions in both of these events.[3] To justify the wedding of the "Myth and ritual school of Mowinckel and the "history of redemption school" of von Rad, Cross took on an analysis of Psalm 24. In doing this, he emphasizes those aspects of the festive celebration of the kingship of YHWH and the commemoration of YHWH's victory in war. Similarly, Miller suggests that the Day of YHWH signals not only YHWH's victory at war, but also the participation of the whole cosmos in the wars of YHWH. It is in the light of these arguments that this study supports von Rad, since it was also noticed that Cross and Miller are yet to produce a systematic study of the Day of YHWH text.

While we revisited the general historical background of Zephaniah, it became necessary to also review specific studies of the prophet Zephaniah. It was discovered that even those scholars, including Marvin Sweeney, who devoted commendable time on specific studies on Zephaniah had their shortcomings. They concentrated on the methodological debates, rather than on the theological values. Sufficient time was not given to a systematic and coherent comprehensive study of the theology of the Day of YHWH in Zephaniah (1:14–18; 3:14–20), as demonstrated in this work. The relevance of Zephaniah for our times and cultures were not adequately stressed.

Demonstrated also in this dissertation was the unity of the Twelve Minor Prophets. Elements of this unity highlighted in our study, included the facts of the scribal practice, size of the book, the MT and

---

3   It is noted in chapter one that the conquest so understood, according to Cross is not a historical event, but a construct of the *Heilsgeschichte* School, hence he feels von Rad fails to deal fully with the origin of the Holy war in Israel, and in turn with the methodological elements in holy war as practiced by earliest Israel, and indeed as practiced by non-Israelite people.

LXX ordering.[4] The presence of catchwords, shared chronology or literary features, and the common theological-eschatological theme of the Day of YHWH, that runs through the Twelve, was also used to support our arguments for the unity of the Twelve Minor Prophets. The Day of YHWH, being our major focus, this theological-eschatological theme with its multiple strands of hope, YHWH alone worship, universalism, judgment, punishment, was presented in this thesis, to have undergone updating, some modifications and contextualizations, in subsequent prophetic messages, particularly in Zephaniah.[5]

In addition, while discussing this overwhelming theme, the general structure of Zephaniah with a detailed exegesis of Zephaniah 1:14–18 became central. Zephaniah's knowledge of the earlier traditions was demonstrated in the course of the exegesis. It showed Zephaniah's understandings of God, His judgment and saving roles in human history. Nouns, verbs and concepts were shared with other OT texts, especially with the texts of the Twelve Minor Prophets, as indicated by Adele Berlin and other scholars mentioned in the study.

The thesis also argued that Zephaniah related his preaching of 1:14–18, with other passages or with the overall materials of his book. For example, Zephaniah 1: 2–3 (universal creation, human and animal); Verses 4–6 (Judah and wealthy class), and particularly verses 7–13 (the Day of sacrifice), all earlier motifs are found reflected in the rhetorical unit of 1:14–18. Zephaniah's hymnic and poetic-alliterative style of his preaching, about the soon-arrival of the Day of YHWH, not only contrast him with Amos, Joel and other prophets, but they help to highlight the uniqueness, modification and contextualizing pattern of his theological language. This is, of course, clearly expressed in verses 15–16, which is characterized, as we saw, with pairs of nominal sentences and contents of paronomasia (vv15–16).

---

4   See the discussion on these ordering in Nogalski and Sweeney "Preface" in *Reading and Hearing the Book of the Twelve*, viii. Here it rightly Hosea, Joel, Amos, Obadiah, Jonah, Micah, Nahum, Habakkuk, Zephaniah, Haggai, Zechariah, and Malachi are listed as MT version of the Twelve as opposed to the LXX ordering: Hosea, Amos, Micah, Joel, Obadiah, Jonah, Nahum, Habakkuk, Zephaniah, Haggai, Zechariah and Malachi.

5   For a further details see, Coogan, *Old Testament*, 316–317.

Theological lessons were drawn from the exegesis conducted in Chapter Two. These included the facts that YHWH intervenes in human activities, in various ways (1:7). YHWH is the sovereign of creation, animal and humans (vv 2–3). YHWH judges and punishes (vv 8–13). His judgment is swift (v 14), and devastating (v 15). It penetrates barriers and fortification of all kinds (v 16), and renders non-repentant people worthless (v 17). YHWH's judgment reaches to the ends of the earth. It touches the rich and the poor (v 18; 2:4–15), regardless of culture and nationality. Yet, mercy would be the final work of YHWH. Zephaniah offers hope for the poor and the remnant of Israel who constantly seek the Lord (1: 4–6; 2:1–3, 4–7, 8–11; 3:9–13, 14–20). Their fortunes shall be restored. And there will be joy, dancing of victory and salvation (Zeph 3:1–20), as discussed.

These motifs of joy, salvation and restoration of fortunes (שבות/ šᵉbût שוב/šûb), constituted the overall exegetical-theological analysis of Zephaniah 3:14–20, which we undertook in Chapter Three. The hope of this restoration was long foreshadowed by Zephaniah 1:14–18. The uniquely poetic and literary features of this unit (3:14–20), separated the creativity of the prophet Zephaniah from those Prophets before him. Verses 15a–16c for instance, brought to lime light the reason for the genre of hymn and psalm of praise, which uniquely characterized the entire pericope of 3:14–20.

Zephaniah 15a–16c further presented the Day of YHWH in an anaphorical and repetitive or alliterative style. The thesis went on to suggest unequivocally, that the joyful cheers (רני) of the humble people, in Zephaniah 3:14–20, reverse the bitter cry of the warrior (מר צרח שם גבור), the wrath (עברה), distress and tribulation (צרה ומצוקה), ruin and desolation (שאה ומשואה), darkness and gloom (חשך ואפלה), the terrible clouds (ענן וערפל), the cry of the war with trumpet blast (שופר ותרועה) and the hostility (צרר) earlier heard in Zephaniah 1:14–18.

The dissertation observed that the phrase (שבות/šᵉbût שוב/šûb), embraces captivity, well being, reversal of misfortunes (bad name, mockery, exile, denial of fundamental human rights) to the good fortunes of the humble, who humbly trust and realize their entire hope in YHWH alone. The prophets including Zephaniah were pastors. They helped Israel to put language on its experiences. They were the conscience of the people and helped to reinterpret Israel's reality. They were Israel's creative, living, challenging and actualizing memory. Hence, Zephaniah not only adapted past traditions but he arose to the occasions of actualizing the concept of the Day of YHWH already extant in the traditions particularly of the prophetic literature.

Such historical traditions in the prophetic literature, especially in the Twelve Minor Peophets, particularly in Amos 5:18–20, where the expression was first explicitly heard in the context of eighth century Israel became the focus of Chapter Four. It was a socio-religious, cultural and political *Sitz-im-Leben*, familiar with the covenant and divine election traditions, as discussed. These traditions understood the popular notion of the Day of YHWH, as that day, when YHWH will not only fight to free his elected people, but would defeat their enemies and restore their fortunes.

We argued that, Amos and his contemporaries, especially the prophets, were familiar with these traditions. They also shared a common socio-political situation. Politically, it was a time of political equilibrium, when Jeroboam II governed in the North (786–746 B.C.E.) and Uzziah ruled in the South (785–733 B.C.E.). Israel's emergence in power and wealth (Amos 6:4) were not only accompanied by all kinds of abuses in the land (5:21–27), but the election theology was taken for granted. Social injustice and abuse of cult and religion became the order of the day. Various kinds of abuses including expropriation, fraud, exploitations and corruption, the dissertation stressed, were practiced. These unethical behaviors, religious mediocrity and class distinctions provoked the condemnation by prophet Amos, who turned the popular rosy notion of the Day of YHWH to that of darkness (Amos 5:18–20).

This work also observed that naturally, it must have been shocking to his contemporaries when Amos prophetically changed the popular and positive, covenant-based notion of the Day of YHWH (divine intervention, blessing and prosperity), to a negative Day of Judgment and punishment of idolaters, corrupt judges, exploiters of the poor and degraders of human dignities. As we saw, Amos presented this so well, with such antithetical motifs of "light" and "darkness" (Amos 5:18; 8:9; 9:1), that left a figurative land mark in the discussion of the theology of the Day of YHWH, in the prophetic literature (Isa 13:10; Ezek 30:3; Joel 2:1–2 and Zeph 1:15).

The benefits of undertaking such a historical investigation of the Day of YHWH in the prophetic traditions other than Zephaniah served to shed more light on, and give a better understanding of the specific growth and unique place of the concept in the theology of Zephaniah, *vis-á-vis* the Twelve Minor Prophets. It also helped to establish the setting for a comparative analysis of the Day of YHWH (יום יהוה), in the Zephaniah with other prophets. It helped to highlight specifically the creative, unique and contextual insight into the theology of Zephaniah which constantly challenges us today to adapt and inculturate the vitality of the word of God in our contexts, as well as seek meaning in history and tradition through faith.

This comparative analysis became the task for Chapter Five. The relationship of our two units under investigations (Zeph 1:14–18; 3:14–20), with other prophets, especially the Twelve Minor Prophets was discussed. Similar comparison was extended to Isaiah, Jeremiah, Ezekiel, to the DH and to the other texts of the OT, particularly Psalm 126, where similar theological language, literary features, theological themes and socio-historical traditions are prominent.

In the light all these, Zephaniah's life situation, the thesis argued, was rooted in the covenant traditions, and with the idea of YHWH as their savior-warrior, deliverer (Exod 14:14; 15:1–23), a source of blessing and prosperity. He was familiar with earlier prophetic traditions. Zephaniah proclaimed the theology of YHWH alone as the sovereign of all creation. He preached the theology of hope, repentance, universalism, judgment, justice and punishment, repentance, covenant renewal and restoration of fortunes. These various strands of Zephaniah's message are delivered in a single theological package of the Day of YHWH. Although these theological strands overlap one another, Zephaniah 1:14–18 and 3:14–20 demonstrate and highlight YHWH as the master of all creation with an unchallenged superiority. YHWH in Zephaniah is the overall judge (1:2–3, 7, 14–18, 3:8). YHWH is not only the King of Israel but He is also the King of the Universe. YHWH's reign extends to all the earth and mercy, the dissertation stressed, would be His final work (3:14–20).

As extensively stressed in Chapter Six, the theological and religious values of Zephaniah cannot be overemphasized. Zephaniah's theology shares common elements with Judaism, Christianity, ATR, and Islam. In terms of justice and worship of YHWH alone, Zephaniah's theology, the thesis emphasized, is constantly relevant to the Church today, particularly the Church in Africa. While Zephaniah, condemned the particular external fault of his day, namely, the worship of false gods (1:4–5), the adaptation of foreign customs (1:8), the perpetration of violence and fraudulent behavior (1:11), the performance of hypocritical rituals and false prophecy (3:4), we underlined that the prophet also preached against the causes of sin, namely, pride (1:16; 2:10, 15; 3:11), rebellion (3:1) and lack of trust in God (1:12; 3:2).

Zephaniah's theology of the Day of YHWH, in conclusion, bears the imprint of past traditions. It is a day of YHWH's intervention in history. It is a day of YHWH's demonstration of his sovereignty, judgment and renewal of his covenant with his people. For Zephaniah YHWH's judgment (1:14–18) is universal, provoked by sin, disobedience and bad choices of human beings. True religion is to seek righteousness and YHWH (2:3). His sovereignty is enduring, and mercy is his final goal. YHWH would hide the remnant under His umbrella when His wrath is delivered. He would restore the fortunes of the poor, the remnant and the humble that place their entire hope in him (3:14–20). In other words, repentance, hope, faith and humble trust in God alone, are the true settings for God's blessings, divine promises, prosperity and restoration of fortunes of the remnant by a God who is always in the midst of his people (vv 15c, 17a). This God brings them home, at that time (3:20a). He gathers his people (v 20b), and makes their name known (v 20c). YHWH would also make his remnant people famous among all the people of the earth (v 20d). He would restore their fortunes before their eyes; since they have humbly sought refuge in the name of the Lord their God (20e).

Like Zephaniah who bore the message of justice, judgment, perseverance in the midst of suffering and who promoted universalism, championed reconciliation, repentance, faith and hopes building for salvation and restoration, single-mindedness in the worship of YHWH alone, it is incumbent on the Church and individual Christians to be the prophetic presence in today's world. This is true since some of those problems addressed by Zephaniah take on new forms today in poverty, war, syncretism, divisions, political instability, abuse of fundamental human rights, and pride of self-sufficiency by political dictators. The Church is invited to persevere in her proclamation to bring about the kingdom of God after the example of Jesus, a manifestation of YHWH preached by Zephaniah. This Kingdom is the source of full liberation, restoration of fortunes, justice and salvation for people of all cultures.[6] Human history finds its true and full meaning in the incarnation of the Word of God, the foundation of hope[7] and restored human dignity. It is through Christ, the new prophet and "image of the invisible God, the firstborn of all creation" (Col 1:15), that the human person is redeemed.[8]

6   John Paul II, *Redemptoris Missio* (7 December 1990), 15: *AAS* 83 (1991), 263, cited in *Ecclesia in Africa*, 53.

7   This hope was extensively discussed alongside desire by Thomas Aquinas in the *Summa Theologica* $I^a II^{ae}$, q. 40, a.1. Here Thomas argues that Hope is like one of the human passions, for example desire or cupidity. Just as desire or cupidity, human hope arises from the natural appetite for happiness. Stressing the Christian hope, the primacy of God, and commenting on Thomas further, A. M. Carre, *Hope or Despair* (trans., René Hague. London: Harvill Press, 1955), 5–13 emphasized that desires is the impulse which drives human beings towards something which appears to them to be a good. A good they do not yet posses, but which is accessible and which can become theirs. Hope is also directed towards a good which is not yet present, but which may be wished for and is attainable. But hope does not come into action unless it becomes apparent that the winning of this good will be arduous. When that is so desire is no longer enough. The good that is envisaged may be accessible and the chance of possessing it may not be distant, but it is not quite within reach; and this element of difficulty, this cleavage between man and the good he desires, is part of the very essence of hope. In other words, rooted in every human being, and bound to him by the will of God, lies a need for fulfillment, a need to blossom in maturity, fundamental and indestructible tendency to persevere to the final term- happiness. Hope shares this same root with desire, but with hope they strike even deeper. See also Benedict XVI, *Spe Salvi*, 16–21, idem *Lent: The Journey to Easter* (London: Catholic Truth Society, 2009), 16–18.

8   *Ecclesia in Africa*, 53.

Zephaniah's contacts with the past prophetic and OT traditions demonstrate that prophets were the conscience of the people of their times. Prophets were consistent in adapting the message that if the experience of the presence of God grounded the promises of encounter, that encounter could mean salvation or judgment. Zephaniah reminds us that YHWH is a God of promise to whom appeal could be made on the basis of known fidelity and obedience to God. This dialectical experience of judgment and restoration has as its basis our call to repentance, as well as our trust in God's love and mercy.

Zephaniah therefore challenges us today, as he challenged his contemporaries, to keep in mind that YHWH is a God of promise to whom appeal could be made on the basis of this known fidelity and obedience to him, who demands from us the constant struggle of faith- actualization. He calls on each and every one of us always to seek the Lord, (2:3) and to live responsibly in the ambience of history, on the dawn of a new tomorrow which we hopefully choose. This choice embodies the pattern of living ethically and fully the Christian and prophetic values of faith, hope, justice, love, worship of the true God and perseverance in the present as foreshadowed by Zephaniah (1:14–18; 3:14–20), in anticipation of the future, enlivened and enabled by the life-giving traditions of the past.

Bibliography

1. Primary Literature, Texts and Translation

ALAND, B. et al., eds., *The Greek New Testament*. 4ᵗʰ Revised Edition. Stuttgart: Deutsche Bibelgesellschaft, 2001.

BERETTA, P. ed., ספר תרי עשר *(Libro Di Dodici Profeti) I Profeti Minori: Osea, Gioele, Amos, Abdia, Giona, Michea, Naum, Abacuc, Sofonia, Aggeo, Zeccaria, Malachia, Ebraico, Greco, Latino, Italiano*. BEI 13; Milano: Edizione San Paolo, 2008.

COOGAN, Michael D. *The New Oxford Annotated Bible: New Revised Standard Version with the Apocrypha*. New York: Oxford University Press, 2001.

ELLIGER, K. et al., eds., *Biblia Hebraica Stuttgartensia*. 5ᵗʰ Edition. Stuttgart: Deutsche Bibelgesellschaft. 1997.

METZGER, Bruce M. *A Textual Commentary on the Greek New Testament*. 2ⁿᵈ Edition. Stuttgart: Deutsche Bibelgesellschaft, 2002.

NESTLE, E. and K. Aland. eds., *Novum Testamentum Graece*. 27ᵗʰ Edition. Stuttgart: Deutsche Bibelgesellschaft, 1998.

RAHLFS, A. ed., *Septuaginta*. Stuttgart: Deutsche Bibelgesellschaft, 1979.

SCOTT, William R. *A Simple Guide To BHS: A Critical Apparatus, Masora, Accents Unusual Letters & Other Markings*. 3ʳᵈ Edition. Richland Hills; TX: Bibal Press, 1995.

SENIOR, D. et al., eds. *The Catholic Study Bible: The New American Bible*. New York: Oxford University Press, 1990.

THE NEW JERUSALEM BIBLE: *The Complete Text of the Ancient Canon of the Scriptures*. Standard Edition. New York: Doubleday, 1999.

WÜRTHWEIN, E. *The Text of the Old Testament*. 2ⁿᵈ Edition. Trans., Erroll F. Rhodes. Grand Rapids, MI: Eerdmans, 1995.

2. Commentaries and Related Works Consulted

BERLIN, A. *Zephaniah: A New Commentary with Introduction and Commentary*. AB. Vol. 25 A, New York: Doubleday, 1994.

BROWN, Raymond E. *The Birth of the Messiah: A Commentary on the Infancy Narrative in the Gospels of Matthew and Luke*. New York: Doubleday, 1993.

—. *Lamentation: A Commentary*. OTL; Louiville/London: Westminster John Knox, 2002.

DAHOOD, M. *Psalms III: 101–150*. AB 17A. Garden City; NY: Doubleday, 1970.

IRSIGLER, H. *Zefanja*. Herders theologischer Kommentar zum Alten Testament; Freiburg: Herder, 2002.

JEREMIAS, J. *The Book of Amos: A Commentary*. OTL. Louisville, KY: Westminster John Knox Press, 1998.

KRAUS, H.-J. *Psalms 1–59: A Continental Commentary*. Trans. Hilton C. Oswald; MN: Fortress, 1993.

—. *Psalms 60–150: A Continental Commentary*. Trans. Hilton C. Oswald; MN: Fortress, 1993.

MAYS, James L. *Amos: A Commentary*. Philadelphia: The Westminster Press, 1969.

RENAUD, B. *Michée – Sophonie, Nahum*. Paris: J. Gabalda, 1987.

ROBERTS, J.J.M. *Nahum, Habakkuk, and Zephaniah*. OTL. Philadelphia: Westminster, 1991.

RUDOLPH, W. *Micha – Nahum – Habakuk – Zephanja*. KAT XIII/3. Gütersloh: Gütersloher Verlagshaus Gerd Mohn, 1975.

PATTERSON, Richard D. *Nahum, Habakkuk, Zephaniah; The Wycliffe Exegetical Commentary*. Chicago: Moody Press, 1991.

PETER, A. *Die Bücher Zefanja, Nahum, and Habakkuk*. Düsserldorf: Patmos-Verlag, 1972.

PETERSEN, David L. *Haggai and Zechariah 1–8: A Commentary*. OTL; Philadelphia: The Westminster Press, 1984.

ROBERTSON, O.P. *The Books of Nahum, Habakkuk and Zephaniah*. NCOT; Grand Rapids, MI: 1990.

SABOTTKA, L. *Zephanja: Versuch einer Neuübersetzung mit philologischem Kommentar*. Biblica et orientalia 25; Rome: Biblical Institute Press, 1972.

SAVOCA, G. *Abdia-Naum, Abacuc-Sofonia: nuova versione, introduzione e commento*. ILB.PT 18; Milano: Paoline Editoriale Libri, 2006.

SHALOM, M. Paul. *A Commentary of the Book of Amos*. ed., Frank Moore Cross. Minneapolis: Fortress Press, 1991.

SKEHAN, Patrick W. and Alexander A. Di Lella. *The Wisdom of Ben Sira*. Anchor Yale Bible 39. New Haven: Yale University Press, 1987.

SMITH, John M.P. *A Critical and Exegetical Commentary on Zephaniah and Nahum.* ICC; Edinburg: T. & T. Clark, 1911.

STONEHOUSE, G.G.V. and G.W. Wade. *The Books of the Prophet Zephaniah, Nahum and Habakkuk.* London: Methuen & Co. Ltd., 1929.

STUHLMUELLER, C. *Amos, Hosea, Micah, Nahum, Zephaniah, Habakkuk.* Collegeville Bible Commentary. Old Testament 15. Collegeville, MN: The Liturgical Press, 1986.

SZÉLES, Maria E. *Wrath and Mercy: A Commentary on the Books of Habakkuk and Zephaniah.* Trans. George A.F. Knight. ITC. Grand Rapids; MI: Eerdmans, 1987.

SWEENEY, Marvin. A. *Zephaniah: A Commentary.* Minneapolis: Fortress Press, 2003.

VLAARDINGERBROEK, J. *Zephaniah.* HCOT. Leuven: Peeters, 1999.

VUILLEUMIER, R. *Michée, Nahum, Habacuc, Sophonie.* CAT XIb. Switzerland: Delachaux & Niestlé, 1971.

WINTON, D. *The Wisdom of Solomon. A New Translation with Introduction and Commentary.* AB 43. Garden City, NY: Doubleday, 1979.

WOLFF, Hans W. *Joel and Amos: A Commentary.* Translated by Waldermer Janzen, S.D. McBride and C.A. Muenchow Jr. Philadelphia: Fortress Press, 1977.

3. References, Methodology and Hermeneutical Literature

ARNDT, W.F., Gingrich, F.W. *A Greek-English Lexicon of the New Testament and other Early Christian Literature.* Third Edition. Revised and Edited by Danker, Frederick William, based on Walter Bauer's *Griechisch-deutsches Wörterbuch zu den Schriften des Neuen Testaments und der frühchristlichen Literatur,* 6th edition, Chicago/London: The University of Chicago Press, 2000.

AUNE, David E. *The Westminster Dictionary of New Testament & Early Christian Literature & Rhetoric.* Louisville: Westminster John Knox Press, 2003.

BALZ, H., and Gerhard S., eds., *Exegetical Dictionary of the New Testament.* 3 Vols. Grand Rapids, MI: Eerdmans, 1990.

BÉCHARD, Dean P. *The Scripture Documents: An Anthology of Official Catholic Teachings.* Collegeville; MN: The Liturgical Press, 2001.

BOTTERWECK, G. Johannes and Helmer Ringgren, eds., *Theological Dictionary of the Old Testament.* Trans. John T. Willis and David E. Green. 16 Vols. Grand Rapids, MI: Eerdmans, 1980.

BROTZMAN, Ellis R. *Old Testament Textual Criticism.* Rapids, MI: Baker Book House, 1984.

BROWN, F., S. Driver and C. Briggs, *The Brown-Driver-Briggs Hebrew and English Lexicon: With an Appendix Containing the Biblical Aramaic*. Peabody, MA: Hendrickson Publishers, 2005.

DANKER, Frederick W. *Multipurpose Tools for Bible Study: With CD-Rom*. Revised and Expanded. Minneapolis: Fortress, 2003.

FITZMYER, Joseph A. *The Biblical Commission's Document "The Interpretation of the Bible in the Church," Text and Commentary*. Subsidia Biblica 18. Rome: Biblical Institute Press, 1995.

FREEDMAN, D.N. et al., eds. *Anchor Bible Dictionary*. 6 Vols. New York: Doubleday, 1992.

HABEL, N. *Literary Criticism of the Old Testament*. Philadelphia: Fortress Press, 1971.

JENNI, E., and Claus W. *Theological Lexicon of the Old Testament*. Trans., Mark E. Biddle. 3 Vols. Peabody, MA: Hendrickson Publishers, 1997.

JOÜON, P. *A Grammar of Biblical Hebrew*. Translated and revised. T. Muraoka. 2 Vols. Rome: Editrice Pontificio Instituto Biblico, 2005.

KIPFER, Barbara A. Ed. Roget's 21st Century Thesaurus in Dictionary Form. New York: The Philip Life Group, 1999.

KNIGHT, D.A. Foreword. *Methods of Biblical Interpretation*. Excerpted from *The Dictionary of Biblical Interpretation*. Edited by John H. Hayes. Nashville: Abingdon Press, 2004.

LAMBDIN, Thomas O. *Introduction to Biblical Hebrew*. Upper Saddle River, New Jersey: Prentice Hall, 1971.

LÉON-DUFOUR, X. *Dictionary of Biblical Theology*. New Revised Edition. New York: The Seabury Press, 1973.

LUST, J., E. Eynikel and K. Hauspie. *Greek-English Lexicon of the Septuagint*. Revised Edition. Stuttgart: Deutsche Bibelgesellschaft, 2003.

MARTHALER, Berard L. et al., eds. *The New Catholic Encyclopedia*. 16 vols. New York: Thomson & Gale, 2003.

MCKENZIE, John L. *Dictionary of the Bible*. New York: TouchStone, 1995.

MCKENZIE, S.L. and S.R. Hynes, eds. *To Each Its Own Meaning: An Introduction to Biblical Criticisms and their Application*. Revised and expanded. Louisville: Jonn Knox Press, 1999.

METZGER, Bruce M., and Michael D. Coogan. eds., *The Oxford Companion to the Bible*. New York: Oxford University Press, 1993.

MITCHEL, Larry A. *A Student's Vocabulary for Biblical Hebrew and Aramiaic: Frequency Lists with Definitions, Pronunciation Guide, and Index*. Grand Rapids, MI: Zondervan, 1984.

MORGAN, R. and John Barton. *Biblical Interpretation*. Oxford: Oxford University Press, 1988

SCHNEIDERS, Sandra M. *The Revelatory Text: Interpreting the New Testament as Sacred Scriptures*. Collegeville: MN: Liturgical Press, 1999.

SMITH, J.P. ed. *A Compendious Syriac Dictionary.* Eugene, OR: Wipf and Stock Publishers, 1999.

SOULEN, Richard N. and R. Kendall Soulen. *Handbook of Biblical Criticism.* 3rd Revised and Expanded Edition. Louisville: Westminster John Knox Press, 2001.

STECK, Odil H. *Old Testament Exegesis: A Guide to Methodology.* Translated by James D. Nogalski. 2nd ed. Resources for Biblical Study 39. Atlanta: Scholars Press, 1998.

TOV, E. *Textual Criticism of the Hebrew Bible.* Second revised edition. Minneapolis: Fortress Press, 1990.

WALTKE, Bruce K., and M. O'Connor. *An Introduction to Biblical Hebrew Syntax.* Winona Lake; IN: Eisenbrauns, 1990.

WRIGHT, P.H. *Greatness, Grace and Glory: Carta's Atlas for Biblical Biography.* Jerusalem: Carta Jerusalem, 2008.

ZIEFLE, Helmut W. *Modern Theological German: A Reader and Dictionary.* Grand Rapids, MI: Baker, 1997.

4. Secondary Literature, Books and Monographs

ALONSO Schökel L. *A Manual of Hebrew Poetics.* Rome: Editrice Pontificio Instituto Biblico, 2000.

ALTER, R. *The Art of Biblical Narrative.* NY: Basic Books, 1981.

—. *The Art of Biblical Poetry.* NY: Basic Books, 1985.

BALL, Ivan J. *A Rhetorical Study of Zephaniah.* Berkeley, California: Bibal Press, 1988.

BARSTAD, Hans M. *The Religious Polemics of Amos: Studies in the Preaching of Am 2, 7B–8; 4, 1–13; 5, 1-27; 6, 4–7; 8, 14.* VTsup 34. Leiden: Brill, 1984.

BEMPORAD, J. ed., *The Inner Journey: Views from the Jewish Tradition.* Parobola Anthology Series; Sandpoint; ID: Morning Light Press, 2007.

BEN ZVI, E. *A Historical Critical Study of the Book of Zephaniah.* BZAW 198. Berlin: Walter de Gruyter, 1991.

BEYERLIN, W. *We Are Like Dreamers: Studies in Psalm 126.* Trans., Dinah Livingstone; Edingburg: T & T Clark, 1982.

BLENKINSOPP, J. *Prophecy and Canon: A Contribution to the Study of Jewish Origins.* Notre Dame, IN: University of Notre Dame Press, 1977.

BORG, Marcus J. *Jesus in Contemporary Scholarship.* Valley Forge, PA: Trinity Press 1994.

BOSSHARD-Nepustil, E. *Rezeptionen von Jesaja 1–39 im Zwölfprophetenbuch.* OBO 154; Fribourg, Switzerland: Universitätverlag; Göttingen: Vandenhoeck & Reprecht, 1997.

BRACKE, John M. "The Coherence and Theology of Jeremiah." PhD diss., Richmond, VA: Union Theological Seminary, 1983.

BRIGHT, J. *Covenant and Promise: The Prophetic Understanding of the Future in Pre-Exilic Israel.* Philadelphia: Westminster Press, 1976.

—. *A History of Israel.* 4th edition. Louisville/London: Westminster John Knox Press, 2000.

ČERNY, L. *The Day of Yahweh and Some Relevant Problems.* Praze: Karlovy University, 1948.

CHILDS, Brevard S. *Introduction to the Old Testament as Scripture.* Philadelphia: Fortress, 1979.

COLLINS, T. *The Mantle of Elijah: The Redaction Criticism of the Prophetical Books* Biblical Seminar 20; Sheffield: JSOT Press, 1993, 59–87.

COOGAN, Michael D. *The Old Testament: A Historical and Literary Introduction to the Hebrew Scriptures.* New York: Oxford University Press, 2006.

CRAIGIE, Peter C. *The Problem of War in the Old Testament.* Grand Rapids, MI: Eerdmans, 1978.

CROSS, Frank M. *Canaanite Myth and Hebrew Epic: Essays in the History of the Religion of Israel.* Cambridge, MA: Harvard University Press, 1973.

CULLMANN, O. *Salvation in History.* Trans., S. G. Sowers et al. London: SCM, 1967.

DE VAUX, Roland. *Ancient Israel: Its Life and Institutions.* Trans. John Mchugh. Grand Rapids, MI: Eerdmans, 1997.

DEVER, William G. *Who Were the Early Israelites and Where Did They Come From?* Grand Rapids, MI: Eerdmans, 2003.

DIETRICH, W. L. שׁוּב שְׁבוּת, *Die Endzeitliche Wiederherstellung bei den Propheten.* BZAW 40, (1925).

DODD, C. H. *The Parables of the Kingdom.* New York: Scribner, 1961.

EDLER, R. *Das Kerygma des Propheten Zefanja.* Freiburg im Breisgau: Herder, 1984.

FEINBERG, Charles L. *The Major Messages of the Minor Prophets: Habakkuk. Zephaniah, Haggai and Malachi.* New York: American Board of Missions to the Jews, 1951.

—. *The Minor Prophets.* Chicago: Moody Press, 1990.

GOWAN, Donald E. *Theology of the Prophetic Books: The Death & Resurrection of Israel.* Louisville: Westminster John Knox Press, 19998.

GERLEMANN, G. *Zephanja: Textkritisch Untersucht.* Lund: C. W. K. Gleerup, 1942.

HAYS, J. D. *From Every People and Nation: A Biblical Theology of Race.* New Studies in Biblical Theology 14. Downers Grove, IL: Inter Varsity Press, 2003.

HESCHEL, Abraham J. *The Prophets.* New York: Haprennial, 1995.

HOLLADAY, William L. *The Root Šûbh in the Old Testament: With Particular References to Its Usages in Covenantal Contexts.* Leiden: E. J. Brill, 1958.

HOUSE, Paul R. *Zephaniah: A Prophetic Drama.* Bible and Literature Series 16. JSOTSup 69. Sheffield: Almond Press, 1988.

—. *The Unity of the Twelve.* Bible and Literature Series 27. JSOTSup 97; Sheffield: Almond Press, 1990.

JONES, B. A. *The Formation of the Book of the Twelve: A Study in Text and Canon.* SBlDS 149; Atlanta: Scholars Press, 1995.

GOWAN, Donald E. *Theology of the Prophetic Books: Death & Resurrection of Israel.* Louisville: Westminster John Knox Press, 1998.

GNUSE, Robert K. *No Other Gods: Emergent Monotheism in Israel.* JSOT 241; England: Sheffield Academic Press, 1997.

HARNACK, von A. *What is Christianity?* Translated by Th. B. Saunders. New York: Harper 1957.

HUNTER, A. V. *Seek the Lord! A Study of the Meaning and Function of the Exhortations in Amos, Hosea, Isaiah, Micah, and Zephaniah.* Baltimore, Maryland: St. Mary's Seminary & University, 1982.

IRSIGLER, H. *Gottesgericht und Jawetag. Die Komposition Zef 1, 1–2, 3 untersucht auf der Grundlage der Literarkritik des Zefanjabuches.* ATSAT 3. St. Ottilien: EOS, 1977.

JENSEN, J. *Ethical Dimensions of the Prophets.* Collegeville, MI: Liturgical Press, 2006.

JONES, Barry A. *The Formation of the Twelve: A Study of Text and Canon.* SBLDS 149; Atlanta: Scholar Press, 1995.

KAISER, Walter C. *Toward an Old Testament Theology.* Grand Rapids, MI: Zondervan Publishing House, 1991.

KAPELRUD, Arvid S. *The Message of the Prophet Zephaniah.* Oslo: Universitetsforlaget, 1975.

KRINETZKI, G. *Zefanjastudien: Motiv- und Traditionskritik + Kompositions- und Redaktionskritik.* Regensburger Studien zur Theologie 7; Frankfurt am Main: Peter Lang, 1977.

KUKEL, James L. *The Idea of Biblical Poetry: Parallelism and Its History.* Baltimore: John Hopkins University, 1981.

LADD, George Eldon. *The Presence of the Future: The Eschatology of Biblical Realism.* Grand Rapids, MI: Eerdmans, 1974.

LANGHOR, G. *Le livre de Sophonie et la critique d'authenticité.* Analecta Lovaniensia Biblica et Orientalia V/17. Louvain: Éditions Peeters, 1967; = *ETL* 52 (1976): 1–27.

LASOR, W. S. D. A. Hubbard and F. W. Bush. *Old Testament Survey.* Grand Rapids, MI: Eerdmans, 1982.

LINDBLOM, J. *Prophecy in Ancient Israel.* Philadelphia: Fortress Press, 1962.

MERRIL, Eugene H. *Kingdom of Priests: A History of Old Testament Israel.* Grand Rapids: Baker, 1987.

MILLER, J. M. and J. H. Hayes. *A History of Ancient Israel and Judah.* Philadelphia: Westminster, 1986.

MOLTMANN, J. *Theology of Hope: On the Ground and the Implications of a Christian Eschatology.* Translated by J. W. Leitch. New York: Haper & Row, 1967.

MOWINCKEL, S. *He That Cometh.* Translated by G. W. Anderson. New York: Abingdon Press, 1954.

MURRAY, Paul. *A Journey with Jonah: The Spirituality of Bewilderment.* Blackrock, Dublin: The Columbia Press, 2002.

NOGALSKI, James D. *Literary Precursors to the Book of the Twelve.* Berlin; New York: Walter de Gruyter, 1993.

—. *Redactional Process in the Books of the Twelve.* BZAW 218. Berlin: Walter de Gruyter, 1993.

PATE, C.M. et al., eds. *The Story of Israel: A Biblical Theology.* Downers Grove, IL: InterVarsity Press, 2004.

REID, David P. *What Are They Saying About the Prophets?* New York: Paulist Presss, 1980.

ROBINSON, H.W. *Inspiration and Revelation in the Old Testament.* Oxford: Oxford University Press, 1946.

ROBINSON, John A.T. *Jesus and His Coming: The Emergence of a Doctrine.* London: SCM, 1957.

ROWLEY, H.H. *The Faith of Israel: Aspects of Old Testament Thought.* London: SCM Press, 1956.

SCHWARZ, Hans. *Eschatology.* Grand Rapids, MI: Eerdmans, 2000.

SCHWITZER, A. *The Mystery of the Kingdom of God: The Secret of Jesus' Messiahship.* Translated by Walter Lowrie. New York: Macmillan 1950.

SEYBOLD, K. *Satrirische Prophetie: Studien zum Buch Zefanja.* SBS 120. Stuttgart: Katholisches Bibelwerk, 1985.

SMITH, Mark S. *The Early History of God: Yahweh and the Other Deities in Ancient Israel.* 2nd ed. Grand Rapids, MI: Eerdmans, 2002.

STECK, Odil H. *Der Abschluss der Prophetie im Alten Testament: Ein Versuch zur Frage der Vorgeschichte des Kanons.* Biblisch-theologische Studien 17. Neukirchen-Vluyn: Nerkirchener, 1991.

SWEENEY, Marvin A. et al., *The Book of the Twelve Prophets.* 2 vols. Berit Olam; Collegeville, MI: Liturgical Press, 2000.

VANGGEMEREN, G.W. *Interpreting the Prophetic Word.* Grand Rapids: Zondervan, 1990.

VON RAD, G. *The Message of the Prophets.* New York: Harper San Francisco, 1965.

—. *Holy War in Ancient Israel.* Trans., and ed., Marva J. Dawn. Grand Rapids, MI: Eerdmans, 1991.

VRIEZEN, Th.C. *An Outline of Old Testament.* Newton, MA: Bradford, 1958.

WATTS, James W., and Paul R. House, eds., *Forming Prophetic Literature: Essays on Isaiah and the Twelve in Honor of John E.W. Watts.* JSOTSup 235. Sheffield: Sheffield Academic Press, 1996.

WCELA, Emil A. *The Prophets: God's Spokesmen through the Years.* God's Word Today III; A New Study Guide to the Bible. New York: Pueblo Publishing, 1980.

WEIGL, M. *Zefanja und das "Israel der Armen."* Eine Untersuchung zur Theologie des Buches Zefanja. ÖBSt 13. Klosterneuburg: Österreichisches Katholisches Bibelwerk, 1994.

WEISS, J. *Jesus' Proclamation of the Kingdom of God.* (1892). Trans., with intro., by Hyde Hiers and David Larrimore Holland. London: SCM, 1971.

WESTERMANN, C. *Basic Forms of Prophetic Speech.* Trans., H.C. White. Philadelphia: The Westminster Press, 1967.

—. *Praise and Lament in the Psalms.* Atlanta: John Knox Press, 1981.

WRIGHT, G.E. *God Who Acts: Biblical Theology of Recital.* SBT 8. London: SCM Press, 1958.

WHYBRAY, R.N. *The Second Isaiah.* New York: T &T Clark, 2003.

ZAPFF, Burkhard M. *Redaktionsgeschichtliche Studien zum Michabuch im Kontext des Dodekapropheton.* BZAW 256; Berlin and New York: Walter de Gruyter, 1997.

ZUCK, Roy B. *A Biblical theology of the Old Testament.* Chicago, IL: Moody Press, 1991.

5. Articles and Other Studies

ALOMMIA, M. "The Psalms of the "Blessed Hope": Comments on Psalm 126." *To Understand the Scriptures: Essays in Honor of William H. Shea.* Ed., David Merling; Berrien; MI: Institute of Archaeology, Andrews University, 1977, 45–56.

ANDERSON, G.W. "The Idea of Remnant in the Book of Zephaniah." *ASTI* 11(1978): 11–14.

ASEN, Bernhard A. "No, Yes and the Perhaps in Amos and the Yahwist." *VT* 43/4 (1993): 434–441.

BARTON, J. "The Canonical Meaning of the Book of the Twelve." *After the Exile.* ed. J. Barton and D.J. Remer. Macon, GA: Mercer University Press, 1996.

BAUMANN, E. " שׁוב שׁבות, eine exegetische Untersuchung," *ZAW* 47 (1929): 17–44.

BENTZEN, A. "The Ritual Background of Amos 1:2–2:16." *Oudtestamenttische Studien* 8 (1950): 85–99.

BEGG, C. "The Non-mention of Zephaniah, Nahum and Habakkuk in the Deuteronomistic History." *BN* 38/39 (1987): 19–25.

BERLIN, A. "Parallelism." *ABD* 5: 155–162.

—. "On Reading Biblical Poetry: The Role of Metaphor." Congress Volume Cambridge 1995. Edited by J.A. Emerton. VTSup, Leden: Brill 1997.

BERTRAM, G. "στρέφω." *TDNT* 7: 714–29.

BIDDLE, Mark E. "The Figure of Lady Jerusalem: Identification, Deification and Personification of Cities in the Ancient Near East." *The Biblical Canon in Comparative Perspective.* Edited by B. Batto et al., Lewiston, NY: Mellen Press, 1991, 173–94.

—. "Israel" and "Jacob" in the Book of Micah: Micah in the Context of the Twelve." *Reading and Hearing the Book of the Twelve.* Ed. James D. Nogalski and Marvin A. Sweeney. Symposium Series 15; Atlanta: SBL, 2000, 146–165.

BORGER, R. "שוב שבו/ית" ZAW 66 (1954): 315–318.

BOSSHARD-Nepustil, E. "Boebactungen zum Zwölfprophetenbuch." BN 40 (1987): 30–62.

BOSSHARD-Nupustil, Eric and R. G. Kratz. "Maleachi im Zwölfprophetenbuch." BN 52 (1990): 27–46.

BRACKE, John M. "Sub s'but: A Reappraisal." ZAW 97 (1985): 233–244.

BRIGHT, W. F. "The Chronology of the Divided Monarch of Israel." BASOR 100 (1945): 16–22.

BRINKMAN, J. A. "Appendix: Mesopotamian Chronology of the History Period." Ancient Mesopotamia: Portrait of a Dead Civilization. ed., A. Leo Oppenheim. Chicago: The University Press, 1964.

BROWN, Raymond E., and S. M. Schneiders. "Hermeneutics." NJBC. ed., R. E. Brown, J. E. Fitzmyer and R. E. Murphy. Englewood Cliffs: Prentice-Hall, 1990), 1146–1165.

BRUGGEMANN, W. "From Hurt to Joy, From Death to Life." Interpretation 28 (2006): 3–19.

BUDDE, K. "Eine folgenschwere Redaktion des Zwölfprophetenbuchs." ZAW 39 (1921): 218–229.

BUSS, J. "The Meaning of 'Cult' and Interpretation of the Old Testament." JBR 32 (1964): 317–225.

CATHCART, Kevin J. "bos'et in Zephaniah." JNSL 12 (1984): 35–39.

—. "Day of Yahweh." ABD 2: 84–85.

CHISHOLM, Robert B. "Theology of the Old Testament." ed., Roy B. Zuck. Chicago: Moody Press, 1991, 397–433.

CHRISTENSEN, Duane L. "Zephaniah 2:4–15: A Theological Basis for Josiah's Program of Political Expression." CBQ 46 (1984): 669–682.

CLIFFORD, R. J. "The Use of Hôy in the Prophets." CBQ 28 (1966): 458–464.

COGGINS, R. J. The Minor Prophets – One Book or Twelve? Crossing the Boundaries: Essays in Biblical Interpretation in Honour of Michael D. Goulder. ed. S. E. Porter, P. Joyce, and D. E. Orton. Biblical Interpretation Series 8; Leiden: Bill, 1994, 57–68.

COUNTRYMAN, William L. Interpreting the Truth: Changing the Paradigm of Biblical Studies. New York: Trinity Press, 2003.

CROSS, Frank Moore, "The Divine Warrior in Israel's Cult." Biblical Motifs: Origins and Transformation, ed., Alexander Altmann. Cambridge: Harvard University Press, 1966, 11–30.

CURFFEY, Kenneth H. "Remnant, Redactor, and Biblical Theologian: A Comparative Study of Coherence in Micah and the Twelve." Reading and Hearing the Book of the Twelve. Symposium Series 15. Edited by James D. Nogalski and Marvin A. Sweeney. Atlanta: SBL, 2000, 185–208.

DE ROCHE, M. "Zephaniah 1:2–3: The "Sweeping" of Creation." VT 30 (1980): 104–109.

DI LELLA, Alexander A. "Wisdom of Ben-Sira." *ABD* 6: 940–945.

—. "Fear of the Lord as Wisdom: Ben Sira 1:11–30." *The Book of Ben Sira in Modern Research: Proceedings of the First International Ben Sira Conference 28–31 July 1996. Soesterber, Netherlands.* ed. Pancratius C. Beentjes. BZNW 255. Berlin: Walter de Gruyter, 1997, 113–133.

—. "God and Wisdom in the Theology of Ben Sira: An Overview." *Ben Sira's God: Proceeding of the International Ben Sira Conference, Durhum-Ushaw College 2001.* BZNW 321. Berlin: Walter de Gruyter, 2002, 3–17.

ESCOBAR, Donoso S. "Social Justice in the Book of Amos." *Review and Expositor* 92 (1995): 169–174.

EVERSON, A.J. "The Days of Yahweh." *JBL* 93 (1974): 329–337.

FARR, G. "The Language of Amos, Popular Or Cultic?" *VT* 16, 3 (1966): 312–324.

FENSHAM, F.C. "A Possible Origin of the Concept of the Day of the Lord." *Biblical Essays.* Bepeck, South Africa: Potchefstroom Herald, 1966, 90–97.

FERGUSON, H. "The Historical Testimony of the Prophet Zephaniah." *JBL* 3 (1883): 42–59.

FICKER, R. "רנן rnn to rejoice." *TLOT* 3: 1240–1243.

FITZGERALD, A. "The Mythological Background for the Presentation of Jerusalem as Queen and False Worship as Adultery in the Old Testament." *CBQ* 34 (1972): 403–416.

FLOYD, Michael H. "Welcome Back, Daughter of Zion!." *CBQ* 70 (2008): 484–504.

FOHRER, G. "Der Tag YHWHs." *BZAW* 196. Ed. Otto Kaiser. Berlin: Walter de Gruyter, 1991, 32–34.

GALAMBUSH, J. *Jerusalem in the Book of Ezekiel: The City as Yahweh's Wife.* SBLDS 130; Atlanta, GA: Scholars Press, 1992.

GASTER, Theodor H. "Two Textual Emendations – Zephaniah iii. 17." *ExpTim* 78 (1966): 267.

GEYER, John B. "Mythology and Culture in the Oracles against the Nations." *VT* 37 (1986): 129–145.

GERSTERNBERGER, E. "The Woe-oracles of the Prophets." *JBL* 81 (1962): 249–263.

GRAY, J. "A Metaphor from Building in Zephaniah II 1." *VT* 3 (1953): 404–407.

HAGG, H. "חמס chāmās." *TDOT* 4: 478–487.

HAUPT, P. "The Prototype of the Dies irae." *JBL* 38 (1919):142–151.

HAYS, J.D. "Racial Issues in the Prophets," in *From Every People and Nation: A Biblical Theology of Races.* NSBT 14. Downers Grove, IL: Inter Varsity Press, 2003, 105–139.

—. "The Ethnic Make-up of the Old Testament World," in *From Every People and Nation: A Biblical Theology of Race.* NSBT 14. Downers Grove, IL: Inter Varsity Press, 2003, 25–45.

HELLER, J. "Zephanjas Ahnenreihe (Eine redaktionsgeschichtliche Bemerkung zu Zeph. I)." *VT* 21 (1971): 102–104.

HIERS, Richard H. "Day of the Lord." *ABD* 2: 82–83.

HEINTZ, Jean-Georges. "Orocles prophetiques et 'guerre sainte' selon les achieves royales de Mari et l'Ancient Testament." *VTSup* 17; Leiden: Brill, 1969.

HOFFMANN, Y. "The Day of the Lord as a Concept and a Term in the Prophetic Literature." *ZAW* 93 (1981): 37–50.

HOLLADAY, William L. "Reading Zephaniah with a Concordance: Suggestions for a Redaction History." *JBL* 120/24 (2001): 671–684.

IHROMI. "Die Häufung der Verben des Jubelns in Zephaniah III 14f, 16-18: rnn, rw ?, śmh 'lz, śwś and g|,,l." *VT* 33 (1981): 102–110.

IRSIGLER, H. "Äquivalenz in Poesie: Die kontextuellen Synonyme ?a ?aqāyalā-šibr gadu (w) l in Zef 1, 10 c.d.e," *BZ*, n.s. 22 (1978): 221–235.

ISHAI-ROSENBOIM, D. "Is Yom H (the day of the Lord) a term in biblical language." *Biblica* 87 (2006): 395–401.

JENNI, E. "יום yōm day." *TLOT* 2: 526–539.

JEPPESEN, K. "Zephaniah I 5B." *VT* 31 (1982): 372–373.

KAPELRUD, Arvid S. "Cult and Prophetic Words." *Studia Theologica* 4 (1950): 5–12.

—. "God as Destroyer in the Preaching of Amos and in the Ancient near East." *JBL* 1 (1952): 33–38.

—. "The Role of the Cult in Old Israel." *The Bible in Modern Scholarship*. Edited by Philip J. Hayatt. Nashville, NY: Abingdon Press, 1965, 44–56.

—. "Eschatology in Micah and Zephaniah," in M. Carrez, J. Doré and P. Grelot, eds., *De la Tôrah au Messie: Etudes d'exégèse et d'herméneutique bibliques offertes à Henri Cazelles*. Paris: Desclée de Brouwer, 1981, 255–262.

KARTVEIT, M. "Daughter of Zion." *Theology of Life* 27 (2004): 25–41.

KING, Greg A. "The Day of the Lord in Zephaniah." *BSac* 156 (1995): 16–32.

—. "The Remnant in Zephaniah." *BSac* 151 (1994): 414–427.

KLEIN, Ralph W. "Day of the Lord." *Concordia Theological Monthly* 39 (1968): 517–525.

KSELMAN, John S. "Zephaniah, Book Of." *ABD* 6: 1077–80.

LANGHOR, G. "Le Livre de Sophonie et la critique d'authenticité." *ETL* 52 (1976): 1–27.

—. "Rédaction et composition du livre de Sophonie." *Le Muséon* 89 (1987): 51–73

LOHFINK, N. "Zefanja und das Israel der Armen." *Biki* 39 (1984):100–108.

—. "Zephaniah and the Church of the Poor." *ThD* 32 (1985): 113–118.

MASON, R. *Review of Zephaniah*, by Marvin A. Sweeney. *Journal of Theological Studies* 55 (October 2004): 618–621.

MELUGIN, Roy F. "Amos in Recent Research." *CR* 36 (1998): 655–101.

MILLER, Patrick M. "The Divine Council and the Prophetic Call to War." *VT* 18 (1968): 100–117.

MOORE, Michel S. "Yahweh's Day." *ResQ* 29 (1987): 193–208.

NOGALSKI, James. D. "The Day (s) of YHWH in the Book of the Twelve," in *SBLSP 1999: One Hundred and Thirty-Fifth Annual Meeting: November 20–23, 1999*. SBL Seminar Paper Series 38. Atlanta, Georgia: Scholars Press, (1999): 617–642.

—. "Joel as "Literary Anchor" for the Book of the Twelve." Reading and Hearing the Book of the Twelve. Symposium Series 15. Edited by James D. Nogalski and Marvin A. Sweeney. Atlanta: SBL, 2000, 91–124.

O'BRIEN, Julia M. "Nahum – Habakkuk – Zephaniah: Reading the "Former Prophets" in the Persian Period." *Interpretation* (2007): 168–183.

PETERSEN, David L. "A Book of the Twelve?" *Reading and Hearing the Book of the Twelve*. Edited James D. Nogalski and Marvin A. Sweeney. Symposium Series 15; Atlanta: SBL, 1990, 3–10.

—. "Eschatology (OT)." *ABD* 2: 575–590.

PREEZ Du, J. "Social Justice: Motive for the Mission of the Church." *JTSA* 43 (1985): 36–46.

PREUSCHEN, E. "Die Bedeutung von שׁוּב שְׁבוּת im Alten Testament." *ZAW* 15 (1895): 1–74.

VON RAD, G. "The Origin of the Concept of the Day of Yahweh." *JSS* 4 (1959): 102–109.

RECTOR, Larry J. "Israel's Rejected Worship: An Exegesis of Amos 5." *ResQ* 21 (1978): 161–175.

REDDITT, Paul L. "The Book of Joel and Peripheral Prophecy." *CBQ* 48 (1986): 225–240.

RENDTORFF, R. "Alas for the Day! The "Day of the Lord" in the Book of the Twelve." *God in the Fray: A Tribute to Walter Brueggemann*. Edited by Tod Linafelt and Timothy K. Beal. Minneapolis: Fortress, 1998, 187–197.

—. "How to Read the Book of the Twelve as a Theological Unity." *Reading and Hearing the Book of the Twelve,* Edited by James D. Nogalski and Marvin A. Sweeney. *SBLSymS* 15, Atlanta: SBL, (2000): 75–87.

RENAUD, B. "Le Livre de Sophonie. Le jour de YHWH theme structurant de la synthèse rédactionnelle." *RSR* 60 (1973): 291–303.

RICE, G. "The African Roots of the Prophet Zephaniah." *JRT* 36 (1979–80): 21–31.

ROBINSON, H.W. "The Day of Yahweh." *Inspiration and Revelation in the Old Testament*. Oxford: Oxford University Press, 1946.

RODAS, C., M. Daniel. "Seeding the Virtues Among the Prophets: The Book of Amos as a Test Case." *Ex auditu* 17 (2001): 77–96.

—. "La ética social de los profetas y su relevancia para América Latina hoy: La contribuición de la ética filosófica." *Kairós* 35 (2004): 7–24.

ROWLEY, H.H. "Ritual and the Hebrew Prophets." *JSS* 1 (1956): 338–360.

—. "The Day of the Lord." *The Faith of Israel: Aspects of Old Testament Thought*. London: SCM Press, 1961, 177–201.

SCHART, A. "Reconstructing the Redaction History of the Twelve Prophets: Problems and Models." *Reading and Hearing the Book of the Twelve.* Edited by James D. Nogalski and Marvin A. Sweeney. Symposium Series 15; Atlanta: SBL, 2000, 34–48.

SCHIMITT, John J. "The Motherhood of God and Zion as Mother." *RB* 92 (1995): 557–569.

SCHWERTNER, S. "סוּר sûr to deviate." *TLOT* 2: 796–97.

SEKINE, M. "Das Problem der Kutpolemik bei den Propheten." *EvTh* 28 (1968): 605–609.

SMART, J. D. "Amos." *IDB* 1. Nashville: Abingdon Press, 1962, 118–120.

SMITH, John. M. P. "The Day of Yahweh." *AJT* 4. vol 5 (1901): 505–33.

SOGGIN, J. A. "שׁוּב Sûb to return." *TLOT* 3: 1312–1317.

—. "Der Prophetische Gedanke über den heiligen Krieg, als Gericht gegen Israel." *VT* 10 (1960): 81–92.

STENZEL, M. "Zum Verständnis von Zeph. III 3b." *VT* (1951): 303–305.

STINESPRING, W. F. "No Daughter of Zion: A Study of the Appositional Genitive in Hebrew Grammar." *Encounter* 26 (1965): 133–141.

STOLZ, F. "צִיּוֹן siyyōn zion." *TLOT* 3: 1071–1076.

STRUGNELL, J. "Note on Psalm 126. 1." *JTS* 7 (1956): 239–243.

SWEENEY, Marvin A. "A Form-Critical Reassessment of the Book of Zephaniah." *CBQ* 53 (1991): 388–408.

—. "Zephaniah: A Paradigm for the Study of the Prophetic Books." *CR-BS* 7 (1999): 119–145.

—. "Sequence and Interpretation in the Book of the Twelve," in *Reading and Hearing the Book of the Twelve.* Edited by James D. Nogalski and Marvin S. Sweeney. Symposium Series 15. SBL; Atlanta: 2000, 49–64.

VOLZ, P. "Die Radikale Ablehnung der Kultreligion durch die alttestamentlichen Propheten." *ZSTh* 14 (1937): 63–85.

VRIEZE, Th. C. "Prophecy and Eschatological." *Supplementum to Vetus Testamentum,* vol. 1, Congress Volume: Copehangen 1953. Leiden: Brill, 1953.

WAGNER, Norman E. "רנה in the Psalter." *VT* 10 (1960): 435–441.

WEIGL, M. "Current Research on the Book of Nahum: Exegetical Methodologies in Turmoil?" *CR* 7 (2001): 81–130.

WEIMER, P. "Obadja: Eine redaktionskritische Analyse." *BN* 27 (1985): 35–99.

WEISER, A. "ἀγαλλιάω agalliaō rejoice, exult, be glad," *EDNT* 1: 7–8.

WEISS, M. "The Origin of the "Day of the Lord" – Reconsidered." *HUCA* 37 (1966): 629–660.

—. "Concerning Amos' Repudiation of the Cult." *Pomegranates and Golden Bells: Studies in Biblical, Jewish and Near Eastern Ritual, Law and Literature in Honor of Jacob Milgrom.* Edited by David P. Wright, David N. Freedman and Avid Hurvitz. Winona Lake, IN: Eisenbrauns, 1995, 93–102.

WILLIAMS, Donald L. "The Date of Zephaniah." *JBL* 82 (1963): 77–88.

WOLFF, Roland E. "The Editing of the Book of the Twelve." *ZAW* 53 (1935): 90–129.

WÜRTHWEIN, E. "μετανοέω." *TDNT* 4: 975–1008.

—. "Amos 5:21–27." *ThLZ* 72 (1947): 143–52.

ZALCMAN, L. "Ambiguity and Assonance at Zephaniah II 4." *VT* 36 (1986): 365–371.

6. Ecclesiastical/Interreligious and Cultural Studies

BENEDICT XVI. Encyclical Letter *Spe Salvi*. Vatican City: Libreria Editrice Vaticana, 2007.

BEVANS, Stephen B. *Models of Contextual Theology: Faith and Culture*. Revised and Expanded Edition. Maryknoll, NY: Orbis Books, 2004.

BEVANS, Stephen B. and Jeffrey G. *Evangelization and Religious Freedom: Ad Gentes, Dignitatis Humanae*. Rediscovering Vatican II; New York: Paulist Press, 2009.

CASSIDY, Edward I. *Ecumenism and Interreligious Dialogue: Unitatis Redintegratio, Nostra Aetate*. Rediscovering Vatican II; New York: Paulist Press, 2005.

D'COSTA, G. *Christianity and World Religions: Disputed Questions in the Theology of Religions*. West Sussex, United Kingdom: Wiley-Blackwell, 2009.

DULLES, A. "The Unity for which we Hope," in *Evangelicals & Catholics: Toward a common Mission Together*. Edited by Charles Colson and Richard John Neuhaus. Nashville: Thomas Nelson, 1995, 115–146.

GAILLARDETZ, Richard R. *The Church in the Making: Lumen Gentium, Christus Dominus, Orientalium Ecclesiarum*. Rediscovering Vatican II; Paulist Press, 2006.

GROS, J., Eamon McManus and Ann R. *Introduction to Ecumenism*. New York: Paulist Press, 1998.

HARRINGTON, Daniel J. *Meeting St. Paul Today: Understanding the Man, His Mission, and His Message*. Chicago: Loyola Press, 2008.

IDOWU, E. B. *Olódùmarè: God in Yoruba Belief*. London: Longmans, 1962.

—. *African Traditional Religion: A Problem of Definition*. London: SCM Press, 1977.

JOHN PAUL II. The Encyclical Letter, *Redemptoris Missio*. Vatican City: Libreria Vaticana, 1990.

—. *Post-Synodal Apostolic Exhortation: Ecclesia in Africa*. Vatican City: Libreria Editrice Vaticana. 1995.

KASPER, W. *That They May all be One: The Call to Unity Today*. London: Burn & Oates, 2004.

KROEBER, Alfred L and Klyde Kluckhohn. *A Critical Review of Concepts and Definitions. (Papers of the Peabody Museum of American Archaeology and Ethnology*. Harvard University 47, n. 1. Cambridge; MA: Peabody Museum, 1952).

MALINA, Bruce J. *The New Testament World: Insight from Cultural Anthropology*. Revised Edition. Louisville, KY: Westminster John Knox Press, 1993.

MBITI, John S. *African Religion & Philosophy*. New York: Praeger, 1969.

—. *The Concept of God in Africa*. New York: Praeger, 1970.

NILSON, J. *Nothing Beyond the Roman Catholicism and the Ecumenical Future*. New Yrok: Paulist Press, 1995.

NYOYOKO, V. "Dialogue and Inculturation," in *Reconciliation and Renewal of Services in the Church: Lineamenta for the First Synod of the Catholic Diocese of Ikot Ekpene*. Uyo, Nigeria: Trinity Press, 2002, 105–130.

PONTIFICAL COUNCIL FOR PROMOTING CHRISTIAN UNITY. *Directory for the Application of Principles and Norms on Ecumenism*. Vatican City: Libreria Editrice, 1993.

RATZINGER, J./Pope Benedict XVI, *Jesus of Nazareth*. Translated Adrien J. Walker; New York: Doubleday, 2007.

SCHREITER, Robert J. *The New Catholicity: Theology between the Global and the Local*. Maryknoll, NY: Orbis Book, 1997.

SEGOVIA, Fernando F. and Mary Ann Tolberts. eds., *Reading from this Place: Social Location and Biblical Interpretation*. 2 vols. Minneapolis: Fortress Press, 1995.

SYNOD OF BISHOPS SPECIAL ASSEMBLY FOR AFRICA. *The Church in Africa and her Evangelizing Mission towards the Year 2000 "You Shall be My Witnesses" (Acts 1:8):* Vatican City: Libreria Editrice Vaticana, 1990.

TANNER, K. *Theories of Culture: A New Agenda for Theology*. Minneapolis: Fortress Press, 1997.

THE PONTIFICAL BIBLICAL COMMISSION. *The Interpretation of the Bible in the Church*. Vatican City: Libreria Editrice Vaticana, 1993.

—. *The Jewish People and their Sacred Scriptures in the Christian Bible*. Vatican City: Libreria Editrice Vaticana. 2002.

—. *The Bible and Morality: Bible Roots of Christian Conduct*. Vatican City. Libreria Editrice Vaticana, 2008.

UDOEKPO, Michael U. *Corruption in Nigerian Culture: The Liberating Mission of the Church*. Enugu, Nigeria: Snaap Press, 1994.

—. *The Limits of a Divided Nation*. Enugu, Nigeria: Snaap Press, 1999.

VATICAN II. *Decree on Ecumenism, Unitatis Redintegratio*. Vatican City: Libreria Editrice Vaticana, 1964.

—. *Dogmatic Constitution on Divine Revelation, Dei Verbum*. Vatican City: Libreria Editrice Vaticana, 1965.

—. *Declaration on the Relation of the Church to Non-Christian Religions, Nostra Aetate*. Vatican City, Editrice Vaticana, 1965.

WITHERUP, Roland D. *Scripture: Dei Verbum*. Rediscovering Vatican II; New York: Paulist Press, 2006.

Index of Authors

This supplements the bibliographical information and leads readers to pages where authors and their views are also listed in the footnotes, but in this case beginning with their surnames as found in the bibliography.

Index of Subjects

331